Friends of the Revolution

Rachel Rogers

Friends of the Revolution
The British Radical Community in Early Republican Paris 1792-1794

BREVIARY STUFF PUBLICATIONS
2021

First published by Breviary Stuff 2021

Breviary Stuff Publications,
BCM Breviary Stuff, London WC1N 3XX
breviarystuff.org.uk
Copyright © Rachel Rogers 2021
The centipede device copyright © Breviary Stuff Publications

All rights reserved. No part of this publication may be reproduced, stored in a retrieval system, or transmitted, in any form or by any means, electronic, mechanical, photocopying, scanning, recording, or otherwise, without the prior permission of Breviary Stuff Publications

A CIP record for this book is available from
The British Library

ISBN: 978-1-9161586-4-1

Contents

About the Author		*vii*
Abbreviations		*viii*
Acknowledgements		*ix*
1	The 'man without a country'? Assessing the British radical community in early republican Paris	1
2	'In defence of their rights': British reactions to the popular revolution of 10th August 1792	15
3	British emigration to early republican Paris in 1792-1793	29
4	Professional lives and projects of British residents in Paris	47
5	*La Société des Amis des Droits de l'Homme*: A political association at White's hotel	67
6	Revising the monarchical constitution of 1791: The writings of Joel Barlow and David Williams on the new republican constitution	85
7	'A state of permanent popular deliberation is indispensable': The constitutional writings of Robert Merry, John Oswald and George Edwards	109
8	British experience in Paris under emergency rule, 1793-1794	137
9	Sketchers of Revolution: Eyewitness histories	161
10	'It would be rash to hazard any prediction of the future': The historical accounts of Helen Maria Williams and Mary Wollstonecraft	181
11	'A spectacle worthy of heaven and earth': Sampson Perry's *An Historical Sketch of the French Revolution* (1796)	203
12	British Girondins?	223

Appendices	235
Map of Paris Showing the Location of White's hotel	237
Short Biographies of British Politicians mentioned	238
Short Biographies of Revolutionary Leaders mentioned	240
Glossary of Revolutionary Terms	243
Timeline of Key Events in Britain and France, 1792-94	246
Engravings from contemporary editions of the newspaper *Révolutions de Paris*	250
Title Pages of Tracts and Pamphlets by British Observers	256
Some Extracts from Manuscript Sources	259
Signatories of the *SADH* Address to the National Convention, 24th November 1792	263
Prison records for British residents of Paris	264
Extract from *La Chronique du Mois; ou Cahiers Patriotiques*	267
Bibliography	269
Index	295

About the author

Rachel Rogers is a lecturer in British history and politics in the English studies department at the University of Toulouse Jean Jaurès and has a particular interest in radicalism, popular political culture and protest. She is the author of a number of articles which explore the involvement of British men and women in the events of the French Revolution, their engagement with the political debates dominating public life, and their collective experience of living and working in Paris during the early years of the first republic.

Abbreviations

CCST	T. B. Howell, *A Complete Collection of State Trials and Proceedings for High Treason and Other Crimes and Misdemeanours from the Earliest Period to the Year 1783, with Notes and Other Illustrations ... and Continued from the Year 1793 to the Present Time*, vol. 25 (London: Longman, Rees, Orme, Brown & Green, 1818)
CWTP	P. S. Foner (ed.), *The Complete Writings of Thomas Paine* (New York: Citadel, 1945)
HMV	Mary Wollstonecraft, *An Historical and Moral View of the Origins and Progress of the French Revolution; and the Effect it has Produced in Europe* (London: J. Johnson, 1794)
HS	Sampson Perry, *An Historical Sketch of the French Revolution: Commencing with Its Predisposing Causes, and Carried on to the Acceptation of the Constitution, in 1795* (London: Symonds, 1796)
LCS	London Corresponding Society
SADH	*La Société des Amis des Droits de l'Homme* (The Society of the Friends of the Rights of Man)
SCI	Society of Constitutional Information

Acknowledgements

This book owes its existence to the help and encouragement of teachers, colleagues, friends and family, without whose support over the years it would not have reached publication. I am grateful also to Paul Mangan and the team at Breviary Stuff for their guidance and interest in this subject.

Jon Mee planted the seed of this research, and his indefatigable enthusiasm in guiding me through those years of postgraduate study in regular cross-Channel meetings was crucial. His generosity in taking me on as a doctoral student and the rigour of his supervision cannot be overstated. Wholehearted thanks also go to Fabrice Bensimon, who never let me forget I had a book to publish and who has nourished my lasting interest in labour history. Thank you to my friends and colleagues at the University of Toulouse Jean Jaurès, to Alexandra Sippel, Nathalie Duclos, Françoise Coste, Helen Goethals and all the participants in the ATHIP workshops, and to Xavier Cervantès who co-supervised my doctoral research. A word of gratitude as well to generous scholars Mary-Ann Constantine, Myriam-Isabelle Ducrocq, David Duff, Jean-François Dunyach, Mathieu Ferradou, Colin Jones and Mark Philp for their precious help and advice at different stages. The archival research for this book would not have been possible without early study grants and support from the CAS research laboratory at Toulouse Jean Jaurès University and the SAES. I also appreciate all the help I was given by the staff at the National Archives in Kew, the Archives Nationales in Paris and in the inter-library loan team in Toulouse.

Some sections of this book are based on talks given at conferences held in Toulouse, Rennes and Bordeaux and subsequently published, including Pascale Antolin, Arnaud Schmitt, Susan Barrett, Paul Veyret (dir.), *"Men without a Country': British Radicals as Vectors in 1790s Paris"*, *La figure du passeur : Transmission et mobilité culturelles dans les mondes anglophones* (Pessac: Presses de la MSHA, 2014), pp. 135-54; "White's Hotel: A Junction of British Radical Culture in early 1790s Paris", *Anglophonia / Caliban* n° 33, (Toulouse: Presses Universitaires du Midi, 2013), pp. 153-72; "Censorship and Creativity: The Case of Sampson Perry, Radical Editor in 1790s Paris and London", *Revue LISA/LISA e-journal* [Online], Vol. XI – n° 1 | 2013; "'Relinquish[ing] all former connections': British radical emigration to early republican Paris" in David Duff & Marc Porée (eds.), *Exiles, Émigrés and Expatriates in Romantic-Era Paris and London* (Prague: Litteraria Pragensia, 2019).

Thank you to Anne and Malcolm, my parents, and to Julien, for understanding my need to write this book and for never tiring of talking about it. A special mention for Corto and Eli who have accompanied this book from the start and who have, even at their young age, put up pretty well with the hours spent in the attic writing it.

I

The 'man without a country'? Assessing the British radical community in early republican Paris

The news of the overthrow of monarchical authority in France, triggered by the siege of the Tuileries on 10th August 1792, and the subsequent establishment of a National Convention and republican rule on 21st September 1792, resonated with a number of British men and women who had followed the progress of the French Revolution closely since 1789 and who were themselves partisans of radical reform in Britain and elsewhere. While visits to and from France did not begin at this stage of the Revolution, and although a number of British nationals had already settled in Paris by then, witnessing the confrontation firsthand, these events, with the eradication of the institution of monarchy and a shift to a greater degree of popular participation in the political life of the nation at their core, aroused the interest of British reformers and, for some, may have precipitated their decision to settle in the French capital.[1] Some of those who took up residence in Paris in late 1792 had been pursued for seditious libel for their unabridged criticism of the British parliamentary model in their editorial work, printing activities or writings and sought refuge and publishing outlets on French shores.[2] Many had endorsed the much-criticised second part of Thomas Paine's *Rights of Man*, published in February 1792 and circulated cheaply by the Society for Constitutional Information. Most combined a firm antipathy to what they saw as a decadent political system in Britain in urgent need of overhaul with a renewed enthusiasm for the potential of the French Revolution to stimulate wide-reaching European improvement. All

---

1   For an account of this 'second revolution', see Marcel R. Reinhard, *La chute de la royauté, 10 août, 1792* (Paris: Gallimard, 1969).
2   The most notable cases of British residents seeking exile in France were those of Thomas Paine and Sampson Perry, both of whom were subject to judicial pursuit in Britain.

arrived in Paris in the knowledge that their presence on French soil, at this turning point in the Revolution, would prompt suspicion and criticism from the ruling authorities at home who had begun to clamp down more heavily on those who expressed a preference for fundamental constitutional and political change.[3]

As close observers of the inauguration of republican government, British nationals in Paris allied professional activities such as property speculation, publishing, journalism and business ventures with political activism, setting up a political society in central Paris in November 1792, just days after the republican army achieved victory over the Austrian forces at Jémappes, a crucial step towards consolidating the international stature of the new regime. Based at a hotel in the centre of Paris in the passage des Petits Pères, run by an English hotelier called Christopher White, the society was registered with the municipal authorities under the name *La Société des Amis des Droits de l'Homme* (*SADH*, The Society of the Friends of the Rights of Man) in January 1793. The members of this group, many of them already acquainted with each other through membership of radical societies in Britain or Ireland, met regularly at White's hotel to discuss news of French affairs, to pursue writing and publication initiatives and to give voice to the collective position of British emigrants on the events of the Revolution's course. British residents of Paris were exercised in particular by the fallout of the August Days, the debates over the form of a new republican constitution in the making and the impact that constitutional changes in France could have both within and outside its borders. The society's members issued a joint declaration of support for the republic on 24th November 1792, only ten days after the Convention had issued a declaration of fraternity to those peoples considered to be struggling under oppressive monarchical government.[4] Some, such as Robert Merry, John Oswald and David Williams, also responded to the invitation from the National Convention to set forth ideas on the best form of government to be implemented by the new republic.

The decision to try the king, and the outcome of the trial, which led to the execution of Louis XVI on 21st January 1793, had a decisive impact on the position of British residents in Paris. Following the declaration of war between France and Great Britain on 1st February 1793 prompting a rallying

---

3   While support for the French Revolution was widespread in Whig and reforming circles in 1789, the events of 1792 contributed to the decline of this broad approbation. Thomas Paine was prosecuted for seditious libel *in absentia* in December 1792 after the publication and cheap circulation of the second part of *Rights of Man* in February of that year and other editors, booksellers and printers were hounded for sedition and found themselves in Newgate prison.

4   Sophie Wahnich highlights how both the need to ensure British neutrality and the legacy of the British influence on actors in the 1789-1790 Constituent Assembly meant that there was a persistent attempt to differentiate between a guilty government and a liberty-loving people. See Sophie Wahnich, *L'Impossible citoyen: l'étranger dans le discours de la Révolution française* (Paris: A. Michel, 1997), in particular pp. 281-310.

of European monarchies to the counter-revolutionary effort, suspicion of the intentions, political affiliations and loyalty to the Revolution of British nationals multiplied. The vast majority would be affected over the course of 1793 and early 1794 by measures put in place to restrict their freedoms as emergency revolutionary government – sometimes known as the Terror – was instituted. In March 1793, foreign residents were required to obtain permission from their local section in order to leave Paris, and local committees held foreigners in greater suspicion. Landlords were required to identify foreign tenants occupying their premises and residents from abroad increasingly had to provide proof of their utility and loyalty to the regime to ensure their safety. By August 1793, subjects of nations at war with France could be targeted for imprisonment, and on 9th October 1793 all British nationals were subject to blanket arrest, their property was confiscated and they were and placed in makeshift prisons across the capital such as the Luxembourg and the Madelonnettes. On 25th December 1793, Thomas Paine and Anacharsis Cloots were expelled from the National Convention and Paine narrowly escaped execution for his suspected Girondin sympathies, having voted for the exile rather than the execution of the king. Under the laws of 26-27 Germinal Year II (15th and 16th April 1794), foreign participation in political societies was outlawed and foreigners had to leave Paris and all frontier towns and ports.

During the course of these months of emergency rule, British residents drew upon their ties in the wider community in Paris – both in their local Sections and in international circles – and called upon their previous revolutionary credentials, in an effort to negotiate passports to leave French shores, to protect their families and livelihoods or later, to secure their release from prison. Some continued their engagement with the Revolution and advanced writing projects while behind bars. After the fall of the revolutionary government on 27th July 1794 (9 Thermidor), most British residents were progressively released from prison and either chose to remain in France, return to Britain, or emigrate to other shores. Their experience of residence, activism and persecution in early republican Paris continued to shape their political outlooks and impacted on their material and social fortunes in the subsequent months and years.

In choosing to begin with the events of 10th August 1792, it can be shown that the popular departure in the French Revolution was a catalyst for a peak of collective interest in the events going on across the Channel among British radical reformers, some of whom made the decision to take up temporary or permanent residence in the French capital in its wake. The evidence points to the period between August 1792 and July 1794 as being of particular significance in terms of the continued, joint and vociferous engagement of British residents with the events and debates of the Revolution. While some British nationals had already arrived before August 1792 and others remained after 9 Thermidor and the fall of the emergency government, the months covered in this book nevertheless represent a period of heightened interest and involvement in the Revolution – with the establishment of a political society a crucial feature – which calls for attention in its own right. It was also a period in which perceptions of the Revolution changed rapidly in Britain and when the anxiety of the ruling administration, under William Pitt the Younger, about the impact of events in France led to measures being taken to restrict freedoms of radical reformers on home shores. Equally, the status of British nationals on French soil shifted dramatically during these months, in accordance with wider diplomatic conflicts and the internal struggles in the revolutionary administration.

The broad aim of this book is thus to shed new light on the experience of the British community in early republican Paris, a subject that remains in the margins of, if not entirely absent from, the historiography of the French Revolution. More specifically, it attempts to highlight the impact of these community ties and of joint residence in the capital, on individual lives, and to delve more thoroughly into the role played by the *SADH* on the Parisian political stage. The book seeks to deconstruct the widely-held view that British participants in the Revolution were sympathetic to one single political grouping, the Girondins, and pulls together evidence to show that there was a strong pull towards more democratic participation in the political sphere among British residents, in tune with their observations of and involvement in local politics on the ground in central Paris. Such admiration for democratic innovation was often written out of British observers' later accounts of their time spent in the French capital. I also put forward the point that British histories of the Revolution, written from the perspective of eyewitness observation, were often more hybrid and discordant in their nature and conclusions than has been admitted. These histories are often the written trace of their authors' attempts to work out the Revolution and capture its elusive nature as it unfolded. They reveal the ambivalence of British residents towards some of the events which characterised the early republic. Some of the conclusions in this book confirm, nuance or revisit earlier interpretations of the British community in Paris which emerged from the late nineteenth century onwards.

RETRACING THE HISTORIOGRAPHY OF THE BRITISH COMMUNITY IN THE FRENCH REVOLUTION

John Goldworth Alger was the first professional scholar to devote particular attention to the activities of the British in Paris in his work on *Englishmen in the French Revolution*, published in 1889. He also wrote a number of other studies in both monograph and essay form.[5] Alger's aim was to recover the

---

5   The main works by Alger dealing with the British emigrant community are *Paris in 1789-94: Farewell Letters of Victims of the Guillotine* (London: Allen, 1902), *Napoleon's British Visitors and Captives, 1801-1815* (New York: AMS Press, 1970), *Englishmen in the French Revolution* (London: S. Low, Marston, Searle and Rivington, 1889), *Glimpses of the French*

experience of British residents of and visitors to France during the revolutionary era from historical obscurity, having lamented the fact that, in the eyes of French historians of the Revolution, British participants were "but imperceptible specks in the great eddy." He regretted that the attention of French historians "is absorbed by their own countrymen; they have none to spare for interlopers, none of whom appreciably influenced the course of events."[6] Alger's portrait of the British, which echoes some of the feverish portraits of British spectators published contemporaneously, set the tone for later representations of British radicals as both fervent idealists and subversive plotters.[7] His account, which includes chapters entitled "Enthusiasts" and "Outlaws and Conspirators", reflects his reading of British secret agent Captain George Monro's dispatches to the Pitt ministry. Monro followed Thomas Paine and John Frost to Paris in mid-September 1792 and sent regular reports back to the British government until he was singled out as a spy and suspected by the emigrant community as well as the French revolutionary authorities in early 1793.[8] Monro depicted a set of violent and subversive conspirators seeking to overthrow the British constitution in collusion with international patriots and French revolutionaries. Yet in somewhat of a paradox, he also emphasised the insignificance of the group in the eyes of the French government as well as their internal disputes and inability to reach consensus. Monro's portrait is ambivalent, combining alarmism over the intentions of the group's members to disrupt the settled constitutional arrangement in Britain with nonchalant dismissal of their effectiveness. Yet his is one of the few accounts recorded at the time and has therefore understandably guided later historical studies.

Alger also emphasised the progressive disillusionment of British witnesses and their embracing of loyalism as the Revolution wore on: "It must be presumed that many of them altered their opinion of their own country's stability and institutions, and learned to prefer even an unreformed

---

Revolution: Myths, Ideals, and Realities (London: Sampson Low, Marston and Co., 1894) and 'The British Colony in Paris, 1792-93', *The English Historical Review* 13.52 (1898) pp. 672-94.

6 Alger, *Englishmen* vi.
7 A report from January 1791 suggested that Helen Maria Williams was "intoxicated with liberty" (*The Gentleman's Magazine*, vol. 61, part 1 (1791) 62) and Anna Seward reproached Williams for her "cold alienation" in a letter of 17th January 1793 (Anna Seward and Archibald Constable, *Letters of Anna Seward: Written between the Years 1784 and 1807*, vol. 3 (Edinburgh: A. Constable and Co., 1811) pp. 44, 209).
8 Captain Monro's despatches are contained in the Treasury Solicitors Papers and Foreign Office deposits at the National Archive in Kew. The Foreign Office papers have also been published under the title of 'Despatches of Earl Gower'. Monro sent an initial report to the Home Office shortly after his arrival in Paris in which he tried to identify the principal figures in the Paris society. He also sent regular reports to the British government until early 1793, tracing the activities of the club from his lodgings at White's hotel. In early 1793 he was singled out as a potential spy and suspected by fellow British guests. By May 1793 he had also come to the notice of the French authorities, who sent a warrant for his arrest.

Parliament to the French Convention."⁹ Such conclusions, which negate the enthusiasm shown by British residents for some of the innovations of the French republic, drew to some extent on the representations of contemporary biographers who wrote with the intention of restoring the reputations of friends or acquaintances that had been tarnished through their continued involvement with France after 1792. Thomas Clio Rickman, in his very partial account, wrote of his friend Thomas Paine as "incorrupt, strait forward [sic], and sincere, he pursued his political course in France, as every where [sic] else, let the government or clamor or faction of the day be what it might, with firmness, with clearness, and without a "shadow of turning.""¹⁰ Many contemporary accounts of the British in the French Revolution were noteworthy for their attempts to write out the initial support of radicals for the republican turn and provide a more moderate portrait of their political inclinations. Focus was also given to the dual persecution suffered by men such as Sampson Perry, who was incarcerated both in Britain and France, and Thomas Paine, whose estrangement from Britain precluded a return to his home country, even after his eventual release from the Luxembourg prison. A contemporary of Alger, Thomas Paine's editor Moncure Conway, categorised British experience in Paris during the Revolution as being that of "the man without a country", and drew attention to the innumerable "griefs" British emigrants endured as a result of their ultimate ostracism from both regimes.¹¹ From these late nineteenth-century accounts, a trend began which considered British participants in the Revolution as plotters on the one hand, outcasts and victims of Pittite repression at home and Terror-driven persecution in France on the other.

Early twentieth-century accounts did little to attenuate the focus on the idealism of British emigrants, their penchant for plotting and their ultimate ostracism from both national communities. A commentator of emigrant Henry Redhead Yorke's letters, writing in 1906, stated, "Redhead threw himself heart and soul with the enthusiasm of youth into a popular movement which he believed was to liberate humanity from every sort of bondage, and bring about a period of quite utopian peace and prosperity."¹² The author highlighted the conspiratorial strain in British activity, defining the *SADH* as "an association at which were discussed such subjects as the advantage of liberating England by the assassination of that harmless

---

9   Alger, *Englishmen*, x.
10 Thomas Clio Rickman, *The Life of Thomas Paine: Author of Common Sense, Rights of Man, Age of Reason, Letter to the Addressers, &c. &c.* (London: Rickman, 1819) p. 136.
11 Thomas Paine's nineteenth-century editor, Moncure Conway, suggested that "nearly all of these men suffered griefs known only to the 'man without a country'." Moncure D. Conway (ed.), *The Writings of Thomas Paine*, vol 3 (New York: G.P. Putnam's Sons, 1899) p. xiii.
12 Henry Redhead Yorke, *France in 1802, Described in a Series of Contemporary Letters* (1804), J. A. C. Sykes (ed.), with an introduction by Richard Davey (London: Heineman, 1906) p. 2.

monarch George III."[13] The emphasis on the dramatic, the treasonable, the naive and the anecdotal endured well into the twentieth century.

Three twentieth-century accounts stand out for their attempts to chart in detail the experiences of the British in Paris. Michael Rapport's book, *Nationality and Citizenship in Revolutionary France: The Treatment of Foreigners 1789-1799*, looks at the treatment of British radicals as part of a wider investigation of the question of nationality in both pre-revolutionary and revolutionary France.[14] Furthermore, Lionel Woodward's study of Helen Maria Williams and her relationship to the French Revolution is noteworthy for its attempt to explore a wider perspective of British involvement in the events. While Woodward devotes a considerable section of his account to Williams' early experiences and her membership of the Dissenting community in London, the chapter focusing on "Miss Williams and the foreign colony in Paris", and two subsequent sections on John Hurford Stone and British imprisonment under emergency rule, give a much broader vision of British experience in Paris. The author retraces much of the archival material first brought to light by Alger, but also explores in detail the British correspondence files held in the *Archives Diplomatiques*.[15]

The most recent biographical study of a British radical in Paris during the revolutionary period to take into consideration the wider picture of British activism is David Erdman's *Commerce des Lumières: John Oswald and the British in Paris 1790-1793*.[16] Erdman places greater emphasis than previous scholars on the routes of transmission opened up between Britain and France through the existence of the *SADH*, which he refers to as the "British Club".[17] He sees the Channel as a passageway of information and propaganda and John Oswald himself as an intermediary, deeply involved in communication and deliberation between the two countries. While insisting on the international dimension of British activities in the French capital, Erdman also highlights the intense secrecy which surrounded the organisation which has made, and continues to make, reconstituting British activities in Paris problematic. He points to the lack of evidence, the ambiguity which characterises the group, the misinformation which circulated and the necessity of basing conclusions partly on conjecture, legend and hearsay. He claims that those historians who have continued to cling to the belief that British radicals turned against the Revolution after the September massacres are mistaken. While several did

---

13 Ibid.
14 Michael Rapport, *Nationality and Citizenship in Revolutionary France: The Treatment of Foreigners 1789-1799* (Oxford: Clarendon, 2000).
15 Lionel D. Woodward, *Une Anglaise amie de la Révolution française: Hélène-Maria Williams et ses amis* (Paris: Champion, 1930).
16 David V. Erdman, *Commerce Des Lumieres: John Oswald and the British in Paris in 1790-93* (Columbia: University of Missouri Press, 1986).
17 I used this name in my PhD thesis, but in particular thanks to discussions with scholars working on Irish involvement in the society, have revised my views on this and now prefer the French appellation given in the official registration of the society with this Paris authorities.

reject the republican departure and radical phase of the Revolution in France, others confronted the growing violence with an open-minded pragmatism which filled many of their contemporaries with horror and which later commentators have sometimes filtered out. Erdman provides insights into the aims of the political society, the idealism at its heart, the republican ambitions of some of its core members, and their gradual divergence from reforming Whig politics throughout the course of their residence in Paris. He places particular stress on the willingness of British emigrants to encourage a French landing on British soil and insists on the diversity of political beliefs which coexisted within the group.

In focusing on John Oswald, Erdman necessarily understates the role of those Oswald associated with. He acknowledges this in the earliest pages of his book, readily accepting that there remains considerable scope for further study of the other members of British community in Paris. He wrote, "A full historical account of British participation in the Revolution has yet to be assembled, but the present undertaking should help prepare the way."[18] It is inevitable therefore that Oswald, in Erdman's study, becomes the pioneering figurehead of the grouping, one of the first foreigners to welcome the French Revolution, achieving fame for his ideas, influential among revolutionary leaders including Nicholas de Bonneville and Jacques Pierre Brissot de Warville, and a prominent secretary of the *SADH*. Although Erdman contests earlier views expressed by Captain Monro and John Goldworth Alger that the society had virtually dissolved by the beginning of 1793, his own work only extends to Oswald's death in the Vendée in September 1793 and does not provide any substantial insights into the experience of its members during emergency rule in the period before Thermidor. Erdman verges on hagiography at times, and his portrayal of Oswald as a "would-be Wolfe Tone for England" does have some shortcomings despite its meritorious attempt to revitalise the debate on the British in Paris and give a vivid portrait of the atmosphere in revolutionary Paris at the time. It is undeniable that Oswald did have a central role and was one of the members of the group known for his ultra-radical leanings, going further than many in articulating a desire for a British revolution and establishment of a republic. Yet, if we rely solely on Erdman's account, there is a danger of exaggerating Oswald's role and influence.[19]

There are also myriad biographical studies which have devoted attention to individual British figures who travelled to Paris, and a number of romanticised revolutionary narratives.[20] Thomas Paine's narrow escape from

---

18　Erdman, *Commerce des Lumières*, p. 2.
19　Alexis Corbière, a political activist for the left-wing political movement, La France Insoumise, devoted a section to Oswald in his recent book, *Jacobins ! Les inventeurs de la République* (Paris: Perrin, 2019).
20　Thomas Paine's French experience has been detailed by only a small number of biographers. His friend and fellow Paris resident, Thomas Clio Rickman gave a detailed account of Paine's life in Paris (see Rickman, *The Life of Thomas Paine*). Alfred Aldridge's

the Luxembourg jail has captured the literary imagination, as has Thomas Muir's extraordinary fate following his transportation to the penal colonies.[21] Members of the emigrant community have also been alluded to in thematic works on newspaper history, the book trade and travel writing.[22] There have been a small number of studies dedicated to the Irish in the French Revolution due to the more explicit affiliation which developed between the French authorities and leaders of the Irish Rebellion in the closing years of the 1790s.[23] Mathieu Ferradou has carried out important work into the specific role of the Irish members of the *SADH*, suggesting that Irish residents of Paris, particularly under emergency government, began to assert a distinctive Irish identity in their appeals to the revolutionary administration. Mary-Ann Constantine has also drawn attention to the Welsh experience in revolutionary Paris. She has shown that, despite the fact that the Welsh were

---

account of Paine's life gives attention to his time in France (see A. O. Aldridge, *Man of Reason: The Life of Thomas Paine* (London: Cresset Press, 1959)). More recent biographies provide insights into Paine's political philosophy and engagement with American and French politics as well as the British reform movement. Gregory Claeys, *Thomas Paine: Social and Political thought* (Boston; London: Unwin Hyman, 1989) tends to emphasise the consistency in Paine's thought, while Mark Philp, *Paine* (Oxford: Oxford University Press, 1989) sees Paine's political ideas as developing according to events and circumstances. John Keane's *Tom Paine: A Political Life* (1995; London: Bloomsbury, 2009) is a more classical biography, seeking to show the different events of Paine's life. More recently, Carine Lounissi has provided a comprehensive study of the development of Paine's political thought in France in a book entitled *Thomas Paine and the French Revolution* (Palgrave Macmillan, 2018). For narratives on individual figures see P. W. Clayden, *The Early Life of Samuel Rogers* (London: Smith, Elder & Co., 1887), Thomas Moore, *The Life and Death of Lord Edward Fitzgerald* (Paris: Baudry's European Library, 1835), and Dumas Malone, *The Public Life of Thomas Cooper, 1783-1839* (Columbia: University of South Carolina Press, 1961).

21 See Peter, Mackenzie, *The Life of Thomas Muir, Esq. Advocate, Younger of Huntershill, Near Glasgow; Member of the Convention of Delegates for Reform in Scotland etc. etc. Who was Tried for Sedition Before The High Court of Justiciary in Scotland, and Sentenced to Transportation for Fourteen Years with a Full Report of his Trial* (Glasgow: McPhun's, 1831) and Christina Bewley, *Muir of Huntershill* (Oxford: Oxford University Press, 1981).

22 See Lucyle Werkmeister, *The London Daily Press, 1772-1792* (Lincoln: University of Nebraska Press, 1963) and *A Newspaper History of England, 1792-1793* (Lincoln: University of Nebraska Press, 1967); see also Jeremy Black, *The English Press in the Eighteenth Century* (Philadelphia: University of Pennsylvania Press, 1987). Madeleine B. Stern, 'The English Press in Paris and Its Successors, 1793-1852', *Papers of the Bibliographical Society of America* 74 (1980), pp. 307-59 and 'The Franco-American Book Trade in the Late Eighteenth and Early Nineteenth Centuries', *Publishing Research Quarterly* 10:1 (March 1994), pp. 47-54; Matthew Bray, 'Helen Maria Williams and Edmund Burke: Radical Critique and Complicity', *Eighteenth-Century Life* 16 (May 1992), pp. 1-24; Steven Blakemore, *Crisis in Representation: Thomas Paine, Mary Wollstonecraft, Helen Maria Williams and the Rewriting of the French Revolution* (Madison: Fairleigh Dickinson University Press, 1997); Deborah Kennedy, 'Responding to the French Revolution: Williams' Julia and Burney's The Wanderer' in Laura Dabundo (ed.), *Jane Austen and Mary Shelley and Their Sisters* (Lanham, New York, Oxford: University Press of America, 2000), pp. 3-17.

23 Marianne Elliott, *Partners in Revolution: The United Irishmen and France* (New Haven: Yale University Press, 1982) and Liam Swords, *The Green Cockade: The Irish in the French Revolution, 1789-1815* (Dublin: Glendale, 1989).

overlooked in the declarations and addresses of the society itself as well as in historical study, a small number of Welsh observers of the Revolution left traces of their views and experiences of the revolutionary arena, sometimes, as in the case of David Williams, playing more official diplomatic roles.[24]

Studies have also been devoted to individual American emigrants in Paris such as Gilbert Imlay and Joel Barlow, while Philipp Ziesche and Yvon Bizardel have carried out research into the wider American community in Paris.[25] Equally, there has been interest in other foreign radicals who established themselves in Paris in the revolutionary years. Georges Avenel wrote a biography of the Prussian-born member of the National Convention, Anacharsis Cloots, in 1865 and Marita Gilli translated and edited a work in French on the German emigrant revolutionary, Georg Forster.[26] Christoph Bode has recently examined the revolutionary enthusiasm of Forster over the years of emergency rule.[27] Finally, there has been some attention paid to the contribution of British radical thinkers in Paris, notably Thomas Paine, to the evolution of revolutionary ideas and political theory.[28] Yet the actual nature of Paine's engagement with his fellow British radicals in France and the intersection of his views with those of his countrymen have provoked less interest.

In French scholarship, allusions to the British community in writings on the Revolution are notably scarce. Historians of the French Revolution, Jacques Godechot and Michel Vovelle, have both insisted on the importance of the events in France to the wider world, but have largely considered this impact from a diplomatic or military perspective rather than in terms of the way in which it affected foreign men and women at the scene.[29] The figure of

---

24 See Mathieu Ferradou, 'Histoire d'un « festin patriotique » à l'hôtel white (18 novembre 1792) : les irlandais patriotes à paris, 1789-1795', *Annales historiques de la Révolution française*, 382 (2015), pp. 123-143, and Mary-Ann Constantine, 'The Welsh in Revolutionary Paris', in Mary-Ann Constantine and Dafydd Johnston (eds.), *'Footsteps of Liberty and Revolt': Essays on Wales and the French Revolution* (Cardiff: University of Wales Press, 2013). The study focuses on a handful of Welsh travellers who recorded their experience in revolutionary France. See also my article on the convergences in British and Irish radical circles in Paris, Rachel Rogers, 'The Society of the Friends of the Rights of Man, 1792-94: British and Irish Radical Conjunctions in Republican Paris', *La Révolution française*, 11 (2016) [online].

25 Richard Buel, *Joel Barlow: American Citizen in a Revolutionary World* (Baltimore: Johns Hopkins University Press, 2011); Wil Verhoeven, *Gilbert Imlay*. See also Philipp Ziesche, *Cosmopolitan Patriots: Americans in Paris in the Age of Revolution* (Charlottesville and London: University of Virginia Press, 2010) and Yvon Bizardel, *Les Américains à Paris sous Louis XVI et pendant la Révolution: notices biographiques* (Paris: Y. Bizardel, 1978).

26 Georges Avenel, *Anacharsis Cloots: L'orateur du genre humain* (Paris: Lacroix, Verboeckhoven and Co., 1865); Marita Gilli, *Un révolutionnaire allemand: Georg Forster 1754-1794* (Paris : CTHS, 2005).

27 Christoph Bode, 'Georg Forster in Paris 1793-1794', *Exiles, Émigrés and Expatriates in Romantic-Era Paris and London*, David Duff & Marc Porée eds. (Prague: Litteraria Pragensia, 2019), pp. 60-74.

28 Carine Lounissi's book, cited above, is a notable example.

29 Jacques Godechot, *La Grande Nation: L'éxpansion révolutionnaire de la France dans le monde de*

the foreigner in revolutionary ideology has been explored by scholars of Marxist persuasion, such as Albert Mathiez and Georges Soboul, and more recently in the works of François Furet, Sophie Wahnich and Lynn Hunt.[30] As Michael Rapport has highlighted, though Alexis de Tocqueville insisted on the transcendental power of the Revolution to unite men through their common humanity and negate national frontiers, later commentators have acknowledged the complex place of the foreigner in revolutionary thinking.

The fact that British experience during the early years of the French Revolution has been relatively sidelined in French historiography is not in itself surprising. In the political heritage of the post-revolutionary era, there has been a clear and unquestionable conjunction between the Revolution and the French nation. If the early message after the fall of the Bastille was that the Revolution represented a victory for humanity at large and was anchored in a pan-European and pan-Atlantic dynamic, 1789 soon became the founding symbol of a particular national form of republicanism. The loose divides which hardened into factional disputes in the National Convention, pitting Girondins against Montagnards, a dichotomy which is still contested by many historians, laid the foundations for nineteenth and twentieth-century political alignments and later historiographical categories. Differing paradigms of political economy, ranging from moderate liberalism to authoritarian socialism were rooted in the different traditions emerging in the revolutionary era. The Revolution therefore dictated thinking on statehood and the nation and became inextricably linked to successive upheavals and experiments, molding French collective memory and identity.[31] The place of foreign onlookers, many of whom remained on the fringes of official diplomacy, has occupied a marginal place in French scholarship.

The material difficulty of accessing manuscript sources on British involvement in the French Revolution is a factor in the neglect of emigrant radicals' place in the Revolution. The tracking of British participation in the republic is fraught with obscurities and practical obstacles and any findings

---

1789 à 1799 (Paris: Aubier, 1956). Godechot devotes several pages to the foreigners based in Paris during the Revolution. Michel Vovelle, *La Révolution française : 1789-1799* (Paris: Armand Colin, 1992). Vovelle considers the role of the Revolution in the wider world, with a significant emphasis on the military conflicts that the revolutionary authorities entered into during the ten-year period of his study.

30 See Albert Mathiez, *La Révolution et les étrangers : cosmopolitisme et défense nationale* (Paris : Renaissance du livre, 1918) and Albert Soboul, *Les sans-culottes parisiens en l'an II: histoire politique et sociale des sections de Paris, 2 juin 1793 au 9 Thermidor an II* (Paris : Clavreuil, 1958). Rapport also gives a brief summary of more recent work inspired by the François Furet school of thought. In particular, see François Furet, *Interpreting the French Revolution*, tr. E. Forster (Cambridge: Cambridge University Press, 1981), Lynn Hunt, *Politics, Culture and Class in the French Revolution* (1984; Berkerley: University of California Press, 2004) and Joan Landes, *Women in the Public Sphere in the Age of the French Revolution* (Ithaca: Cornell University Press, 1988).

31 I am grateful to Colin Jones of Queen Mary, University of London, for sharing his views on the instability of a Montagnard-Girondin dichotomy and suggesting essential reading on the French constitutional heritage.

must be gleaned from a patchwork of inchoate, scattered sources. Traces of British activities can be found in the letters in the archives of the *Comité de Salut Public* or *Comité de Sûreté Générale*, in records of foreign correspondence and in the recorded reports from state trials. Many of these sources have already been noted by historians such as John Goldworth Alger, Lionel D. Woodward and David V. Erdman and many more remain unearthed.[32] The charting of British activities was often the prerogative of spies recruited by the British government to monitor expatriate activities, such as Captain Monro, or Charles Ross who reported back to the Home Office, or of the French revolutionary authorities whose stance towards British sympathisers shifted with the outbreak of war. Their experience is therefore filtered through the lens of suspicion. As Erdman says of the *SADH*, "Its activities, indeed, were kept so secret that even the surface evidence has been ignored by most historians."[33] Such dilemmas continue to thwart attempts to gain a better understanding of the British emigrant community.

This book seeks therefore to revisit the history of a community that has been overlooked in the scholarship of both the British radical movement of the early 1790s and the French Revolution.[34] It pays attention to the complex

---

32 Most of the archival sources I have studied are those referred to by Lionel Woodward and David Erdman. Unfortunately John Alger did not cite the location of his sources in his major monograph, though it seems that many of the manuscripts that he used, from subsequent matching, were found in the Archives Nationales in Paris. I was also helped immensely by Michael Rapport's detailed footnotes and recording of sources he used in his study of nationality and citizenship. Occasionally while leafing through papers in the files mentioned by the above authors, I came across documents which were either overlooked or left unexploited by these authors. The prison records for British residents such as Robert Rayment, Robert Smith, and Christopher White receive little attention in previous studies yet sometimes add qualitatively to the perspective of British experience during the months of emergency rule. Equally, some of the pamphlets written by British residents during the constitution debate have never been properly exploited. The tracts of Robert Merry and George Edwards, apart from the mention of their existence in Alger, have not been analysed, while John Oswald's pamphlet on the new republican constitution was not given detailed attention by Erdman. Mary Wollstonecraft's *An Historical and Moral View of the French Revolution* (1794) is one of her least-studied tracts and Helen Maria William's *Letters Written in France* from 1793-94 have attracted much less attention than her first volume, written in 1790, and her later commentaries on the reign of Robespierre. Finally, Sampson Perry's monumental *An Historical Sketch of the French Revolution* (1796) has gone practically unnoticed, apart from a cursory mention in Jacques Godechot's *La Grande Nation*. Iain McCalman, in his portrait of Perry in the *Dictionary of Literary Biography*, called for more detailed study of Perry's historical account. See Iain McCalman, 'Sampson Perry, Jacobin Doctor and Journalist', *Dictionary of Literary Biography* 158, *British Reform Writers, 1789-1832* (Detroit: Gale Research, 1995). McCalman's entry on Perry is, to my knowledge, the only scholarly piece that has so far been published on the radical editor.

33 Erdman, *Commerce des Lumières*, p. 3.

34 Much historical enquiry into the revolutionary era in British academic circles has centred on the French Revolution *per se* or the influence of the French Revolution on popular politics on home soil rather than on the cross-fertilisation generated by the movement of British radicals between Britain and Paris. In the field of popular politics, E. P. Thompson's ground-breaking study *The Making of the English Working Class* (London:

political and social lives of those who took up residence in Paris, their networks, wider influences, collaborative writing projects, residential arrangements and their collective attempts to contribute to and disseminate commentary on the Revolution. Attention to these associational traits of British activism allows for insights into the continuance of Enlightenment traditions of rational exchange in the late eighteenth century but also to the ways in which such traditions were questioned, disrupted or consolidated in revolutionary Paris. It also allows us to consider the *SADH* as a much more complex and eclectic community, both politically and ideologically, than has previously been suggested.

Victor Gollancz, 1963) clearly has a legacy on British historical research today. Thompson provided a provocative interpretation of the emergence of a self-conscious working class over the period spanning the end of the eighteenth through to the mid-nineteenth century. His identification of a continuous strain of Jacobin thought through the 1790s, re-emerging in later periods of reform agitation, has been contested by some scholars. John Belchem has stressed that the literal meaning of radicalism is "to go back to the roots" in his *Popular Radicalism in Nineteenth-Century Britain* (Basingstoke: Macmillan, 1996). Belchem's suggestion is that "radicals sought almost without exception to extend and redefine, not to challenge and subvert, the proud political heritage of constitutional rights and parliamentary government." (Belchem, *Popular Radicalism*, p. 1). Radicals were renovators, not innovators, committed to appeals to history and precedent, rather than natural rights. Paineites were exceptions rather than the rule and adherents of reform were more firmly concerned with establishing themselves as the true defenders of the British constitution than denying its very existence. Such dualism, pitting rationalism against constitutionalism, has been contested by James Epstein whose work tends to demonstrate that radical discourse conjugated both emerging theoretical claims of natural equality, not necessarily themselves indicative of more radical intentions, and constitutional language inherited from 1688 and earlier. See, for example, James Epstein, *Radical Expression: Political Language, Ritual and Symbol in England, 1790-1850* (Oxford: Oxford University Press, 1994).

2

'In defence of their rights'
British reactions to the popular revolution of 10th August 1792

The dismantling of absolute monarchy in 1789 was widely celebrated in Great Britain within both Whig and radical circles. The changes being enacted in France to curtail the remit of monarchical rule were seen by reforming Whigs as the adoption in France of a constitutional framework that had been pioneered in Britain during the settlement reached after the Glorious Revolution of 1688.[1] British observers watched with interest as the

---

[1] By the mid-to-late eighteenth century, the revolutionary Whig discourse of the 1690s had been absorbed into the mainstream political language of Britain's ruling elite. Tyranny, as the narrative went, had been suppressed peacefully and moderately through the 1688 settlement. Englishmen benefited from a parliamentary system which restrained the crown, they had the right to expect trial by jury and could claim freedom of expression. Whigs continued to insist on the need to watch over the constitutional settlement to guard against abuse, yet any change would be restorative rather than innovative. The British constitution was seen as the most perfect constitution in the modern world. Montesquieu had come to prefer the British mixed constitution after failing to find a working example of good republican government during his European travels, and he was not alone among Enlightenment thinkers to hold up Britain's system of government as a model to other states. The French Revolution brought into question the Whigs' status as the party of dissent and renewal. Edmund Burke's outspoken criticism of the events of 1789 provoked a crisis at the heart of the party. Foxite Whigs opposed Burke's apparent defence of royal despotism in France, while the "New Whigs", under the leadership of Charles Grey, founded the Society of the Friends of the People and tabled a more radical reform agenda. For a brief period, animated by the success of the French Revolution, Grey and other 'new' or 'reforming' Whig members of the Friends of the People began to advocate reform of the British constitution, and found themselves on common ground with emerging popular radical societies who were arguing for more far-reaching change. Yet the Society of the Friends of the People, was in truth less about attempting to secure real reform than trying to preclude more deep-seated institutional change of the type supported by the popular reforming societies.

French Revolution unfolded and commented on the attempts to reach an agreement with a king who, on a number of occasions, demonstrated his antipathy to the demands being made to curb his sovereign power. Despite the king's attempted escape from France via Varennes in June 1791, his placating of refractory priests who had refused to sign the Civil Oath and his fundamental opposition to the principles inscribed in the new constitutional settlement, leading figures in the Constituent Assembly desperately wanted to bring some stability to the new regime. Thus, the monarchical constitution was signed in September 1791, the result of a compromise which ultimately satisfied few.[2] British onlookers noted the inherent fragility of the new regime. The British ambassador in Paris predicted, "The present constitution has no friends and cannot last,"[3] while David Williams, accepting his nomination for French citizenship on 26th October 1792, wrote, "It is not wonderful the first attempt [at a Constitution] should not have fully succeeded."[4]

Throughout 1792 threats to the constitutional settlement emerged from within and without. In June, a crowd of people marched to the Tuileries in an act of defiance towards the king, but were pacified by Louis XVI and his ministers. The king's dismissal of his Girondin counsellors on 16th June, as well as the Duke of Brunswick's declaration determining to restore absolute monarchy and punish rebellious citizens, which reached in Paris in late July, contributed to creating a climate of unrest in the capital. The shortage of food and the effects of the ongoing war with Austria and Prussia generated significant hostility towards the king and served as catalysts for the events of 10th August 1792. What became known as the 'August Days' was a popular uprising orchestrated and enacted by the militias of the sections of Paris and some from the provinces. It was the expression of mounting frustration at the behaviour of the king towards the people and the perceived failure of abortive legislative solutions to restrict his power. Louis XVI had lost what confidence remained after his attempted flight out of France the previous year. Despite the Assembly proclaiming him inviolable and therefore exempt from prosecution for his actions, many revolutionaries in the Paris Commune and the local sections had begun to discuss the merits of republican government free of monarchy. Some activists drew inspiration from earlier Cordeliers texts such as those by Louis de la Vicomterie and Pierre-François Robert. Rachel Hammersley states, "Robert's pamphlet *Républicanisme adapté à la France* is a prime example of republican propaganda designed to help its readers overcome the psychological barriers to imagining

---

2   In particular, the decision to adopt a royal veto was a source of dispute. While many monarchists in the Assembly, including Lafayette, advocated the adoption of an absolute veto, republican activists objected to the very notion of a veto.
3   Quoted in William Doyle, *The Oxford History of the French Revolution* (Oxford: Oxford University Press, 1989), p. 158.
4   Whitney R. D. Jones, *David Williams: The Anvil and the Hammer* (Cardiff: University of Wales Press, 1986), p. 119.

a French republic."⁵ The confrontation which took place between the Parisian militias and the king's Swiss Guard on 10th August forced the king to take shelter in the National Assembly. Following the events of that day, members of the Assembly, under pressure from the Revolutionary Commune of Paris, decided to detain the king and his family in the prison of the Temple, leading to the downfall of constitutional monarchy. Following a general purge of the Paris prisons at the start of the month, known as the 'September massacres', in late September 1792 "Year One" was declared, representing a break with past political forms and evoking what Benedict Anderson has termed the "sublime confidence of novelty."⁶ For Carol Blum "a whole new political and moral frame of reference had come into existence" with the founding of the French Republic on 21st September 1792.⁷

The dismantling of kingship was denounced by the majority of observers in Britain and saw reforming Whigs progressively draw back from open support for the Revolution's republican direction. Edmund Burke published a heavily critical account of the events of 10th August in his *Annual Register*. He emphasised the summary justice of the "multitude" towards those whose protection had previously been assured by the court. Priests were "cut in pieces with sabres", and the "vigorous resistance" of one of the king's bodyguards "only rendered his death more cruel." Another guard, a Monsieur Suleau, was "butchered without mercy." These acts of cruelty are contrasted with the clemency of the Swiss Guard who valiantly respected the instructions given by the king not to fire on the people, even though they were far outnumbered by the plundering "insurgents" invading the Tuileries. Burke focused on the uncompromising nature of popular vengeance and the lack of empathy shown by the militias for their victims who were "put to death in the most unfeeling manner" and, even when on their knees begging for mercy, were "seized in that attitude, and instantly thrown out of the windows into the court below."⁸

In a similar vein to Burke, Anna Seward, writing later in January 1793, denounced the "brutal indecency" of the National Convention and the "narrow-hearted and cruel policy" instituted there.⁹ She remembered the people "butchered" in their defence of Louis XVI and noted the "murderous stroke" which eventually brought an end to the monarchical dynasty in France. Cruelty, rashness and heartlessness characterised popular justice, while the monarchy and its protectors were portrayed as

---

5   Rachel Hammersley, *French Revolutionaries and English Republicans: The Cordeliers Club 1790-1794* [Rochester, NY: Boydell Press: 2005], p. 41.
6   Benedict Anderson, *Imagined Communities: Reflections on the Origin and Spread of Nationalism* (London: Verso, 2006), p. 193.
7   Carol Blum, *Rousseau and the Republic of Virtue: The Language of Politics in the French Revolution* (Ithaca: Cornell University Press, 1986), p. 171.
8   See *The Annual Register or a View of the History, Politics and Literature For the Year 1792. Part I: History of Europe* (London: Rivington, 1798), pp. 519-20.
9   Letter LXII, 17th January 1793, *Letters of Anna Seward* 3, p. 209.

demonstrating all the restraint necessary for enlightened leadership. The radical phase of the Revolution which began with the events of 10th August was also caricatured by artists such as Thomas Rowlandson, whose *The Contrast 1792. Which is Best?* (1792) drew a Manichean distinction between British civility and French barbarity. Rowlandson pitted British "loyalty", "morality", "obedience to the laws", "justice", and "happiness" against French "liberty", epitomised by "atheism, perjury, rebellion, treason, anarchy, murder, equality, madness, cruelty, injustice, treachery, ingratitude, idleness, famine, national and private ruin, misery."[10]

More accounts of events in France came out a few weeks later, in reaction to the Paris prison massacres. Most reports circulating in Britain emphasised the barbarity of the actions taking place in Paris and the dishonourable treatment of the French monarchy and aristocracy by a rampant and uncivilised mob. Lord Auckland wrote that those who took part in the prison massacres were "amused by shedding blood."[11] One of Lord Auckland's informers wrote of "new massacres; of 160 priests being butchered in a church; of all the prisoners confined in all the prisons having been deliberately and in orderly succession put to death."[12] The stories of the attacks on the French prisons in early September contributed to discrediting the latest developments in the Revolution in Britain by the end of 1792. Sir James Bland Burges, writing from Whitehall in early September 1792, only days after the massacres noted, "The French excesses, I fancy, have made a great impression here. Everything with us is quieter than ever, and a general indignation seems to prevail amidst all descriptions of men, whenever the conversation turns on the recent transactions at Paris."[13] Yet Bland Burges remained concerned about British emigrants in the French capital. He wrote to Lord Auckland warning that members of the English and Scottish contingent in Paris were "at present employed in writing a justification of democracy and an invective against monarchy in the abstract which is to be printed at Paris, and dispersed throughout England and Ireland. The names of some of them are Watts and Wilson, of Manchester, Oswald, a Scotsman; Stone, an Englishman, and Macintosh, who wrote against Burke."[14] It is not clear which text is being referred to, if indeed it existed, but the letter gives a stark indication of the anxiety British presence in Paris in early September 1792 provoked within the ruling administration.

---

10 Thomas Rowlandson, *The Contrast 1792. Which is Best?* (1793).
11 *Journal and Correspondence of William, Lord Auckland*, vol. 2 (London: Bentley, 1861-1862), p. 438.
12 Ibid, p. 440.
13 Bland Burges to Lord Auckland, Whitehall, 7th September 1792, ibid, p. 378. Sir James Bland Burges was writing in the wake of the September massacres, an event which helped to alienate the bulk of the British population from the Revolution and its violent excesses. The papers of Bland Burges, who was under-secretary of state for Foreign Affairs between 1789 and 1795 and who went on to work with David Williams on the Literary Fund, are held in the Bodleian Library, Oxford.
14 Mr. Burges to Lord Auckland, Whitehall, 4th September 1792, ibid, p. 438.

The response of the king's guards towards the people of Paris on 10th August made a lasting impression on British residents of the capital and governed many of their subsequent reactions to the next stages of the Revolution. Their reactions could not have been more different to those of Burke, Seward and Burges. Four residents who would go on to join the *SADH*, including Robert Rayment and James Gamble, orchestrated a fundraising initiative – acknowledged and praised by the National Convention – in the wake of the clashes, to raise money for the widows and orphans left without means because of the deaths of those whom Rayment described in a later statement as "the heroes of the *journée* of the 10th August."[15] The episode was recorded later in Rayment's prison file, where it was noted that "on the fourth day after the memorable victory at the Tuileries, he appeared with other Englishmen, republicans at heart, at the bar of the National Assembly to present their fraternal donations to the widows and orphans of the free men who died for their country on the 10th August."[16] One of the donors was Sir Robert Smith, former Member of Parliament for Colchester. Smith, incarcerated under the emergency measures introduced against foreign residents of Paris in 1793, claimed in his prison deposition to have donated 1,910 *livres* to, among others, the cause of the victims of the Tuileries.[17]

The ascendancy of popular sovereignty in France, manifested on 10th August, caused concern among Whig reformers in Britain who did not wish to see any outbursts of unrestrained popular activism undermine reforming initiatives at home. The Society of the Friends of the People, a Whig outfit established in April 1792 and finding common cause at its inception with the London Corresponding Society and the Society for Constitutional Information, progressively distanced itself from both radical reform societies, who had supported part two of Paine's *Rights of Man*, and the events of the Revolution during the latter months of the year. Sampson Perry noted the waning support of the Whig society for radical reform in a column published in November 1792, just before he left for Paris:

> We at first observed of this Society, that it appeared to us to be designed as a conductor to turn away the lightening accompanying the thunder of the Public for a reform of abuses in Government ... we hope they will [now] lay aside their violent fears, at least those expressed for the several classes of men whose interest they profess to have at heart. There is no occasion for apprehensions from Mr. Paine's advice on the score of Economy and Reform.[18]

---

15 Robert Rayment makes reference to his support for the widows and children of the Tuileries in his prison declaration. See AN F7/4774/88.
16 AN F7/4774/88.
17 AN F7 4775/20/3, the file is recorded under the name of Smyth.
18 *The Argus*, 16th November 1792, quoted in Jon Mee, 'The Magician No Conjuror: Robert Merry and the Political Alchemy of the 1790s' in Paul A. Pickering and Michael T. Davis (eds.), *Unrespectable Radicals?: Popular Politics in the Age of Reform* (Aldershot, England:

Some members of the Friends of the People, such as Perry, Robert Merry, Lord Edward Fitzgerald, D. E. MacDonnell and John Hurford Stone, who established themselves in Paris and contributed to setting up the English-speaking society in the capital, rescinded their membership of the Whig society over the following months, disillusioned at its lack of support for more far-reaching reform.[19]

For those British residents who had witnessed the August Days and who put their observations to paper, their accounts were often written with the broad intention of correcting what they saw as the misinformation circulating in their home country about the behaviour of the people of Paris. In volume IV of her *Letters from France*, British resident and reformer, Helen Maria Williams, who had watched the events from her window at rue Hélvetius, within viewing distance of the royal palace, explained the outbreak of violence in the prisons on the 2nd September by reference to the sentiment of injustice that prevailed in the wake of the clashes on 10th August. Williams denied the portrait circulating in London of "a mere wanton and unprovoked effusion of the cruelty and ferociousness of the French populace," and set out the rational basis of the actions as well as their place in the annals of human history.[20] Rather than being proof of the unprecedented depravity of an entire population, the prison massacres were the explicable result of the "wrath and fury" of the victims of 10th August.[21] Williams emphasised what she saw as the understandable impatience of the people, who had been kept waiting too long for justice after the August Days, when husbands, brothers and fathers had been killed. One eighteen-year-old "had lost two brothers the tenth of August, and was resolved to revenge their death."[22] Williams drew the conclusion that the prison massacres could not be blamed on the perpetrators themselves but on the chain of betrayals that preceded and thus prompted the actions: "I must believe that the treachery of the court made the tenth of August – the tenth of August made the foundation of the second of September – and the Duke

---

Ashgate, 2008), p. 49.

19 A number of the members of the Paris society had been involved in the early meetings of the Society of the Friends of the People. John Hurford Stone, D. E. MacDonnell, Sampson Perry, Robert Merry and Lord Edward Fitzgerald were all either among the society's members or had initially expressed support for its objectives. Merry, Fitzgerald, Stone and MacDonnell all signed the Friends of the People declaration of 11th April 1792 but all were absent at the signing of the address printed on 30th April 1793. By late 1792, these central figures of the Paris contingent no longer held out any hope for elite Whig assistance in the cause of political reform and were disappointed by the society's refusal to support the SCI's collaboration with Paine.

20 Helen M. Williams, *Letters from France: Containing A Great Variety of Interesting and Original Information concerning the most important events that have lately occurred in that country, and particularly respecting the campaign of 1792* (London: G. G. and J. Robinson, 1793), p. 182.

21 Ibid, vol. IV, p. 191. Williams was critical also of leaders of the Paris Commune, who included members of what would later be termed the Montagne who she considered gave their tacit consent to the killings.

22 Ibid, vol. IV, p. 206.

of Brunswick provoked the execution of it."[23] William Johnson, a member of the *SADH* may have been the author of an eyewitness account covering the period from December 1791 to February 1793. Although critical of the "treacheries" of the king, the account was more uncompromising that Williams' piece in denouncing the excesses of violence of the Paris populace towards those considered close to the court. He wrote how "grown arrogant in destruction and insolent in the exercise of lawless power, they resolved on the commission of crimes that will be an everlasting blot in the annals of France."[24] Opinions diverged therefore among British observers who had witnessed the August Days firsthand.

A CIRCUMSTANTIAL HISTORY OF THE TRANSACTIONS AT PARIS ON THE TENTH OF AUGUST

It is likely that British resident of Paris, Robert Merry, was the author of *A Circumstantial History of the transactions at Paris on the tenth of August* (1792).[25] An enthusiast of the French Revolution, Robert Merry, who had also been a member of the Society of the Friends of the People and the Society for Constitutional Information, went to France to witness the events of 1789 before returning again in 1791 and settling for a longer spell in 1792. He appears to have been in Paris by the time of the arrest of the king, and he went on to join the *SADH* from its inception in November, attending weekly meetings at White's hotel and presiding over a gathering of the society on 16th December 1792. David Erdman considers Merry to have been a member of the central revolutionary committee of the society and this seems to be confirmed by his place on the list of loyal British citizens drawn up in March 1793 by Merry's own translator, Irish resident Nicholas Madgett.[26]

The anonymous pamphlet was published by radical publishers H. D. Symonds, Robert Thomson and R. Lyttlejohn in early September 1792. It had initially been sent to a newspaper editor as a riposte to a report vilifying the people after the 10th August.[27] On 11th September 1792 *The Times* advertised the imminent appearance of "A PARTICULAR ACCOUNT of the Rise,

---

23 Ibid, vol. IV, p. 207.
24 *A genuine narrative of the proceedings at Paris from the 16th of December, 1791, to the 1st of February, 1793: containing, among other interesting anecdotes, a particular statement of the memorable tenth of August and third of September. To which is annexed the life, trial, and execution, of Louis XVI. By Mr. Johnson, Who was an Eye-Witness of the Whole of the Transactions* (London: Turner, 1793), p. 21.
25 Robert Merry [?], *A Circumstantial History of the Transactions at Paris on the Tenth of August Plainly Shewing the Perfidy of Louis XVI, and the General Unanimity of the People, in Defence of their Rights* (London: Symonds, 1792).
26 David Erdman, *Commerce des Lumières*, p. 234. Erdman refers to an announcement in *The Manchester Herrald* of 1st December 1792 which named Merry, Hurford Stone, Fitzgerald and Paine as among the individuals worthy of attention.
27 Symonds also published Sampson Perry's *An Historical Sketch of the French Revolution* in 1796.

and also of the Fall of Despotism in Paris, on the 10th of August, and the Treasons of Royalty, anterior and subsequent to that period. By Robert Merry, Esq."[28] *The Morning Chronicle* and *Lloyd's Evening Post* also advertised the publication the same week. Although the title is different, no other tract by Merry of the August Days has been located. In addition, the particular contents of *A Circumstantial History* suggest that it was published by a pro-revolutionary British writer who had been a witness to the events, evidence which points to Merry's authorship. The fact that it was published by radical printers H. D. Symonds and Robert Thomson would also tend to suggest that the author was known to the radical community. According to Alger, Thomson had denounced Captain Monro as a spy in Paris in early 1793 and, if this was the case, would probably have met Merry at White's hotel. Such evidence gives further weight to the presumption that Merry was the anonymous author.[29]

The tract is a vindication of the popular intervention in the Revolution, manifested on 10th August, and a condemnation of Louis XVI and Marie Antoinette. Published only weeks after the arrest of the royal family, it is divided into two parts: a preface, or address "to the public", in which the author explains his reasons for writing, followed by an account of the events themselves. While the preface is the work of the author, the account of the events at the Tuileries, as stated by the author in the address, was taken almost word for word from an edition of the weekly newspaper *Révolutions de Paris*, covering the week of 4th to 11th August 1792.[30] The journal, founded in 1789, was a radical publication under the editorship of Louis-Marie Prud'homme.

The author's stated intention in publishing the tract was to allow people in Britain to "hear the other side" of the story of the August Days, given the "imperfect details" which had lately reached London. He wrote because of his "surprise" and "sorrow at seeing the accounts given in papers in Wednesday and Thursday last, of the events which took place here in the 10th August."[31] The author was receiving the British daily newspapers relatively soon after their publication and determined to pen a riposte within the month. The accounts contained in these publications had, according to the author, "industriously suppressed everything which might appear like a justification of the conduct of the people."[32] His aim was to contrast the

---

28 *The Times*, 11th September 1792.
29 My thanks go to Jon Mee for drawing my attention to this tract, the newspaper announcements and the probability of Merry's authorship.
30 The account is faithful to the original report contained in *Révolutions de Paris, dédiées à la nation et au district des petits-augustins, quatrième année de la liberté française* 161, 4-11th August 1792, pp. 229-39. The report in the French journal also goes on to discuss the days which followed the 10th August. These following reports are not retranscribed in *A Circumstantial History*. The account is almost entirely faithful to the original apart from the omission of one or two paragraphs which does not alter the main message of the text.
31 Merry [?], *A Circumstantial History*, p. 17.
32 Ibid, p. v.

"perfidy" of the king with the "general unanimity of the people in defence of their rights," something the newspapers in Britain had failed to do. He also advised that the standards of British political life should not be imposed on France because of the "widely different manner in which political parties are circumstanced in that country and our own."[33] He intended to correct the errors circulating in Britain by those "venal prints with as little regard to decency and to truth."[34] The French nation would be shielded from reproach and the people, struggling for their freedom, vindicated.

Like other British writers based in Paris who wrote about what they witnessed, the author of *A Circumstantial History* attempted to provide what he considered to be a just account of the advent of popular sovereignty to counter the false reports widely available in Britain and correct prevailing public opinion: "The least informed amongst us, if candour guides his judgment, must recant the unfavourable sentiments which from the first *exaggerated* view of the late melancholy events, he may have been led to entertain of the French people, or the present ruling party in that country."[35] These faulty reports were propagated by a misguided reporter whose other interests in Paris "have prevented him from viewing this great event on all its sides, or on the side that he ought."[36] If eyewitness observation could be held up as a source of authority by some British writers at the scene, not all firsthand accounts were deemed reliable. Those who did not have liberty as an object and who were prejudiced against the changes taking place in France could not, in the author's view, be relied upon to convey a true account of the events.

Although the report revises prevailing perceptions of the battle at the Tuileries, the author does not deny that "horrors" and "cruelties" were perpetrated. Yet he accepts these as "the effects of a just and *necessary* self-defence on the part of the people."[37] The integrity and courage of the populace is contrasted with the venality of the nobility and the behaviour of the king, depicted as a "weak, voluptuous man." In a similar way to Sampson Perry, whose later work, *An Historical Sketch of the French Revolution*, would retrace similar themes of a virtuous people struggling against the hypocrisy of the privileged classes, the author considered that popular vengeance would not have been required had the enemies of the Revolution not plunged the country into war on all fronts and had the privileged given up their titles willingly. The clergy and nobility were intriguers who had concerted with foreign powers and insidious monarchs to orchestrate the downfall of the Revolution.

The author of *A Circumstantial History* concludes the preface with an optimistic view of the advent of republican government, stating that "by the

---

33 Ibid, p. iv.
34 Ibid, p. iv.
35 Ibid, p. vi.
36 Ibid, p. 18.
37 Ibid, p. vii.

general diffusion of knowledge, the political mists are fast dissipating, which have hitherto obscured the minds of men in general." The author confirms his belief that man's knowledge was advancing. Such progress is attributed to the work being done in France but also to the uncovering of the myth of British freedom and rights which had blinded people to the need for reform at home.[38] The appeal "to the public" is itself an assertion of the importance of popular understanding of the Revolution, over and above the necessity of convincing foreign governments of the justice of the changes taking place in France. While the ruling ministry could conclude that the events of the 10th August were manifestations of popular insubordination and barbarity, it was important to educate the British people as to the true nature of the Revolution and disclose what was seen as a conspiracy to keep the people in ignorance.

The preface therefore outlines the author's views and aims at vindicating the expression of popular sovereignty manifested on 10th August which had received broadly negative press in Britain. The reader is warned not to be "deceived by empty sounds" and the widespread use of the term "faction" to describe the current French government is denounced as an insidious strategy to discredit legitimate opposition to established rule. This is an echo of the epigraph chosen for the account. The author quotes Harrington's maxim that "Treason ne'er prospers – what's the reason? If it prospers – none dare call it treason!" Although it is attributed to Jonathan Swift on the title page, the reflection on the justice of opposition to tyranny was also part of a long-standing English republican tradition stretching back to the mid-seventeenth century. Radical writers would often note how simple opposition to established forms could be passed off as sedition or treason by the ruling authorities, intent on quelling all forms of dissent. Writers therefore took every opportunity to highlight the workings of this mechanism in their public addresses. Thomas Paine in "An Address to the Addressers" had argued that his suggestions for improvement in government had simply been dismissed as libel so that the ruling ministry could avoid having to contend with the legitimate claims he had advanced. If all the reforms he argued for were libel, he claimed, "let the name of libeller be engraved on my tomb."[39] Equally, Mary Wollstonecraft, in her account of the French Revolution, described how Chief Justice Mansfield, responsible for sedition trial proceedings in Britain, "established it as a law precedent, that the greater the truth the greater the libel."[40] A common trait therefore in radical texts was to

---

38 Ibid, p. xv.
39 Paine, 'An Address to the Addressers', in *CWTP* vol, 2, p. 488.
40 Mary Wollstonecraft, *An Historical and Moral View of the Origins and Progress of the French Revolution; and the Effect it has Produced in Europe* (1794) in Janet M. Todd and Marilyn Butler (eds.), *The Works of Mary Wollstonecraft: An Historical and Moral View of the French Revolution. Letters to Joseph Johnson. Letters Written in Sweden, Norway and Denmark* (London: Pickering, 1989), p. 117.

expose charges of sedition, or even treason, as tools employed by the ruling authorities to silence those who challenged the status quo.[41]

The preface is followed by a detailed account of the August Days, based entirely on the version of events published in the *Révolutions de Paris* only days after the invasion of the Tuileries. The epigraph of the journal was *Les grands ne nous paraissent grands que parce que nous sommes à genoux. Levons-nous!* ("The great only appear great to us because we are on our knees. Let us rise up!") Writers on the paper included Elisée Loustalot, Sylvain Maréchal, Pierre Gaspard Chaumette and Philippe Fabre d'Églantine. The latter was involved in the Revolutionary Tribunal and went on to be accused and executed with the Dantonists in April 1794. Loustalot was a radical editor of the paper but died from illness in 1790 and Maréchal, a journalist and spokesman of the disaffected masses and adherent of Babeuf after 1794, militated for the cause of atheism and agrarian reform to help the poor. The final contributor, Chaumette, had been involved in promoting the cause of social reform and was ultimately executed because of his democratic tendencies, having associated indirectly with Jacques Hébert, who would also be guillotined in early 1794 for espousing even more extreme views than the *Comité de Salut Public*. He was a severe critic of the Girondin members of the National Convention and sympathised with the cause of the lower classes.

These preoccupations – the moral superiority of the people, the condemnation of the repression of the lower classes, the right to resist kingly oppression and militate for wide-reaching political and social reform – are clearly discernable in the report of the August Days republished in *A Circumstantial History*. The *Révolutions de Paris* version was translated and reprinted in English with some annotated comments by the British author. The engravings included in the edition – depictions of the removal of royal statues from two sites in Paris, the stand-off between the people of Paris and the Swiss Guards and of the funeral pyre of the victims who fell in the struggle – were also strongly supportive of the popular seizure of power. They were not however reproduced in *A Circumstantial History*. The account blames the insurrection on the cowardliness of the "insidious" Louis and the hypocrisy of his ministers.[42] It even suggests that the ministry was attempting to foment rebellion by detaining Jérôme Pétion, the mayor of Paris, whose influence over the people was substantial. The author highlights the dishonourable conduct of the king's guards who targeted women and children when firing from their protected positions within the palace walls.

---

41 John Barrell has also studied this trait of British radicalism, highlighting how "the notion that the political conflict of the period was to be regarded as a conflict, among other things, about the meaning of words, was a theme of numerous liberal or radical texts of the 1790s." See John Barrell, *Imagining the King's Death: Figurative Treason, Fantasies of Regicide, 1793-1796* (Oxford: Oxford University Press, 2000), p. 1.

42 Merry [?], *A Circumstantial History*, p. 21.

The subservience of the king's guards ("savages in black") is brought into sharp contrast with the bravery of the men who led the siege of the palace.[43] Their ardour and spirit contributed to the overwhelming of the royal force, despite the underhand tactics used such as "false patrols", who pretended to be at one with the people but whose actual aim was to assassinate Pétion. The report emphasises the orderliness of the people, their capacity for rational decision-making and prudent voting behaviour. Their violence and vengeance are not downplayed however, and the account describes how the militia members systematically pursued and put their enemies to death for their crimes. In their victory, the people showed restraint, "moderation", and "generosity", claiming some remnants of their victory but not resorting to looting.[44] They deposited the treasures found in the palace in the National Assembly rather than dividing them up as spoils.

The account is annotated with personal remarks from the British author on the details given in the official report from the French newspaper in the form of footnotes. In one such note, the author claims to have met with Jérôme Pétion on 9th August 1792. It was quite likely that Merry would have met with the mayor of Paris on arriving in Paris or even earlier, on his visit to London in 1791, as Merry spent much of his time over the years 1791 to 1793 travelling back and forth between the two capitals. The British residents in the French capital were on good terms with Pétion and some had met him during his 1791 visit to Britain. Several, including John Hurford Stone, Thomas Christie and David Williams, wrote to him during the course of 1792 to praise his conduct in re-establishing order in the capital based on firm but just principles. The editorial notes also corroborate the assertion made in the report that it was the royal guards who had provoked the assault on the Tuileries rather than the people. The author describes walking through the streets near the Tuileries before the events, where he "saw not the least appearance of a tumult. The alarm-bell was sounding, and the drums beating, but everything else was still as death. I could not help observing at the time, that the intention seemed rather to be to form a riot than to quell one."[45] The footnotes also confirm the view put forward in the report that the guards lacked honour and rectitude. Far from meeting the standards of chivalry and bravery expected of an elite force, they ran away through the palace once they realised their positions have been overcome.[46] The editorial notes consolidate the portrait of the bravery of the people, who entered the palace and resisted fire: "I could not have conceived that it was possible, had I not witnessed it, that there could have been found men so prodigal of life, as those who first entered the garden."[47]

---

43 Ibid, p. 34.
44 Ibid, p. 35.
45 Ibid, p. 21, note 2.
46 Ibid, p. 32, note 6. For a pro-royalty version of these events, see Grace Dalrymple Elliott, *Journal of my Life during the French Revolution* (London: Rodale Press, 1859).
47 Merry [?], *A Circumstantial History*, p. 33, n. 7.

The notes are a resounding validation of the version of events presented in the translated text from the *Révolutions de Paris*. The portrait of the scene at the end of the day is deemed "perfectly exact".[48] This description, which closes the text, depicts with pathos the anguish of those who had lost relatives during the siege and their determination to locate the corpses of loved ones. The author recalls the individual cases of women lifting up the heads of the dead, surveying the grounds for signs of members of their families, and taking away the wounded and those who had perished. This final focus on the devastation caused to the poor, who lost members of their intimate families, confirms the intention of the author to bring to the fore both the courage but also the humanity of the ordinary people of Paris compared to the regime under which they struggled. The version of this scene published in *A Circumstantial History* may have influenced other British writers and editors who wrote of the August Days in their own testimonies. Sampson Perry's account, published in *An Historical Sketch of the French Revolution* in 1796, is almost identical in tone and emphasis.

The tract attempted to undermine the accounts circulating in the British press of the events of 10th August 1792, in particular one published in "a morning paper" whose identity is not revealed. It was a defence of the people's justice and a condemnation of the king, his guards and his ministers. By using a translated version of the *Révolutions de Paris* report, the author not only showed his approval of the radical reading of the day's occurrences put forward by a newspaper with ties to *sans culotte* activism, but revealed that he had direct access to the principal news sources of Paris and could discriminate between those of merit and those of little value. This position is clearly visible in the footnote commentaries which corroborate the original report. British observers were anxious to prove the validity of their accounts in the face of widespread scepticism towards the unfolding Revolution and their own place at the scene. The decision to use reports from on the ground, which had been translated from the French, was a way of emphasising the reliability and accuracy of their writings. The choice to use this particular account – one which was uncompromising in its support for the people and on the radical wing of the revolutionary movement – was also loaded with political significance.

If *A Circumstantial History* was indeed the account by Robert Merry advertised in the British press in early September 1792, it is a testimony to the determination of British emigrants to publicly, and in print, support events which had been vilified by newspapers at home and which may have guided prevailing attitudes to French affairs in their home country. In the column adjacent to the September 1792 advertisement of the account of the August Days, published in *The Times*, is included a strong denunciation of the prison massacres committed by a "sanguinary mob" only a week earlier. The displaying of heads on pikes to the Queen, the King and their children steals

---

48 Ibid, p. 36, n. 9.

the headline and the editors add in square brackets, "We have noticed this remark, in order to shew the base calumnies that are propagated concerning these August Personages."[49] *The Times* was a newspaper which strongly supported the official government line and was openly hostile to the Revolution at this stage.

The August Days provoked mixed responses in Great Britain. While the popular assault on royal power and arrest of the king was seen by some in Whig ranks as an indication that the French Revolution was moving further away from a revered British constitutional model, there were also expressions of support, in particular from within the growing pro-revolutionary emigrant community resident in Paris, some of whom progressively abandoned Whig reforming groups over the course of late 1792 and 1793. The events may also have played a part in encouraging some radical reformers in Britain to take up residence in the French capital. What appears certain is that the events of the 10th August – which recast the people as sovereign within the nation – resonated with the British community in Paris and were inextricable therefore from their hopes for transformation on home soil. It also provides further evidence of a trait common to a large number of British revolutionary sympathisers who took up residence in Paris in late 1792; a willingness to countenance a greater degree of popular participation in the political life of a country than was admitted – and widely desired – in the strictly delineated, property-based electoral system and parliamentary model of Great Britain.

---

49   *The Times*, 11th September 1792.

3

British emigration to early republican Paris in 1792-1793

A number of men and women crossed the Channel to take up residence in Paris in late 1792. For British emigrants, stays could vary from a few months to decades with some visitors making numerous trips backwards and forwards. Others embarked on one visit which would never be repeated, while several made Paris their permanent residence, enduring and sometimes exploiting the uncertainties of the revolutionary and imperial regimes. Some British residents of Paris had had previous experience of emigration and had been active in European radical circles, although for the majority their residence in Paris appears to have been one of their first expeditions abroad. Thomas Paine had recently returned from the new American republic and Robert Merry had played a key role in the founding of the Della Cruscan poetic circle in Florence in the late 1780s and, while in Italy, may have militated for Florentine independence.[1] For many however, France was the first direct contact they had had with an alternative regime and their first experience of radical activism outside Britain.

John Hurford Stone travelled between London and Paris until 1793, when he set up an English printing press and began a period of permanent residence. Helen Maria Williams first went to Paris in July 1790, returning to London in September of the same year to publish her first volume of letters. She returned with her mother and sisters in 1792. Stone and Williams lived out the rest of their lives together in the French capital, under changing regimes. Stone was buried in Père Lachaise cemetery on his death in 1818 and Williams lived until 1827, finishing off a final account of her memories

---

1   M. Ray Adams, 'Robert Merry, Political Romanticist', *Studies in Romanticism* 2 (New York, 1965), p. 25.

29

of the revolutionary age, which was translated by her nephew and published in 1828 in a French edition under the title of *Souvenirs de la Révolution française*.²

Thomas Christie made three visits to Paris, first in 1791, when he embarked on a translation of the new monarchical constitution into English, then later in 1792, and finally again in the spring of 1793. Sampson Perry visited France twice, once for a short visit in October 1792, when he tried to generate interest in a project to publish his newspaper *The Argus*. He left London for a longer stay at the end of the year. Perry would stay in Paris until November 1794, when he was released from prison. For fourteen months of this stay he was lodged in Paris jails. After a few months in Paris, Irish resident Robert O'Reilly went to Britain briefly in 1793 to attend a trial before returning to Paris and establishing himself as an inventor and editor of the *Annales des Arts et Manufactures* journal, while John Frost made two short visits to Paris, firstly accompanying Thomas Paine in mid-September 1792 and again in November 1792 as part of the Society for Constitutional Information delegation.³ He returned to London in February 1793. Robert Merry had visited France on at least two occasions, first over the course of 1788 and 1789 and again in 1791, before making a longer visit spanning mid-1792 to May 1793. Even during this stay, he returned to Britain between the end of September and October 1792, attending an SCI meeting on 28th September and sitting on the committee chosen to consult the London Corresponding Society on a congratulatory address to the National Convention.⁴ Despite having settled in France and founded a journal entitled the *Universal Patriot* in 1790, John Oswald continued to write for the *Gazetteer* in Britain until June 1791. He died fighting for the French republic during the Vendée uprising in September 1793.

Such individual examples point to the fact that the nature of emigration to Paris varied and highlight how most radicals who settled in France during this period continued to pursue activities in both countries. Identifying a pattern to stays in Paris is problematic as the length, nature and motivation of visits were invariably determined by individual circumstances. Yet what seems undeniable is that British reformers visiting Paris initially opted for short, exploratory trips before making any attempt to settle in the French capital and their stays could vary from a few weeks to several years,

---

2   Helen Maria Williams, *Souvenirs de la Révolution française* (Paris: Dondey-Dupré, 1828).
3   See AN F7/4412. O'Reilly suggests that his return to Britain was to attend the trial of Richard Sheridan, the famous Whig theatre proprietor. Sheridan, though heavily involved in campaigns for the liberty of the press and a campaigner against the war with France, was not brought to trial. There is a possibility that O'Reilly wanted to attend a trial where Sheridan was to be called as a witness, or that he simply used the excuse of a trial as a pretext to temporarily leave the country while tensions mounted against foreigners.
4   See James Clifford, 'Robert Merry, A Pre-Byronic Hero', *Bulletin of the John Rylands Library* 27.1 (December 1942), pp. 74-96. Merry was in Paris from May to October 1788 and visited again after the fall of the Bastille in summer 1789 when he attended debates at the National Assembly. See also Jon Mee, 'The Magician No Conjuror'.

depending on imperatives at home and both opportunities available and obstacles encountered in Paris. They continued to be involved in both British and French editing, publishing and reforming networks as they travelled and took part in a two-way transfer of knowledge and news that the short distance across the Channel allowed.

The pattern of returning to Britain from France was more predictable, and there were two major waves of departures. A considerable number of British residents took the decision to leave Paris permanently in the spring of 1793 once their status in the capital began to be brought into doubt and as draconian measures began to be taken against both their Girondin acquaintances in the French revolutionary administration and against citizens of countries at war with France. Robert Merry left Paris in May 1793 after hastily negotiating a passport from his friend, Jacques-Louis David, while Charlotte Smith and Robert O'Reilly secured temporary passports to leave in late spring 1793, both promising to return at a later date. George Edwards took the opportunity to flee Paris in July 1793, having offered his views on the new constitution and political affairs of France in published essays.[5] For those who remained after mid-1793, most would go on to have some experience of incarceration, and the next opportunity afforded them to leave either permanently or temporarily, was in the months following Thermidor.[6] After July 1794, apart from those whose case was put forward for special residence permission, most took the opportunity of the relaxation of emergency measures and liberation from imprisonment to travel on elsewhere, sometimes to Switzerland, Hamburg or the United States. Others returned to Britain to either remain indefinitely or later seek emigration elsewhere. Some, such as Henry Redhead Yorke, went back to Paris during the brief cessation of hostilities between Britain and France that began in 1802 with the Treaty of Amiens.

Others would go on to experiment with transatlantic travel. Thomas Cooper went to America after a brief stay in France. He would later compare the French Revolution unfavourably to the American Revolution, despite his earlier optimism. Sampson Perry arrived in France with an initial plan of making his way via the continent to American shores, yet his plan never came to fruition, probably thwarted by his prolonged detention in French jails from 1793 to 1794 and the financial hardship he endured. Robert Merry

---

5   See AN F7/4412. Edwards asked for a passport out of France, stating that he had all the required documents. He also insisted that, if necessary, he could prove his loyalty to the French Revolution and the "spotlessness" of his political principles by reference to his tracts previously presented to the Convention.

6   The fall of Robespierre on 9 Thermidor An II is often seen as a pivotal moment, signalling not only the end of the Terror, with public opinion resolutely rejecting the continued pursuit of radical revolutionary justice and emergency governance, but also the beginning of the end of the Revolution. However, there were many extremists among the Thermidorians and little concern was paid initially to the fate of British residents in French jails. Some, such as Robert Rayment and Thomas Paine, remained behind bars for months before their petitions were recognised and their freedom secured.

did eventually emigrate to America, after returning to England from France in the summer of 1793. He made the transatlantic crossing with his wife in 1796. Helen Maria Williams and John Hurford Stone were forced into a protracted stay in Switzerland after being marked out as suspects by the French authorities in April 1794, and Mary Wollstonecraft undertook a mission from France to Sweden, Denmark and Norway on behalf of Gilbert Imlay, before returning to London in 1795. While some members of the *SADH* were seasoned international travellers who had occasionally been involved in earlier revolutionary struggles, the prior experience of the majority of British visitors to Paris was restricted to the domestic reform scene.

For British men and women with radical sympathies who were seeking emigration, two choices opened up to them in 1792. While some chose to settle in France, a significant number decided to take up residence in the new American republic. Michael Durey has carried out a comprehensive investigation of the reasons for British emigration to America in the late eighteenth and early nineteenth century and he identified different factors prompting departure. There were those of a radical background who withdrew from Britain or Ireland to gain tactical advantage and renew their forces for the next move, fully intending to return once the time was right. This group included Irish militants such as Archibald Hamilton Rowan who were planning for an Irish uprising with French backing. A significant number chose exile as the only alternative to the scaffold or transportation to Botany Bay, particularly after the failed Irish Rebellion of 1798. Others, such as Joseph Priestley, chose exile to America because of persistent intimidation by loyalist gangs in Britain. Priestley's home had been attacked by Church and King rioters in Birmingham in July 1791 and Priestley was cast as a national pariah in the subsequent months. Finally, those who turned informers and spies often sought refuge in America once their identity and safety had been compromised.

America boasted a host of attractions for British and Irish radicals. It was seen as a neutral country amid the conflicts of European war which had broken out in 1792. It conjured up visions of prosperity and liberty and was considered the most promising asylum for those fleeing persecution. Many had trade or family connections already established and therefore drew on those networks in seeking refuge outside the British and Irish Isles. The American political system was also considered a model of democracy and moderate republicanism, and was brought into sharp contrast with France once the emergency rule of the *Comité de Salut Public* began in 1793.

The American republic may therefore have proved attractive to those of more temperate radical leanings. Durey suggests that "John Thelwall, probably the most erudite of the LCS political thinkers, noted that more advanced radicals were impressed by France, the moderate by America."[7]

---

7 Michael Durey, *Transatlantic Radicals and the Early American Republic*, (Lawrence: University

While the American republican model became associated, for some, with a quasi-monarchical form of republicanism with a powerful executive office, by mid-1791, on the other hand, the French Revolution had started to take a more radical direction after the king's abortive flight to Varennes and republican voices had begun to be heard with greater urgency. After the events of late 1792 and early 1793, it became clear that the republican shift in France would be of an entirely different character than that of America. Most British activists arrived in Paris at this crossroads and their decision to emigrate to France might point to the fact that they were prepared to witness, encourage and participate in a radical republican experiment with a greater degree of popular involvement in political affairs than that underway across the Atlantic.

Men and women who spent time in Paris, such as Robert Merry and Mary Wollstonecraft, were also sceptical about whether the cultural and social life developing on American soil would be able to rival that of Europe. They doubted the capacity of the American republic to offer the same potential for literary, cultural and intellectual betterment as Europe. France in the early years of the 1790s still inspired idealism as to the political and cultural progress it might encourage, hopes which had slowly dissipated across the Atlantic. Unease at the cultural repercussions of an advanced, predominantly commercial society, which relied on trade and speculation for its riches, dampened enthusiasm for emigration to America. Mary Wollstonecraft chastised Gilbert Imlay in successive letters for his blind pursuit of wealth to the detriment of personal fulfilment and simpler pleasures. She reiterated this contempt for commerce in her *Letters Written in Sweden, Norway and Denmark* (1796), where she seemed to dismiss all ideas she may have had of emigrating to America. Interest in industry and knowledge prompted equivocal reactions during the early Revolution yet proliferated under the Directoire and Empire.[8] While it is possible that Wollstonecraft's distaste for commerce was tied up with her disapproval of Imlay's repeated absences, (and the different view given in her *An Historical and Moral View of the French Revolution* that "the friction of arts and commerce have given to society the transcendentally pleasing polish of urbanity" would support this argument), she may also have had deeper cultural reservations about the potential for the progress of knowledge and manners across the Atlantic.[9]

A major attraction of France, in comparison to the American republic, was its proximity. Travelling to the French capital demanded planning, but it was considerably more convenient than a trans-Atlantic crossing. Visits to

---

Press of Kansas, 1997), p. 166.
8 See Jean Tulard, *Les Thermidoriens* (Paris: Fayard, 2005). Tulard's study shows, among other things, that the Thermidorian years saw an exponential growth in industry, the arts and intellectual pursuits, leading to the establishment of many enduring institutions which are not conventionally associated with this period of French history, such as the *Arts et Métiers*.
9 *HMV*, p. 16.

France could be impromptu and temporary, without necessitating the sort of forward-thinking and uprooting of family life that was inevitable in emigration to America. In contrast to those who took up residence across the Atlantic, those who settled in France could envisage making shorter exploratory visits before opting for a longer stay and often managed to travel back and forth between London and Paris, continuing ventures in both cities. The reservations that radicals felt about going to America therefore combined ideological difference and cultural anxiety with the practical obstacles of long-distance travel.

Those of radical sympathy who went to Paris to investigate the Revolution at close hand varied in age and experience. One of the youngest to briefly take up residence in the French capital was Henry Redhead Yorke, who was seventeen at the time of the fall of the Bastille and who went to Paris at the end of 1792.[10] Francis Tweddell, a signatory of the 1792 British and Irish address to the National Convention, was "a lad of about eighteen" when he arrived in Paris with Joel Barlow and John Frost in November 1792.[11] The main contingent of the international reforming society, however, seem to have been aged between their mid-twenties and mid-forties at the time of the Revolution. Leading members such as John Hurford Stone and Edward Fitzgerald were twenty-six in 1789 while other key figures, such as Robert Merry, John Oswald, Sampson Perry and John Frost were in their mid- to late-thirties or early forties when they arrived in Paris. As Peter Clark has noted in his study of the English-speaking associational world, such wide age spans were relatively common in clubs and societies of the era.[12]

This age spread suggests that many of the British who took up short-term residence in Paris were youthful, yet with not inconsiderable professional and political experience. They had invariably reached adulthood by the outbreak of the American Revolution and some had already registered significant achievements in fields such as law, commerce, poetry, theatre, medicine, the military or journalism. Their decision to go to France was in all likelihood a carefully conceived one. It would undoubtedly have been tinged with idealism, probably prompted by membership of Dissenting or reformist circles and heavily inspired by an adventurous temperament which had swelled with the French Revolution, coming on the heel of the American War of Independence. Yet it was less naïve than maturing and worldly individuals who formed the core nucleus of the international radical community in Paris. Many had already acquired a significant degree of political experience, pedigree or notoriety in London reforming circles and some had been thwarted from advancing their professional pursuits and social status further under the Pitt ministry, which had become increasingly

---

10 Henry Redhead Yorke, *France in 1802, Described in a Series of Contemporary Letters* (1804), J. A. C. Sykes (ed.), with an introduction by Richard Davey (London: Heineman, 1906), p. 2.
11 Captain Monro, 6th December 1792, TNA TS 11/959.
12 Peter Clark, *British Clubs and Societies 1580-1800: The Origins of an Associational World* (Oxford: Oxford University Press, 2000).

hostile to proponents of reform. These constraints ultimately galvanised radicals' courage, both in seeking emigration and exploiting the opportunities it provided.

While a number of radicals went to Paris unaccompanied, others set off with, or were later joined by, family and domestic staff, while several also departed with colleagues and acquaintances. Collective departures may have been spurred by a number of considerations. Visits had the potential to be extended indefinitely and kin may have been dependent on the departing member for material survival. Robert Merry set off for the French capital again in the summer of 1792, with his wife Anne Brunton, having already visited Paris on two occasions, while Robert Smith and Robert Rayment both settled in Paris with their wives and children.[13] John Hurford Stone's wife, Rachel Coope, accompanied him to Paris, though after the settling of their divorce in June 1794, Hurford Stone's relationship with Helen Maria Williams was openly acknowledged, and he probably moved into her lodgings later that year. Williams herself departed for Paris for the first time in her late twenties with her mother and sisters. Mary Wollstonecraft met her American partner, Gilbert Imlay, soon after arriving in Paris and was shielded from some of the effects of measures taken against British nationals by her association with the American trader. Robert Merry and Charlotte Smith both employed chambermaids and servants during their stay in France and showed concern for their well-being when applying for passports to leave France in the spring and summer of 1793.[14] Robert Smith also troubled himself about the safety of a number of elderly French men and women in his charge when he was imprisoned from late 1793 onwards.[15] Thomas Christie went to France with his wife Rebecca, as well as his sister, and employed a French servant while based there.[16] Evidence for the employment of domestic staff corroborates the view that many radicals who emigrated to France, while sympathetic to fundamental changes in social and political organisation, themselves hailed from a professional or bourgeois background and, at least initially, could finance the outlay of maintaining servants.

LANGUAGE AND INTERPRETING

Some British residents of Paris, such as John Hurford Stone, were proficient in French and would have assisted those fellow foreign residents who

---

13 The *Monthly Magazine* biographical notice of Merry reads, "They both returned from the continent in the summer of 1793 (for Mrs. Merry had accompanied him to France)." *The Monthly Magazine*, vol. 7 (April 1799), p. 257. Robert Smith had three children, aged ten, eleven and twelve. (See AN F7/4775/20/3).
14 In their petitions for passports, both Merry and Smith included their serving staff in their bid for passage back to Britain. See AN F7/4412.
15 AN F7/4775/20/3. See Smith's petition to the committee of his Le Pelletier section, written on 12th September 1793.
16 See AN F7/4648, in particular the file on Thomas Christie.

encountered problems. Stone may have had some input in the translation of key addresses and letters, and his wife, Rachel Coope, acted as an interpreter for Joel Barlow and Samuel Blackden.[17] Robert Smith also mastered the French language, his friend and collaborator, Thomas Paine, describing him as "a man of letters and of leisure" who "understands several languages." Smith helped Paine to read the texts in French that the latter was using as source material for his writing. Paine wrote, "[Smith] assists me in examining sundry authors, as well ancient as modern, in the National Library, which I could not accomplish without that assistance."[18] Smith's prowess in French, as well as being an essential aid to Thomas Paine, may also have proved useful in negotiations with the ruling authorities when he was imprisoned under emergency rule. Another member of the *SADH*, Irish radical Nicholas Madgett, translated Robert Merry's tract on republican government which was presented to the National Convention in late 1792.[19] He also served as an intermediary between British petitioners and the revolutionary administration, explaining, excusing and occasionally denouncing appeals from his British and Irish acquaintances. John Oswald, also adept in the French language, translated texts during his service on the editorial committee of *La Chronique du Mois*, notably Jean-Marie Collot d'Herbois's *Almanach du Père Girard*.[20] Sampson Perry was fluent enough in French to find employment in translation on his return to Britain, after his release from Newgate jail, and gave evidence in French public trials without the aid of an interpreter.[21] Finally, James Watt, representing the Manchester Constitutional Society at the Jacobin Club in April 1792, showed his proficiency in French to the audience of revolutionaries. Watt, whose three years of schooling in Geneva had made him fluent in the language, was equal to the occasion. Springing on the platform, he pushed Robespierre aside, and "in a short but vehement speech completely silenced his formidable antagonist, carrying with him the feelings of the rest of the audience, who expressed their sense of his honest British spirit in a loud burst of applause."[22] Such eloquence in

---

17 Woodward, *Une Anglaise*, p. 77. According to Woodward, Coope acted as a translator for Barlow and Blackden while they lodged together at a hotel on rue Jacob.
18 AN AF III 1808/369/79. The file contains a plea from Thomas Paine on behalf of Robert Smith to extend his residence in Paris.
19 *The Monthly Magazine* printed a biographical notice of Robert Merry in the April 1799 edition following his death in December 1798 in Baltimore, USA. Reporting on his activities in Paris, the magazine reported that "while in that city, and under the invitation given by the French legislature to all foreigners, to favour them with their sentiments on the erecting of a free constitution; he wrote a short treatise in English, on the nature of free government. It was translated into French by Mr Madget [sic], and presented in the same manner as the Laurel of Liberty to the Convention Nationale: "honorable mention" being made of it in their journals." (*The Monthly Magazine*, vol. 25 [1799], p. 257).
20 See Erdman, *Commerce des Lumières*, pp. 125-8.
21 *The Gentleman's Magazine* obituary of Perry notes that "During this period he maintained his wonted spirit, and employed himself translating from the French, and in a variety of literary works." (*The Gentleman's Magazine*, vol. 134 [1823], p. 281).
22 Quoted in Alger, *Englishmen*, p. 47. Alger doesn't mention the source of his quote but it is

the French language often inspired confidence, respect and attentiveness among members of the revolutionary leadership.

Other emigrants had much greater difficulties in conversing, exchanging and making themselves understood and in deciphering the cultural norms of their adopted country. This could sometimes lead to diplomatic incidents that severely compromised relationships. David Williams' poor grasp of the French language led the future mayor of Paris, Jérôme Pétion, to describe his meeting with the Welsh radical, before the latter's trip to Paris in late 1792, as having "lacked the vivacity and interest which it could have had if we could have spoken the same language."[23] According to Captain Monro, Thomas Paine, himself inhibited by his poor command of French, helped delegates, Joel Barlow and John Frost, to get the SCI address translated, yet even this did not prevent a series of misunderstandings from occurring at the moment of the presentation of the address to the Convention on 28th November 1792. The intention of the delegates had been to present the congratulatory address and inform the French assembly of the offer of a gift of a thousand pairs of shoes from the London SCI, a gift to be renewed and repeated over the following six weeks to help the efforts of the revolutionary armies. However, the War Secretary (perhaps disingenuously) mistook Frost for a shoemaker who had come to request a contract, another told him he had come to the wrong department, while a third told him to apply to the Convention. Monro attributes the misunderstanding to the "confused state of the different departments of the present French Government and the bad French all these gentlemen spoke."[24] Thomas Paine and others "encouraged him in his enterprize; and after some little arrangement had taken place, he ... presented his address on the 28th, and at the same time his shoes."[25] Monro noted that Frost was unable to either read or converse in French.

The desire to communicate did not necessarily translate into smooth verbal exchange. Mary Wollstonecraft complained bitterly in her letters to her sisters of her frustration at her inability to speak the French language, confiding to Everina that she felt uncomfortable amongst the "flying sounds."[26] She reiterated her irritation in a letter to Ruth Barlow, dated February 1793:

> I am endeavouring to acquire the language, I mean that I should not be content to speak as many of the English speak, who talk away with an unblushing face, and I am exceedingly fatigued by my constant attention to words, particularly as I cannot yet get rid of a

---

probably from the records of the Jacobin Club.
23 This episode is recounted in Whitney R. D. Jones, *David Williams: The Anvil and the Hammer* (Cardiff: University of Wales Press, 1986), p. 119.
24 Captain Monro, 6th December 1792, TNA TS 11/959.
25 Ibid..
26 Mary Wollstonecraft to Everina Wollstonecraft, Paris, 24th December 1792, Wollstonecraft, *Collected Letters*, p. 214.

foolish bashfulness which stops my mouth when I am most desirous to make myself understood, besides when my heart sinks or flies to England to hover round those I most love all the fine French phrases, ready cut and dry for use, fly away the Lord know where.[27]

Wollstonecraft wanted to acquire more than just the bare rudiments of the language that she believed so many English people settled for and expressed her desire to find a place within French society. However, by October 1794, she was writing to Gilbert Imlay, informing him of her progress in the French language which had allowed her to make new acquaintances and converse with a judge on the Revolutionary Tribunal.[28]

Welsh visitor, Morgan John Rhys, an acquaintance of *SADH* member James Gamble, found out about travelling in France from the experience of fellow countrymen congregating in one of the hotels open to foreign residents. Yet as soon as he began to seek private accommodation, he recognised the need for a better command of the French language: "Next morning I deliver'd my letter & was recommended to private lodgings – I was now under the obligation of learning a little French."[29] Proficiency, or at least rudimentary ability in the French language, was a necessary asset for residents and travellers hoping to remain in Paris for a certain length of time.

Thomas Paine, although he helped to find translators for fellow radicals, had a notoriously poor command of French which inhibited his communication both in the National Convention and in private with members of the revolutionary government. It was a lacuna that Paine never reconciled himself to and which was frequently brought up in letters and conversations. Paine's flawed French was seized upon by Jacques Thuriot and Jean-Paul Marat during the tense final stages of the trial of Louis XVI. The French representatives challenged the accuracy of the translation of Paine's speech on 23rd January 1793 after it had been delivered to the Convention, a pretext for discounting the value of his political opinion. Paine's view that the king should not be executed but rather imprisoned for the duration of the war and then exiled once peace had been established, was unacceptable to the Montagnard members of the Convention. Thuriot asserted that the language used in the speech was not that of Thomas Paine, while Marat contested the exactitude of Paine's point of view, claiming that it had been inaccurately translated: "I denounce the intermediary, and I maintain that this is not the opinion of Thomas Paine. It is a vicious and unfaithful

---

27 Mary Wollstonecraft to Ruth Barlow, 1-14th February 1793, Wollstonecraft, *Collected Letters*, p. 220.
28 Mary Wollstonecraft to Gilbert Imlay, 26th October 1794, Wollstonecraft, *Collected Letters*, p. 270: "I have therefore employed and amused myself since I got rid of – and am making a progress in the language amongst other things."
29 BM Add. Ms 25388.399-404. 402. Letter from Morgan John Rhys to the Reverend John Rippon, from France, dated 23rd November 1791. I am grateful to Mary-Ann Constantine for providing me with her transcripts of these letters.

translation."³⁰ Paine's opponents in the Convention were able to exploit his linguistic failings to political advantage and Paine, unable to reply to his detractors swiftly and eloquently, laboured to respond through interpreters.

Paine regularly prefaced his letters to French revolutionary leaders with an acknowledgement of his inability to speak the French language, a handicap that inhibited his communication on a number of levels. Writing to Condorcet, Bonneville and his own translator François Lanthenas in June 1791, he offered his assistance in the drafting of a republican manifesto: "Unfortunately all my productions have been composed in English, and can be of slight advantage to the cause, except through the medium of translation, so that, I suppose, the services I would render can never be commensurate with my desires."³¹ He admitted that his contributions would be of lesser value because of the obstacle posed by language. Paine's faltering French often led him to request face-to-face meetings with the aid of an interpreter rather than proceed by written exchange. He wrote to Foreign minister Lebrun on 4th December 1792 on the question of Irish affairs. In his request for a meeting he explained, "I wish to confer with you on that subject, but as I do not speak French, and as the matter requires confidence, General Duschastelet has desired me to say, that it you can make it convenient to name a day, to dine with him and me at Auteuil, he will, with pleasure, do the office of interpreter."³² Paine also wrote to Bertrand Barère in September 1793, after an accidental meeting in the street, stating he was "sorry that we cannot converse together."³³ Paine felt deep frustration at having to operate in politics at the highest level without the necessary tools to flourish in oratory or even engage in one-to-one discussion.

Paine wrote to Louis-Guillaume Otto at the foreign affairs division on 2nd October 1793 to request reimbursement for the costs incurred during Colonel Eleazer Oswald's mission to Britain. Oswald had been sent to judge the readiness of the British people for revolution. The sensitivity of the subject prompted Paine to request the services of a government mediator who was above suspicion: "As it is not proper that any interpreter should act in this business but a confidential person, and as you are the most proper person to communicate between him and the Minister. I wish you would undertake to forward the settlement of his accounts, I will call you on Monday, in company with Col. Oswald."³⁴ The context of war meant that

---

30 *Le Moniteur Universel*, vol. 15, Wednesday 23rd January 1793.
31 Paine, "To Messieurs Condorcet, Nicolas de Bonneville and Lanthenas", Paris, June 1791, *CWTP* vol. 2, p. 1315.
32 Archives Diplomatiques, Affaires, Étrangères, Correspondance Anglaise, vol. 584 folio 150, quoted in Lionel D. Woodward, 'Les projets de descente en Irlande sous la Convention, et les réfugiés irlandais et anglais en France: d'après des documents inédits'. *Annales historiques de la Révolution française* 8 (1931), p. 4.
33 Paine, "To Citizen Barère", 5th September 1793, *CWTP* vol. 2, p. 1333.
34 Archives Diplomatiques, Correspondance Anglaise, vol. 588, folio 8. Quoted in Woodward, 'Les Projets de Descente'. Woodward converts the republican calendar date to 28th June 1793, which seems erroneous. I have gone by the republican date to find the

language took on heightened sensitivity. The accuracy of the translation was crucial, as was the need for personal trust when the likelihood of incomprehension was high. Paine found great relief in being able to communicate in English. In a letter to Georges Danton from early May 1793 he began his letter with "As you read English, I write this letter to you without passing it through the hands of a translator."[35] Paine expressed his concern at the disputes in the National Convention which would eventually lead to the expulsion of the Girondin members at the end of the month and the consolidation of Montagnard control.

Thomas Paine's political role in France cannot be judged without some consideration being given therefore to his persistent struggle to communicate, to achieve the flair and fluency demanded by the codes of the French Convention, and to reassure himself of the confidence and understanding of his interlocutors. These obstacles severely impeded his political effectiveness, particularly in the months of 1793 when political realignments occurred frequently and when tensions were high. Rudimentary French was not enough to convey a firm impression of loyalty to the republic, and those who were adept at speaking the language tended to prove more able at negotiating their status and liberty than those who had very little working knowledge. John Hurford Stone, though briefly imprisoned twice, faced little real danger. Partly through his capacity to defend his position and communicate effectively, he was exempted from many of the more stringent conditions faced by his fellow countrymen and women.

RESIDENCE AND LODGING: MAPPING THE BRITISH IN PARIS

White's hotel, located at 7 passage des Petits Pères, provided accommodation for visitors arriving in the capital and guests may have invited friends to dine while they rented quarters there. The hotel was just off the place des Victoires and a few minutes' walk from the Palais Royal, the residence of the Duc d'Orléans and hub of café and literary culture in Paris. George Edwards and Lord Edward Fitzgerald both had rooms at 7 passage des Petits Pères and Stephen Sayre stayed at the hotel for a number of months.[36] Fitzgerald, writing from the hotel on 30th October 1792, described his own sociable routine: "I lodge with my friend Paine, – we breakfast, dine, and sup together."[37] Sampson Perry recounted how he "breakfasted with Paine about this time, at the Philadelphia Hotel." Perry was seeking Paine's advice on how to establish oneself in America without any means of subsistence.[38]

---

corresponding date in October 1793, two months before Paine's imprisonment.
35 Paine, "To George Jacques Danton," Paris, 6th May 1793, *CWTP* vol. 2, p. 1335.
36 See John R. Alden, *Stephen Sayre: American Revolutionary Adventurer* (Baton Rouge and London: Louisiana State University Press, 1983), p. 164.
37 Moore, *The Life and Death of Lord Edward Fitzgerald*, pp. 73-4.
38 See *HS* I, pp. 9-10.

Many former guests of White's, who went on to take up semi-permanent residence in Paris, found accommodation in neighbouring streets, not far either from the Tuileries and the Palais du Louvre, once home to the royal court but, from 1793 to 1795, the seat of the *Comité de Salut Public* and *Comité de Sûreté Générale*. Robert O'Reilly found lodgings at rue de Buffaut at the house of a citizen known as Aimée. Charles and Elizabeth Churchill and their children, a family well-acquainted with Christopher White, took up a tenancy agreement with citizen Jacquin at 63 rue de la Roquette. The Churchills, like White, had been in Paris since before the Revolution, settling there in 1783, probably for commercial reasons.[39] It is unlikely that Charles Churchill was a member of the political society at White's, although he may have had some contact with the group, since he had donated shoes and guns to the revolutionary armies. Robert Rayment took up lodgings at 3 rue Neuve St Augustin and Helen Williams' salon was located at 105 rue Hevétius, where she had a view overlooking the Tuileries gardens. Robert Smith lived on rue de Choiseul, at the corner of one of the major Parisian boulevards and James Gamble took up residence at 12 rue des Piques. Here Gamble played host to the Welsh Baptist preacher, Morgan John Rhys, who had come to France on a religious mission.[40] John Hurford Stone moved into Helen Maria Williams' residence in 1794 after his divorce from his wife, Rachel Coope, had been finalised.

The cartographical representation of the British in Paris therefore shows a high concentration of activity and lodgings around the Palais Royal and the Tuileries, sites of political importance during the years in which the *SADH* was active. Because of their physical proximity to these centres, some British residents were sometimes witnesses to political actions in the district, including the storming of the Tuileries on 10th August 1792. According to Richard Buel, the area was the site of "incessant carnival."[41] This proximity of a thriving hub of social life as well as the Duke's early sympathy with the radical direction of the Revolution, may have contributed to the frequency of British visits to the gardens and streets around the palace, as well as to the palace itself. Yet the living quarters around the Palais Royal were not considered particularly desirable. The American couple Joel and Ruth Barlow took up residence on the top floor of a building where they were visited by Samuel Breck in February 1791. Breck described how "in order to reach the

---

39 Elizabeth Mayne Churchill was originally from Boston, America, though the nationality of her husband Charles is not mentioned in the official record. She had two young children and was arrested during the last months of 1793. Her husband, though having no clear involvement with radicalism, was considered a loyal partisan of the Revolution and had provided shoes and guns for the revolutionary armies. They had a good relationship with their local section and no reason had been identified for doubting their loyalty to the republic. See AN F7/4648/3.
40 For an account of Morgan John Rhys's mission to France, see Mary-Ann Constantine, 'The Welsh in Revolutionary Paris'. I am grateful to Mary-Ann Constantine for allowing me to mention the example of Tilly Matthews in this book.
41 Buel, *Joel Barlow: American Citizen*, p. 140.

apartment of Mr. Barlow, I was obliged to pass through the door of a great gambling establishment that occupied the floor immediately below his." He also judged that "the poet's poverty consented [to such quarters] rather than his will."[42] If the residential arrangements were insalubrious, the site offered the best view of revolutionary action and the opportunity for regular contact with representatives of both local and national government.

Those who met at White's hotel would have been in frequent contact with the bustle and animation of the gardens where Camille Desmoulins had exhorted crowds to insurgency after the expulsion of Necker from Louis XVI's counsel, just before the taking of the Bastille, and where commerce was pursued amid political addresses, prostitution and gambling in an environment which was free of literary censorship. Arthur Young described the scene in June 1789, on the eve of Revolution:

> Is it not wonderful, that while the press teems with the most levelling and even seditious principles, that if put in execution would overturn the monarchy, nothing in reply appears, and not the least step is taken by the court to restrain this extreme licentiousness of publication. It is easy to conceive the spirit that must thus be raised among the people. But the coffee-houses in the Palais Royal present yet more singular and astonishing spectacles; they are not only crouded [sic] within, but other expectant crouds [sic] are at the doors and windows, listening à gorge deployé to certain orators, who from chairs or tables harangue each his little audience: the eagerness with which they are heard, and the thunder of applause they receive for every sentiment of more than common hardiness or violence against the present government, cannot easily be imagined. I am all amazement at the ministry permitting such nests and hotbeds of sedition and revolt, which disseminate amongst the people, every hour, principles that by and by must be opposed with vigour, and therefore it seems little short of madness to allow the propagation at present.[43]

The Palais, formerly a seat of the monarchy until Louis XIV gave it to the House of Orléans, had been reinvested under the Revolution. Its grounds became known as the "jardins de la Révolution" after 1791 and its name changed to Palais Egalité in 1792. Mary Wollstonecraft gave a different portrait of the atmosphere around the Palais to that of Young in her *An Historical and Moral View*:

> At this juncture also, a spacious square, equally devoted to business and pleasures, called the *Palais Royale*, became the rendezvous of the citizens. There the most spirited gave lectures, whilst more modest men read the popular papers and pamphlets,

---

42 Ibid, p. 134.
43 Arthur Young, *Arthur Young's Travels in France during the years 1787, 1788, 1789*, Miss Betham-Edwards (ed.) (London: George Bell and Sons, 1906), pp. 153-4.

on the benefits of liberty, and the crying oppression of absolute governments. This was the centre of information; and the whole city flocking thither, to talk or to listen, returned home warmed with the love of freedom, and determined to oppose, and the risk of life, the power that should still labour to enslave them.[44]

For Wollstonecraft, this hub of literary and political life was a microcosm of the spirit of liberty which was transforming the French nation.

Kevin Hetherington describes the Palais as a site of "heterotopia," understood as "spaces of alternate ordering," sites of convergence where marginal groups could meet and mingle with the highest orders of society. For Hetherington, the Palais was "a site of openness, tolerance and civility as well as a space for rational and enlightened debate that played a significant part in the emerging civil society of the bourgeoisie."[45] Yet he also sees the site as "carnavalesque; a space of playful cultural inversions, with the highest and lowest strata of society able to mingle, which offered a moment of freedom from some of the hierarchical constraints of French society."[46] It was a space that encouraged social mixing and vibrant exchange and contributed to the emergence of a self-conscious bourgeois public culture. Yet by 1793, the gardens were generally associated with secrecy, plotting and assassination. Jules Michelet summed up this vision of the 1793 Palais as a place of "life, death, quick pleasures, rude, violent, fatal pleasure."[47]

Not all British emigrants resided close to this centre of public activity however. Some lived much further out, perhaps for financial reasons or, by 1793, in the hope of finding some respite from the political turmoil to write or simply to shield themselves from suspicion. Mary Wollstonecraft, after a period living in central Paris, moved to Neuilly-sur-Seine during the most intense months of emergency rule before returning to central Paris, during one of Imlay's prolonged absences, to take up residence with a German woman whose tariffs were reasonable. Thomas Paine, after a brief spell at White's, moved to a hotel near rue Richelieu. David Williams also took up residence at a hotel on rue Richelieu, probably the same as Paine, where he was not far from Madame Roland's salon, located on rue Neuve des Petits

---

44 *HMV*, p. 76.
45 Kevin Hetherington, *The Badlands of Modernity: Heterotopia and Social Ordering* (London; New York: Routledge, 1997), p. 2.
46 Ibid, p. 3.
47 "Ce n'étaient plus ces premiers temps du Palais Royal, où ses cafés furent les églises de la Révolution naissante, où Camille, au café de Foy, prêcha la croisade. Ce n'était plus cet âge d'innocence révolutionnaire où le bon Fauchet professait au Cirque la doctrine des Amis, et l'association philanthropique du *Cercle de la Vérité*. Les cafés, les restaurateurs, étaient très-fréquentés, mais sombres. Telles de ces boutiques fameuses allaient devenir funèbres. Le restaurateur Février vit tuer chez lui Saint-Fargeau. Tout près, au café Corraza, fut tramée la mort de la Gironde. La vie, la mort, le plaisir rapide, grossier, violent, le plaisir exterminateur, voilà le Palais Royal de 93." Jules Michelet, *Les femmes de la Révolution* (Paris: Chamerot, 1863), p. 245.

Champs.[48] Paine finally settled further out of Paris at 63 rue du faubourg Saint-Denis in 1793, where he occupied shared apartments with society members William Choppin and William Johnson. In his lodgings at the Hôtel Richelieu, Paine had been "so plagued and interrupted by numerous visitors, and sometimes by adventurers, that in order to have some time to himself he appropriated two mornings in a week for his levee days."[49] Thomas Rickman described how Thomas Paine withdrew from the hub of sociability at White's as conditions became more stringent during 1793. With "a good garden well laid out" in rue du faubourg Saint-Denis, he would rise at seven in the morning and breakfast with Johnson, Choppin and "two or three other Englishmen" before spending some time in the grounds.[50] He also received a number of friends, a "chosen few", with whom he "unbent himself." These callers included Brissot, the Marquis de Châtelet le Roi, Jean-Henri Bancal des Issarts, General Miranda, as well as some English acquaintances such as Thomas Christie and his family, Mary Wollstonecraft, the "Stones" (by which he probably meant Hurford Stone and his wife Rachel Coope), Gilbert Imlay and Joel Barlow. In a letter to the Irish revolutionary, James O'Fallon, written from "Passy, near Paris", Paine describes being "at my little retreat, a few miles from Paris, where I expect some American friends to dinner."[51] Rickman paints a rather improbably idyllic portrait of Paine in his final days of liberty before he was arrested and incarcerated in the Luxembourg:

> The little happy circle who lived with him here will ever remember these days with delight: with these select friends he would talk of his boyish days, play at chess, whist, piquet, or cribbage, and enliven the moments by many interesting anecdotes: with these he would play at marbles, scotch hops, battledores, &c. on the broad and fine gravel walk at the upper end of the garden, and then retire to his boudoir, where he was up to his knees in letters and papers of various descriptions. Here he remained till dinner time; and unless he visited Brissot's family, or some particular friend in the evening, which was his frequent custom, he joined again the society of his favourites and fellow-boarders, with whom his conversation was often witty and cheerful, always acute and improving, but never frivolous.[52]

Sociable practices and private enterprise could also provide occasions for British and Irish residents to come into contact with each other. The Carmelites convent on rue d'Enfer brought Nicholas Joyce and Christopher White into frequent proximity and they may have been occasionally joined by

---

48 See Jones, *The Anvil and the Hammer*, p. 122.
49 Rickman, *The Life of Thomas Paine*, p. 129.
50 Ibid, p. 130.
51 Thomas Paine to Doctor James O'Fallon, 17th February 1793, *CWTP* vol. 2, p. 1330.
52 Rickman, *The Life of Thomas Paine*, pp. 135-6.

business partners John Hurford Stone and James Gamble. Hurford Stone's printing press was located from 1793 to 1804 on rue de Vaugirard, one of the major arteries running through central Paris. It is likely that the printing press would have been another of the locations where some residents, keenly involved in writing, editing and publishing, would have met.[53] Helen Maria Williams' salon on rue Helvétius served as a location for sociable encounters which were not restricted by the same codes as more formal assemblies and would frequently involve women. M. Ray Adams argues that "few Englishmen of importance came to Paris in the years after the beginning of the Revolution without calling on Helen Maria Williams. Her home was a sort of political and literary clearing-house for her countrymen on the continent."[54] Williams' salon welcomed French and foreign guests, including Thomas Paine. Charles Fox also visited Williams' salon during one of his visits to Paris. One frequent visitor to Williams' salon was Mary Wollstonecraft, who arrived in Paris in December 1792. Shortly after her arrival she met Gilbert Imlay with whom she would be intimately linked until 1796. Imlay had a close business relationship with Joel Barlow and Wollstonecraft frequently wrote to Barlow's wife while she was still in London. She found herself spending evenings with members of the American emigrant community during her days in Paris and later at Neuilly-sur-Seine. She would also breakfast with John Hurford Stone's wife, Rachel Coope, and Helen Maria Williams would call from time to time at Neuilly after her release from prison. Helen Williams claimed her fellow compatriots spent evenings gathered at a club (possibly White's) to read the daily newspapers and discuss politics.[55]

British men and women would also gather in public venues. Sociable outings could also allow British residents to connect with each other outside the framework of political gatherings, for instance in trips to the theatre or opera. John Hurford Stone went to the theatre "when we saw the representation of Brutus, just after the tenth of August." At the performance, he heard a version of *La Marseillaise* sung "with so much accompaniment."[56] Stone also went on at least one occasion to the opera, an

---

53 Perry's lodgings were located at no. 225 rue du petit Vaugirard, faubourg Saint-Germain. This street became the rue du Cherche-Midi in 1823. Perry's address is specified in the testimony about his role in the Marat affair, see AN W 269/16/29.

54 M. Ray Adams, 'Helen Maria Williams and the French Revolution', *Wordsworth and Coleridge: Studies in Honour of George McLean Harper*, Earl Leslie Griggs (ed.) (Princeton: Princeton University Press, 1939), p. 89.

55 Woodward, *Une Anglaise*, p. 56: "Ce qui l'étonnait, c'était de n'y trouver fort peu de ses compatriotes, qui, selon elle, perdaient beaucoup en n'y assistant pas, puisque les hommes forment un club tous les soirs, quand on lit les journaux du jour et qu'on discute la politique."

56 This recollection is included in Stone's letter written from Verdun on 16th October 1792 while he was travelling with the revolutionary armies and following the progress of hostilities with the Prussian and Austrian forces. The letter was included in Helen Maria Williams' third volume of letters, under the title of *Letters from France: containing A Great Variety of Interesting and Original Information concerning the most important events that have lately*

activity disliked by Helen Maria Williams. Accompanied by Lord Edward Fitzgerald in November 1792 after the latter's recent arrival in Paris, Stone went to see a performance of *Lodoïska*, a heroic comedy by Luigi Cherubini. It was first performed at the Théâtre Feydeau in Paris on 18th July 1791 and ran for two hundred shows. It is likely Stone and Fitzgerald attended one of these first inaugural performances. Fitzgerald described his activities in Paris in a letter to his mother: "I pass my time very pleasantly, read, walk, and go quietly to the play."[57] Helen Maria Williams lamented the irregular attendance of her fellow countryfolk at the Lycée, where she attended lectures on philosophy, the arts, science, history and poetry. She suggested that some British guests were not devoting the required zeal to enhancing their cultural knowledge.[58] Williams admired how "learning seems stripped of its thorns, and decorated with flowers," and described it as a place where "the gay and social Parisians cultivate science and the belles letters, amidst the pleasures and attractions of society."[59] Such enjoyment through education contrasted with the English tradition where learning had to be in "sober meditation, and serious solitude."[60] Williams suggested that such an initiative would make a welcome change in London from fashionable but vapid conversation and endless card assemblies. Political encounters and sociable outings appear to have connected British residents of Paris, supporting the assertion that the emigrant society forged at White's hotel also served to provide a degree of solidarity, means of sociable introduction and mutual sustenance for British guests recently settled in Paris.

---

been occurring in that country, and particularly respecting the campaign of 1792, vol. III (London: G. G. and J. Robinson, 1793), p. 147.
57 Moore, *The Life and Death of Lord Edward Fitzgerald*, p. 73-4.
58 H. M. Williams, *Letters from France: Containing Many New Anecdotes Relative to the French Revolution, and the Present State of French Manners*, vol. II (3rd edition; London: G. G. and J. Robinson, 1796), p. 133.
59 Ibid, pp. 129-30.
60 Ibid, p. 130.

4

Professional lives and projects of British residents in Paris

The activities of British radical residents of Paris were as diverse as their reasons for taking up residence and, for many, the motives and pursuits that prompted their departure sustained their lives and livelihoods in Paris. Emigrants were involved in a range of ventures, from printing and publishing to entrepreneurship, military service, journalism and political activism. With the exception of titled men such as Lord Edward Fitzgerald and Sir Robert Smith, most of the radical emigrants to Paris were men of letters and of the professions or from an entrepreneurial background. They were often, to differing degrees, reputed within international philosophical circles and well-connected both in London and Paris. They were also primarily an urban set. Many had already met figures from the French and American Revolutions before arriving in Paris and a large number were members of different radical societies in London.

The *SADH* was also given impetus by men and women who had achieved some celebrity in the field of publishing, journalism, authorship or editing. Some had already played roles within the European intellectual Enlightenment. Their legitimacy had frequently been challenged by the Pitt government operating an increasingly intolerant policy towards determined radicals who continued to look to the French precedent. Thomas Christie was a writer for, and some-time editor of, the *Analytical Review*, and, though not an acknowledged signatory of the British and Irish address to the National Convention, mixed with a number of its members. John Hurford Stone, Mary Wollstonecraft, Thomas Paine, Sampson Perry, Robert Merry, Robert O'Reilly, Henry Redhead Yorke, David Williams, Thomas Cooper and John Oswald were among those associates or members of the society whose primary activities centred on the publishing world, journalism or pamphleteering.

Others had established themselves in more overtly commercial lines of activity or in the field of medicine. Before turning to journalism, Sampson Perry had been a surgeon, writing a tract on bladder and kidney disease, and William Choppin, who shared lodgings with Thomas Paine in Paris, had worked as a chemist in London prior to his departure.[1] The third resident in the triumvirate living in rue du faubourg Saint-Denis was William Johnson, a doctor.[2] George Edwards had also practised medicine in both Barnard Castle and London and had written a treatise based on the work of Benjamin Franklin, while Robert O'Reilly was known in the scientific world. His inventions and experiments came to light in Paris under his editorship of the *Annales des Arts et Manufactures* in the Napoleonic era.[3]

A number of members of the *SADH* also played an active role in the French revolutionary armies. Henry Redhead Yorke suggests that Robert O'Reilly "fought against England in the French armies, and glories in the fact."[4] In 1792 John Oswald became a commander of a battalion in the Paris Volunteers and tried to persuade the revolutionary government to order a descent on London to aid a British rising. Captain Monro reported that another society member, Doctor Maxwell, "has at last obtained a company in the French Service, and I understand is soon to have this to join the army."[5] Maxwell had also tried to raise subscriptions for the French before departing for Paris, but his house was mobbed by loyalist opponents, an event which precipitated his hasty departure. William Newton joined the French dragoons on 5th March 1793 but was denounced to the *Comité de Sûreté Générale*, whose members ordered his dismissal from the army. Newton was eventually executed by orders of the Revolutionary Tribunal. William Ricketts, of the *SADH*, also petitioned the Convention to allow his enrolment in the French navy in November 1792.[6]

---

1 Sampson Perry, *A Disquisition of the Stone and Gravel; with Strictures on the Gout, When combined with those Disorders, The Seventh Edition improved and enlarged*, (London: Reynell, 1785). See also Iain McCalman's portrait of the radical editor in the *Dictionary of Literary Biography*, 158.

2 See TNA TS 11/965/3510/A2: Memorandum from Ross to Nepean, Friday 13th November 1792: "Since my last Clio received a letter from a Mr Choppin late a chymist of London."

3 O'Reilly appears to have been managing editor on the journal from 1801 to 1806. He also provided a substantial number of entries for the magazine. He is noted as having either "invented, perfected or described the procedure" of just under one hundred manufacturing techniques (*Annales des arts et manufactures* vol. 36. Paris: Imprimerie de Chaigneau Ainé, 1810, pp. 106-8). The range of subjects is eclectic, including English stationary, how to whiten straw, the making of portable kitchens, a machine for crushing oats, English cast iron, a water purifying machine and worms which eat into ships' hulls.

4 Yorke, *France in 1802*, p. 228.

5 17th December 1792, Captain Monro to Lord Grenville. TNA FO 27/40 Part 2.

6 See Erdman, *Commerce des Lumières*, p. 217.

SAMPSON PERRY AND BRITISH JOURNALISM IN PARIS

Although he was pushed into exile after successive threats of prosecution for libel, Sampson Perry saw emigration to France as a way of exploiting opportunities he had been denied in Britain. Having specialised in surgery before serving in the army during the American Revolution, Perry had failed to secure the military promotion he believed he deserved and harboured bitterness towards those he was convinced had impeded his social ascension. He elaborated on his misfortune in the introduction to his later account of the French Revolution: "I have detailed the particulars of my civil persecution; I shall therefore finally wind up the whole, by painting, in few words, my *military proscription*."[7]

Perry had taken up the editorship of *The Argus* in March 1789. At this time, the newspaper was considered as under the umbrella of the Whig opposition, along with four other publications, *The Gazetteer*, *The General Advertiser*, *The Morning Chronicle*, and *The Morning Post*. The paper, under Perry's editorship, adopted a conventionally reformist posture and was generally supportive of liberal reforming initiatives. Yet his journal became increasingly critical of the status quo. Adopting a more radical platform, the newspaper published the opening address of the LCS in full in January 1792 and noted the appearance of Part Two of Paine's *Rights of Man* in February of the same year, a gesture which did not endear him to the ruling authorities. Distancing itself increasingly from Whig circles, *The Argus* became the mouthpiece of more radical reforming ideas over the course of 1792. Concerns for the freedom of the press gave way to calls for universal suffrage and The Argus became one of the regular sources of news for the journal *Le Courier de l'Europe*.[8] The Anglo-French newspaper published an extract from *The Argus* from 17th January 1792 in which the writer predicted and approved of the strengthening of the international revolutionary spirit and the assertion of the authority of free governments over empires.[9] It was Perry's open admiration for the changes occurring in France which earned his publication a reputation as "a scandalous paper ... which, at the commencement of the French revolution, was distinguished for its virulence and industry in the dissemination of republican doctrines."[10]

---

7   *HS* I, p. 28
8   *Le Courier de l'Europe ou mémoires pour servir à l'histoire universelle puis gazette anglo-française* (London: Cox, 1776).
9   "Les événemens de chaque jour tendent à justifier ce que nous avons souvent dit, que les révolutions se propageront, & que les gouvernements se multiplieront; & y a-t-il un vrai philosophe, un ami du genre humain "qui ne désire l'accomplissement de cette prophétie?" (*Le Courier de l'Europe*, Friday 20th January 1792).
10 *A Biographical Dictionary of the Living Authors of Great Britain and Ireland; comprising literary memoirs and anecdotes of their lives; and a chronological register of their publications* (London, 1816), p. 270. This report was also printed as part of Perry's obituary in *The Gentleman's Magazine* vol. 134 (1823), p. 280.

The Argus was not only becoming an official mouthpiece of radical reform by mid-1792, but it was circulating increasingly widely. Thomas Paine, writing to Lord Onslow in June 1792, referred to his letter which "has since appeared in the "Argus" and probably in other papers."[11] At a meeting of the SCI on November 23rd 1792 it was "ordered that the advertisement relative to the submission for assisting the efforts of the Friends in the Cause of Freedom be published every day during the next week in *The Argus*."[12] A month earlier, on 12th October 1792, it had been "ordered that the secretary be directed to transmit a copy of the *Argus* of tomorrow to each of the members of this society."[13] *The Argus* was being used by the SCI to publish its motions for reform and its circulation among a larger reading public was being encouraged by its leading members. Edward Fitzgerald, writing to his mother, the Duchess of Leinster, in October 1792 just before his departure to France, remarked that "the joke, in *The Argus*, of the *invincible cavalry* of Prussia being totally *eat up* by their infantry, is not a bad one."[14] *The Argus* was revelling in French victories in the revolutionary wars, a stance which earned Perry the reputation among ministerial representatives as a seditious editor. The paper was targeted for libel at the height of its popularity among leading radicals, at a moment when it was circulating among an increasingly large audience and when it was regularly publishing pro-revolutionary articles.

Critics suggested that Perry, along with the editor of *The Morning Chronicle*, was already subsidised by the French government before his departure to Paris in late 1792.[15] In response, *The Morning Chronicle* published a comment which read:

> A morning paper says, that there are two daily Journals of London actually bribed by the Jacobins of France, to spread sedition in England – and that one of them, in particular, has 10,000 livres per month for its treason. It would have been a faithful service to their country to have named the particular Journals, so infamously corrupted by foreign gold…that the Crown officers may bring the abandoned writers to legal punishment.[16]

The paper chided those responsible for spreading ministerial hearsay about the French bias of the Opposition press for failing to openly accuse

---

11 Paine, Letter to Onslow Cranley, London, 21st June 1792, *CWTP*, p. 460.
12 TNA TS 11/965/3510. This document was part of the informant reports sent to under-secretary of state at the Home Office, Evan Nepean.
13 TNA TS 11/962/3508.
14 Quoted in T. Moore, *The Life and Death of Lord Edward Fitzgerald*, p. 73-4.
15 Werkmeister quotes a letter from William Augustus Miles to Charles Long. Writing on 24th September 1792, he claims to have had "several hints … from Frenchmen in constant relation and intimacy with M. de Chauvelin [the French Minister Plenipotentiary] and his family, that the editors of the 'Morning Chronicle' and of the 'Argus' have received considerable sums of money, and that they have each of them a large monthly allowance," Werkmeister, *A Newspaper History of England*, p. 113.
16 Werkmeister, *A Newspaper History of England*, p. 113.

newspapers of disloyalty and therefore bring them to justice. Whether Perry was in the service of the French authorities is difficult to determine as the counter-propaganda campaigns waged by the ruling administration were overtly aimed at destroying the patriotic credibility of Opposition editors and therefore must be viewed with caution.

Perry had a history of acrimonious encounters with the Pitt administration. The editor was first indicted in November 1790 for "a scandalous libel, charging Administration and particularly Mr Pitt with falsehood, corruption, and fraud."[17] He was convicted in February 1791. He was tried for a second libel in June 1791 and in July was brought again before the King's Bench on three different counts. On the first charge of libel against the editor of *The Times*, Perry refused to make a public apology thereby avoiding prison, claiming that everything he had said in *The Argus* was true. He was sentenced to six months in the King's Bench prison. He pleaded guilty to a second and third charge of libel, on a member of the aristocracy and the Government respectively. Perry acted on his own counsel, despite the recommendations from the judge to seek legal advice. On 12th July 1791 he was sentenced to another six months in prison and fined £200. The *Evening Mail* reported Perry's 1791 conviction, summing up that "the Court – the Bar – the Jury and the Auditors all coincided in one opinion – that the whole of the publications were the most scandalous and atrocious libels that ever made their appearance in Print."[18] In a decision taken in November 1791 on the third count of libel, he was only fined £100, possibly because the court had reason to believe the paper would tone down its criticism of the administration. Yet *The Argus* continued while Perry was in prison, renamed *The Argus of the Constitution* and still defiantly critical of the Government. One day after his release on 9th July 1792, Perry was again indicted for libel for stating that the Commons was not composed of the people's representatives and that the people were to be condemned for their docility in submitting to its laws. He suggested, in an echo of Paine, that a Convention was necessary because the people had played no part in electing their representatives. He was warned that he would be arrested, deprived of writing materials and held without bail. Faced with the probability of total isolation from the world of print journalism and harsher conditions compared to his earlier periods of incarceration, Perry agreed to leave the country after two years of open combat with the ruling administration. Shortly after his departure to France in late 1792, his newspaper was brought to a close by Government officials. On its premises, an official pro-governmental publication, the *True Briton*, was set up in January 1793.

Perry's decision to leave the country was inseparable from the sustained pressure he suffered at the hands of the Pitt government over the course of 1791 and 1792. Following his emigration, his detractors at *The World* rejoiced

---

17 Werkmeister, *The London Daily Press*, p. 336.
18 *The Evening Mail*, 15-17th June 1791.

that "The Sampson of the Argus was found too weak to carry off the pillars of the Constitutional Fabric, although he made several ineffectual attempts."[19] Perry recalled his fugitive existence as he set off from Britain in his later account of the French Revolution:

> I put a shirt and a pair of stockings in my pocket, and with only eleven guineas in my purse, I set off to Brighthelmstone; at which place I had not arrived an hour, before I was told that a boat was just sailing to Dieppe, with half a dozen French gentlemen; and that, if I chose, I might be one of the party.[20]

In France, the editors of *La Chronique du Mois* described Perry as "having only escaped the executioner by flight," and a letter written and used as evidence in the trial of Jean-Paul Marat depicted Perry as "a gallant man, a victim of his love for the French Revolution, he fled his country where there was a price on his head for having defended republican principles in a paper he wrote under the name of the argus of the people."[21] Perry's case was so notorious that it has even been used as a benchmark for libel prosecutions against radical writers in the eighteenth century: "The stringent measures adopted towards Sampson Perry, the editor of the "Argus", sufficiently betrayed the disposition of the reigning powers to punish such free-writers as publicly avowed their works."[22] Perry's arrival in Paris was closely linked therefore to the ministerial pressure he had been subject to.

Perry appears to have been planning his exile for some time, despite the impression given by newspaper reports of the time and subsequent scholarly works that he was forced into fleeing out of the imminence of further libel action. His plan had been progressively emerging at least from the moment of his release from prison on 10th July 1792, when he was again charged with libel. Perry was nominated for membership of the SCI on 27th April 1792 by a future fellow compatriot in Paris, Robert Merry, and Perry's SCI affiliation was secured the following week. He attended his first meeting at the Crown and Anchor Tavern in London only ten days after his release from prison. During the summer months, Perry was in close contact with Thomas Paine, who would depart for France in September. One informant for the Home Office reported, "On Friday last Capt'n Perry (Editor of the Argus) was with P_ in his room for a considerable time."[23] There is a strong case for concluding that it was Paine with whom, in 1792, Perry was in communication.

---

19 *The World*, Monday 10th December 1792.
20 *HS* I, p. 7.
21 *La Chronique Du Mois; ou, Cahiers Patriotiques* (January 1793) 80; see also the letter from Citoyenne Moreau, Affaire Marat, AN W 269/16/30: "un galant homme victime de son amour pour la révolution française il a fui son pays où sa tête est mise à prix pour avoir défendu les principes républicains dans une feuille qu'il rédigeait sous le nom de l'argus du peuple."
22 *The Mirror of Literature, Amusement, and Instruction*, vol. 2, part 2 (1844).
23 Charles Ross to Evan Nepean, Wednesday 8th August 1792. TNA TS 11/965/3510/A2.

Perry attended another SCI gathering at the Crown and Anchor Tavern on 28th September 1792. He was not present throughout the entire month of October, but resumed attendance on three successive occasions in November, just before his departure to Paris.[24] Perry was actually in France in October 1792, attempting to secure an agreement for the publication of his newspaper. Government spy Charles Ross informed Evan Nepean, Under-Secretary at the Home Office, that, "Captain Perry of the *Argus* is gone to France in order to establish Correspondents for his Paper, which in his absence is conducted by Mr. Oldfield."[25] Perry's departure later that year does not seem to have been simply a desperate attempt to seek refuge from imminent prosecution, but the culmination of a carefully devised plan which would combine the prospect of political exile with creative promise, in a nation which was favourable to the ideas Perry was espousing and his own distinctively irreverent way of voicing them.

The editor had carefully sounded out acquaintances in Paris about the publication of his banned newspaper before he embraced emigration. He seems to have had some success, judging by an entry in *La Chronique du Mois* in January 1793, which vowed to publish his "persecuted journal" with the help of the English Society of the Rights of Man (probably the *SADH*) and Thomas Paine, who would "zealously participate."[26] The announcement was followed by an appeal from Perry himself who announced the imminent appearance of his journal in Paris:

> It must however give some satisfaction to the advocates for European freedom, and to the friends of the human race in general, should they find that their Argus is not banished from the world, but that it has only been transplanted from the region of tyranny, injustice and oppression to his happy soil of Liberty, Equality.[27]

If the physical apparatus of his printing venture had been taken over by the loyalist press in London, Perry believed the spirit of his journal could survive

---

24 Perry's attendance is detailed in the minutes of the SCI meetings from 9th December 1791 to 9th May 1794. TNA TS/11/962/3508.

25 Charles Ross to Evan Nepean, 9th October 1792. TNA TS 11/965/3510/A2.

26 *La Chronique du Mois* (January 1793), p. 80. "To the Friends of Truth. Sampson Perry, auteur d'un journal républicain, en Angleterre, The argus of the People (La Sentinelle du Peuple) pour avoir défendu avec énergie les droits de l'homme, la révolution françoise, Horne-Tooke et Thomas Payne, son ami, n'a échappé que par sa fuite à des bourreaux. Perry et un autre écrivain anglois, Merry, célèbre par une pièce de théâtre, des vers républicains, et autres écrits philosophiques que nous ferons connoître, sont venus trouver de francs amis, chez les Directeurs de l'Imprimerie du Cercle Social, qui vont publier en France, le journal persécuté, The Argus of the People, la société angloise des Droits de l'Homme, et Thomas Payne et autres y contribueront avec zèle. Amis de la liberté vous leur devez secours, alliance et fraternité. Voilà la lettre de Sampson Perry, à ses amis persecutés à Londres."

27 *La Chronique du Mois* (January 1793), p. 80.

and his enterprise be relocated to Paris. Captain George Monro wrote in early January 1793:

> The society of our friends here presented an address to the Jacobin Club last night and mean to present a similar one to the Convention Nationale today. The nature of these addresses I have not been able as yet to learn, but hope by next post to give you some account of them. I think I told you that Mr Frost and a number of our other friends have withdrawn from this society, but they have been reinforced by Capt. Perry who means to publish his Argus here.[28]

The Times noted that Sampson Perry was intending to publish his banned journal in the French capital. It reported that "the Conductor may there give unlimited scope to his treasonable abuse of our Government."[29] Whether Perry was successful in establishing his newspaper in Paris is difficult to judge, as no copies of *The Argus* are traceable in Paris, only rumours and statements of intended publication. He clearly hoped to secure the publication of his newspaper at the printing house of the *Cercle Social*. One of Perry's fellow British radicals in Paris had suggested in October 1792 that it was difficult to get hold of a copy: "Mr Choppin mentioned in his letter that he would not get at a perusal of an *Argus* in all Paris, that he had read a proof copy of Paine's *Address to the Addressers* and which is very severe upon Mr Burke."[30] Despite there being no physical trace of *The Argus*, it seems there was an expectation of being able to locate copies of the paper in Paris. This was before Perry begun his concerted campaign to secure a French publisher. Some British newspapers did find their way to France therefore, despite the repressive measures in place to restrict the circulation of radical literature.

Although the Pitt administration and Government press tried to portray emigration as fearful flight from justice, the reasons behind radicals' decisions to leave their home country were often more complex. In Perry's case, France provided a timely opportunity for him to cast off the stranglehold of what he saw as the narrow hierarchical system of social ascension in Britain. He joined fellow reformers from the SCI in the *SADH* and worked hard to try to publish his banned journal in Paris. Despite his griefs during emergency rule and ultimately unsuccessful newspaper project, Perry never lost sight of a belief in the egalitarian quality of French society under the revolutionary momentum.

Other associates and members of the *SADH* were active throughout the intense period of activity from 1789 through to 1793, contributing to British

---

28 Captain Monro to Lord Grenville, Paris, 7th January 1793. TNA FO 27/41. Monro provides details on the proceedings in the National Convention and the king's trial.
29 *The Times*, 5th January 1793, quoted in Werkmeister, *A Newspaper History of England*, p. 197.
30 Charles Ross to Evan Nepean, 9th October 1792. TNA TS 11/965/3510/A2.

journals, setting up newspapers in the French capital or contributing articles to already established publications. John Oswald was, according to David Erdman, one of a "set of Gentlemen, Britons, by birth" who launched a twice-weekly English-language newspaper as early as May 1790, to be distributed in both capitals, under the title of the *Universal Patriot*. The newspaper was quickly suppressed by the British government, with only the prospectus still featuring in library holdings. Oswald soon got involved in a further project as one of the fourteen editors of *La Chronique du Mois*, a publication orchestrated by the members of the *Cercle Social*. According to Gary Kates, the *Cercle Social* was an intellectual grouping whose members, though in favour of liberating the voice of the people, did not go as far as advocating a role for the people in law-making. As Kates notes, "the function of the Cercle Social was precisely to decipher the will of the people through the study of their writings; the group acted as a kind of enlightened window through which the desire of the people could be more clearly seen."[31] Yet after the king's flight to Varennes in June 1791 the *Cercle Social* consolidated a nascent pact with the more radical Cordeliers Club activists, proponents of greater decision-making emanating from the districts and critical of representative democracy. It was at this transitional phase in the evolution of the club that both John Oswald and Thomas Paine took up positions on the editorial committee of *La Chronique du Mois*, the group's new publication which replaced the previous journal *La Bouche de Fer*. Paine was already collaborating with some members of the editorial committee, including Bonneville, on *Le Républicain*. Paine and Oswald, though joint editors of *La Chronique du Mois*, diverged in their political views. While Oswald followed the popular democratic ideals of the Cordeliers, Paine, who would be heavily involved in the conception of the Girondin plan for a constitution at the turn of '93, promoted the case for the establishment of reformed representative government.

Mary Wollstonecraft intended to continue her writing for the *Analytical Review* whilst in Paris, having agreed to provide reports on the state of French affairs to Joseph Johnson. Yet she devoted most of her time in Paris to writing her history of the Revolution and penning an educational plan commissioned by the National Convention. Wollstonecraft as well as Thomas Paine, Sampson Perry, Joel Barlow and Helen Maria Williams, sometimes in collaboration with John Hurford Stone and Thomas Christie, all devoted considerable time and energy to more long-term publication projects, attempting to assemble sketches, histories and views of the Revolution. These writing and publication projects were often the fruit of collective encounters and initiatives, although members of the *SADH* seemed to have fiercely resisted any requirement of consensus in their written production, editorial decisions or printing contracts. This embracing

---

31 Gary Kates, *The Cercle Social, the Girondins and the French Revolution* (Princeton: Princeton University Press, 1985), p. 56.

of difference was one of the key characteristics of the British contributions to the debate on the embryonic French republic, as well as the nature of British activism activity more generally.

The English-language newspaper published in Paris in 1792, the *Paris Mercury*, drew together society member Thomas Marshall and Irish editor Robert Taylor in another joint publication initiative, aiming, in Simon Macdonald's words, to provide "speedy reportage from Paris", but also epitomising the "claim that Paris had superseded London both as a place of news interest and as a centre of uninhibited journalistic production".[32] Cross-national initiatives therefore found their place easily in the early republic.

JOHN HURFORD STONE'S ENGLISH PRINTING PRESS IN PARIS

John Hurford Stone was a key member of the British radical community in Paris, acting as president of the *SADH* when the address of solidarity was delivered to the Convention in November 1792. He was also a former member of the Society of the Friends of the People and the Revolution Society. He had a number of skills which proved of use to the new French administration and which facilitated his establishment in 1793 as a niche printer in Paris, specialising in radical publications in the English language. With a secure knowledge of European languages, he had already expressed his readiness to serve the French administration on one of the French diplomat Talleyrand's trips to London in February 1792. He was a member of Richard Price's Unitarian congregation at Hackney and, like other British Dissenters, would not have had access to the same privileges and benefits of social ascension as those of Anglican faith.[33] He described in a letter to Jérôme Pétion, mayor of Paris, on 12th February 1792, how he had also been singled out for suspicion after papers had been found at Joseph Priestley's house following its sacking by Church and King rioters in July 1791:

> In the Birmingham affair, when the house of Dr. Priestly was sacked, my letters were found and given to the Secretary of State, and were found to contain material of a criminal nature such as perhaps, as I don't remember, that we always [? think] tyrants when those who are persecuted or abused speak the truth. I was threatened, but I [? am not concerned], it interferes however with my ability to serve in this negotiation, besides, I would be

---

32 See Simon MacDonald, 'English-language Newspapers in Revolutionary France', *Journal for Eighteenth-Century Studies* Vol. 36 No. 1 (2013).

33 Attempts to repeal the Test and Corporation Acts had once again failed in 1791 leaving those of Non-Conformist background disillusioned and with little hope of being able to accede to positions in politics, public administration and the universities.

extremely flattered to pay all the compliments that we are, me and my patriotic friends, able to give.[34]

Stone also went to Paris with the intention of setting up in chemical production. This was only the first of many business ventures he embarked on while in the French capital.[35] His talent for languages, his Non-Conformist heritage and his penchant for business speculation were all factors leading him to emigrate.

Hurford Stone was one of a number of British residents in the French capital who became involved in the book and publishing trade, setting up a venture which would endure through the revolutionary years and into the era of the Directoire and Consulat. Stone is listed in the *Biographie Universelle* as a "learned printer" who, in 1806, became the official printer of the *Administration des Droits Réunis*, a branch of the finance department under Napoleon which drew together major legal texts relating to taxation in order to tackle the public debt. Yet Stone had established his "English Press in Paris" over a decade earlier, in 1793, just as other commercial projects he had embarked on were running into difficulties.[36] The printing press would change name and address a number of times. Initially located on rue de Vaugirard, where it remained until 1804, its location later changed to rue de l'Echiquier and then by 1810 to rue de Bondi.[37] Joel Barlow may have bought the *hôtel particulier* on rue de Vaugirard, where the printing press had previously been located, in 1805.

Stone, despite having grand designs for his printing outlet, only published a small and select group of texts and authors. Joel Barlow's *Vision of Columbus* came out in July 1793, and this was followed in September of the same year by Barlow's second part of *Advice to the Privileged Orders*. Sonnets by Helen Maria Williams were also published at the press.[38] Madeleine Stern suggests that Stone may have printed Part One of Paine's *Age of Reason*, the manuscript for which had been given to Barlow on Paine's arrest in December 1793.[39] He also published Paine's *Dissertation on First Principles of Government* and its French translation, in 1795. After a period in prison in 1794, prompted by the accusatory statement filed by a spy who went by the

---

34 AN F7/4774/70/459: "Dans l'affaire de Birmingham, quand la maison de Dr Priestley était pillée, on a trouvé mes lettres, qu'on a remises au secrétaire d'état et qu'on a trouvées contenants de matière criminelle telle peut-être, car je ne m'en souviens, que [on penseront?] toujours les tyrans quand ceux qui sont persécutés et injuriés parlent la vérité. J'ai été menacé, mais c'est ce que je ne [regarde?], il empêche pourtant ma capacité de service dans cette négotiation [sic], d'ailleurs, je serai fort flatté de rendre à M. Talleyrand toutes les civilités, dont nous sommes, moi et mes amis patriotiques, capables."

35 *CCST*, p. 1329.

36 Although one of Stone's first publications was Joel Barlow's *Vision of Columbus*, John Oswald's tract sent to the constitutional committee was also published by the English Press in 1793.

37 Stern, 'The English Press in Paris and its Successors, 1793-1852', p. 316.

38 *CCST*, p. 1225.

39 Stern, 'The English Press in Paris and its Successors, 1793-1852', p. 325.

name of 'Citizen Arthur', who had socialised with the British contingent at White's hotel, Stone was released and subsequently gained recognition as a printer-bookseller in the Mucius-Scaevola section.[40] In 1795 he printed a work by his friend General Francisco de Miranda and also produced a translation of Helen Maria Williams' *Letters Written in France*.[41] In 1796 Stone printed a letter from himself to Joseph Priestley and in 1801 he organised for the reproduction of Thomas Jefferson's Inaugural Address.

The first years of the press were particularly frenetic and Stone devoted considerable energy to finding buyers, researching possible texts to be translated into French, and sending samples via Le Havre and his brother William to Britain. In late 1793 he contacted his brother, requesting information on the likelihood of his printed books being well received in Britain and may have sent across some samples as illustrations. William Stone was acting on his brother's behalf in the quest for information on the prospective British market. Hurford Stone wrote, "I have received your letter, which gives me accurate information respecting my literary enquiries."[42] As Stern notes, his plans for conquering the European market seem to have been "grandiose".[43] In one letter to his brother, Hurford Stone wrote, "as this place will be the emporium of literature, as well as of everything else, it is impossible to say what may not be done, especially with the assistance of men, as well instructed as Mr. Gillet appears to me to be, to help forward the machinery of it."[44] Mr. Gillet, also an acquaintance and business associate of John Oswald, seems to have been Stone's principal contact and advisor on the book market. Stone may also have engaged in a venture with Helen Maria Williams to publish a magazine for national circulation:

> Miss H. M. Williams will be the conductor in chief. As it will be a national work, you may be sure it will be most magnificent. This (short-hand characters) of safety, will intrust [*sic*] its regulation to her; and she will choose the proper assistants. You may therefore hint this to Gillet, if you can make out my writing, which no one else will.[45]

Stone's relationship with Helen Maria Williams may also have prompted his growing interest in the translation market as a source of business for the

---

40 AN F7/4773/23. This information is included in Stone's arrest file.
41 General Miranda was a Venezuelan revolutionary whose commitment to universal liberty led him to fight in both the American revolutionary war and in the struggles of the French revolutionary army. He was considered a sympathiser of the Girondins and was brought to trial in 1794. John Hurford Stone and Joel Barlow both testified at his trial, where he was acquitted. See Pérez C. Parra, *Miranda et la Révolution française* (Paris: Dumoulin, 1925).
42 *CCST*, p. 1215.
43 Stern, 'The English Press in Paris and its Successors, 1793-1852', p. 319.
44 *CCST*, p. 1215.
45 Ibid, p. 1218.

printing press. He asked his brother to inquire of Mr. Gillet "whether the plan he prepared for literary translation from French into English cannot be inverted with respect to this country – whether he cannot furnish us with the means of getting books of merit which may come out, to translate from the English into French." Stone had been in touch with "a bookseller and a printer of eminence" who had shown interest in such a translation project and who could guarantee "a speedy sale." The buyer was primarily interested in travel literature and Stone pressed on his brother to persuade Mr. Gillet that the investment would be profitable and that the press "can now make a catalogue of twenty or thirty different articles, one of which 4 vols. of 500 pages each." He informs his brother that trade had been busy, "as ours is the most complete press here for certain books."[46] Stone's editing and printing venture exploited the demand for travel literature as well as French translations of works written in English, a market which he seems to have successfully tapped into by calling on the translation skills of Helen Maria Williams. Stone had an astute business mind and only invested in projects which would secure a profit for himself and his intermediaries. Yet he also seems to have restricted his printing ventures to works which reflected his own radical opinions.

COMMERCIAL AND PRIVATE INTERESTS

Some British, Irish and American residents pursued private commercial interests while in Paris which sometimes took precedence over, or at least intersected with, their political activities centred on White's hotel. Richard Buel has suggested that American resident Joel Barlow "seems to have been more preoccupied with exploring economic opportunities than observing the revolutionary drama playing out in Paris."[47] Stephen Sayre, an American member of the society, renowned republican and signatory of the British and Irish address to the Convention, ran a snuff and tobacco shop from White's, combining political activism with lucrative commercial practice.[48] Sayre had already set up a snuff manufacturing enterprise in 1790 or 1791 with an associate, yet the partnership came to an end in 1792.[49] Sayre probably established his own business in May 1792, using White's as an outlet.[50] He advertised his activity in the *Journal de Paris* on 25th May 1792,

---

46 Ibid, pp. 1223-4.
47 Buel, *Joel Barlow: American Citizen*, p. 139.
48 Captain Monro, 6th December 1792, TNA TS 11/959.
49 Stephen Sayre to George Washington, 2nd July 1791, Department of State, Miscellaneous Letters quoted in Alden, *Stephen Sayre*, p. 162. Sayre mentions his snuff manufacturing in his letter to the American president.
50 Alger, 'The British Colony in Paris, 1792-1793'. Alden also suggests that Sayre set up a factory at 7 passage des Petits Pères. As this is the address of White's hotel it is perhaps more likely that he ran his distribution activity from the hotel, but perhaps carried out the manufacturing elsewhere. There is also the possibility that other activities were carried out at the same address.

emphasising the excellent quality of the tobacco on offer.[51] Sayre wrote to Lord Stanhope in October 1792 informing him, "I have a part of White's Hotel, his first floor is as yet unoccupied."[52]

Buel argues that Sayre and Gilbert Imlay "used the clichés of revolutionary republicanism to promote their own interests," exploiting economic opportunities under a veneer of activism.[53] Yet most society members hailed from the urban bourgeoisie and could envisage conjugating commercial enterprise and republicanism without any perceived ideological contradiction. Stephen Sayre's biographer emphasises the complex nature of the American's engagement with France, pointing out that "his troubles in English society and his failure to secure recognition and employment from the republic across the Atlantic enhanced the fascination that the continuing French Revolution exerted on him, but he was also seeking economic opportunity."[54] Emigrants in Paris often conformed to this loose model of the entrepreneur-activist whose hopes of private personal advancement had been frustrated in their home country, leading them to embrace emigration for ideological reasons but also because it allowed them to pursue economic gain and professional standing.

James Gamble, a British resident of Paris who also put his name to the address to the National Convention in November 1792, set up a paper manufactory in Paris, also combining political and commercial endeavour, and may have assumed co-ownership of White's hotel after the landlord, Christopher White, who had called on Gamble to be his guarantor, got into financial difficulties in 1793.[55] Gamble was also recognised as an inventor of coloured engravings.[56] According to Alger, Gamble had been licensed to publish a collection of engravings in May 1789 and with a partner he had subsequently portrayed revolutionary scenes and allegories. On 18th January 1795 the two engravers presented an allegorical scene of Brutus condemning his son to death. Gamble was one of the British contingent whose interests in politics (he contributed to the initiative to raise money for the widows and children of the victims of the 10th August 1792) intersected with his commercial activities in Paris.

---

51 See Alger, *Paris in 1789-1794*, p. 352.
52 Letter from October 28th 1792, quoted in Alden, *Stephen Sayre*, p. 173. Sayre also tried to persuade Stanhope to visit Paris to see for himself events taking place in the capital: "You will be well received here by all the leading characters, you will return with accurate information, may meet Parliament with advantage and confidence, and render service to the world."
53 Buel, *Joel Barlow: American Citizen*, p. 164
54 Alden, *Stephen Sayre*, p. 161.
55 John Goldworth Alger, 'The British Colony in Paris, 1792-1793'. See also Citizen Arthur's declaration, AN F7/4775/23: "Gamble, anglais imprimeur en taille, douze rue des piques, au coin du boulevard est copropriétaire de la maison With...il n'a pris intérêt dans cette maison que depuis With, dont il était la caution, a fait la Banqueroute."
56 See Alger, 'The British Colony in Paris', pp. 682-3.

John Hurford Stone, as well as establishing a printing venture in Paris, was also a speculator, pursuing different projects in the French capital. He set up a cotton manufacturing industry in Paris and became "tolerably rich" through his business pursuits.[57] He also became involved at various times in the banking, chemical and wine sectors.[58] Hurford Stone and Joel Barlow exploited openings in the real estate field following the flight of French *émigrés* to British shores. Barlow purchased his Paris house at a price far below its value, after it had been confiscated by the revolutionary authorities and turned into national property.[59] Hurford Stone mentioned his own intention to purchase an abandoned property at low cost in a district close to his latest manufacturing interest: "I have some thought, of buying one of those Emigrants houses on the side of the city, where our business will be carried on, as there is no doubt of these houses being sold very cheap, and as national property, not to be paid for under 12 years."[60] Stone, though closely involved in the political initiatives of the *SADH*, aimed at exploiting the economic opportunities presented by the Revolution in a series of experimental business plans.

Thomas Christie, a business associate of Stone, combined political journalism with mercantile activities. In Paris, he represented Turnbull, Forbes and Co., a company which sent grain and wheat to France during periods of severe dearth after 1789, despite the uncertainty which reigned in Britain as to the outcome of events across the Channel.[61] Christie, in a letter to Jérôme Pétion of February 1792, suggested that it was faith in the justice of the French nation that had fuelled the risky business venture. The company had sent supplies to Dieppe, Rouen and Paris to help alleviate the food shortages afflicting the country. Business investment was therefore directly linked to political sympathy. Christie made numerous trips to France in the ensuing years, partly out of interest in the Revolution, partly as an ambassador for his employer, charged with recovering outstanding sums of money owed by the different French districts in exchange for the goods supplied. Christie was even imprisoned for a few days in late 1793 under the measures adopted against British subjects, yet his release was secured when his mission to claim outstanding debt from the municipal government was acknowledged. In a similar vein, James Watt was to promote Thomas Walker's commercial interests in France while also leading a delegation to the Jacobin Club. Watt, after his stay in Paris, intended to "visit different parts of France, for the purpose of extending the commercial connexions of my Brother and myself with a Nation for which we have the highest esteem."[62]

---

57 *CCST*, p. 1218.
58 Ibid, p. 1337.
59 Yorke, *France in 1802*. See chapter entitled 'Thomas Paine, Jack Barlow. The Abbé Costi. Dr. Sudaeur'.
60 *CCST*, p. 1301. Letter dated 24th October 1792.
61 Correspondence of Thomas Christie in AN F7/4648/3.
62 AN F7/4774/70/464. The file contains an undated letter from Thomas Walker to Jérôme

Political missions could be used as pretexts for consolidating or establishing business connections.

Robert Rayment, one of the least well-documented of the British radicals in Paris, described his profession as a merchant and agriculturalist to his captors during his incarceration from late 1793. Rayment went to France to present an economic proposal relating to the fabrication of copper currency to the revolutionaries and publicise his ideas on agrarian improvement. While he was in France he was recruited as a representative of a French banking establishment, the *Caisse d'Escompte*, to gather information about the organisation and running of the Bank of England. Yet Rayment also seems to have combined economic endeavour with political activism, being one of the principal figures behind a plan to provide relief for the widows and orphans of those who died at the Tuileries in August 1792 and signing the British and Irish address of support to the National Convention in November 1792. Rayment, along with Thomas Marshall, another signatory of the address, devised a plan to increase the value of *assignats* and to lower the price of foodstuffs in an attempt to relieve the financial distress of the less well-off among the French population. Copies of the plan were circulated to the departments of France.[63] Rayment was not unique among his British associates to be active in searching for practical ways of alleviating the distress of the poor or vocal in calling for the end of the oppression of the destitute by the rich. Mary Wollstonecraft bewailed the persistence of poverty as a barrier to the moral improvement of French society, asking, "How, in fact, can we expect to see men live together like brothers, when we only see master and servant in society? For till men learn mutually to assist without governing each other, little can be done by political associations towards perfecting the condition of mankind."[64] If British emigrants were interested in commerce and speculation, not all believed that economic activity should be unlimited. For Wollstonecraft, commercial activity was a way of securing the general improvement of society and should not be conducted to perpetuate economic inequality between the wealthy and the poorest.

Christopher White, the proprietor of the hotel which became the meeting ground for British activists in Paris, was first and foremost a businessman, setting up a hotel and brasserie in Le Havre in 1786 with his wife and two children after receiving inviting offers from several tradesmen and negotiators to establish himself in the northern French port town. He

---

Pétion.

63 The material held on Robert Rayment in the National Archives in Paris is extensive. See AN F7/4774/88. Rayment distinguished himself by successive petitions for his release, supported by testimonies from members of his section who seemed to consider him a loyal citizen and adherent of the Revolution. The Thomas Marshall mentioned in the information relating to the *SADH* does not seem to be the same Marshall who was a close friend of William Godwin and who translated the works of Volney.

64 *HMV*, p. 46.

transferred his livelihood to Paris in 1790, renting a house for ten thousand francs per year and furnishing it at great expense. Though essentially spurred to set up his hotel for economic gain, White exploited the Revolution's attractiveness to foreigners to populate his hotel. He encouraged members of the *SADH* to hold their twice-weekly meetings on his premises and allowed Paine, Fitzgerald and others to make the hotel their temporary residence. Nevertheless, White also had a number of less enthusiastic observers of the Revolution on his guest register. Foreign-Office spy, Captain Monro, also stayed at the hotel during his mission on behalf of the British government.

Despite White's concessions to the radical core of British emigrants, his primary interests remained in entrepreneurship. After the flight of most foreigners from Paris in mid to late 1793, which precipitated the collapse of his hotel venture, despite James Gamble's attempts to rescue the operation by taking a part share in the hotel, White set up in business with another compatriot and society member, Nicholas Joyce, renting the Carmelites convent and establishing a cotton factory.[65] White's share in the venture was the equivalent of the sum already owed to him by his partner Joyce. The factory was about to be opened when the Convention declared the wholesale arrest of British citizens in October 1793. White's arrest and imprisonment seem to have ended his commercial aspirations in France, though little is yet known of his fate after the Luxembourg.[66] John Hurford Stone mentions in a letter of December 1793 that "we have engaged in a manufactory of English fashion cotton hose".[67] Considering Stone was a speculator in Paris and attended meetings at White's hotel on a regular basis, he may have also been involved in White and Joyce's cotton enterprise. It is also likely that a trade in English clothing items was taking place a couple of doors down from White's hotel, at 9 passage des Petits Pères, as the sale of second-hand English ties and flannel at a price thirty per cent lower than the retail price was announced in *Le Moniteur Universel* in late November 1792.[68]

---

65 Nicholas Joyce was probably a signatory to the address of 24th November 1792. Although David Erdman reads the first name on the address as "Rich" for Richard, the first four letters given could equally be "Nich" for Nicholas. This would make sense, considering that Nicholas Joyce was White's business partner and that I have found no records under the name of Richard Joyce.

66 Christopher White's career in France is outlined in some detail in the submissions he made to the *Comité de Sûreté Générale* while imprisoned in the Luxembourg prison. See AN F7/4775/52 70-81. White's depositions are made largely in support of an application for the freedom of Nicholas Joyce's orphaned children, one of whom, the eldest, was held in detention with the White family. Joyce had died in the Benedictine prison on 25th February 1794.

67 *CCST*, p. 1214.

68 27th November 1792, *Le Moniteur Universel*, vol. 14. "Au grand balcon, rue et passage des petits pères, no.9, au premier. La société qui tient l'entrepôt de marchandises d'occasion, à 30 pour cent au-dessous du prix de fabrique, prévient ses concitoyens qu'elle a reçu un grand assortiment de marchandise de tout genre, et particulièrement pour l'hiver…Idem vrai anglais… cravates anglaises…flanelle vraie anglaise."

There were some contemporary critics, however, of this enthusiasm for combining entrepreneurship and revolutionary adherence. One of the perennial themes in Mary Wollstonecraft's letters to Gilbert Imlay was her disapproval of his penchant for commerce which she considered as both antithetical to a fulfilling life in the present and morally reprehensible. After Imlay's extended stay in Le Havre she wrote to him with the expectation that he would "make a power of money to indemnify me for your absence."[69] Joel Barlow and Imlay were involved in a risky project to evade the British blockade of Toulon and import grain, soap and iron. Wollstonecraft repeatedly reproached Imlay for his attachment to speculation, conveying her concern that he was excessively consumed by monetary accumulation. On 29th December 1793 she wrote, "Be not too anxious to get money! – for nothing worth having is to be purchased."[70] Three days later she reiterated her view on his business ventures stating, "I hate commerce."[71] As her frustration with their protracted separation continued, Wollstonecraft began to accuse Imlay of having been "embruted by trade and the vulgar enjoyments of life," and a day later articulated her lack of admiration for his "commercial face."[72] The theme is persistent in her letters and, although her frustration was evidently motivated by the spectre of her estrangement from Imlay, the tension that emerges between the coveting of present time and immaterial joys and the pursuit of commercial gain also had a philosophical slant. As Wollstonecraft notes in her *An Historical and Moral View*, the German model of moral and cultural advancement was laudable not only because it was pursued with "simplicity of manners, and honesty of heart," two virtues crucial to her vision of moral improvement, but the situation of the country "prevents that inundation of riches by commercial sources, that destroys the morals of a nation before it's [*sic*] reason arrives at maturity."[73] Commerce was not a curse in itself, but it was unhelpful in the early stages of cultivating a polished society. She did not criticise commerce *per se* in her history of the Revolution, in fact she suggested the liberating of trade was a necessary step in the advancement of civilisation. Yet she criticised "the destructive influence of commerce" on men whose state of moral infancy led them to partake in an "aristocracy of wealth" and "exchange savageness for tame servility" rather than cultivating "the urbanity of improved reason." It was the slavishness that commerce engendered in degenerate European man, and the way it displaced honest husbandry, which she objected to rather than commerce as an ideal form of rational human exchange. The debate over the virtue of commerce belied divisions over the interpretation of republicanism that continued to have relevance during the 1790s. While

---

69 To Gilbert Imlay, 29th December 1793, Wollstonecraft, *Collected Letters*, p. 235.
70 Ibid.
71 To Gilbert Imlay, 1st January 1794, Wollstonecraft, *Collected Letters*, p. 238.
72 To Gilbert Imlay, 23rd September 1794, Wollstonecraft, *Collected Letters*, pp. 264, 265.
73 *HMV*, p. 116.

commerce and republicanism had hitherto been seen as antithetical, their conjunction began to be accepted and justified.[74]

What stands out from these cases is that, on the whole, adherence to the goals of the Revolution was not seen as incompatible with financial speculation or industrial and manufacturing innovation. On the contrary, there was much to justify their merger. Speculation, experimentation and the embracing of novelty were key features of revolutionary thinking, distinguishing adherents of the Revolution from more sceptical observers. As Roger Chartier has shown, the "certainty of inauguration" and the "illusion of a new departure" were essential aspects of the Revolution.[75] Commentators in Britain noted British emigrants' propensity for innovation. At the trial of William Stone, Sergeant Adair speaking for the prosecution, suggested that the defendant's brother, John Hurford Stone, was "a man of a fervid imagination, and a restless mind, rather with a turn inclined to speculation and theory, ready to enter into any projects, and to have no great objection to innovation".[76] The terms 'speculation', 'novelty' and 'projects' were used in relation to British emigrants, and invoked the threat posed by the questioning of the status quo. The term "projecting" also conjures up the "Academy of Projectors" in *Gulliver's Travels*. In Swift's satire, the Academy develops theories to improve society and puts them into practice without testing them beforehand which results in failure. "Projecting" was therefore associated with the rejection of practice in favour of abstraction.[77] As Lord Auckland noted in a letter to William Pitt, despite the general antipathy to 'Jacobinism' in Britain, "there prevails among us a growing disposition to innovation; and we must not conceal from ourselves (what we certainly shall experience most sensibly) that this attachment of the country at large to Government is naturally weakened by the long course of calamities which has baffled and disappointed all the measures of Government."[78]

The latitude accorded to foreign residents to engage in lucrative commercial ventures would change radically once the more open cosmopolitanism of the first three years of the Revolution began to disintegrate and when experimentation and speculation began to be

---

74 See Mark Philp, 'English Republicanism in the 1790s', *The Journal of Political Philosophy* 6:3 (1998), pp. 235-262. Philp suggests, "In many ways, one of the most shocking of eighteenth-century innovations was to find in the conduct of commerce and the accumulation of wealth symptoms of civic health and strength, rather than of corrupt self-seeking", p. 242.

75 Roger Chartier, *Les origines culturelles de la Révolution française* (Paris: Seuil, 1991), pp. 28-9.

76 *CCST*, p. 1328.

77 Unlike the Projectors, Lord Munodi, ruler of Lagado in Balnibarbi, applies tried and tested methods and as a result the community he governs thrives. I am grateful to Andrew McKenzie McHarg of the University of Erfurt, Germany for pointing me in the direction of Swift's text as an example of early eighteenth-century satire on the notion of projection at the *Conspiracies Real and Imagined* Conference in York in September 2011.

78 *Correspondence of William Lord Auckland* 2, p. 272.

associated with deviance and counter-revolution. Yet the combining of economic interest with support for the Revolution was not in itself contradictory. Although some radicals, in particular Mary Wollstonecraft, were sceptical about the moral implications of commerce in rational, enlightened human society, others saw no friction between the two, and their residence in Paris was characterised by private profit-making as well as public political activism.

5

La Société des Amis des Droits de l'Homme
A political association at White's hotel

The sources which allow scholars to access the precise nature of the society established in Paris under the name of *La Société des Amis des Droits de l'Homme* are scarce and scattered, and there are no official minutes or records to testify to the nature of its proceedings. The reports sent by British agent Captain George Monro are helpful yet must be treated with caution. We can glean information about the club from the addresses and petitions sent to the National Convention during the course of late 1792 and 1793. The official address was a key instrument of political influence exploited by the society, a form which, during the course of 1793, as British residents' status and legitimacy was cast into doubt, could sometimes take the guise of a petition or a plea. Details of the members of the society can also be found in the writings published by its members while in Paris or from the prison records held at the *Archives Nationales*. Letters also survive, as do some later references to the society in autobiographical writings, newspapers and obituaries. Occasionally the society is mentioned in tracts and treatises published by the members of the emigrant community, but these allusions are few and far between. Hazarding any firm assertions on the nature of the group, its organization and its functioning is thus a perilous endeavour, and any offerings here are made with the caution that such a patchy record necessitates. Yet what does emerge from the archive is a picture of a group admirative of the changes wrought by the French Revolution, some of whose members were sympathetic to, and intent on implementing in practice, ideas of a greater degree of popular participation in the public sphere. It was also a club whose links across the Channel to reforming societies in Britain remained strong and whose specific activities were defined by those connections as well as by new synergies created in the French capital.

The first meeting of the English-speaking society was recorded on 18th November 1792 when a group of British and Irish residents of Paris met over dinner at White's hotel and selected a committee to draft an address that same evening to be presented to the National Convention, publicly endorsing the new republican departure in the Revolution.[1] In a letter to the Home Office in early December, spy Captain Monro suggested that the initial gathering was attended by nearly eighty people "of various ranks and descriptions."[2] He singles out Edward Fitzgerald, Robert Smith, John Hurford Stone and "a few others" as the principal actors and suggests that the committee set up to frame the address consisted of some fifteen members, led by a "Mr. McDonald who is concern'd in the Morning Post."[3] Monro probably made an error here, as it was more likely D. E. MacDonnell, the editor of the Opposition newspaper, *The Morning Post*, who signed and drew up the address to the Convention.[4] He states that Sir Robert Smith had "a great share in all their committees and accompanied the address to the bar" and, like Hurford Stone, was notable for his subversive views towards his home country. Other figures he considered of significance were Robert Rayment, Nicholas Joyce, the American Stephen Sayre, James Gamble and John Oswald. He also mentions Henry Yorke and John and Henry Sheares, and later Sampson Perry, whose addition to the ranks reinforced the club in early 1793.[5] Lesser respected members, according to Monro, included Irishman Robert O'Reilly, William Newton, whose abilities "neither do much harm nor good," and Dr. William Maxwell.

At the gathering on 18th November, both Sir Robert Smith, former Member of Parliament for Colchester, and Lord Edward Fitzgerald cast off

---

1 The donations that had been offered by British residents to help the widows and children of the victims of the Tuileries assault was perhaps also an early manifestation of collective action which would provide impetus for the creation of the society. The architects of the Tuileries scheme – Robert Rayment, James Gamble and Sir Robert Smith would go on to help set up the *SADH*.
2 TNA TS 11/959.
3 Ibid.
4 AN C11/278/40. The *SADH* address is not signed by a McDonald, but by a D.E. MacDonnell. Erdman mistakes a D for a J and misspells his surname. Werkmeister suggests in *A Newspaper History of England* that MacDonnell was probably editing the *Morning Post* in 1792. MacDonnell also edited *The Gazetteer* and *The Telegraph* over the course of 1791-1796. See Robert Haig, *The Gazetteer 1735-1797: A Study in the Eighteenth-Century English Newspaper* (Carbondale: Southern Illinois University Press, 1960), pp. 232-9 and pp. 250-3. He was also a journalistic acquaintance of Robert Merry and may have acted as a go-between in a dispute between the poet and John Taylor of the Drury Lane theatre. See John Taylor, *Records of My Life*, vol. 2 (New York: Harper, 1833), pp. 272-8.
5 TNA FO 27/40 Part 2. See the letter from Captain Monro, written from Paris on 17th December 1792. See also the letter from Captain Monro to Lord Grenville, written at Paris on 13th January 1793, which mentions Perry. TNA FO 27/41

their titles in a show of solidarity with the egalitarian impulses characteristic of the new republic. Sampson Perry noted the change in his account of the Revolution. He wrote, "It ought not to be omitted in mention, that this convention, still more strongly imbued with the principle of equality than either of its predecessors, resolved the same day to disuse the title of *monsieur*, and take the plain one of citizen."[6] Monro reported that "After a dinner a variety of toasts were given, and Lord Edward Fitzgerald, and Sir Rob't Smith propos'd laying down their titles, and are now actually call'd by this sett Citoyen Fitzgerald, and Citoyen Smith."[7] This is corroborated in a letter from Fitzgerald himself to his mother from Paris, which he signed off "Le citoyen Edouard Fitzgerald."[8] Fitzgerald took to dressing more informally in France, following the revolutionary custom, wearing his collar high, his hair short and unpowdered and donning a simple jacket. Fitzgerald and Smith were the only two titled members of the club, as the majority hailed from the gentry or professional classes, yet their gesture of opposition to social rank and distinction was hailed by their compatriots. Robert Merry praised the conduct of members of the nobility who "cordially acquiesced in the new order of things, and by a glorious effort of enlightened benevolence, chearfully [*sic*] sacrificed the empty gewgaws of aristocracy to merit the most substantial and only noble distinctions of a patriot and a philanthropist."[9] Emigrants in Paris, often hailing from a reforming Whig background, embraced some of the more democratic initiatives underway under the early republic. For this, they were criticised by loyalist commentators at home for their renunciation of the established order. *The Annual Register* published this view of Merry:

> Before the lamentable disorders of France, he was highly esteemed by numerous and respectable friends, who admired him for his knowledge, humour, and companionable qualities; but the change in his political opinions gave a sullen gloom to his character, which made him relinquish all his former connections, and unite with people far beneath his talents, and quite unsuitable to his habits.[10]

As J. G. A. Pocock has noted, "Eighteenth-century fears of revolution regularly took a Catilinarian form; some member of the inner circle might betray his class."[11]

---

6 *HS* II, p. 265.
7 Captain Monro, 6th December 1792, TNA TS 11/959.
8 Moore, *The Life and Death of Lord Edward Fitzgerald*, pp. 73-4.
9 Merry [?], *A Circumstantial History*, pp. vii-viii.
10 *The Annual Register* (1799) p. 350.
11 J. G. A. Pocock, *Virtue, Commerce, and History: Essays on Political Thought and History, Chiefly in the Eighteenth Century* (Cambridge: Cambridge University Press, 1985), p. 245. Catiline had opposed Cicero in his bid to become Consul under the late Roman Republic. He had renounced his aristocratic background to champion the cause of reform for the poor, promote debt relief and orchestrate attacks on property and wealth.

The address drawn up by the committee on the 18th November was signed at a subsequent gathering six days later, on 24th November, by fifty men. On 20th November, the National Convention had pledged to "grant fraternity and assistance to all people who wish to recover their liberty" and shortly after the French ambassador, the Marquis de Chauvelin, promulgated the Edict of Fraternity which declared France's willingness to aid sovereign nations in securing their freedom from tyranny.[12] Included among the signatories of the foreign address were a large number of Scottish and English men such as Robert Merry, John Oswald, William Choppin and Robert Rayment, as well as former or current students of the Irish colleges, Jeremie Curtayn, Bernard MacSheehy, Edward Ferris and William Duckett. American resident Stephen Sayre also signed the address.[13] Members of the society were therefore drawn from across the English-speaking nations of Britain, Ireland and America, and the association may also have attracted some French adherents.

The society began to attract attention and an entry in *Le Moniteur Universel* on 26th November 1792 announced that a meeting had taken place in the preceding days:

> Those English residents of Paris gathered a few days ago at White's Hotel, passage des Petits Pères, to celebrate the victories of the French republican armies and the triumph of liberty. Foreigners from different European countries were invited to this celebration and shared the joy which moved the Assembly. Thus are strengthened each day the bonds of universal fraternity which the French have extended to all peoples and on which they stake their lives.[14]

On 28th November, the address from the "English, Scots and Irish, residents of Paris" was presented to the representatives of the Convention by secretary Robert O'Reilly at the head of a delegation of twenty men, who "were all afterwards admitted to the honour of France."[15] Although Captain Monro dismissed him as "of little consequence either one way or the other", O'Reilly's position as secretary at the head of the delegation indicates his

---

12 See the transcription of the declaration of the National Convention of 20th November 1792 in TNA TS 11/965/3510/A2. For a discussion of the Edict of Fraternity, see Boyd Hilton, *A Mad, Bad, and Dangerous People?: England, 1783-1846* (Oxford: Oxford University Press, 2006), p. 66.
13 For a full list of signatories, see page 260.
14 *Le Moniteur Universel*, vol. 14, Monday 26th November 1792. "De Paris – Les Anglais demeurant à Paris se sont assemblés, il y a quelques jours, à l'hôtel de Withes, passage des Petits-Pères, pour célébrer les victoires des armées de la république française et le triomphe de la liberté. Des étrangers de différentes contrées de l'Europe ont étés invitées à cette fête, et ont pris part à la joie qui transportaient l'assemblée. Ainsi s'étendent chaque jour les liens de la fraternité universelle à laquelle les Français ont invité tous les peuples, et qu'ils veulent établir au prix de leur sang."
15 TNA TS 11/959.

centrality within the club was perhaps greater than Monro admits. He was also a figure who was well-respected within the revolutionary administration.

The declaration was presented along with an address from the SCI delivered by Joel Barlow and John Frost.[16] In the Paris society address, the signatories congratulate the republic on its recent military victories and hold up the principles of the French Revolution as an example for the rest of Europe. The constitutional settlement of Britain, long seen as a model of moderate monarchical government in Europe, and even presumed initially to have inspired the events of 1789, is not referred to. The authors claim to have "always applauded the sacred principles" on which the French representatives have pledged to found their government. The future enfranchisement of the people of Europe is anticipated and the union between the French republic and "the English, Scottish and Irish nations" is celebrated.

Not only does this statement of unity between the peoples of Britain and Ireland coincide with the sentiments articulated in the address sent by the SCI but it also echoes the toast made at a dinner of the Revolution Society on 16th November 1792, two days before the first meeting of the *SADH*, to call for "equal rights for the Irish people" as well as "unity between the people of Britain, Ireland, France and America".[17] The Paris society declaration outlines an ideal vision of liberty in the spirit of the universalism of the early Revolution. The text is also free from all reference to a specific national constitutional tradition, enabling reformers of British and Irish descent to rally round its central message.

Further meetings of the political society took place over the course of December, probably on a bi-weekly basis, on Sundays and Thursdays, though Helen Maria Williams suggested that at times the meetings, some of which took place outside White's hotel, would be nightly. Citizen Arthur, who later denounced John Hurford Stone as a British spy, suggests that a man going by the name of Milne provided dinner at the hotel almost every week for British guests.[18] Dinners at the hotel would often be the occasion for socialising and the broadening of networks. This regularity of assembly during the latter months of 1792 is confirmed in Hurford Stone's letters to his brother William, in which he described evenings spent with fellow British men and women reading the national papers and toasting the cause of liberty.[19]

On 16th December 1792, only days after the king's trial had begun in the Convention, a meeting of the society was chaired by Robert Merry. At the

---

16 Henry Redhead Yorke also brought an address from Derby which Monro mentions in his Foreign Office correspondence. See the letter dated 17th December 1792 in TNA FO 27/40 Part 2.
17 Quoted in *Le Moniteur Universel*, volume 14. The Revolution Society had a much more Whig-oriented reform agenda in late 1792 than the SCI or the LCS.
18 See AN F7/4775/23.
19 *CCST*, p. 1215.

gathering Merry and Thomas Paine suggested presenting a second congratulatory address to the Convention, although this motion was objected to by other members, including John Frost, Henry Yorke and D. E. MacDonnell. Monro suggests that tension over the planned declaration was so high that "the debate nearly ended in blows."[20] Members increasingly disagreed, it would appear, over the extent to which support for the developments under the new republic should be publicly proclaimed, with some favouring a more cautious approach and others more fervent in their commitment. Monro suggests that MacDonnell "is look'd up to by the party but is more moderate than many."[21] In his report of 27th December, Monro added that "Mr F__t and Tom Payne are not on such good terms as they were; the Député treats his friends with much *hauteur*."[22] This animosity may have been the result of the fall-out at the meeting two weeks earlier. John Frost was conscious of the outstanding warrant for his apprehension in Britain and this may have impacted on his willingness to put his name to overt declarations of support for the republic as the king's trial progressed.[23] Yet despite Frost's apparent reticence about further public engagement with the Revolution, he still attended the trial of Louis XVI in January. He was however increasingly suffering from financial hardship and had moved out of White's hotel by the end of the year. According to Monro, "Frost's remittances I suppose are not large from his employers, for he has left this hotel and gone to one which he pays extremely cheap."[24]

The main event of the evening on 16th December however was the presentation of an address from the president of the place des Fédérés section to the foreign audience. The subject of the speech is unknown, yet the very presence of a Section leader at a society gathering provides evidence that the British were mixing with local representatives, seen as the voice of *sans-culottes* activism. A number within the ranks of the society were closely involved with figures in the Parisian Sections. Both Robert Rayment and Robert Smith received glowing character references from local leaders (Guillaume Tell and Le Pelletier sections respectively) in later pleas for release from prison. Emigrants' involvement with local political organisation and preference for direct appeals to local districts for consent on laws was

---

20 Captain Monro to Lord Grenville, 27th December 1792, *The Despatches of Earl Gower, English Ambassador at Paris from June 1790 to August 1792 (Cambridge: Cambridge University Press, 1885)*, p. 268. See also Captain Monro's letters in TNA FO 27/40 Part 2.
21 TNA TS 11/959.
22 Captain Monro to Lord Grenville, 27th December 1792, *The Despatches of Earl Gower*, p. 268.
23 Captain Monro to Lord Grenville, 17th December 1792, TNA FO 27/40 Part 2. Monro wrote that "Mr Frost has left this house and seldom makes his appearance. He is however one of the Society. He appears however a good deal alarmed at his situation, as he told me a reward was offered for apprehending him."
24 Captain Monro to Lord Grenville, Paris, 31st December 1792. TNA FO 27/40 Part 2. The transcription of this letter in *Despatches to Earl Gower* reads "he lives extremely cheap", p. 269.

also in evidence in later political writings.²⁵ Such contact with local Parisian activism may also have led to certain practices being put in place within their own political association, some of which drew criticism from within the membership as well as at home. John Taylor contended that Robert Merry had "imbibed all the levelling principles of the most furious democrat," and had become an outright enemy of the British government.²⁶ One opposition newspaper also lamented his "associating with the last dregs of human nature."²⁷ *The European Magazine*'s portrait of Merry from December 1793 suggested, "Having passed the greater part of his life in what is called high company, and in the *beau monde*, he became disgusted with the follies and vices of the Noblesse, and is now a most strenuous friend to general liberty, and the common rights of mankind."²⁸

As well as, or perhaps in part because of, their openness to democratic initiatives, emigrants were portrayed by those monitoring their actions and critical of their stance as being part of a wider insurrectionary underground whose intentions stretched to the subversion of the monarchy and constitution of Great Britain. On 6th December 1792 Captain Monro reported:

> I here beg leave to remark that the people concern'd in these addresses extend their views in the most culpable degree far beyond simply a mere reform in the more equal representation in Parliament; they extend their damnable ideas to the tottal [*sic*] subversion of Royalty, and the entire overthrow of the present British Constitution on which they mean to form a Republic. There are people in power in France now backing them in their diabolical schemes, and I dare say will gladly give them every assistance in their power to carry them into execution.²⁹

Monro noted how the members of the *SADH* "extend their views in the most culpable degree far beyond simple a mere reform" and that they would "stand at nothing" to achieve their aims.³⁰ The agent concluded his report of the 6th December by reassuring ministers of the fact that the members of the Paris society were "contemptible for their numbers as consequence" yet warning that "such people have in general been the beginners of Revolutions on republican principles, and when their Doctrine becomes popular then people of greater consequence step forward." Monro, in the pay of the

---

25 Haim Burstin's book, *Une révolution à l'œuvre. Le faubourg Saint Marcel 1789-1794* (Seyssel: Champ Vallon, 2005) illuminates this tension between initiatives of the revolutionary authorities and the gradual politicisation and radicalisation of this particular Paris district (faubourg Saint Marcel) after the August Days.
26 John Taylor, *Records of my Life* 2: 274, quoted in Mee, 'The Magician No Conjuror', p. 43.
27 Quoted in Werkmeister, *A Newspaper History of England*, pp. 94-5.
28 'Some Account of Robert Merry, Esq.', *The European Magazine* 24 (December 1793), p. 411.
29 Captain Monro, 6th December 1792, PRO TS 11/959.
30 Ibid.

British state and therefore with a material interest in providing evidence of the need for continued surveillance, recommended that the government keep "a watchful eye" on the group who he considered would "stand at nothing" in the pursuit of their "diabolical plans."[31]

On 21st December Monro wrote again to Lord Grenville at the Foreign Office. He added that, "their dispositions are such that I am however sure they would, with the assistance of France, put anything in execution that could injure their country" and advised that "England ought to be on their guard against such parties."[32] The spy described Sir Robert Smith as "exerting every nerve to ruin his country" and Robert Rayment as "not only an enemy to the Minister, but to his country."[33] While dismissing the talent of Nicholas Joyce, Monro signalled his "strong propensity to ruin his country."[34]

At the end of the month, Monro sent a further despatch to Lord Grenville, reiterating the violent nature of the group's intentions, despite their diminishing numbers and impact. He wrote, "We have however still many enemies here, who would stand at nothing to ruin their country."[35] Monro's reports from December therefore, as the trial of the king continued and as diplomatic tension between Britain and France mounted, accentuate the conspiratorial streak in British radical politics in France and depict the group as an ultra-violent fringe of the reform movement whose members, heavily involved in French networks, were actively plotting against their own country.

In the climate of diplomatic tension, frictions within the society appear to have reached their height. Both Citizen Arthur and Captain Monro suggested that the discussions and meetings at White's hotel during the course of December were fraught with brimming animosity. Citizen Arthur recounts one evening when during one of the "orgies" of political debate, an argument broke out between Thomas Paine and another British resident. The latter punched Paine in the face and fled before later returning to make amends. Monro also depicted a group riven by dissension, contending that the members were "jealous of one another, differing in opinions."[36] He recalls how the support of certain members for the turn of events in France had "occasioned Sir Rt. Smith to quit their party as well as many others."[37] While Smith seems to have welcomed the eradication of titles, he was perhaps more reticent, faced with the impending judgement to be meted out

---

31 Ibid.
32 George Granville Leveson-Gower, Duke of Sutherland, *The Despatches of Earl Gower*, p. 263.
33 Captain Monro, 6th December 1792, TNA TS 11/959.
34 Ibid.
35 Captain Monro, 27th December 1792, *The Despatches of Earl Gower*, p. 268.
36 Captain Monro to Lord Grenville, 27th December 1792, *The Despatches of Earl Gower* 268. See also Captain Monro's letters in TNA FO 27/40 Part 2.
37 Captain Monro to Lord Grenville, 21st December 1792, *The Despatches of Earl Gower*, p. 263

against the king. Smith was a close acquaintance of Paine and worked in tandem with him on some of his later publication ventures. Like Paine, he may have had reservations about the suitability of a democratic political model in the new republic. Tensions also arose between American and British members, with a motion being passed to expel members from America as subjects of another state, a gesture which went contrary to earlier celebrations of universal fraternity in the society's ranks and hints at the difficulties encountered by foreign residents whose nationality was increasingly held up as a mark of potential counter-revolutionary design.[38]

Despite accounts of such strain from within the informant cell, in early January *Le Moniteur Universel*, the French government's official news outlet, announced the club's registration with the Paris municipal authorities, a sign that the enthusiasm of emigrants for the Revolution had not entirely waned as the king's trial progressed. The paper reported that "foreigners, for the most part English, Scots and Irish, resident in Paris, have addressed themselves to the city council, and declared that, in accordance with the law, they will meet every Sunday and Thursday, under the name of the Society of the Friends of the Rights of Man, at White's English hotel, 7 passage des Petits Pères."[39] The explicit reference to the English, Scots and Irish might show that those who continued their engagement with the club in early January were more committed to an agenda which combined the priorities of both British and Irish radicals and which may have been more overtly democratic in character. A further address was presented to the Jacobin Club on 12th January, and another to the Convention on 22nd January 1793, according to Erdman.

By the turn of the year, spies began to be suspected within the community gravitating around White's, and by mid to late January, Captain Monro had considered it wise to withdraw, being "noticed and observed by his rascals of countrymen."[40] Mr Somers, one of Monro's fellow informants in Paris who disguised his role by declaring his trade as "negotiator", wrote on 20th January: "I shall wait your further orders – I hope I have nothing to fear and the private and obscure retreat I have chosen put me above or below suspicion – I am glad Mr Monro set off for England – he was not only suspected but marked here."[41] Monro had to petition a friend of Lord

---

38 Captain Monro to Lord Grenville, 31st December 1792, *The Despatches of Earl Gower*, p. 269.
39 Monday 7th January 1793, "France Commune de Paris, du 5 janvier : Des étrangers, pour la plupart Anglais, Ecossais et Irlandais, résidant à Paris, se sont présentés au secrétariat de la municipalité, et ont déclaré, suivant la loi, qu'ils se réuniront tous les dimanches et jeudis, sous le nom de Société des Amis des Droits de l'Homme, à l'hôtel anglais de White, no. 7, passage des Petits-Pères."
40 "My Lord ... La situation de cette malheureuse ville est bien critique. Tellement que Mr Monro le juge prudent de se retirer ... il est déjà remarqué et observé par des scélérats ses compatriotes ... s'il se retire ... j'aurai soin de vous instruire de tout, peut-être mieux que lui." TNA FO 27/41 folio 82.
41 Letter from Mr. Somers, 20th January 1793, TNA FO 27/41. By 5th June 1793, Somers

Grenville's for the fifty pounds outstanding on his hotel bill at White's, and Monro's successor, Somers, ended his report of 20th January 1793 with a request for twenty to thirty pounds, having "been at some expenses to get at information here."[42] Henry Redhead Yorke apparently left the club after a "violent quarrel" with Henry and John Sheares over his objection to an assault on the British monarch and would later be denounced to the National Convention by fellow member, Robert Rayment.[43] Yorke himself, who renounced his radicalism on his return to Britain, wrote in 1802 of how Robert O'Reilly quarrelled with two members of the club, leading to their expulsion: "As citizen O'Reilly, in the year 1792, he succeeded in expelling two Englishmen from White's in the Rue des Petits Pères, because they opposed the manic Irish propositions of Citizen Lord Edward Fitzgerald and the two unhappy Sheares, all of whom met a tragic fate in Ireland."[44] Questions remain over the veracity of the supposed divide in early 1793 between more moderate British members and their allegedly radical Irish counterparts. The evidence points to there being a range of positions within the British community at the turn of 1793 and some, such as Perry, Merry and Oswald, may have allied themselves more clearly with a more radical republican position taken by some members of the group. Other members attended gatherings less frequently, perhaps due to the strain within the community or because they had secured more lucrative individual positions within the administration. Monro suggests, "Mr Raymond [sic] [Rayment] scarcely attends any of their meetings, I have an idea he has got employed in the finance department, many others have left them, and those that remain are constantly quarrelling among themselves."[45]

Dissension, forthright disagreement and even physical blows were therefore an integral part of proceedings of the Paris society. Such confrontations, though portrayed by Monro as revealing the club's inherent fragility, the violent pathologies of its members and their propensity for plotting the downfall of their country, may rather show that the *SADH* conformed to some of the conventions governing Enlightenment networks of improvement in a broader sense. Clubs were seen by their members,

---

had also been granted a passport to return to Britain by the French government, negotiating his passage out of France by describing himself as a "merchant." See AN F7/4412.

42 Captain Monro to Lord Grenville, 31st December 1792, *The Despatches of Earl Gower*, p.269; letter from Mr. Somers, 20th January 1793, TNA FO 27/41.

43 Henry R. Yorke, and J A. C. Sykes, *France in 1802: Described in a Series of Contemporary Letters* (London: Heinemann, 1906), p. 2. This portrait of Yorke, a virulent democrat turned defender of royalty, denounced by a fellow British resident in Paris, seems exaggerated and there is little evidence to suggest that the club was planning any sort of coherent assault on George III, despite their reconnaissance missions to gather evidence of the readiness of the British people for a revolution.

44 Yorke, *France in 1802*, p.228.

45 Captain Monro to Lord Grenville, 31st December 1792, *The Despatches of Earl Gower*, p. 269.

many of whom derived from the professional middling classes, as places where minds and ideas could collide. Such groups were arenas where a whole spectrum of diverging opinions could be expressed, characterised by William Godwin in his *Enquiry Concerning Political Justice* of 1793 as "unlimited speculation."[46] Clubs, although encouraging free expression, were restricted in membership and operated with strict codes of behaviour. Not all minds could meet. Latent in these circles was the fear of popular disruption of the codes of polite, refined society. Even if some members of the society advocated a greater degree of popular involvement in politics, and were willing to accept the potential disruption of received codes of conduct that such democratic departures would entail, some members and associates feared the descent of enlightened discussion into popular anarchy. Godwin himself warned, "We must therefore carefully distinguish between informing the people and inflaming them. Indignation, resentment and fury are to be deprecated; and all we should ask is sober thought, clear discernment and intrepid discussion."[47] At the heart of the club there might have been discord over the prevailing question of the early republic: how far the involvement of the people in government could be sanctioned and to what extent the Revolution cautioned the disruption of elite codes of association and decision-making that such democratic developments prompted. To a certain extent therefore, strains with the society mirrored tensions in wider French politics – between so-called Girondins and Montagnards – over the extent of popular participation desirable in a future republic.

LINKS WITH THE SOCIETY FOR CONSTITUTIONAL INFORMATION

An examination of the minute book of the London Society for Constitutional Information from the years 1792 to 1794 shows that at least thirteen individuals who were either members or close associates of the *SADH* were also adherents of the SCI. The Society was initially founded in 1780 with the aim of bringing the middle orders into the political sphere. The SCI was guided at its inception by men such as John Horne Tooke and the Whig politicians Capel Loffe and John Cartwright. Although associated in its early stages with a Whig reform platform and drawing its membership from among the middle to upper classes, the society began to embrace more radical reforming ideas from early 1792. The decision to endorse the publication and distribution of Thomas Paine's Part Two of *Rights of Man* in February 1792 was the most visible sign of its movement towards a platform which was more far-reaching in its calls for constitutional change and democratic reform. The decision led to the gradual departure of some of its Whig members during the course of 1792, seeing that the priorities and

---

46 William Godwin, *An Enquiry Concerning Political Justice, and its influence on general virtue and happiness* (London: G. G. and J. Robinson, 1793), p. 21.
47 Ibid, p. 203.

principles of the society were diverging from their own.⁴⁸ The support given to Paine's pamphlet also encouraged men from the middling ranks and the lettered classes to join the society. As a result, the social composition of the SCI changed considerably from 1792 to 1794. It began to renew its membership, alter its political priorities and find more common ground with the London Corresponding Society.

The members of the SCI who helped to found the *SADH* in Paris society had for the most part joined the London society after its endorsement of Paine, over the spring and summer of 1792. Those who were members of both societies included Robert Merry, Thomas Paine, William Maxwell, George Edwards, John Frost, Henry Yorke, William Choppin, Francis Tweddell, Lord Edward Fitzgerald, Sampson Perry, Joel Barlow, William Watts and Thomas Cooper. The "Rev Mr. Joyce" listed in the minutes on of the meetings of 8th and 15th June 1792 is more likely to be the Unitarian preacher and radical Jeremiah Joyce than the Nicholas Joyce listed in the British and Irish address, though a question mark remains for the "Mr Joyce" listed on 5th October of the same year.⁴⁹ John Hurford Stone had also been a member of the Friends of the People, along with Robert Merry. Yet like Merry, Stone withdrew his support from the Whig society as his involvement in popular reform increased and as the Friends of the People drew back from a radical reform platform in early 1793. Sampson Perry also attended meetings of the LCS and was present at a meeting of the SCI on 1st April 1792, a little less than a month before he was nominated by Robert Merry to membership of the society. John Frost had been attending SCI gatherings since 1785, well before the society began to widen its membership in mid-1792, but he was also one of the few longstanding members to approve of the more radical turn taken by the society. He was regularly present at the society's gatherings from December 1791 to July 1792. In September 1792 Frost accompanied Thomas Paine to France, also delivering a message to the mayor of Paris that the sum of £1000 had been raised as a patriotic gift. He returned to chair SCI meetings on 26th October and 2nd November 1792.⁵⁰ His last attendance at the SCI was on 16th

---

48 The minutes of the SCI meetings from 1792 show a clear shift in membership around mid-March, when Thomas Paine began to attend the gatherings. Also, in May 1792, meetings began to be held at the Crown and Anchor Tavern in the Strand rather than at John Horne Tooke's court at Chancery Lane. This decision perhaps indicates that the society had pretensions to open its doors to a wider population.

49 TNA TS 11/962/3508. The SCI minute book details the men who attended SCI gatherings but also gives vital information on the intimacy of certain acquaintances through records of membership nomination. We also gain an insight into those figures who held some sway within the association through the details given on those who chaired the weekly meetings. John Frost was a regular chair, and William Choppin assumed the chairmanship very soon after being nominated as a member.

50 See TNA TS 11/962/3508 for the record of SCI meetings in London from Friday 9th December 1791 to Friday 9th May 1794. For details of John Frost's case, see John Barrell, 'Coffee-House Politicians' in *The Spirit of Despotism: Invasions of Privacy in the 1790s* (Oxford: Oxford University Press, 2006), pp. 75-102, and James Epstein, "'Equality and

November 1792, before he left for France again, accompanying Barlow as the SCI's co-delegate to Paris.

At a meeting of the SCI on 12th October 1792, Joel Barlow's *Letter to the National Convention of France on the defects in the Constitution of 1791 and the extent of the amendments which ought to be applied* was read to those gathered.[51] A week later, Barlow, having impressed the society with his tract, was appointed to the committee, along with Charles Sinclair and John Tuffen, which would draw up an address to the National Convention.[52] The following week, on 9th November 1792, it was decided that Barlow and John Frost would be charged with delivering the address on behalf of the SCI. Richard Buel suggests that Barlow was seen as an ideal candidate because he was being considered for French citizenship and was in the process of translating his *Letter to the National Convention* into French. Equally, allying Frost with Barlow "underscored the fraternal connection between peoples of different nations."[53] They set off on their mission in early November and presented the SCI address to the Convention on the 28th of the same month, at the same sitting as the address from the *SADH*. A letter read at the SCI gathering of 7th December 1792 confirmed the deposition of the address at the bar of the Convention.

Although the Paris society was not simply an offshoot of the SCI, the overlap in membership with this particular association suggests that there was a significant degree of concordance between the priorities and membership of both societies. Like the SCI, the *SADH* was not a popular radical society, although its members also showed a degree of openness to the more radical constitutional changes that were underway in France at the end of 1792.

MEMBERSHIP OF THE LITERARY FUND

A number of members of the Paris society had also been involved in the Literary Fund, an initiative begun by David Williams in 1790 at the Prince of Wales Coffee House after a long incubation period, during the 1770s and

---

No King": Sociability and Sedition: The case of John Frost' in Gillian Russell and Clara Tuite (eds.), *Romantic Sociability: Social Networks and Literary Culture in Britain 1770-1840* (Cambridge: Cambridge University Press, 2002), pp. 43-61.

51 Barlow's tract was published by Joseph Johnson in 1792 under the title *A letter to the National Convention of France: on the defects in the constitution of 1791, and the extent of the amendments which ought to be applied*. It was translated into French by Wilhelm Ludger and published as *Lettre à la Convention nationale de France sur les vices de la Constitution de 1791 et sur l'étendue des amendements à y porter* (1792).

52 Barlow had impressed the society with his *Letter to the National Convention* in which he outlined a republican framework for France after carefully suggesting a number of ways in which the mixed monarchical plan of 1791 could be improved. He addressed a letter to the SCI on 4th October 1792, thanking the society for his honorary membership and presenting the members with a copy of his letter addressed to the Convention. (See PRO TS 11/962/3508).

53 Buel, *Joel Barlow: American Citizen*, p. 156.

1780s during which he attempted to secure backing for the venture. The Fund was set up "to support authors in distress; and to afford temporary relief to the widows and children of those who have any claim on public gratitude or humanity, from literary merit or industry."[54] It aimed to "withdraw the dreadful apprehensions and prospects which warp integrity and pervert genius, and to produce candor and harmony in the provinces of literature."[55] The Fund would provide assistance to "properly recommended" authors, while subscribers would have to contribute a minimum of one guinea per annum and more to the Fund if their means allowed it. Those who donated more than ten guineas were considered subscribers for life.

The Fund carefully drew up its constitutions and gave a list of its different echelons of responsibility, including the president, vice-presidents, committee members, treasurers, registers and subscribers. Of those who would go on to join the *SADH*, seven had some involvement with the early Literary Fund, either as associate members or as recipients of aid. Robert Merry and David Williams served on the committee from 1790, while Thomas Christie, George Edwards, and John Hurford Stone were all subscribers, contributing one pound and one shilling to the Fund. John Oswald was a beneficiary, receiving ten pounds in a vote on 4th May 1792. David Williams sent the ten pounds to John Oswald in Paris via John Hurford Stone's publishing partners, Mr. Gillet and George Mead. The sum had been allocated as a relief grant for Oswald and his family.[56] Sampson Perry's widow would later receive a sum to alleviate her distress, years after her husband's death. Both Williams and Merry were actively engaged in drawing up the constitutions of the Fund and Merry was charged with both approaching the Duke of Leeds for his support in the enterprise and contacting the Drury Lane theatre with the aim of putting on a play for the benefit of the Fund. John Hurford Stone seems to have attended for the first time in April 1791, while Edwards went to the meeting on 4th May 1792 when Oswald received relief.

Of those who departed for Paris in mid to late 1792, few would go on to be active in the Literary Fund again on their return. By mid-1794 the Fund had shed its radical reputation and begun to be conducted by a David Williams whose support for the Revolution had severely flagged after his return from Paris in February 1793. John Reeves and Bland Burges, one a figurehead of the loyalist reaction against radical activism, the other a member of the Pitt government, would also take on roles in the Fund in the later 1790s, ensuring its full transformation from organ of radical reform to pro-loyalist institution. Thomas Morris, a biographer of David Williams and member of the Fund, wrote that Williams had to "work with jarring materials" on the Fund, probably alluding to the diversity of its membership.

---

54 *Literary Fund, The Constitutions of the Society; Alterable only at the Desire of a General Meeting* (London, John Nichols, 1795), p. 1.
55 *Literary Fund*, p. 2.
56 See Erdman, *Commerce des Lumières*, pp. 160-1.

Morris insisted on the harmonious union that was produced through the convergence of men from different backgrounds and the exclusion of partisan political affiliation in an association where "the cabals of political and religious parties" were excluded and "persons of all opinions, professions, and ranks zealously unite."[57] Many members of the Paris society were veterans of the associational world the Literary Fund was a part of, conjugating philanthropic and political interests and using the opportunities such activities provided for social advancement and self-improvement. Peter Clark contends, "By 1800, clubs and other forms of association had become a vital component of the social life of the educated English-speaking classes, whether at home or abroad."[58]

CROSSOVERS BETWEEN PARIS AND LONDON

Members of the *SADH* were drawn therefore from the London reform scene, but also from the Irish radical movement, the American contingent in Paris and internationally-minded French revolutionaries, and many of them had already established close links with each other prior to their arrival in Paris. Henry Redhead Yorke may have been induced to join the Paris society by Irish brothers Henry and John Sheares, who would later be involved in the Irish Rebellion.[59] The arrival of some emigrants was facilitated by friends and acquaintances from Britain who were already established in Paris and who were willing to provide letters of introduction, temporary accommodation or company for the journey. Captain Monro described the arrival of John Frost and the SCI delegation at the end of November 1792: "This Gentleman did not arrive in Paris till three days after me, he was attended by a Mr. Joel Barlow, the author of some inflammatory pamphlets and an American by birth, and a Mr. Twedall, of the County of Cumberland, a lad of about eighteen and a diligent pupil of Frosts."[60] The "Mr. Twedall" of Monro's report is in all likelihood the Francis Tweddell noted in the SCI minute book. Tweddell and Frost probably knew each other through attendance at meetings of the SCI. Robert Merry had already formed a close working relationship with the editor Sampson Perry before they reunited in Paris after Perry's arrival in late 1792. Merry contributed satirical columns to *The Argus* in 1791-92 and nominated Perry for SCI membership on 27th April 1792.[61] Both Perry and Merry were well-acquainted with Thomas Paine from the London radical reform sphere. William Johnson, the young surgeon

---

57 Thomas Morris, *A General View of the Life and Writings of the Rev. David Williams Drawn up for the Chronique du Mois, A French Periodical Publication, at the Request of Messrs. Condorcet, Clavière, Mercier, Auger, Brissot, &c. Editors of that Work* (London: Ridgway, 1792), p. 19.
58 Peter Clark, *British Clubs and Societies 1580-1800: The Origins of an Associational World* (Oxford: Oxford University Press, 2000), p. 3.
59 See Yorke, *France in 1802*, p. 2.
60 George Monro, 6th December 1792, TNA TS 11/959.
61 TNA TS 11/962/3508.

from Derby with whom Thomas Paine would later share lodgings, also accompanied Henry Redhead Yorke to Paris.

In departing for France, British radicals knew that they would be welcomed by friends and acquaintances and would find a well-established circle of individuals with whom to exchange news, seek professional and personal assistance, and engage in debate about the political developments occurring across Europe. Those members remaining in London were also provided with regular updates from their colleagues across the Channel. At a meeting of the SCI on Friday 7th December 1792, a letter was read from Joel Barlow and John Frost "with the address to the National Convention of France and the answer of the president."[62] William Choppin forwarded a rough sketch of the diplomatic situation of the French armies to Thomas Rickman, to whom he sent regular reports of events in France from the perspective of the British contingent.[63] The sketch was taken from a plan originally sent to Thomas Paine who himself had received it from a member of the Convention. Spy Charles Ross, who intercepted the letter, wrote, "This was copied from a rough sketch sent from Mr Choppin in France to Mr. R_ and which he mentions was copied from a Plan sent to Mr Paine with whom he is very intimate. Received in London Monday Oct 8th 1792."[64] Choppin's drawing, initially intended for Paine's friend and publisher Rickman, found its way into the hands of Ross, a British informant who was in close contact with Rickman and monitoring his movements, sending regular updates to Evan Nepean, under-secretary of State for the Home Office. Ross refers to further letters from Choppin to Rickman, one of which was sent on 30th October 1792 in which Choppin "mentioned he was in company with Paine in Paris the preceding day."[65] There is little evidence to suggest that Choppin had become acquainted with Paine before their meeting in Paris and it appears that their residence in Paris forged a friendship between the two men which would culminate in their taking shared private lodgings in 1793.

There are a number of interesting points to draw from Ross's correspondence with Nepean. The first confirms the prevalence of spies and informers within both British-based radical reforming societies and the English-speaking community in Paris.[66] Rickman was the subject of a sustained surveillance operation, much of which was aimed at discovering the activities of reformers in Britain and Paris, and of the communication

---

62 Charles Ross to Evan Nepean, Friday 7th December 1792, TNA TS 11/962/3508.
63 William Choppin's strategic map of the dividing line between France and the Lowlands and details of French military preparations was copied by Charles Ross and sent with his despatch of 9th October 1792 to Evan Nepean. TNA TS 11/965/3510/A2.
64 Charles Ross to Evan Nepean, 9th October 1792, TNA TS 11/965/3510/A2.
65 Charles Ross to Evan Nepean, 13th November 1792, TNA TS 11/965/3510/A2.
66 A study of the papers of the LCS shows that espionage was deep-rooted in London debating societies. For a comprehensive survey of this aspect of the reform movement, see Mary Thale (ed.), *Selections from the Papers of the London Corresponding Society 1792-1799* (Cambridge: Cambridge University Press, 2008).

between them. Reformers' opinions on Thomas Paine were meticulously recorded, as were their views on the French Revolution and the success of the French armies.[67] Ross's memoranda reveal the extent to which radicals based in Paris corresponded with their acquaintances back in London, contributing to the unofficial flow of information between the two countries. Rickman would eventually follow Paine, Choppin, and others to Paris, but while he remained in Britain, he received the latest information about British activities directly from SCI members who had emigrated to France. Ross notes that Rickman would attend SCI meetings and this would have been the occasion for him to share the details of his correspondence with his fellow members, thus disseminating news even further.[68] British radicals departing for Paris did so, therefore, with a clear view provided by residents of what they were to expect on arrival. Those who remained in Britain were sent precise and often personal news relating to those who had emigrated and the scenes they witnessed.

John Frost and Henry Redhead Yorke are the only society members who returned to the SCI after their stay in Paris. The SCI itself would soon be threatened by governmental repression and former Paris residents may have lost much of their initial faith in the society as a vehicle of radical reform. Frost was present at the meeting at the Crown and Anchor Tavern on 15th February 1793, not long after he and Yorke apparently clashed with some remaining members of the Paris society over the latter's involvement with the work of the National Convention. Frost attended SCI meetings regularly until May 1793, when he was tried and sentenced to six months in prison and one hour on the pillory for uttering seditious words. He seems to have returned immediately to the SCI the following January, when he made two last appearances before giving up attendance altogether.

Melvin Edelstein has argued that the clubs and sections of French towns were more pivotal in urging forward the expansion of political participation in late 1792 than the widely heralded municipal elections held on the basis of quasi-universal manhood suffrage held from September the same year.[69] In many ways, the *SADH* took inspiration from the models of local activism that emigrants had witnessed on their arrival in Paris, and whose organs their own society drew upon for support, material aid and ideological sustenance.

---

67 Ross recalls a society gathering in the Old Jewry where "liberty sentiments were given and Paine's health drank with cheers." See Charles Ross to Evan Nepean, 1st November 1792, TNA TS 11/965/3510/A2.

68 Charles Ross to Evan Nepean, 22nd October 1792, TNA TS 11/965/3510/A2. Ross notes Rickman's attendance at a meeting of the Constitutional Society on "Friday evening last."

69 Melvin Edelstein, "'Une élection purement populaire': l'impact de la démocratie sur les élections municipales dans les plus grandes villes à l'automne 1792', *Annales historiques de la Révolution française*, 349 (2007), pp. 29-49. Edelstein argues that despite the advent of wide manhood suffrage in September 1792, it was the local sections and their influence through the club network, which had the greatest impact on ushering in more democratic participation in politics.

The Paris emigrant society was also influenced by the changes that had occurred in the membership and priorities of the Society for Constitutional Information over the course of 1792. Momentum was also provided by Irish members, which allowed for new connections to be forged between radicals of the nations of Britain and Ireland on French soil.[70]

Members of the society trialed their own participative structures in practice, using their nascent political organisation as a laboratory of rotating leadership, committee-driven collective decision-making and joint or polyvocal authorship, the experience of which may have gone some way to shaping their views on the very form of republican government that the new nation should adopt in a future constitution. British contributors to the debate on the new republican constitution emerge, in this portrait, as increasingly embedded in a Parisian public scene animated as much by deliberation in the Convention as local section militancy. Such a portrait also tends to support the view that British emigrants in Paris were drawn to defining their own positions in relation to the deepening schisms in French politics, diverging amongst themselves on the central question of the role of the people in the new republic. Writing projects were often the fruit of collective encounters and initiatives, and their authors seem to have fiercely resisted any requirement of consensus in their written production, editorial decisions or printing contracts. The *SADH* allowed for connections to be made which went on to guide individual submissions to the revolutionary authorities.

---

[70] For further details of Irish involvement in the activities at White's hotel see Mathieu Ferradou, 'Histoire d'un 'festin patriotique' à l'hôtel white (18 novembre 1792): les Irlandais patriotes à Paris, 1789-1795', *Annales historiques de la Révolution française* 382 (2015), pp. 123-43. See also Rachel Rogers, 'The Society of the Friends of the Rights of Man, 1792-94: British and Irish Radical Conjunctions in Republican Paris', *La Révolution française* 11 (2016) [online].

6

Revising the monarchical constitution of 1791
The writings of Joel Barlow and David Williams

A committee was established by the French National Convention in early October 1792 to make recommendations to its representatives on the form of a new, republican constitution. The resulting document was presented to the Convention in February 1793, and became known as the 'Girondin Constitution,' largely due to the committee's composition, since Condorcet, Brissot, Sièyes, Barère and Thomas Paine were among the nine members. The committee opted for universal suffrage but drew back from giving any direct legislative power to the electorate, preferring a representative model. It nevertheless recommended open citizenship qualifications in line with the cosmopolitan designs of its members. The blueprint was studied for two months, but by April 1793 members of the Montagne, objecting to some of the draft's principal clauses, had set to work on writing a different proposal and the Convention itself had decided to set up another committee to review the first document. The resulting Montagnard version, presented by Hérault de Séchelles to the Convention in June 1793, was much more wide-reaching in its democratic intentions. It confirmed the principle of popular sovereignty, yet narrowed the possibilities for open citizenship articulated by the first constitutional committee, in accordance with the increasing suspicion of foreigners prompted by the climate of revolutionary war. Saint-Just articulated his vision in a speech to the Convention in late April. At the heart of his address was a mistrust of power and permanence in governmental structures and a faith in the natural goodness and virtue of the people in a state of nature. For Saint-Just, laws had to be the expression of the "general will" of the people and the interest of citizens in decision-making should be "active," not "passive."[1] He criticised the constitutional committee's version, calling it "Athens voting near its end, without democracy, and decreeing the loss of its liberty."[2]

In Carol Blum's view, the Montagnard drafters set out with the intention of rooting out all monarchical social structures and engendering a more far-reaching change in the social fabric of the country.[3] Vigour and starkness were preferred to intellectualism and the celebration of the values of the European Enlightenment. Saint-Just denounced the way the constitutional committee had "considered the general will in terms of its intellectual relationship." As a result, "laws were the expression of taste rather than the general will."[4] Condorcet, the principal author of the February version, criticised in turn the Montagnard draft. Maurice Cranston summarises Condorcet's view on both constitutions: "Whereas the former could be relied on to ensure the accurate expression of the public reason, the latter, he argued, would maximise the probability of erroneous decisions and provoke an endless conflict of wills."[5] Thomas Paine was a member of the constitutional committee which signed off the first draft. Like Condorcet, he showed hostility to active popular involvement in government and preferred a representative system, with trusted lawmakers making sense of the preferences of the people. In his speech during the trial of Louis XVI, he explained why he had voted against a popular referendum (*un appel au peuple*) on the fate of the king and reiterated his mistrust of primary assemblies, preferred by the Montagne and called for by the Parisian sections. He saw the representatives in the Convention as having been elected in order to make decisions on behalf of the people.[6]

The principal battlegrounds in the constitution debate were thus the method of discovering the "general will" of the people, the precise role of citizens in decision-making, and the place of representatives in governmental structures. The debate over the desired extent of popular involvement in law-making had already animated discussion within the Parisian sections and popular societies over the course of 1792. Cordeliers writer Théodore Le Sueur presented a tract entitled *Idées sur l'espèce de gouvernement populaire qui*

---

1 Saint-Just, 'Discours sur la constitution et essai', *Saint-Just: théorie politique*, Alain Liénard (ed.) (Paris: Seuil, 1976), p. 193.
2 Ibid, p. 192: "C'est Athènes votant vers sa fin, sans démocratie, & décrétant la perte de sa liberté."
3 Blum, *Rousseau and the Republic of Virtue*, pp. 182-3.
4 "Il m'a paru que le comité avoit considéré la volonté générale sous son rapport intellectuel ; ensorte que la volonté générale, purement spéculative, résultant plutôt des vues de l'esprit que de l'intérêt du corps social, les lois étoient l'expression du goût plutôt que de la volonté générale." Saint-Just, 'Discours sur la constitution et essai', p. 192.
5 Maurice Cranston, *Philosophers and Pamphleteers: Political Theorists of the Enlightenment* (Oxford: Oxford University Press, 1986), p. 151. Condorcet went into hiding after publishing the pamphlet in which he makes this claim. Although the pamphlet, *Aux citoyens français sur la nouvelle constitution*, was anonymous, he realised that his authorship would be recognised.
6 *Le Moniteur Universel*, vol. 15, 23rd January 1793.

pourrait convenir à un pays de l'étendue et de la population présumée de la France to Pétion in the autumn of 1792. Rachel Hammersley suggests that "the work was concerned with refuting the pessimistic views of Montesquieu, Rousseau and many revolutionaries by demonstrating how a democratic republic could be built in late eighteenth-century France."[7] Le Sueur, like other Cordeliers activists, some of whom went on to join the Montagnard grouping in the Convention, and whose political opinions had been cultivated in local activism, favoured some form of direct democracy over the representative model preferred by members of the *Cercle Social*, themselves more closely associated with the representatives from the Gironde.[8] While the February 1793 version limited the direct involvement of the people in the legislative process, the Montagnard draft made some provision for popular assent. By the time of the institution of the Thermidorian constitution in 1795 however, the debate had shifted and the post-Thermidorian republicans argued that terror was the natural consequence of allowing the people a role in the political life of the nation.[9] As Gwyn Williams aptly put it, "the republic which the Directory tried to create was built precisely upon the exclusion of this 'people.'"[10]

The fact that the 1793 constitution was quickly suspended has tended to deter later scholars from considering addresses and depositions intended to

---

[7] Rachel Hammersley, *French Revolutionaries and English Republicans: The Cordeliers Club 1790-1794* (Rochester: Boydell, 2005), p. 124. "Modern" republics were defined in opposition to "ancient" republics or city-states such as Athens. While in ancient republicanism, monarchy as an institution was inextricably bound up with tyranny and despotism, in "modern" republicanism, contained monarchical rule was acceptable as a way of ensuring stability and continuity. Whereas democracy in ancient terms was translated as popular participation in the making of laws, democracy under modern republican rule was representative. This was the form of government chosen by the nascent American republic and also the form preferred by the drafters of the French monarchical constitution of 1791, the Girondin constitution of 1793 and the longer-lasting Thermidorian constitution of 1795. Only some members of the Cordeliers Club espoused a more classical form of republicanism in the early 1790s, entirely free of a monarchical element and reliant on direct democracy. The republics of the modern era were thus, apart from the short-lived period of Jacobin ascendancy in France, characterised by realism, pragmatism and pessimism rather than idealism. Man's complex and flawed nature prompted revolutionary thinkers to favour compromise, limited public intervention and the delegation of sovereignty. For Antoine Compagnon, modern republics were inspired more by pragmatic counter-revolutionary compromise than the idealism at the heart of the Revolution itself. See Campagnon, *Les Antimodernes: de Joseph de Maistre à Roland Barthes* (Paris: Gallimard, 2005).

[8] For a study of the relatively unknown Le Sueur, see Hammersley, *French Revolutionaries and English Republicans*, pp. 116-35.

[9] Pierre Serna has argued that, despite the rhetoric of moderation and peace, the ordinary people of Paris suffered more during the winter of 1795, under the Thermidorian regime, than they had during the emergency measures instituted over 1793 and 1794. See Pierre Serna, *La république des girouettes. 1789-1815 et au-delà. Une anomalie politique : la France de l'extrême centre* (Paris: Champ Vallon, 2005).

[10] Gwyn A. Williams, *Artisans and Sans-Culottes: Popular Movements in France and Britain During the French Revolution* (London: Libris, 1988) p. xviii.

influence it. Neither Condorcet's February 1793 proposal nor the Montagnard draft later the same year culminated in an official and durable arrangement, and the next constitution to replace the monarchical settlement of 1791 was the Thermidorian constitution of 1795.[11] Historical discussions of the 1793 constitutional drafts are therefore conducted against the backdrop of their suspension. Nevertheless, the consultation orchestrated by the first constitutional committee over the course of late 1792 and early 1793 drew the attention of British residents of Paris, and coincided with the inception and hiatus of the English-speaking political society in the capital. Alger identified two British contributions to the discussion on the creation of a republican constitution in France; Robert Merry's *Réflexions politiques sur la nouvelle constitution qui se prépare en France, adressées à la république* (Political Reflections on the new constitution being prepared in France, addressed to the Republic) was penned in October 1792, and a tract by George Edwards, entitled *Idées pour former une nouvelle constitution et pour assurer la prospérité et le bonheur de la France et d'autres nations* (Ideas for forming a new constitution and for assuring the prosperity and happiness of France and other nations), which was published in early 1793.[12] Yet Merry and Edwards were not the only British residents of Paris to take an active interest in the constitution debate and write tracts to be offered to the drafting committee. John Oswald also presented his views in a short pamphlet entitled *Government of the People, or a Sketch of a Constitution for the Universal Commonwealth*, printed at John Hurford Stone's English Press in 1793 and the Welsh Dissenting reformer David Williams, invited over to France by Brissot, also expressed his opinion in *Observations sur la dernière constitution de la France, avec des vues pour la formation de la nouvelle constitution* (Observations on the last constitution of France, with views on the formation on the new constitution). Finally, although Joel

---

11 For an account of the Thermidorian regime, see Biancamaria Fontana, 'The Thermidorian republic and its principles' in Biancamaria Fontana (ed.), *The Invention of the Modern Republic* (Cambridge: Cambridge University Press, 2004), pp. 118-38. Fontana sees the Thermidorian regime instituted after the fall of Robespierre as having an essential legacy for modern republicanism as it defined and reworked itself in the nineteenth and twentieth centuries. It would lay the basis for future European democracies characterised by large territorial states, advanced commercial development, a wide popular electorate and constitutional guarantees inscribed in law. Pragmatism was an essential characteristic of the modern political formation therefore. Germaine de Staël supported republicanism in 1795 not out of principle, but because it was the form of government already in existence and would therefore encourage stability and longevity and provoke the least disruption. She also believed that citizens of a modern state would be less inclined to sacrifice their independence and way of life for the sake of a collective purpose. In the modern era therefore, the classical ideal of a virtuous citizenry steeped in glory, heroism and sacrifice was substituted by an awareness of the place of the individual, the ascendancy of delegated, representative modes of government and the primacy of economic independence over collective public spirit.

12 Robert Merry, *Réflexions politiques sur la nouvelle constitution qui se prépare en France adressées à la république* (Paris: J. Reyner, 1792) and George Edwards, *Idées pour former une nouvelle constitution et pour assurer la prospérité et le bonheur de la France et d'autres nations* (Paris: H. J. Jansen, 1793).

Barlow was an American citizen, there is a case for considering his *Letter to the National Convention on the Defects in the Constitution of 1791, and the Extent of the Amendments which Ought to be Applied* in the context of British representations in view of his close involvement prior to arriving in Paris with London reforming clubs, and his role as a delegate for the SCI.[13] His *Letter* will therefore be considered along with the other tracts published by British reformers at the turn of 1793. All authors with the exception of Barlow had been involved in the Literary Fund, either as committee members, subscribers or recipients of aid.

Other tracts on the constitutional settlement in the making were also published. Richard Price's nephew, George Cadogan Morgan, a witness at the fall of the Bastille, wrote an anonymous account of the fall of the French monarchy and urged the French to institute a republican form of government. Entitled, *An address to the Jacobine and other patriotic societies of the French urging the establishment of a republican form of government*, his tract argued for the abolition of monarchy but stepped back from calling for the execution of the king.[14] The Whig politician, Capel Loffe, who was a member of the Revolution Society, also offered his views on the constitution. Spy Charles Ross suggested that "Clio has received a letter from Mr Capel Loffe who informed him he had written (twenty-five sheets) to the Convention, his sentiments respecting their form of Government."[15] British residents may also have had some unofficial involvement with the work of the constitutional committee. Sampson Perry recalled in later writings how he dined with a number of the members of the committee during his stay in Paris: "This party was formed, not from convivial consideration, but to call together the committee for drawing up the plan of a constitution, of which, four of the persons I have mentioned were members, the other two came in as we rose from the table, and, after taking coffee, the whole six retired into a closet to their work."[16] The work of the committee may have been carried out at times in the wings of sociable gatherings. Such occasions appear to have been opportunities for those who were not members of the committee, including visiting radicals, to converse with the members responsible for

---

13 John Oswald, *The Government of the People, or a Sketch of a Constitution for the Universal Commonwealth* (Paris: The English Press, 1792). David Williams' tract, *Observations sur la dernière constitution de la France, avec des vues pour la formation de la nouvelle constitution* was translated by Citizen Maudru and printed at the Imprimerie du Cercle Social in 1793. The original manuscript is conserved at Cardiff Public Library. Joel Barlow's tract was translated into French and published as *Lettre à la Convention nationale de France sur les vices de la Constitution de 1791 et sur l'étendue des amendements à y porter, traduite de l'anglais*.

14 Cadogan Morgan's letters have recently been edited and published. See Mary-Ann Constantine & Paul Framed (eds.), *Travels in Revolutionary France and A Journey Across America* (Cardiff: University of Wales Press, 2013). Morgan's experience is also discussed in Mary-Ann Constantine, 'The Welsh in Revolutionary Paris'.

15 Although the Whig politician seems to have provided the Convention with his views, I have not found any surviving copies. See Ross to Nepean, Friday November 13th 1792, TS 11/965/3510/A2.

16 Perry, *An Historical Sketch* I, p. 11.

working on a republican settlement. Mary Wollstonecraft, herself commissioned to draw up a plan of education for the Convention, was also following the "public news" over the course of February 1793, which included the fact that "the new constitution will soon make its appearance."[17]

The imminent establishment of a new constitutional settlement was closely followed among radical reformers back in Britain. A Revolution Society gathering of 16th November 1792 proposed a series of toasts, the thirty-first of which included "that the new constitution of France be the most perfect that the human mind can create, that it serve as a model for all nations!"[18] Much was expected of the new republican constitution, particularly since the compromises that had been accepted in the framing of the American constitution had provoked disappointment in some quarters. The institution of a presidential office in the American republic was perceived by some as a quasi-monarchical departure from the early promise of the Continental Conventions, despite John Adams' justification of the federal arrangement in his *A Defence of the Constitutions of Government of the United States of America*.[19] Carol Blum suggests, "It was as if the fall of Louis XVI released great surges of authorial energy that had remained in check as long as the dynasty was still, however marginally, on the throne."[20] Yet despite the hopes both among European intellectual circles and within the French nation, the process of devising a new constitution was beset by difficulties. The settlement was being drafted against a backdrop not only of internecine conflict within the Convention, but also of European conflict and imminent war with Britain. Captain Monro wrote in early January 1793:

> The prospect of a war with England of course creates a good deal of conversation here, the people speak for and against it according to the party they are of. The King's friends of course wish it, in hopes of creating a counter-revolution; and the Republicans sensible how materially it may affect their strange Constitution wish by every means to avoid it... It is the opinion of most people here that [war] will effectually ruin France and their new Constitution.[21]

For Alger, foreign activists' willingness to offer their thoughts on the French constitution under consideration at the turn of 1793 was as a sign of the tenacious cosmopolitan openness which accompanied the early idealism of

---

17 Mary Wolstonecraft to Ruth Barlow, 1-14th February 1793, Wollstonecraft, *Collected Letters*, p. 221. Wollstonecraft informed her friend Ruth Barlow, "I am, besides, writing a plan of education for the Committee appointed to consider that subject."
18 *Le Moniteur Universel*, vol. 14, Friday 23rd November 1792.
19 Adams was on a diplomatic mission to London when he wrote his defence of the American constitution. The three-volume work was published in New York and Philadelphia in 1787 and defended the constitutional settlement from European criticism, asserting in the process the primacy of representation.
20 Blum, *Rousseau and the Republic of Virtue*, p. 182.
21 Captain Monro, Paris 7th January 1793, *The Despatches of Earl Gower*, p. 273.

the Revolution. In the enduring spirit of international brotherhood "all the world was invited to offer suggestions for the constitution, and two Englishmen – George Edward[s] and Robert Merry – accordingly did so."[22] Thomas Paine, addressing the people of France for the first time as member of the Convention in September 1792, likewise saw no narrowing of the internationalist spirit: "I feel my felicity increased by seeing the barrier broken down that divided patriotism by spots of earth, and limited citizenship to the soil, like vegetation."[23] Joel Barlow petitioned the Convention in September 1792 with his advice on the new constitutional settlement. He asserted, "I not only consider all mankind as forming but one great family, and therefore bound by a natural sympathy to regard each other's happiness as making part of their own; but I contemplate the French nation at this moment as standing in the place of the whole."[24] For foreign patriots the declaration of the republic and the practical establishment of a constitution befitting the new nation was the proof that the Revolution continued to have resonance for peoples outside France.

Yet the motivations behind the National Convention's invitation to foreigners to contribute to the discussion on the new constitution were not entirely disinterested or ideological. Like the foreign nominations for French citizenship brought before the Convention and ratified in August and September 1792, the apparent cosmopolitanism of the deliberations also masked the underlying expedient concerns of the revolutionary authorities. At the time the Convention was loosely dominated by deputies from the Gironde who were seeking to legitimise the deposition of the king, the establishment of a republic and the decision to declare war on Austria and Prussia in the face of mounting domestic and international unrest.[25] Armand de Kersaint drew on the examples of Joseph Priestley, Thomas Paine, Thomas Cooper and James Watt during his speech in the Convention on 3rd January 1793, in advance of war with Britain, using their persecution in their home country as a diplomatic weapon to justify the outbreak of hostilities.[26]

---

22 Alger, *Glimpses of the French Revolution*, pp. 61-2. George Edwards also addressed an accompanying letter to the legislators of the Convention, entitled, *Adresse au Corps Législatif contenant l'exposé d'un nouveau système politique*, which was written from the Hôtel Anglais, passage des petits-pères. Edwards is less well-known than the other British petitioners. Though a resident of White's hotel until July 1793, when he applied successfully for a passport out of France, he did not sign the November 1792 address nor was his name mentioned by Monro in his observations.
23 Paine, 'Address to the People of France', 25th September 1792, *CWTP* vol. 2, p. 538.
24 Barlow, *Letter to the National Convention*, pp. 4-5.
25 As Michael Rapport points out, the decree of 26th August 1792, naturalising eighteen prominent foreign sympathisers of the Revolution, was both an expression of internationalist cosmopolitanism and a declaration of France's leadership in promoting the rights of man. On 25th September 1792 others were added, including Thomas Cooper, John Horne Tooke, John Oswald, Thomas Christie, Joseph Warner and Joel Barlow. Priestley was described by the revolutionary Chabot as "cosmopolitan and *therefore* French." (Quoted in *Rapport, Nationality and Citizenship*, p. 138).
26 See the speech by Kersaint in the National Convention: "Qui peut voir la liberté de la

Internationalism had pragmatic uses therefore, yet this international openness was beginning to jar with the evolving status of foreigners. For in order for war to be waged successfully, the Revolution and the French nation had to be defined in opposition to the British state and its people.

British residents were conscious that the early euphoria and relative consensus engendered by the fall of the Bastille and the commemorative *Fête de la Fédération* the following July were giving way to a more complex set of political alliances which would require caution and dexterity in engaging with the Revolution. Thomas Paine acknowledged that he was beginning his term of office in the Convention in September 1792 "in the stormy hour of difficulties," while an informant for the British government had learnt of mixed views among British radicals in Paris on the progress of the Revolution.[27] Charles Ross pointed out to his Whitehall contacts how William Choppin had "mentioned he was in company with Paine in Paris the preceding day. Paine was then going to dine with Lord Lauderdale, he exults in the success of the French arms, but laments at the instability of the Convention."[28]

There were also those in the Convention itself who were beginning to temper their internationalist fervour. Alger contended that its membership "was tired of the nonsense of British addresses, perceiving the insignificance of the persons who presented them."[29] Robespierre offered a derisive assessment of petitions of support for the republic in the wake of the judgment meted out to Louis XVI: "The punishment of the tyrant made the principles of equality real. Since then a great number of those who used to blaspheme against the republic have been reduced to rendering homage to it, as hypocrisy renders homage to virtue, by adopting its forms and stammering its language."[30] International cosmopolitanism was still central to republican discourse and useful in helping the republic to legitimise its existence. Yet there was increasing wariness of the motivations of foreigners who remained within the French nation. Protestations of international solidarity began to be interpreted as hollow attempts at feigning support from those suspected of providing information to their own governments. Foreign residents had to negotiate these pressures when voicing their views on the new constitutional settlement.

---

    presse et la liberté des opinions bannies de cette terre où ces deux palladium de la liberté publique ont été forgés par le génie tutélaire des droits de l'homme, le philosophe Priestley persécuté, Thomas Payne proscrit, Cooper et Walker assiégés dans leurs maisons pour avoir cru que les hommes sont égaux et libres ?" *Le Moniteur Universel*, vol. 14, Thursday 3rd January 1793.

27 Paine, 'Address to the People of France', 25th September 1792, *CWTP* vol. 2, p. 538.
28 The information from Choppin is contained in a report from Ross to Evan Nepean, Friday 13th November 1792, TNA TS 11/965/3510/A2.
29 Alger, *Englishmen*, p. 99.
30 Quoted in Blum, *Rousseau and the Republic of Virtue*, p. 195.

JOEL BARLOW, *LETTER TO THE NATIONAL CONVENTION OF FRANCE ON THE DEFECTS IN THE CONSTITUTION OF 1791 AND THE EXTENT OF THE AMENDMENTS WHICH OUGHT TO BE APPLIED* (1792)

Joel Barlow was an American entrepreneur and speculator whose activities on behalf of the Sciotto Company led him to Europe to attempt the ill-fated sale of American lands in Ohio to French men and women seeking exit out of revolutionary France. Yet Barlow also acquired a reputation in politics and was honoured by the National Convention with French citizenship in 1793. Prior to his nomination for citizenship, he had been posted to the Savoy in November 1792, where he had been charged with overseeing the institution of French administration in the former principality of the kingdom of Sardinia. Barlow supported the early republican drive in France and became acquainted with Brissot, whose *Nouveau Voyage dans les Etats-Unis* (1788) he began translating in spring 1791. In 1791 and for some of 1792 Barlow was in London, mixing in British radical circles and making a reputation for himself through the publication of his *Advice to the Privileged Orders* and the poem, *Conspiracy of Kings*. These works "brought Barlow the official recognition from English radicals that until then had been only informally his."[31] He was nominated for SCI membership by John Horne Tooke on 9th March 1792 and was toasted by an SCI gathering on 13th April of the same year. Philipp Ziesche suggests that Barlow was a man for whom the Revolution provided an opportunity for radical self re-definition which included the transformation of his political outlook from "a defender of American class privilege to the spokesman of the illiterate European masses."[32] M. Ray Adams identifies a similar transformation in the political outlook of Robert Merry, who "was still until the actual outbreak of the Revolution apparently satisfied with the British brand of liberty."[33] Presence in Paris during the Revolution could be a politicising experience and motor of personal renewal. Barlow, though an American citizen, was closely involved in London-based radicalism and also played a role in the *SADH*. He was the confidante to whom Thomas Paine trusted his manuscripts on the night of his arrest in Paris and his views were widely considered among the British ruling authorities to be as insidious as those of Paine himself.[34]

Barlow's *Letter to the National Convention* is a radical text framed in pragmatic and diplomatic language. The author examines the constitutional settlement already in place in France and suggests ways in which they must be revised. He uses the constitution of 1791 as a starting point, one which

---

31 Buel, *Joel Barlow: American Citizen*, p. 148.
32 Ziesche, *Cosmopolitan Patriots*, p. 68.
33 M. Ray Adams, 'Robert Merry, Political Romanticist', pp. 26-7.
34 As mentioned earlier, Barlow's pamphlet, *Advice to the Privileged Orders* was considered a seditious work. Those reformers who had read the work were readily associated with treason during the treason trials of radical reformers in London in 1794.

93

had value, but which contained defects incompatible with free government. In his *Letter to the National Convention*, Barlow states his "veneration" for the Constituent Assembly that had drafted the constitution of 1791 and suggests that the constitution should be "revised" rather than begun on fresh ground. The 1791 settlement had been a step in the right direction and the skill of the drafters had been negated by subsequent commentators: "Perhaps the merits of that body of men will never be properly appreciated."[35] These men had done the essential groundwork on which the foundations of the new republic would be laid. They had overturned "abuses" and "prejudices", "open opposition of interests", "corruption", "faction", and all the things "which escape our common observation."[36] Barlow, writing in the autumn of 1792, recognised that the status and contribution of the Constituents would eventually be overlooked or sullied by history. The "legacy" of their "deliberative capacity" would remain "a lasting monument to their praise."[37]

Yet despite Barlow's high opinion of the members of the Constituent Assembly, his vision was far from conservative in scope. Barlow puts forward a model for the root-and-branch overhaul of the existing system of government and lays much greater emphasis on the role of the people, on representation and the need to eradicate all vestiges of monarchical rule. Barlow insists on the incompatibility between monarchy and free government, marvelling at the fact that this was not recognised sooner. He associates republicanism with simplicity, monarchy with complexity, asserting, in the same way as Thomas Paine, that kingship was wrong in principle. If there had been any good done by retaining monarchy longer than necessary in France, "it has taught them a new doctrine, which no experience can shake, and which reason must confirm, *that kings can do no good.*"[38]

After coming down unequivocally on the side of republicanism and criticising the continued pursuit of a monarchical settlement after the king's flight to Varennes, Barlow then addresses the issue of representation. He denies the idea that the wise and virtuous should make laws for the rest. It is "the people at large, ignorant and vitious [*sic*] as they are" who are the real lawmakers, through their representatives. For Barlow, laws originated in the people through representation. He does not advocate direct democracy, in which the people would decide the formulation of laws for themselves, but suggests that the act of electing representatives was a means for the people to make their voice heard. Representatives were chosen by the people and were therefore "organs" of the general will. He states, "I am confident that any people, whether virtuous or vitious [*sic*], wise or ignorant, numerous or few, rich or poor, are the best judges of their own wants relative to the restraint of laws, and would always supply those wants better than they could

---

35 Barlow, *Letter to the National Convention*, p. 5.
36 Ibid, p. 6.
37 Ibid, p. 6.
38 Ibid, p. 12.

be supplied by others."³⁹ It did not matter that the people were not virtuous, educated or ready for liberty, they were still the best-qualified to decide on the public good. With echoes of Rousseau, he emphasises the centrality of the "general will" of the people and suggests that "the sure and only characteristic of a good law is, *that it be the perfect expression of the will of the nation*; its excellence is precisely in proportion to the universality and freedom of consent."⁴⁰ Therefore if Barlow reiterated the importance of delegation and highlighted the role of war in provoking national revitalisation, issues that reflected his role in the American Revolution, it seems clear that his ideas were nonetheless coloured by the particular circumstances in which he was writing.

Barlow also concurred with Paine on the importance of present generations being able to legislate for themselves. In a section on the difference between framing constitutions and laws he writes:

> To suppose that our predecessors were wiser than ourselves is not an extraordinary thing, though the opinion may be ill-founded; but to suppose that they can have left us a better system of political regulations than we can make for ourselves, is to ascribe to them a degree of discernment to which our own bears no comparison; it supposes them to have known our condition by prophecy better than we can know it by experience.⁴¹

Like Paine in *Rights of Man*, and in the same vein as Thomas Jefferson's later reflections, Barlow insists that constitutions should be open to change and not the instruments of forebears bent on ruling from the grave over succeeding generations. Constitutions should be subject to amendments and people should be able to exercise their "irresistible right of innovation, whenever experience should discover the defects of the system."⁴²

In the *Letter* he sets out fourteen essential points to be guaranteed in the constitutional code and shows a shrewd awareness of the diplomatic dilemmas facing those charged with drafting a new constitution. He also defends his right as a foreigner to engage in the debate on the French constitution:

> But my intentions require no apology; I demand to be heard, as a right. Your cause is that of human nature at large; you are the representatives of mankind; and though I am not literally one of your constituents, yet I must be bound by your decrees. My happiness will be seriously affected by your deliberations; and in them I have an interest, which nothing can destroy. I not only consider all mankind as forming but one great family, and therefore bound by a natural sympathy to regard each other's

---

39 Ibid, p. 19.
40 Ibid, p. 21.
41 Ibid, pp. 28-9.
42 Ibid, p. 29.

happiness as making part of their own; but I contemplate the French nation at this moment as standing in the place of the whole. You have stepped forward with a gigantic stride to an enterprise which involves the interests of every surrounding nation; and what you began as justice to yourselves, you are called upon to finish as a duty to the human race.[43]

Barlow's text echoes the principles expressed by Thomas Paine in *Rights of Man* and shows deference to the previous governing body, the Constituent Assembly, and its members. He was also reticent on the role of the people in law-making, though he still expressed some radical ideas on the dangers of kingship and the readiness of the people for citizenship. He showed the influence of Paine and the Jeffersonians in his views on constitution-making, and his approach to political representation was inspired by the American example. His proposal was above all anchored in the practical reality of the mission facing the new Convention and its constitution-makers and took its lead from the 1791 settlement.

Barlow went on to publish again while he was a resident of Paris. Part II of the *Advice to the Privileged Orders* was "a universalistic program for the regeneration of mankind through fiscal reform of the European states" and much more utopian and wide-ranging that his *Letter to the National Convention*.[44] In the later months of 1793, he managed to weather the storm of emergency rule through prudent publication decisions and astute political decision-making. He signed an address to the radical Réunion section of Paris in December 1793 along with fellow Americans Mark Leavenworth, James Swan and Colonel Blackden. This address tacitly excused the excesses of emergency government in the larger struggle for freedom from tyranny and recommended the drafting of a lasting republican constitution to secure the longevity of the Revolution. Despite his preference for representation over popular democracy and his pragmatic way of dealing with the debate on the republican constitution, with an emphasis on building upon rather than overhauling the constitution of 1791, Barlow was on the radical wing of the emigrant community. His status as an American citizen protected him from accusations of counter-revolution while his British counterparts found themselves increasingly the object of suspicion.[45]

---

43 Ibid, pp. 4-5.
44 Buel, *Joel Barlow: American Citizen*, p. 172.
45 Nevertheless, the situation of American emigrants in France was increasingly problematic. America's tardiness in paying back debts amassed during the War of Independence and equivocal support for the Revolution meant that, despite the shared revolutionary and republican heritage, Americans were not above suspicion or reproach.

DAVID WILLIAMS, *OBSERVATIONS SUR LA DERNIÈRE CONSTITUTION DE LA FRANCE, AVEC DES VUES POUR LA FORMATION DE LA NOUVELLE CONSTITUTION* (1793)

David Williams' tract on the constitution was written at the behest of key members of the first constitutional committee following his nomination for French citizenship in August 1792 and invitation to France by Roland and Brissot in November 1792 as an advisor to the drafting committee. Like Paine, Williams was an associate of the Girondin members of the Convention and had been in close correspondence with Brissot in the years preceding the Revolution. Madame Roland recounted how "he was invited by the government to repair to Paris, where he passed several months, and frequently conferred with the most active representatives of the nation."[46] Despite Williams' contribution to the debates in France and his growing reputation as a revered political thinker amongst French statesmen, his constitutional analysis has been largely sidelined in favour of studies of his diplomatic role across the British-French divide once war had broken out. As his namesake, historian David Williams, wrote in 1938:

> He did not take part in the deliberations of the constitutional committee, but was requested to write out a criticism of the Constitution of 1791, which he was to discuss with Condorcet, Gensonné and Brissot. This he did under the title of 'Observations on the Last Constitution of France' which was translated by Maudru and published in French. But the labours of the committee were overshadowed by the trial of the king and by the imminence of war with England, and it was in the latter connection that Williams's presence in France became of some diplomatic importance, and that his autobiography has some value in indicating the attitude of the Girondist leaders towards the war.[47]

Despite the overshadowing of Williams' role in the constitutional debate by his status as a diplomat, there have been some studies of Williams' involvement as an advisor to the Convention. Franck Alengry has assessed the importance of Williams' work to Condorcet's constitutional thought and Whitney Jones discusses *Observations* at some length in his biography of the Welsh reformer.[48] Jones suggests that "much of Condorcet's thought runs parallel with that of David Williams," and places him firmly in the Girondin

---

46 Manon Roland, *An Appeal to Impartial Posterity*, part 1. Translated from the French (London: Johnson, 1795), p. 42.

47 D. Williams, 'The Missions of David Williams and James Tilly Matthews to England (1793)', *The English Historical Review* 53.212 (1938), p. 655.

48 See Frank Alengry, *Condorcet: guide de la Révolution française* (Paris: Giard et Brière, 1904) and Whitney R. D. Jones, *David Williams: The Anvil and the Hammer* (Cardiff: University of Wales Press, 1986).

camp.⁴⁹ James Dybikowski has analysed Williams' political thought and engagement in a recent biographical account, laying emphasis on the recurrence and development of particular philosophical themes in the educationalist's work. Although *Observations* was the only text that Williams published while in revolutionary Paris, Dybikowski prefers to consider this work in the context of other writings on themes such as representation, government and liberty rather than in the context of productions on the French constitution debate. Yet he does pay particular attention to the relationship between Brissot and Williams in the run-up to and during the French Revolution, noting their lengthy correspondence and Williams' view that he had played the role of mentor to the notable revolutionary. Dybikowski considers Williams a "wary radical."⁵⁰ Although he was as scathing of the English constitution as many a hardened reformer, criticising Montesquieu's reverence for British mixed monarchy, Williams kept his distance from "organised reform."⁵¹ This is mirrored in his lack of direct engagement with the *SADH*, which was at its most dynamic and influential during Williams' brief stay in Paris.

Williams went to republican France in late 1792 for a month as the particular guest of Brissot and Roland, both of whom sent him invitations and guaranteed his subsistence costs while in Paris. Brissot had met him in London in 1783-84 and again in 1788 on his return from America. They had corresponded regularly before and during the early stages of the Revolution when Williams expressed his thoughts on the hostile reaction to the Revolution in Britain and wrote on the theme of constitutions. Williams later shared his belief that his own ideas had materially influenced the first French constitution drafters. Dybikowski argues that "from the outset Williams provided Brissot with advice on improving the political and constitutional position of France."⁵² He had already published a number of works on constitutions and government, in particular his *Letters on Political Liberty* (1782) and *Lessons to a Young Prince* (1790), in which he gave an account of the early stages of the French Revolution. He expanded his views on constitutional issues in the second edition of *Lessons to a Young Prince*. He deplored the federation of disparate interests under the new American constitution and believed the emerging constitution of France could correct some of the errors committed across the Atlantic. One of his objections to the representative systems in both America and Britain was the fact that constituency boundaries were decided at random rather than being based on the rule of principle. Yet despite the fact that the American model of commercial republicanism, where individuals were interested and involved in but not preoccupied or submerged by political concerns, may have been an

---

49 Jones, *The Anvil and the Hammer*, p. 131.
50 James Dybikowski, *On Burning Ground: An Examination of the Ideas, Projects, and Life of David Williams* (Oxford: Voltaire Foundation, 1993) , p. 160.
51 Ibid, p. 161.
52 Ibid, p. 202.

influence on Williams, he did not go as far as to suggest that France should apply the lessons of American constitutionalism. In previous writings he had also criticised American federalism. Nevertheless, Williams saw the first French constitution as being a reworking of and improvement upon the settlement across the Atlantic which, in its turn, had erased some of the more pernicious elements of the unreformed British system.

In *Observations* Williams emphasises the importance of preserving the right to liberty, property and security as well as equality before the law, but sees no justification for doing away with social hierarchy, concluding that equality would lead to disorder:

> In England, the opinion of equality is on this account generally resisted or despised. In France, it is dreadfully misunderstood; no declaration having oftener met my ear, than the following, that the people should be equal in fact as well as in words, & that agitations and tumult would never cease until all usurping intriguers be reduced to a level with their fellow citizens."[53]

Observations was translated into French by Citoyen Maudru and published in January 1793 by the Imprimerie du Cercle Social, the printing press of the Girondin grouping. Williams was dissatisfied with his finished text, claiming that he had not been allowed to compose his thoughts at leisure, hampered as he was by endless visits from acquaintances. He had been constrained by the shortness of his visit and regretted the absence of his books. He also considered that his work, once written, would probably have been rendered superfluous by the writings of others. These admissions appeared in the manuscript of the tract but were omitted from the final published version. Williams was also frustrated by the apparent descent of French politics into faction and his inability to access the records of the constitutional committee which hindered his progress:

> The general spirit of Faction, so completely pervaded the pretended Statesmen, that my Invitation and Business were known only to a Part of the Executive Council, by whose order my expences were to be defrayed – I had therefore no access to the Minutes of the Committee of Constitution; & was requested only to write down my Objections, Condorcet, Gensonné, & Brissot were to converse with me. In a few days I delivered to Brissot the annexed "Observations"[54]

---

53 MS.2.192, Williams, *Observations on the Late Constitution of France*, pp. 2-3. For all quotes from Williams' tract I have used his original manuscript text, conserved at Cardiff Public Library. All page numbers therefore relate to this manuscript rather than the printed translation. In the translated version "word" is replaced by the French for "law" i.e. "droit".

54 D. Williams, *Incidents in My Own Life Which Have Been Thought of Some Importance*, Peter France (ed.) (Brighton: University of Sussex Library, 1980) , p. 28, also quoted in Jones, *The Anvil and the Hammer*, p. 122.

In the foreword to *Observations*, Williams explained the task he set out to achieve:

> I came to France with the idea, that the little assistance I might afford, would be applied to the labours of the Committee of Constitution, which I supposed to have made considerable progress in their work – & unprepared by previous reading & meditation for the formation of a plan, – the task that has been assigned me. I have therefore re-perused the late constitution, & introduced my ideas of a new structure, among my remarks on the foundation of the old.[55]

His own interpretation of the mandate he received from Brissot and Roland changed over time. He initially wrote that he had been asked to analyse the defects in the existing constitution before providing an outline of a new draft. Yet by the time he published his later autobiographical account, he was contending that his mission had been restricted to commenting on the old constitution.[56]

Williams' approach to the task in hand was dictated therefore by the mandate set out by his French commissioners. Thus, he grounded his analysis in a detailed consideration of the existing arrangements conceived by the Constituent Assembly before providing his own views on how it could be improved. Williams began by criticising the *Declaration of the Rights of Man and of the Citizen*, not solely for its content, but because its rigid form precluded the elaboration of reasoned arguments.[57] In his view, a declaration resists the type of rational demonstration needed in a constitutional text. He goes on to dissect the declaration and then the monarchical constitution article by article, basing his advice and observations less on abstract principles than on a careful reading of the political circumstances in which he was writing and a blunt refusal, despite it being the "fashion", to criticise the work of those who had gone before.

Williams' chief concern is the issue of representation and the role of the people in law-making. He expresses views which were very different to those of fellow radical reformers in Paris, Robert Merry and John Oswald who

---

55 MS.2.192, Williams, *Observations on the Late Constitution of France*.
56 Dybikowski, *On Burning Ground*, p. 203. See footnote 56.
57 The Declaration was approved by the National Assembly on 26th August 1789 and contained seventeen articles. The preamble read, "The representatives of the French people, organised as a National Assembly, believing that the ignorance, neglect, or contempt of the rights of man are the sole cause of public calamities and of the corruption of governments, have determined to set forth, in a solemn declaration, the natural, unalienable, and sacred rights of man, in order that this declaration, being constantly before all the members of the Social body, shall remind them continually of their rights and duties; in order that the acts of the legislative power, as well as those of the executive power, may be compared at any moment with the objects and purposes of all political institutions and may thus be more respected, and, lastly, in order that the grievances of the citizens, based hereafter upon simple and incontestable principles, shall tend to the maintenance of the constitution and resound to the happiness of all."

advocated the noisy, vociferous place of the people in ratifying laws in vocal neighbourhood assemblies. Williams draws back from recommending such direct involvement of individuals in the legislative process, believing the "general will" of the people could not be gauged by an aggregate of loud voices but was distilled from a rational process of delegation and consultation. The people were too influenced by local concerns; their views therefore needed arbitration and had to be rationalised through delegation. Vocal citizens, voicing their opinion and giving credence to laws through physically gesturing their assent or disapproval, have no place in Williams' vision of government. Not only would such a settlement preclude the efficient delivery of laws and therefore be detrimental to the running of state affairs, but it would also distract individuals from their own private industry and endeavour, activities at the heart of the Dissenting philosophy that Williams espoused. Although he favoured representative government, like Godwin he was also an advocate of private self-improvement.

While some contributors to the constitution debate argued that popular participation in law-making was the mark of an engaged citizenry, for Williams, influenced by Brissot and Roland, a representative model founded on the principle of "delegation" – a term also used by Paine – was preferable. Not only would this make for an organised, clearly visible decision-making procedure and banish the threat of intrigue, which festered in the British system, but it would allow individuals to have a say in the running of government through restricted primary assemblies while not removing them from their private – commercial – activities. If for proponents of greater popular involvement in government, the duty to take part in votes on each proposed law was the mark of a newly mobilised population, for Williams it was an unnecessary distraction from industrious personal pursuits. While Williams criticises the veering of representation into impenetrable cabals and cliques, its fate in Britain, he sees the American remedy as providing the necessary model for revolutionary France.

Williams was influenced by Rousseau and the latter's views on the general will, morality and the inalienability of sovereignty, and referred to the philosopher's "brilliant imagination" in *Observations*.[58] Yet Williams was wary about the impact of a heightened role for the people in decision-making, and this reticence about democratic forms of government comes across in his notes. Williams thought large gatherings inspired tumult and disorder. Thomas Morris, who had collaborated with Williams on the Literary Fund, noted, "He is fond of company and conviviality, but he hates boisterous noise, ill-natured disputes, and the affectation of knowledge in long speeches."[59] In *Observations*, Williams contends that large assemblies were

---

58 Jones, *The Anvil and the Hammer*, pp. 164-65. MS.2.192, D. Williams, *Observations on the Late Constitution of France*, p. 5.

59 Thomas Morris, *A General View of the Life and Writings of the Rev. David Williams Drawn up for the Chronique du Mois, A French Periodical Publication, at the Request of Messrs. Condorcet, Clavière, Mercier, Auger, Brissot, &c. Editors of that Work* (London: Ridgway, 1792) , p. 20.

"always tumultuous" and "express only some prevailing passions, never a general judgment."[60] He considers the people of France to be accustomed to "larger assemblies", "the love of talking", and "the ambition of oratory" but believed such spontaneous oral forms led to cunning and intrigue.[61] It was this type of distaste for loud and lengthy verbal exchange that Madame Roland would later note as his major criticism of the debates taking place in the Convention:

> I saw him, from the very first time he was present at the sittings of the assembly, uneasy at the disorder of the debates, afflicted at the influence exercised by the galleries, and in doubt whether it were possible for such men, in such circumstances, ever to decree a rational constitution. I think that the knowledge which he then acquired of what we were already, attached him more strongly to his country, to which he was impatient to return. How is it possible, said he, for men to debate a question, who are incapable of listening to each other? Your nation does not even take pains to preserve that external decency, which is of so much consequence in public assemblies-: a giddy manner, carelessness, and a slovenly person, are no recommendations to a legislator; nor is any thing indifferent which passes in public, and of which the effect is repeated every day. —Good heaven! what would he say now, if he were to see our senators drest, since the 31st of May, like watermen, in long trowsers, a jacket and a cap, with the bosom of their shirts open, and swearing and gesticulating like drunken *sans-culottes*?[62]

There are two strands to this distaste for large, noisy gatherings. The first is a cultural objection. Williams considered French debate to be characterised by disorganised and riotous talking which could not lead to a rational or considered outcome. Yet, behind this disapproval of large assemblies, lay ambivalence about the readiness of the people for engagement in political decision-making. While he argues forcefully that all men and all unmarried women, even servants, should be citizens and able to exercise their right to vote for the constitutional and legislative delegations, he does not provide a role for the people in the law-making process. He insists that "reason, judgement, and the public virtues require a minute and capillary organisation, by which they can regularly and silently influence the whole community."[63] Popular involvement in decision-making assemblies would also be a harmful distraction from private endeavour: "The general industry, sobriety and morals of the people can never be preserved, if they are frequently induced to quit their employments, & to mingle in distant and tumultuous

---

60 MS.2.192, D. Williams, *Observations on the Late Constitution of France*, p. 14.
61 Ibid, p. 16.
62 Manon Roland, *An Appeal to Impartial Posterity*, pp. 41-2.
63 MS.2.192, D. Williams, *Observations on the Late Constitution of France*, p. 15.

assemblies."[64] While the people should be "assiduously instructed" in all aspects of government and should "comprehend" everything in order to be able to take reasoned decisions, the general will would be enacted through a system of deputation rather than through direct involvement in decisions.[65]

In the manuscript edition of Williams' tract, but pointedly absent from the published version, Williams envisages a role for the clergy in instructing the people, not solely in religious matters but in the civil and moral responsibilities needed in a republican citizenry. Sunday would be the ideal day of the week for such an educational mission as it was already designated as a day of worship. Under the new republican system, people would combine their private religious duties with learning about issues of state and citizenship. The omission of this advice from the published tract is not surprising. It is likely that Williams began to doubt the wisdom of providing for a significant role for the clergy in the new republic while the general trend was towards the replacement of religious orders by secular institutions. The question of religion was a perpetual problem in the relationship of Dissenting reformers in France to the Revolution. As Brian Rigby has argued, "despite the progressive, unorthodox views of some dissenters, and despite the way in which anti-Jacobins branded them as infidels, most Unitarians were still very much part of a pious and strict non-conformist culture which considered that fundamental religious and moral principles should be widespread in the population at large."[66] British radicals in Paris struggled to reconcile their religious views with the trend towards secularisation and Williams' last-minute decision to erase the provision for a role for the clergy from his advice on the constitution is a clear example.

In his writings prior to *Observations*, Williams had, like Paine, denied the existence of a British constitution. Equally, like the author of *Rights of Man*, he believed that the settlement of 1688 was far from being the apotheosis of liberty but had eclipsed the people in an arrangement which had consolidated the power of the propertied class. Like Paine, he was sceptical of the true reforming pretensions of the Whigs. In *Observations*, he develops his notion of conventions more fully, suggesting, again as Paine had done, that governments could not effectuate reform from within but needed an overseeing body – a convention – to establish or modify a constitution. He suggests that the principle of delegation should be applied both to the constitutional and legislative bodies. While the legislature would make laws and the convention would determine constitutional issues, there would equally be a constitutional council charged with conveying the results of deliberations to the people in their primary assemblies. People would assemble in small primary divisions to elect their delegates. A maximum of

---

64 Ibid, p. 14.
65 Ibid, pp. 18, 24.
66 Brian Rigby, 'Radical Spectators of the Revolution: The Case of the *Analytical Review*' in Ceri Crossley and Ian Small (eds.), *The French Revolution and British Culture* (Oxford: Oxford University Press, 1989), p. 69.

three delegates would be sent per department, meaning that the national decision-making assembly would be manageable and not prone to the type of disorder that had characterised national debate thus far. Each delegate would be "merely messengers" of the people.[67] A convention would be elected every four years by the departments to review the constitution and laws of the legislature. Deputies should be citizens but also free of "imputations of infamous vices," they should be acquainted with the arts, agriculture and manufacturing and "without obstinate entanglements from particular interests."[68] Delegates would have salaries and all ties of patronage would be removed, again ensuring that politics would not descend into cabal and intrigue. Such a system, in contrast to large gatherings which led to oligarchy, would ensure the "will of the majority of all the people" was distilled.[69] The move away from the term "general will" is interesting. Williams now considered it impossible to form a whole out of the plethora of individual desires. They were fundamentally irreconcilable; hence the need for arbitration and the discovery of the will of the "majority" of the people rather than one single will.

Unlike some of his compatriots in Paris, Williams considered that some good could be derived from careful observation of the political system in Britain. Oligarchic corruption was to be avoided, yet certain aspects of British custom were to be celebrated. Williams suggests that in practice a local manufacturer or tradesman would rarely represent his county in a political capacity ensuring that parochial interests seldom interfered with wider politics. Equally, he argues that the example of British reserve about the use of the term "equality" should be heeded in France. While equality before the law was surely to be welcomed, real equality – the dissolving or levelling of social status – was illusory and courted the danger of subversive turbulence within the social fabric and the destruction of property. For Williams, like Mary Wollstonecraft, the maintenance of property was essential to achieving reform without the destruction of order.

These allusions to existing forms of government, whether reformed or unreformed, highlight the importance Williams attached to history, experience and precedent. In this he returned to a theme he had pursued in earlier work, in which he celebrated the essential justice of the system of government created under Alfred the Great before the Norman Conquest and criticised the subjugation of British freeborn rights in post-1688 society. For many reformers in Britain, the myth of the Norman yoke and a halcyon age of pre-conquest liberty and justice were powerful rhetorical weapons used to justify their support for reform and distance their ideas from French influence. Although appeals to Britain's ancient constitution were rare among emigrant radicals, who tended to reject the British constitutional paradigm

---

67 MS.2.192, D. Williams, *Observations on the Late Constitution of France*, p. 18.
68 Ibid, p. 21.
69 Ibid, p. 27.

outright, Williams was one of the few who cited Britain as a potential model for the new French constitution.

In *Observations*, Williams does not, however, restrict his appeal to history to Britain, but draws on a pan-European past, citing Saxon, German and French historical practice to provide examples of good governance. He suggests that the new French constitution could not simply be anchored in theory but must take account of "custom." The new constitution would have to take inspiration from history and it was folly to argue that the different proposals put forward for reforming the constitution were anything other than "ancient materials variously adjusted." He denies the "pretences of originality" and criticises the "projecting dogmatists" who simply remoulded the thought of classical, Saxon and French writings and "formed them into various & fanciful systems." Tacitus, Cesar, Selden, the Saxon Chronicle, Hottman's *Franco-Gallia* and Wilkins' collection of *Anglo-Saxon Laws* are held up as the traditions on which all new experiments should rely. This confirms the expedient streak identified by Dybikowski in Williams' *Philosopher*, where Williams had called upon English political history in search of solutions to the question of governance. In this work, the fictional philosopher states "that in religion, as well as in politics, I am not imagining the best that may be conceived, but the most expedient and practicable in our circumstances."[70] In contrast to many British radicals on French soil, who preferred to consider the issue of constitutions in the abstract and who sought to pursue novel ideas of constitutional form, Williams denied the very possibility of originality in the drafting of a new constitution. All settlements were simply reconfigurations of previous orders and therefore had to be rooted in those traditions.[71]

While tracts such as that of Williams, overtly republican and critical of the vein of corruption associated with the British system of parliamentary representation and organisation, would have been considered radical on the British mainland, in the context of the nascent French republic, such hesitancy about the application of theoretical models, refusal of direct popular participation and attachment to custom would have courted accusations of conservatism and even counter-revolution, at least for those revolutionary figures of the Montagne, influenced by the Parisian sections and with increasing political sway after January 1793. Although France had the opportunity to develop a more progressive, improved form of

---

70 Dybikowski, *On Burning Ground*, p. 150.
71 Although the writings of Burke on the French Revolution are sometimes seen as heralding an era of British conservatism and appeals to ancient rights, Gerald Newman has suggested that many of Burke's arguments hail from earlier British radical culture. He notes "The truth is that Burke, defending the upper classes against a much exaggerated 'French' radical threat, in fact borrowed his organicist ideas from the English radical writings of the pre-1789 period. The idea of a native social compact, enshrined in history and passed down as an inalienable inheritance through the generations, was scarcely original with him." G. Newman, *The Rise of English Nationalism: A Cultural History 1740-1830* (London: Macmillan, 1997) , p. 228.

representation, Williams harboured a deep scepticism for some of the mechanisms at work in the Revolution and, like Mary Wollstonecraft, who wrote *An Historical and Moral View of the French Revolution* in 1794, was cautious about the merits of innovation. Projects were dangerous as they were the fruit of theoretical inquiry detached from empirical observation.

Madame Roland sang his praises, Brissot was his personal friend and correspondent, Roland sent him an official invitation and his views were published by the Imprimerie du Cercle Social; if any British figure was distinctly associated with a particular political grouping it was Williams. He was also commissioned to take part in a diplomatic mission on behalf of his Girondin associates to try and forestall the advent of war with Britain. The failure of this mission and Williams' disengagement from the Revolution is recorded in his later autobiographical text. Williams certainly felt the same kind of mistrust of popular intervention in politics that united the Girondins. It was also the kind of social exclusiveness and refusal to entertain popular radical reform for which John Thelwall would upbraid William Godwin.[72] John Hurford Stone criticised Williams' nomination for citizenship, noting scathingly that "They are wretchedly informed respecting characters in England; and from this sample they will get themselves laughed at."[73] Hurford Stone had collaborated with Williams on the Literary Fund in 1792, yet he did not hold the same political views as the Welsh reformer and had little esteem for him. Williams' views erred on the conservative side when seen from a radical republican perspective in France and from the point of view of more radical British emigrants in Paris. This earned him an ambiguous reputation among fellow reformers. He certainly avoided contact with members of the *SADH*, wary of their pretensions at organised politics on French soil and courting of the local sections. Yet viewed from the vantage point of the British authorities, Williams' stance was still radical. He was a staunch republican who had written to Pétion in March 1792 after the death of Leopold of Austria and as opposition to the continued office of kingship was mounting, to defend the severe punishment of treacherous monarchs:

> I congratulate you on the death of the Emperor and on the impeachment of the King's Ministers. Let them be punished legally but exemplarily:- and if the king be a traitor, notwithstanding his numerous Perjuries now is the moment to decide on his fate, by a truly national judgement.[74]

---

72 Michael Scrivener suggests that Thelwall occupied "an especially dangerous place between the polite world of Godwin and the popular world of Spence." See Michael Scrivener, *Seditious Allegories: John Thelwall & Jacobin Writing* (University Park, PA: Pennsylvania State University Press, 2001), p. 260.
73 *CCST*, p. 1298.
74 David Williams to Jérôme Pétion, March 1792, AN F7/4774/70/463.

This extract seems to anticipate the later events of January 1793, which Williams would stay in Paris to witness. The execution of Louis XVI would be seen by many as a "national judgement" meted out to a treacherous king.

Williams left France before the Girondin constitutional proposal was officially tabled, his residence in France being curtailed by the original terms of his mission but also by his awareness of the narrowing scope for freedom of debate in a Revolution that had taken a more radical direction. He would later criticise the Girondins for their "involuntary" error of seeking "a perfect political constitution" rather than heeding his advice on practicability.[75]

Back in Britain after leaving Paris in February 1793, Williams lost much of his early enthusiasm for the Revolution. His later political writings embraced the balance of the British constitution and celebrated its empirical foundations, a position which Madame Roland had anticipated in early 1793. He would go on to criticise the lack of expediency of the French leaders he had encountered and regret the overthrow of the 1791 constitution, whose dissolution he had nevertheless openly approved of and agreed to comment on in late 1792. Dybikowski points to the disparity between Williams' actual behaviour during the Revolution and his rewriting of his position in his later autobiography. Jones, however, suggests that Williams did retain a certain degree of coherence in his political thought despite his reorientation towards an establishment bias in his post-revolutionary career. Yet there can be little doubt that Williams, who worked with the loyalist leader John Reeves on the Literary Fund from the mid-1790s and accepted commissions to write government press articles, rebuked his earlier support for the Revolution. Yet this later position should not blind us to the fact that Williams was an enthusiastic supporter of the Revolution at the turn of 1792, when the republic had already been announced and violent acts been accepted as part of the drive towards ridding France of monarchy. It was in this context that he had accepted a mission to advise the constitutional committee on a settlement for the new republic and in which he published the tract offered to the Convention.

---

75 Quoted in Dybikowski, *On Burning Ground*, p. 216.

7

'A state of permanent popular deliberation is indispensable'
The writings of Robert Merry, John Oswald and George Edwards

The majority of British residents who commented on the new French republican settlement, with the notable exception of David Williams, found common ground in their shared belief that the British representative system could not be held up as a model for constitutional change in France. Disillusionment with the British apparatus of government was a binding force which united British radicals in Paris and was perhaps the most powerful motor driving their political engagement in the French constitution debate at the turn of 1793. In tune with this collective criticism of British representation, any lingering reverence for British constitutional arrangements had also been exorcised from the French public scene after the popular overthrow of the monarchy on 10th August. Speaking during the trial of Louis XVI, Bertrand Barère dismissed the "shapeless shadow of representation" that had been established under what he described as Oliver Cromwell's elite revolution.[1]

On the matter of which type of system would best suit the French state, however, British radicals did not agree. Although some emigrant commentators, such as Joel Barlow and David Williams, took the monarchical settlement as a starting point in their recommendations for the

---

[1] "L'événement actuel ne ressemble en rien à l'événement de l'Angleterre. A Paris, le peuple a lui-même détrôné le roi et l'a fait prisonnier en l'accusant. A Londres, ce fut le parti de Cromwell, et il fallut empêcher que le peuple ne s'élevât contre cette faction, qui avait contre elle une grande partie de la nation anglaise. Ici c'est une grande représentation nationale qui doit prononcer : en Angleterre, c'était une ombre informe de représentation, ou plutôt une commission nommée par l'infâme et ambitieux protecteur!" Speech by Bertrand Barère, published in *Le Moniteur Universel*, vol. 14, Monday 7th January 1793.

new constitutional arrangements, for others the downfall of monarchy was an opportunity to articulate a blueprint for republican government entirely free of precedent. As Sampson Perry wrote in 1796, "the arguments for and against the proposed articles of the [monarchical] constitution, as offered at various times by the committee, though containing a considerable portion of reason and eloquence, are become less important to the reader, from the total supercession of that constitution by the republican one which succeeded it too [*sic*] years after."[2] This was not a position that sat comfortably with a British reforming tradition. As Günther Lottes has suggested, "while English radicals could and had to refer to an existing representative system, French radicals breathed the purer air of theoretical discourse."[3] Some British petitioners to the committee however, themselves influenced by the theoretical discussions taking place in their local section committees and in the Convention, and invigorated by the potential for deep-seated change that the popular revolution afforded, articulated constitutional plans for the new republic with the principle of popular sovereignty at their core. For such commentators, such as Robert Merry and John Oswald, their stance on the question of the place of the people in government, law-making and the constitutional process was at the heart of their recommendations for the new republic. Others, such as George Edwards, saw the changes underway in France as having universal application.

ROBERT MERRY, *RÉFLEXIONS POLITIQUES SUR LA NOUVELLE CONSTITUTION QUI SE PRÉPARE EN FRANCE, ADRESSÉES À LA RÉPUBLIQUE* (1792)

Robert Merry offered his views to the constitutional committee in late 1792. In John Alger's reading, Merry's tract on the constitution juxtaposes France's emerging status as a beacon of liberty with England's inexorable moral decline.[4] Alger evoked the tract's concluding passage which celebrates the emergence of a new Eden of republican plenty in France: "In Paris he wrote odes on the Revolution, [and] also in 1793 a pamphlet in which he spoke of England as rushing towards an ignominious fall, while France was rapidly rising to a pinnacle of glory and splendour, unmatched even by Athens at the meridian of its greatness."[5] In the copy of the tract held at the Bibliothèque Nationale in Paris, the printed date of 1792 is crossed out and replaced with 1793. This is possibly why Alger gave the latter date. Yet it is

---

2   *HS* II, p. 153.
3   Günther Lottes, 'Revolution and Political Culture: An Anglo-French Comparison', Mark Philp (ed.), *The French Revolution and British Popular Politics* (Cambridge: Cambridge University Press, 1991), p. 81.
4   I have not found any surviving copies of Merry's original English manuscript version. In the absence of this document, I have worked exclusively from the published version in French.
5   Alger, *Englishmen*, p. 101.

more likely that Merry wrote the tract in October 1792. In the final paragraphs of the text, the author refers to the considerable advances made in the "two months" since the storming of the Tuileries on 10th August.[6] It was therefore a relatively early contribution to the constitution debate, following that of Barlow, whose *Letter to the National Convention* was published in September 1792 and before that of Williams. Although Alger's evaluation is an over-simplification of Merry's treatise, the historian was right to highlight the comparison made between the decline of Britain and the progress of France. The treatise seems to have attracted little attention in Britain at the time of publication, although it was mentioned in an obituary of Merry published in *The Monthly Magazine* in April 1799:

> While in the city, and under the invitation given by the French legislature to all foreigners, to favour them with their sentiments on the erecting a free constitution; he wrote a short treatise in English on the nature of free government. It was translated into French by Mr. Madget [*sic*], and presented in the same manner as the Laurel of Liberty to the National Convention: "honourable mention" being made of it on their journals.[7]

Merry played no official role in the French administration and was thus able to adopt a position of relative independence on the issues he addressed in *Réflexions politiques*, a pamphlet which was published by J. Reynier's publishing house, and not by the more well-known Imprimerie du Cercle Social. Not adhering to a particular political or philosophical trend, he provides a series of ideas drawing on Enlightenment and proto-democratic traditions as well as an empirical assessment of the British system. He offers a reading of the French constitution debate which, in contrast to other texts, excludes all reference to the previous arrangements of 1791. Although Merry's stated purpose is to aid French legislators in drawing up a constitutional settlement based on principles of liberty and direct democracy, he also illuminates the frailties of the British model, bolstering the case for constitutional reform in his home country.

Though his text is directed at the members of the constitutional committee, Merry refrains from explicitly addressing his observations to the representative body on the title page. His thoughts are for the republic in its widest, and perhaps most democratic, sense, and potentially for republican sympathisers outside France. He sees the republican turn as an opportunity for fundamental change, unencumbered by the piecemeal compromises of the past. While Merry presents his views as "reflections" – or "thoughts" – alluding to the realm of ideas and philosophical abstraction, Barlow's address

---

6   Merry, *Réflexions politiques sur la nouvelle constitution*, p. 18.
7   'Biographical notice of Mr. Robert Merry', *The Monthly Magazine*, vol. 7 (April 1799), pp. 255-6. The "Mr. Madget" mentioned in the notice is Nicholas Madgett, a member of the *SADH* and translator for the revolutionary government. I have not been able to locate the original English version mentioned in the advertisement.

was in the form of an official "letter" and Williams offered his "observations", conclusions drawn from scrutiny of the existing arrangement and close adherence to its discursive structure. Merry envisions the new French constitution as anchored in ideas alone and therefore applicable to other nations intent on reform.

Merry's influences are varied and he draws on different traditions depending on the issue addressed. On questions such as capital punishment, the arts and sciences and the perfectibility of human society, his proposals fuse with those of French philosophers such as Condorcet, whom he knew personally, and he puts forward an essentially optimistic view of the potential for human regeneration. Yet, on preferred modes of government, the question of representation and the people's role in law-making, which are the principal elements of the pamphlet, his views diverge from Girondin views of enlightened commercialism and the superiority of representative government. Merry was wary of the rule of educated elites, identifying considerable scope for corruption and abuse in such a framework. In his articulation of an ideal form of government, he reiterates some of the arguments being put forward by members of the Cordeliers Club, who were committed to far-reaching democratic overhaul.[8] Similarly, in his use of classical texts and examples of the virtue of the republics of Antiquity, Merry echoes Cordeliers activists and some Montagnards, who would take control of the National Convention in June 1793.[9] The text rarely meditates on practical implementation, except in the outline of the executive branch. The question of citizenship, a major preoccupation of Barlow's, is not tackled and the place of foreigners within the republic is given no attention.

In calling for the abolition of the death penalty, Merry appeals to the humanity of the French people but also to justice and reason. The death penalty was established by despots, in his view, and perpetuated fear rather than corrected vice. In condemning the moral decadence of state-induced violence, Merry aligns himself with Enlightenment thinkers from Montesquieu and Voltaire through to Condorcet, distancing himself in the process from the Rousseauian view later adopted by Robespierre and Saint-Just and the leaders of the *Comité de Salut Public* on the interdependence of virtue and terror.[10] Condorcet was a vehement critic of capital punishment and maintained this ideological opposition to the death penalty during the vote on the fate of Louis XVI. Merry sees no utilitarian argument for preserving capital punishment as, in his view, it has no benefit to society and lends itself to vice rather than utility. He highlights the example of the

---

8 For an account of the way in which Cordeliers thinkers drew on the English republican tradition for inspiration and to justify their democratic theories, see Hammersley, *French Revolutionaries and English Republicans*.

9 It is not known whether Merry actually met Camille Desmoulins, although Sampson Perry, a close acquaintance of Merry, certainly did. Perry had close contact with both Desmoulins and Georges Danton, founding members of the Cordeliers Club.

10 Robespierre stated that "virtue without terror is impotent, terror without virtue is malignant." Quoted in Blum, *Rousseau and the Republic of Virtue*, p. 30.

Emperor Leopold of Tuscany who, after abolishing the death penalty, saw a reduction of the crime rate throughout his territory.[11] All crimes are the result of ignorance for the author, and error should be corrected by instruction rather than punishment. Merry evokes the need for clemency, belying tendencies which would make him stop short of condoning violence in the pursuit of revolutionary goals.

Merry shared the essentially optimistic view of human progress of Condorcet who thought man could be led to perfection.[12] He lends weight to this position, arguing that "the rights of man will always triumph, their reign will only become brighter and longer-lasting, the principles of liberty and equality will be spread to all corners of the globe."[13] He goes on to suggest that the Revolution will undo kingly rule, giving the example of King Canute, who was known as the monarch who attempted to master the tides in vain. The image of a British king resisting the advances of the waves was far from neutral in late 1792 and would have given weight to loyalist accusations that British emigrants were fomenting insurrection against their native state and countenancing the idea of a foreign landing.

The aristocracy had predicted that the Revolution would engender the decline of the arts and sciences, but Merry defends the pretensions of the republic to refined manners, morals and the progress of human knowledge. In this sense, he was closer to the Brissotin position than that of the Montagnards, who punished membership of the academies, considering such loyalties as rivalling those of the state for a citizen's attention. The artist Jacques-Louis David, Merry's acquaintance from his Della Cruscan days in Florence, saw membership of the academy as revealing a lack of patriotic vigour.[14] Merry, a recognised though struggling poet, laments the obscurity of men of letters and philosophers under royal despotism.[15]

---

11 The use of the Florentine example was no coincidence as Merry had spent time in the Italian city in the mid-to-late 1780s and was familiar with the reforms that the Grand Duke Leopold of Tuscany had implemented in Florence before becoming Holy Roman Emperor.

12 For an account of Condorcet's political theory see Maurice Cranston, *Philosophers and Pamphleteers: Political Theorists of the Enlightenment* (Oxford: Oxford University Press, 1986). See also Frank Alengry, *Condorcet: guide de la Révolution française* (Paris: Giard et Brière, 1904).

13 Merry, *Réflexions politiques*, p. 18. "Les droits de l'homme triompheront toujours, leur règne n'en deviendra que plus brillant et plus durable, les principes de la liberté et de l'égalité se propageront dans toutes les parties du globe; tous les efforts employés pour en arrêter les progrès retomberont sur leurs auteurs; la vérité, si long-tems continue par la cruauté et par la superstition, n'aura pas plutôt vaincu ces digues, que se répandant sur la terre comme un fleuve bienfaisant, portera par-tout les germes vivifians de la fertilité et de l'abondance; les tyrans auront beau s'opposer à l'inondation, ils auront beau, dans le délire de leur orgueil, imiter cet extravagant Canut* qui, assis sur la plage de la mer, défendit aux ondes d'approcher de sa personne sacrée: l'onde montera toujours et enveloppera dans un déluge commun, eux, leurs flatteurs et leurs folles prétentions."

14 See Blum, *Rousseau and the Republic of Virtue*, p. 8.

15 As mentioned in chapter one, Merry had been a committee member of the Literary Fund for struggling artists and their families.

There are clear Rousseauian echoes to Merry's view on the nature of primitive society and the origin of kingship. His views are aligned with a more radical revolutionary narrative, which insisted that men needed to realise that their personal interest was wedded to the general good. Merry expresses a vision of civilisation as a destructive force, oppressing the noble indigenous peoples ignorant of European progress. This moral turbulence created the "strange cure" of kingship. Monarchy was not a logical response, but an aberrant solution to civil strife. He goes on to explain the rationale behind the appointing of one man over all, namely that this man would rule with only the general good in mind. However, despotism and abuse had quickly followed and the human race soon realised its error. Under royalty, civil society was in a state of slavery and it was tyrannical kings who were the catalysts of conflict between nations. He denies the Hobbesian idea that man is naturally belligerent, arguing that violence was inherent in kingly rule, not in human nature. For Merry, the union of kingly tyrants and the priesthood had perpetuated the absurd notion that the suffering of man had ben willed by heaven. The belief in man's natural wickedness is rejected therefore, and Merry holds up the awaited constitution as promising to be "the cherished and revered gospel of nations."[16]

If Merry echoes Condorcet and earlier Enlightenment thinkers in opposing violence, promoting the arts and sciences and sustaining a belief in human perfectibility, his vision of government is much more closely aligned with that of prominent democratic thinkers of the era, who preferred direct, participatory democracy over representative government. It is problematic trying to situate Merry within this range of opinions, and 'representative government' had very different meanings according to the model drawn upon, be it the unreformed British parliamentary system or the new American republic. Merry, open to experiments in democratic reform, and persuaded of its necessity through his witnessing of events in France, erred on the side of popular sovereignty:

> It appears that people today agree, on the whole, that a purely representative government is a masterpiece of perfection. However, if we carefully examine the principles with strict impartiality, I suspect we will find some great evils, evils which will necessarily destroy that particular effect that was envisaged by its adoption, and what's more, that if it is not restricted to simple agency, it will deliver a fatal blow, sooner or later, to equality, liberty and the rights of man.[17]

---

16 Merry, *Réflexions politiques*, p. 6. "La nouvelle constitution, que la France prépare, va devenir l'évangile chéri et révéré des nations."
17 Ibid. "Il paroit qu'on s'accorde assez généralement aujourd'hui, à regarder un gouvernement représentatif comme un chef-d'œuvre de perfection. Cependant, si on veut examiner les principes de près et avec une stricte impartialité, je ne doute pas qu'on n'y découvre de grands vices; des vices tels que nécessairement ils détruiroient le seul effet que l'on se seroit proposé en l'adoptant; tels encore, que s'il n'étoit pas restreint à une

It was not simply the practical degeneration of representation in real government that prompted concern, but the very principles of representation which were at fault.

Merry also addresses a question that Enlightenment philosophers had consistently grappled with, that of the practicability of instituting republican government in a state the size of France. Montesquieu and Rousseau had concluded pessimistically that such nations were incompatible with effective republican government, and Brissot and Condorcet were convinced that an elite bureaucracy would be needed to stabilise a republic of such vast proportions. In his tract, Merry refutes the claim that a nation could only be managed through representation rather than direct or semi-direct democratic government. Even in an extensive republic all individuals could be invested with legislative power. He adheres to views that had been expressed by Pierre-François Robert and René Girardin, namely that the districts should veto or approve laws before they came into effect.[18] All rejected laws and articles could be rewritten and sent again for approval by the districts. Even the most detailed articles of new laws should be subject to the assent of the people:

> It should be the case therefore that each law which goes through the representative assembly be immediately printed, published and sent to the primary assemblies to be taken into consideration; and that at the end of each year, or at the moment set for the election of members, all the citizens of the districts should individually veto or approve each of the laws. And, in truth, this method of ratifying or rejecting laws is as easy as that of electing members.[19]

This was a radical proposal in favour of a democratic form of government which delved into the detail of how to achieve its application, an issue which John Oswald would also address in his tract on the constitution. Neither Barlow nor Williams substantially dealt with the issue of representation. Barlow was more concerned with morality, public instruction and the exercise of active citizenship, and David Williams' overriding concern was with the importance of ancestral practices in the conception of new constitutional forms. Merry is explicit: citizens should not only be active and virtuous, they should also be intimately and directly involved in the legislative process. Yet, despite this radical suggestion, he does take into account issues

---

simple agence, il porteroit, tôt ou tard, un coup mortel à l'égalité, à la liberté et aux droits de l'homme."

18 Girardin's *Discours sur la nécessité de la ratification de la loi, par la volonté générale* (1791) put forward the view that citizens should approve all legislation.

19 Merry, *Réflexions politiques*, p. 7. "Il convient donc que tout décret passé par l'assemblée représentative soit immédiatement imprimé, publié, et envoyé aux assemblées primaires, pour y être pris en considération ; et qu'à la fin de chaque année, ou au tems fixé pour l'élection des députés, tous les citoyens des districts émettent individuellement leur veto ou leur approbation sur chacun de ces décrets. Et dans le fait cette manière de ratifier ou d'annuller [sic] des décrets est tout aussi simple que celle d'élire les députés."

of practicability. He concedes the need for government efficiency and despatch, issues which had been at the heart of constitutional debates in the new American republic. Laws should take immediate effect until accepted or rejected by primary assemblies.

Merry's view of the corrosive effect of representative government cannot be divorced from his pessimistic reading of the British constitution. He refutes the Montesquieuian view of the superiority of the British mixed combination of Commons, Lords and Monarchy and highlights the decadence of British aristocratic government. Parliament, for Merry, was an organ of oppressive oligarchy rather than an instrument of just governance. In evoking the civil wars of the mid-seventeenth century in Britain and Ireland, it is the Long Parliament rather than the personal rule of Charles I that he denounces. Elected bodies could be just as despotic as absolute monarchy if the conditions were not in place to restrain them. For Merry, there was no likelihood that monarchy would be reinstated in France. He moves rapidly from arguing on the defects of kingship to warning his readers of the malignancy of parliamentary abuse, which he sees as the more insidious source of danger to free government and general liberty.

In Merry's judgement, elected representatives are delegates of the people. The people must constantly watch over their representatives in order to prevent factionalism and intrigue and elected members cannot simply be left to rule for the general good. The people must be active agents – citizens – zealous in the protection of their own sovereignty:

> Then, therefore, absolute power associated with representation is destined to degenerate gradually into tyranny, unless the general will is constantly active in order to contain and rule it. It follows that a state of permanent popular deliberation is indispensable in order to oppose all the decrees that partiality and injustice could offer to the representative assembly with an efficient veto.[20]

Citizens would be mobilised on a permanent basis, never allowed to sink into disinterest. Concern over the apathy of ordinary people was a perennial theme in the writings of British radicals over the period.[21] In the same vein as Cordeliers thinkers, Merry also advocates the regular rotation of assembly members, to ensure democratic vigour and instil a sense of citizenship in the people:

---

20 Ibid. "Puis donc que le pouvoir absolu annexé à la représentation ne peut que dégénérer graduellement en tyrannie, à moins que la volonté générale ne soit dans une activité constante pour contenir et pour commander, il s'ensuit qu'un état permanent de délibération populaire devient absolument indispensable pour opposer un veto efficace à tous les décrets que la partialité ou l'injustice pourroient suggérer à l'assemblée représentative."

21 See Rachel Rogers, "The definition of a virtuous man': British Radicals' Views of Citizens and Citizenship in the French Revolutionary Era', *Revue Française de Civilisation Britannique*, XXI-1 (2016) [online].

The re-election of national assemblies should take place every year, the reason being that the more often a whole nation is mobilised, the more public liberty is safeguarded. Incidentally, frequent primary assemblies familiarise the people with the ease of debating and make them more conscious of the extent of their duties and their own significance.[22]

On executive government, Merry outlines a more extensive practical strategy. He warns against the permanence of emergency solutions and counsels against the degeneration of government into partiality. He makes a direct appeal to the French people to guard against incursions into their natural sovereignty:

> Reject therefore, French people! Reject for ever a form of government which would put the mass of people at the mercy of a handful of individuals.[23]

The executive branch should obey and serve the people and should not have the power to legislate outside the bounds of the national will. This branch would, according to Merry, consist of thirty-six members from the representative assembly. Such a general council would be subdivided into six special councils headed by six ministers. At the end of each month six new members would be elected to the councils by ballot. In that way the entire committee would be renewed every six months without any interruption in the conduct of public affairs. In the course of one legislature, no member would be elected twice to the council. They would be held to account by the public will and obliged to execute their orders without prevarication. Merry insists on the obligation of the committee to publish a list of the available civilian and military vacancies every fifteen days. The most virtuous and meritorious citizens would play the most important roles:

> It is a sure mark of the purity and perfection of a government to see within it men of proven virtue, of true merit, and of incorruptible patriotism: instead of deceitful governments, which resemble a fermenting liquor, only bringing to the surface the bubbles of madness, the froth of ignorance and the dregs of vice.[24]

---

22 Merry, *Réflexions politiques*, p. 8. "La réélection des assemblées nationales devroit avoir lieu tous les ans, par la raison que plus souvent une nation entière est mise en action, plus la liberté publique est en sureté. D'ailleurs la fréquence des assemblées primaires habitue le peuple à une plus grande facilité dans ses délibérations, et lui fera mieux sentie l'étendue de ses obligations et sa propre importance." Rachel Hammersley has shown how Jean-Jacques Rutledge and Theophile Mandar drew on theories of rotation of office developed by Marchamont Nedham and Rousseau. See Hammersley, *French Revolutionaries and English Republicans*.

23 Merry, *Réflexions politiques*, p. 9. "Rejettez donc, François! Rejettez pour toujours une forme de gouvernement qui mettroient la masse entière du people à la merci d'un petit nombre d'individus."

24 Ibid, p.14. "C'est une marque de la pureté et de la perfection d'un gouvernement que d'y

Merry's blueprint for the executive branch is perhaps the most detailed section of his treatise and, once again, he stresses the need for an active citizenry to ensure the application of laws and for representative roles to be open to people on the basis of merit and virtue alone.

Merry joined Barlow in denying the need for a standing army, which would engender slavishness and obedience, states of mind that should be avoided by active citizens of a republic seeking to attain heights of virtue to emulate the classical city states of Athens and Sparta. Even the most virtuous men are fatally transformed under a system which tends towards oligarchy and excludes them from the legislative process. Man's natural tendency towards vice should be circumvented by political mechanisms, as there was no greater threat to liberty than the power exercised by virtuous and patriotic men. Merry revisits republican arguments brought forward in the Commonwealth era. John Milton had seen virtuous kingship as even more insidious than despotic kingship, as it blinded the people to the nature of tyranny inherent in the institution of monarchy. Merry does not suggest that the people could be led towards virtue, but argues for protecting them from the inevitable vices of human nature.[25]

In the epigraph to his treatise, Merry quotes a line from Sallust's *The War Against Jugurtha*. It read, *quos neque armis cogere neque auro parare queas: officio et fide pariuntur*. ("These you can neither acquire by force of arms nor buy with gold; it is by devotion and loyalty that they are won.") He was writing in the aftermath of the French army's entry into war against Austria and Prussia, a decision supported by the Girondin grouping in the Convention but criticised by many of the Parisian sections and the more radical members who would go on to form the Montagne. The epigraph seems to denounce war and commerce and elevate loyalty and devotion, virtues on which the classical republics stood and which came to be more easily associated with the Montagnards. Rather than adhering to modern principles of commercialism and education, Merry sides with those of democratic affiliations. He lauds "the simplicity of the austere principles of republicanism," a vision which would have jarred with Girondin views of a flourishing commercial republican society.

---

voir furnager les hommes d'une vertu éprouvée, d'un mérite non factice, et d'un patriotisme incorruptible : au lieu que les gouvernements vicieux, semblables à une liqueur en fermentation, ne font monter à la surface que les bulles de la folie, l'écume de l'ignorance et la lie de tous les vices."

25 Rachel Hammersley gives the example of Rutledge, who adopted a Harringtonian view of the desirability of a political system which would preclude the need for self-regulated civic virtue. According to Carol Blum, Robespierre and Saint-Just saw the people as one unique entity capable of forming one virtuous city, with egotism and impurity banished outside. See Hammersley, *French Revolutionaries and English Republicans* and Blum, *The Republic of Virtue*.

Merry also celebrates the printing press as the vehicle of liberty in a free republic and associated the liberty of the press with the groundswell of ideas which precipitated the Revolution:

> Freedom of expression by way of the press is the true palladium of freedom; it is the surest channel by which philosophy can penetrate the minds of men: we could date the French Revolution back to the glorious invention of the printing press and that spirit of reform which is generally gripping Europe.[26]

Some restrictions on freedom were needed, however, to avoid defamation. He also denounces the pretensions of the English nation to uphold the free circulation of ideas and the repressive policy of the British government, which punished those who expressed simple opposition to the norms established by the ruling ministry:

> The jurisprudence currently established in England on the liberty of the press is what has led me to the thoughts that I have just presented. Posterity would have difficulty believing that in a century of enlightenment, and in a nation which boasts so much of its freedom, that there we have had the shamelessness, in contempt of the eternal principles of reason and equality, to institute the maxim that a piece of writing which contains only truth, is nonetheless a libellous text: yet, to add insult to injury, the most horrible deceptions, the most shameless lies, provided that they are in favour of the government, can be published, and are published daily with the greatest impunity.[27]

The most vehement passage of Merry's text is a long discussion of the state of affairs in Britain. Although *Réflexions politiques* is ostensibly a contribution to the debate on the republican constitution in France, the tract addresses matters which preoccupied the proponents of radical reform in Britain, such as parliamentary corruption, press censorship and moral regeneration. Merry emphasises the potency of the constitution debate as a catalyst of renewal in Britain. On occasions, this connection to British political affairs is explicit and France is put forward as a blueprint for reform in Britain:

---

26 Merry, *Réflexions politiques*, p. 14. "La libre communication des pensées par les moyens de la presse, est le vrai palladium de la liberté; elle est le plus sûr canal par où la philosophie puisse s'insinuer dans l'esprit de l'homme: on peut faire remonter à l'invention de l'imprimerie la glorieuse révolution de la France, et cet esprit de réforme qui s'empare généralement de l'Europe."

27 Ibid, p. 15. "La jurisprudence actuellement établie en Angleterre, sur la liberté de la presse, est ce qui m'a conduit aux réflexions que je viens de présenter. La postérité aura peine à croire que dans un siècle de lumières, et chez une nation qui se targue tant de sa liberté, on ait eu l'impudeur, au mépris des principes éternels de la raison et de l'équité, d'ériger en maxime qu'un écrit pour ne contenir que la vérité n'en est pas moins un libelle: et cependant, pour comble d'infamie, les impostures les plus odieuses, les mensonges les plus impudens, pourvu qu'ils soient en faveur du gouvernement, peuvent être publiés, et se publient tous les jours avec la plus grande impunité."

Let's suppose that the French constitution had established an executive power independent of the nation, let's suppose even that this power, instead of being entrusted to pure hands, had fallen into the possession of false patriots, the most undesirable consequences would result, not only for the French republic itself, but also for all the countries of Europe that aspire to become free. England, for example, will no longer have any hope of recovering its rights: the two factions which divide this nation will, acting separately, or uniting perhaps in a formidable coalition, seek, by secret emissaries, and by all possible means of corruption and intrigue, to form a treaty with the executive council of France whose principal objective will be the mutual guarantee of the English constitution and in consequence, the loss of British liberty.[28]

Merry feared the degeneration of French liberty if it was not harnessed by those who were truly patriotic and saw in the potential failure of French freedom the subsequent loss of the promise of reform in Britain. He warns against the influence of pretended patriots who did not have liberty at heart, a concern shared by his compatriot Sampson Perry. Merry incites the French constitution-makers to finalise the constitution as it was the only way to provide certitude for their "brothers in England". He emphasises the urgency, as "the dangers are gathering all around us" and the enemies of the constitution were actively seeking to undermine the advances.[29] Merry draws on the British case to provide examples of bad practice. The parliamentary system is an "oppressive aristocracy" and the British press punishes dissent and stifles truth. He concludes the tract with a concern for the eventual enfranchisement of the people of England. Royalty and aristocracy had kept his compatriots in servitude and silenced the constitutional vigour which Britain prided itself on. It is the passage which most struck Alger, the depiction of the soaring human potential of France, in the image of the classical Greek republic of Athens, and the endemic and inexorable decline of Britain, wallowing in shame and self-pity. Merry had already replaced the tree of Eden by the tree of science, he had rewritten the gospel as a

---

28 Ibid, p. 11. "Supposons que la constitution françoise eût établi un pouvoir exécutif indépendant de la nation, supposons encore que ce pouvoir au lieu d'être confié à des mains pures, fût devenu le partage de gens qui n'eussent que le masque du patriotisme, il en résulterait les conséquences les plus facheuses, non-seulement pour la république françoise elle-même, mais encore pour toutes les contrées de l'Europe qui aspireroient à devenir libres. L'Angleterre, par exemple, n'auroit plus d'espoir de recouvrir ses droits: il arriveroit que les deux factions qui divisent cette nation, agitant séparément, ou se réunissant peut-être en une formidable condition, chercheroient, par des émissaires secrets, et par tous les moyens de la corruption et de l'intrigue, à former avec le conseil exécutif de France un traité dont l'objet principal seroit la garantie mutuelle de la constitution angloise et par conséquent la perte de la liberté britannique."
29 Ibid, p.12. "Les dangers se multiplient autour de nous."

republican text and he concludes by defining France as the new Promised Land, the epitome of plenty and a haven of freedom:

> England is hurtling towards a shameful decline, while France is soaring to a degree of glory and splendour, that even Athens at the height of its greatness, never enjoyed. This happy country will become from now on a promised land; its inhabitants, surrounded by plenty, will enjoy the gentle fruits of liberty and equality: we will see only men distinguished by their talents and virtue taking their place in the academies; the pleasing sincerity of free men will triumph over all the small-mindedness of trivial and ridiculous etiquette, the temples of liberty and peace will be decorated by the hands of nature: a pure joy and unlimited goodwill will be the gentle fruits of general prosperity.[30]

In his model of free government, Merry accentuates France's role as a beacon of liberty in Europe. The French experiment in republican government was a necessary step to liberating all the enslaved peoples of the continent, not least the subjugated people of Britain, dependent on the French constitutional settlement to recover their own rights. He calls on the French to recognise their international duty to other European states, notably Britain, and in doing so reiterated the message voiced in the edicts of fraternity circulated internationally by the National Convention.

In his tract on the constitution, Merry evaded the type of political alignments which ultimately proved fatal for some of his compatriots or which stifled the conceptual audacity of others, and drew on intellectual and political traditions without being constrained by them. Merry conjugated a watchful interest in French affairs with an unmitigated desire for root-and-branch political change at home. Although he was one of the more radical British activists in Paris, Merry departed in May 1793. He may have anticipated that foreign residents would begin to suffer materially in the French state, even those whose revolutionary credentials were faultless. On returning to Britain, Merry found no respite from the troubles that had afflicted him prior to his departure. Bankrupt, ostracised and subject to repression of all kinds, he embarked for America in 1796, where he died two years later. Robert Merry had already taken significant steps towards embracing civilisation in its widest and most democratic sense before taking up residence in Paris. Yet his radical reading of constitutional justice and his

---

30 Ibid, p. 19. "C'est ainsi que l'Angleterre se précipite vers une honteuse décadence, tandis que la France s'élève avec rapidité à un degré de gloire et de splendeur dont Athènes, au méridien de sa grandeur, n'a jamais pu jouir. Cette heureuse contrée deviendra désormais une terre de promission; ses habitans, dans le sein de l'abondance, jouiront des doux fruits de la liberté et de l'égalité : on ne verra siéger dans ses académies que des hommes distingués par leurs talens et par leurs vertus: la franchise engageante des hommes libres triomphera de toutes les petitesses d'une étiquette frivole et ridicule; les temples de la liberté et de la paix seront ornés par les mains de la nature; une joie pure et une bienveillance sans bornes seront les doux fruits de la prospérité générale."

increasingly bitter perception of representative government in Britain were all products of an experience in France which shaped his political outlook.

JOHN OSWALD, *THE GOVERNMENT OF THE PEOPLE, OR A SKETCH OF A CONSTITUTION FOR THE UNIVERSAL COMMONWEALTH* (1793)

Born in Edinburgh, John Oswald was a poet and pamphleteer who was involved in the radical press on both sides of the Channel. According to his biographer, David Erdman, he wrote for the *British Mercury* (which he created), the *London Chronicle* and the *Political Herald and Review* and was instrumental in setting up the English-language newspaper in Paris, the *Universal Patriot* in 1790. He collaborated as an editor for the *Cercle Social* publication *La Chronique du Mois* from 1791 to 1793 and by 1792 was permanently settled in France, serving as a secretary for the *SADH*. In the same year he published *Review of the Constitution of Great Britain* and was made commander of the First Battalion of Pike-bearers in October 1792.[31]

Explicit in the title of Oswald's tract on the republican constitution of France is the guiding principle that permeates the entire work, that government should be predicated on popular rather than parliamentary sovereignty. What marks the pamphlet out is, firstly, an attachment to popular involvement in both law-making and elections, secondly the irreverent style in which the tract is written and, thirdly, the universalist foundations of the ideas expressed. Like the vast majority of his fellow British nationals in Paris, Oswald was an internationalist whose faith lay in the potential for a universal brotherhood of men whose binding principles would transcend the frontiers of nations.

The tract was printed by John Hurford Stone's English Press in Paris, which contributed extensively to the dissemination of English-language material in France. According to Madeline Stern, Stone's press was one of the "instruments of international understanding" in the Anglo-French publishing world.[32] Stone was probably sympathetic to Oswald's views on the role of the people in government. As Jack Censer has argued more broadly, "Since the newspaperman was proprietor, he saw little reason to produce what was not of personal interest, and in revolutionary situations, what could concern one more than one's own opinions."[33]

For Oswald, man should be governed by his will and a government's sole role was to ascertain and execute the will of the people. In *Government of the People*, law-making is conceived as a threefold process in which the people first assemble, then deliberate and finally decide. While deliberating should be carried out in primary assemblies, the act of deciding, or legislating – an act of power – should occur within smaller units, or "townships." Here the

---

31 Erdman, *Commerce des Lumières*, p. 183.
32 Stern, 'The Franco-American Book Trade', p. 47.
33 Censer, *Prelude to Power*, p. 6.

people would gather and shout their approval or groan their dissent. The act of law-making is conceived as a vociferous, vocal and visual occasion, far from the restrained and practised eloquence of national debate. For Oswald, human understanding stemmed from discussion, and he contends that when discussion begins, revolution follows, for when men begin to understand their wretched condition, they are compelled to overturn it. Oswald's language is irreverent, designed to reveal the inherent foolishness of instituting a form of government whereby man acts by proxy. If man cannot urinate by proxy, he reasons, man cannot vote or deliberate by proxy since natural man and intellectual man are inseparable. Citizenship is a habit to be learned and needs practice and constant attention, otherwise "we insensibly unlearn to think altogether."[34] In his vernacular mode, Oswald mirrors the style of Thomas Paine who, particularly in his tract on the American condition, *Common Sense*, had used examples drawing on human physicality to highlight the absurdity of the colonies' remaining under Britain's tutelage.[35]

Yet diverging from Paine's actual views on French republicanism, Oswald questions the merits of representation as a form of government: "I confess I have never been able to consider this representative system, without wondering at the easy credulity with which the human mind swallows the most palpable absurdities." Representation is denounced as imposture, "a specious veil under which every kind of despotism has been introduced, and all political frauds are enacted."[36] Oswald suggests that so-called representatives were guilty of blinding the people in the same way as kings and priests under monarchical government. Under such a system, the people are "moon-struck", "dazzled", and "blinded."[37] They are the "audience" who, instead of taking an active, thinking role, assume the place of the "wonder-struck spectator", who are entertained and discouraged from thinking for themselves.[38] For Oswald, "the representation supplanted the reality, the shadow swallowed up the substance."[39] Representative government was not an ideal to be sought-after but a form of artifice, a way of seducing and tricking the people into thinking they had a grasp on power. He directs his criticism against the "political mountbacks" in Britain who maintained their position of authority through the use of "a jargon peculiar

---

34 Oswald, *The Government of the People*, p. 5.
35 In particular Paine used the metaphor of the mother and the suckled child to put forward a case for American independence: "I have heard it asserted by some, that as America hath flourished under her former connexion with Great-Britain, that the same connexion is necessary towards her future happiness, and will always have the same effect. Nothing can be more fallacious than this kind of argument. We may as well assert, that because a child has thrived on milk, that it is never to have meat; or that the first twenty years of our lives is to become a precedent for the next twenty." (Thomas Paine, *Common Sense* [1776; Harmondsworth: Penguin, 1976], p. 83).
36 Oswald, *The Government of the People*, p. 5.
37 Ibid, p. 6.
38 Ibid, p. 6.
39 Ibid, p. 7.

to themselves."⁴⁰ The people's attention was thus deflected from the reality of the political landscape and power was channelled into the hands of an unscrupulous elite. Representation is equated with falsehood, theatre and the art of conjuring rather than the rational and just manifestation of the voice of the people. While representatives elevated the sovereignty of the people in their discourse, they acted differently, like the drunken sailor in *The Tempest* who announced "I shall be vice-roy over you."⁴¹

The metaphor of the theatre was a particularly potent one in late eighteenth-century British political culture. Gillian Russell has argued that "political debate in Britain after 1789 was focused around the competing claims of two forms of theatre – Burke's theatre of order and tradition which clothed the state in the 'decent drapery' of respect, veneration, and awe, and Paine's 'open theatre of the world' in which the mechanisms of power were completely open to the scrutiny of the people."⁴² Paine's theatre would remove the mystery of the stage, thereby making it less an instrument of dissembling than an activity which tallied with the Revolution's concern for integrity and transparency. As Russell observes, in line with Rousseau's mistrust of theatre, the revolutionaries believed the stage was "an unreliable medium for political expression."⁴³ So while Oswald criticised the representative mode of government as being akin to the falsehood of theatrical play, he concurred with Paine on the importance of broadening political culture to include the dispossessed, who had been prevented from occupying a civic role through the conjuring tricks of their rulers.

Oswald sought to show how the people would not have any agency under a system of representative government. He does not make the distinction between ideal representative government (understood by Thomas Paine and others as the type of representation practised in America) and the debased representation considered to characterise British government. While Paine understood republicanism as "nothing more than representative government conducted in the public good," Oswald evokes the need for a mode of popular government based on the loud and noisy participation of the people in the act of legislating.⁴⁴

Though Oswald makes little reference to the earlier developments in the Revolution before the advent of republicanism, he does criticise the mixed monarchical settlement reached between the king and the Assembly in 1791, arguing that if the people had been asked to deliberate on whether the king should have a suspensive veto or not, they would never have assented to such a constitutional remedy. With the king overthrown and those who negotiated with the king discredited, Oswald was free to criticise a settlement

---

40 Ibid, p. 8.
41 Ibid, p. 9.
42 Gillian Russell, *The Theatres of War: Performance, Politics, and Society, 1793-1815* (Oxford: Clarendon Press, 1995), p. 85.
43 Ibid.
44 Philp, 'English Republicanism in the 1790s', pp. 245-6.

which had attempted to reconcile monarchy and popular sovereignty. Oswald suggests that "the jugglers of the Constituent Assembly borrowed the jargon of their elder brethren of England. They declared, that the government of France was representative, that is to say, that the government should not in reality belong to the people, but only in representation or shew; – in short, it was to be a sham government of the people."[45] Oswald shows no reverence towards the former deputies of the National Assembly, unlike Joel Barlow and Sampson Perry. Barlow expressed his veneration for the work undertaken by the Assembly in his tract to the Convention and Perry praised the members for their statesmanship and virtue in his *Historical Sketch*. For Oswald however, the 1791 solution had only been possible because the nation was "reeling" from revolution. Such ideas of representative government could no longer be accepted now that stability had been restored:

> I will venture to predict, that if the second Constituent Assembly should form a constitution, founded on what is called the principles of representation, that it will not last so long as the first. In a short while, the true principles of legislation will be clearly understood, and the people will be satisfied with nothing short of a real and actual exercise of the Sovereignty established on the Will of the People, unequivocally collected and indubitably ascertained.[46]

Oswald provides a democratic alternative to representation. Under such a system, the National Assembly would be entirely dependent on the will of the people. Debate across the nation would be possible through what he terms the "neighbourhood" system:

> The neighbourhoods would instantly take into deliberation the question agitated by the National Assembly, and the whole understanding of the nation, would, at the same moment, be exercised upon the same point.[47]

There would be simultaneous study of the different proposals in widespread local assemblies:

> To deliberate is an operation of the understanding, performed in small assemblies, to decide, on the other hand, is an *Act of Power*, a Declaration of the Public Will, a Demonstration of the *Common Sense* of the Nation, which requires the enforcement of the many, and the support of the mass.[48]

---

45 Oswald, *The Government of the People*, pp. 8-9.
46 Ibid, p. 9.
47 Ibid, p. 10.
48 Ibid, p. 10.

Oswald describes in detail the system of popular decision-making he envisaged through the network of townships filled with active and armed citizens. Questions discussed in primary assemblies would be presented by National Assembly for the endorsement of the people: "A shout of approbation shall sanction, or a groan of disapprobation reject the decrees." The verdicts of the townships would be transmitted to the National Executive Council and they would each send an armed deputation to the capital, swearing to uphold the "Will of the People."

Visual modes of approbation are preferred and decisions should be physically seen and heard: "The decrees shall then, in the midst of the most profound silence be read over, or rather, they shall be lifted up, inscribed upon standards, and displayed to the sight."[49] This visual manner of decision-making would be the only way to avoid pretence and Oswald recommends constant communication between the National Assembly and the townships, and between the townships and the primary assemblies. Voices must be heard, known and circulated, not restricted to the corridors of national forums. He favours the dissemination of knowledge amongst the widest possible audience, echoing George Edwards' view in his tract to the constitutional committee in which he put forward the need for the wide circulation of legal texts.

For Oswald, the executive had to be "*actually* and *immediately* chosen by the people."[50] To be a member of the National Assembly, a delegate had to be chosen three times at three different levels, the primary, the township and the national. Elections would be frequent, taking place every three months in the primary assemblies, every six months in the townships and every twelve months at national level. Oswald concentrates on the layers of government and the importance of communication between them. Representatives would have to undergo "the trial of public opinion."[51] Through a system of multi-layered election and decision-making, the people would be able to exercise their sovereignty in the establishment of laws and in their free choice in the election of "public agents", a term he preferred to "representatives."

Oswald anticipates three possible objections to his form of government. Detractors might suggest that the process of decision-making would be too long, that there would be too much discord, or that the people would have no time to attend to private concerns if they were perpetually involved in public duties. In answer to the first objection, he suggests that the process would not be long if it "proceeds with the rapidity of thought, unshackled, unimpeded, and shaped towards one object."[52] If the people were free and uninhibited in their debate, the process would be short and private responsibilities would not be neglected. As for the fear of dissension, he argues that at least the system he had articulated would crush aristocratic

---

49 Ibid, p. 11.
50 Oswald, *The Government of the People*, p. 12.
51 Ibid, p. 14.
52 Ibid, p. 15.

conspiracies "under the great mass of the National Common Sense." Finally, as regards the question of public service deflecting men from individual concerns, Oswald states:

> I have remarked, that this objection is commonly found in the mouths of men, who yet think it no waste of time that the people should dance attendance at the heels of the Priest for six months in the year. They think it perfectly fit, that the people should pass their time in the performance of barbarous ceremonies, too ridiculous for the practice of a dancing dog; but they cannot bear that they should assemble for any purpose that comes home to the business and the bosoms of men. They will not permit them to meet together to exercise their reason; but they encourage them to assemble, in order to profess their submission to a religion, which demands an absolute surrender of the human understanding![53]

For Oswald, it was only those who believed that the people were not ready to take an active role in law-making, elections and government who put forward the argument that men would no longer have time for their private lives. He denounces the influence of church ceremony over the public mind. On this question he differed from David Williams and George Edwards, both of whom believed that religious instruction could have a role in conveying republican values.

Oswald relied on the ideas of those on the democratic fringe of the British and French reform movements, dismissing representative government and favouring a longer, yet more participative system of direct democracy, involving the people in the process of law-making. Oswald had, like Paine, been on the editorial board of the *Cercle Social*'s magazine, *La Chronique du Mois*. The editors of the publication, while progressively radicalised over the course of 1791-92, still favoured some enlightened steering of popular participation. Yet from Oswald's tract, it appears that he did not see any incompatibility between his editorial role on the board of *La Chronique du Mois* and his own private views, which took inspiration from other sources. Unlike Williams, he chose not to publish his tract at the *Cercle Social*'s publishing house. Like Merry, with whom he undoubtedly conferred at White's hotel, Oswald developed an individual position. What united these two activists was their respective mistrust of the corrupt practices of representation, epitomised by the British oligarchic system, and their lack of reverence for precedent, particularly the work of the Constituent Assembly, which had been discredited and replaced by the National Convention. Oswald went further, both in the impertinent style of writing he adopted, but also in the degree of popular involvement in government he advocated. Merry was more reticent, his proposal conjugating elements of an energetic form of representation with measured openness to democratic involvement.

---

53 Ibid, pp. 15-16.

GEORGE EDWARDS, *IDÉES POUR FORMER UNE NOUVELLE CONSTITUTION ET POUR ASSURER LA PROSPÉRITÉ ET LE BONHEUR DE LA FRANCE ET D'AUTRES NATIONS* (1793)

George Edwards is the least known of the contributors to the constitution debate and one of the more obscure members of the *SADH*. As the contributor to the *Dictionary of National Biography* put it in the late nineteenth century, "it does not appear that Edwards attracted any attention."[54] David Erdman only fleetingly refers to him in his study of Oswald's compatriots. Yet, over the course of his lifetime, Edwards was probably the most prolific writer of all the emigrants affiliated to the Paris society, covering a wide range of interests and topics in his written output. The British Museum counts forty-two separate publications by Edwards among its collection.[55] Later esoteric offerings however, such as *Effectual Means of Relieving the Exigencies and Grievances of the Times, or of Introducing the New and Happy Era of Mankind* and *A Certain Way to Save our Country, and make us a more Happy and Flourishing People, than at any Former Period of our History* led critics to doubt his sanity.[56] Prior to his visit to France at the end of 1792, he had already written tracts on agricultural improvement and on the constitutional regeneration of Great Britain.[57] He had also published work on how to perfect national finance, the art of improving land, how to perfect medical practice in line with the ideas of Benjamin Franklin, a way to allow a declining town and its surroundings to flourish and a plan for a universal patriotic society.[58] He would present all of these works to the National Convention in early 1793, along with his tract written specifically for the constitution-makers. In the latter, he synthesised all his previous thought on the general improvement of

---

54 See *Dictionary of National Biography*, vol. 17 (1885-1900), p. 118.
55 For a brief summary of Edwards' many publications, see the entry in the *Dictionary of National Biography* 1885-1900.
56 *Effectual Means of Relieving the Exigencies and Grievances of the Times, or of Introducing the New and Happy Era of Mankind* (London: [publisher unknown], 1814) and *A Certain Way to Save our Country, and make us a more Happy and Flourishing People, than at any Former Period of our History* (London: Printed for the Author, 1807).
57 *Some Observations for Assisting Farmers and Others to Acquire the Knowledge of their Business ... as delivered January 18, 1779, at the anniversary meeting of the Medical Society of London* (London: [publisher unknown], 1779); *A Plan of an Undertaking Intended for the Improvement of Husbandry, and for Other Purposes* (Newcastle: Saint, 1783); *The Royal and Constitutional Regeneration of Great Britain: or, properly speaking, the effectual advancement of all the different national interests of the kingdom...being the discovery of the practical means of advancing and completing the political economy, the national improvements and civilization; the church, medicine, and law; the government, politics, and finances of the kingdom* (London: Debrett, 1790).
58 In his tract to the constitutional committee, Edwards drew attention to his previous publications and enclosed them with his address. Although I have been unable to locate all of these treatises, the pamphlet discussing the creation of a universal society was published in 1792 under the title of *Form and Foundation, Views and Laws Proposed for the Consideration of the Members of an Universal Society, or of a Society to be Established by some Similar Name, for the Purposes of Advancing and Completing Public Welfare, Private Happiness and Universal Peace* (London: [publisher unknown], 1792).

humanity and suggested his ideas could be applied without difficulty to France.

Little is known about Edwards apart from sparse biographical accounts and one or two appearances at London associational gatherings in 1792. Born in 1752, possibly of Welsh origin, he studied at Edinburgh University and practised medicine both in County Durham and London.[59] Like Robert Merry, he had joined SCI gatherings before his visit to Paris and was in attendance at a meeting at the Crown and Anchor Tavern on 9th March 1792. The only other future member of the *SADH* at that meeting was John Frost, whom he would have come into contact with again in the French capital. Two months later, on 4th May 1792, Edwards was again active on the London associational scene, this time taking part in a meeting of the Literary Fund at Wood's hotel in Covent Garden, where he would have encountered David Williams and Robert Merry, who were also in attendance that day.[60] Edwards was listed as one of the subscribers to the Fund in the statutes of the society. Despite his relative anonymity in the history of British radicalism, Edwards seems to have been closely involved in the activist network in the early 1790s and was keenly interested in the way in which collective efforts could generate momentum for social change.

Alger notes that by mid-December 1792 Edwards was in Paris. He probably took up immediate residence at White's hotel, as his pamphlet on the constitution, published in early 1793 from Henrik Jansen's publishing house at the Cloître Saint-Honoré, was signed off from there. He was still in the French capital in March 1793, when his name featured on the list of loyal foreign citizens drawn up by Nicholas Madgett. Although Erdman suggests that the mention of "Edwards" may in fact have been a reference to Lord Edward Fitzgerald, it seems more likely that it was George Edwards who had staked his claim to a place among the inner circle of international sympathisers.[61] Edwards, still residing at White's hotel, filed for a passport on 7th July 1793. The Convention had chosen not to take him up on his offer to work in the service of the Revolution on his agricultural, educational or public health schemes. In submitting his application for departure, he reminded President Jacques Thuriot and the other members of the *Comité de Salut Public* of his previous contribution to the debate over the new constitution and reiterated his belief in "true republicanism".[62] The

---

59 The conclusion that he was Welsh is suggested by an entry under "?George Edwards, M.D., 1752-1823; physician and writer on social economics" contained in Sir Evan Davies Jones and Herbert M. Vaughan (eds.), *The Welsh Book-Plates in the collection of Sir Evan Davies Jones, bart., M. P. of Pentower, Fishguard; A Catalogue, with Biographical and Descriptive Notes* (London: Humphreys, 1920), p. 21.
60 See the notes of attendance in the Royal Literary Fund Committee Minute Book, folio 22.
61 David Erdman did not acknowledge the place of George Edwards in the British society and it is probably for this reason that he suggests the name on the list may have been Lord Edward Fitzgerald.
62 See the passport request at AN F7/4412. Edwards' application was signed off by three members of the committee.

application was accepted by three members and Edwards probably left shortly after.

Following his return to Britain, Edwards continued to publish widely on topics ranging from the means of alleviating food scarcity to how to negotiate peace and prosperity and further British imperial interests.[63] These later publications, their titles revealing the grandiose hopes of their author to offer a complete system to regenerate humanity, prompted commentators to question his mental state. An obituary in *The Gentleman's Magazine* suggested that "his publications savour more of visionary theory, than sound reasoning," while a later commentator summed up: "It may be conjectured that his sanity was imperfect. He died in London on 17 Feb. 1823, in his seventy-second year."[64]

The features of Edwards' expansive vision of human regeneration are all present in his tract to the representatives of the National Convention entitled *Idées pour former une nouvelle constitution et pour assurer la prospérité et le bonheur de la France et d'autres nations*. He introduced his more substantial work in a short address in which he outlined his general argument. Concerned with "national regeneration", "perfection", and the means of creating a society which would ensure man's happiness, he addressed both the structure of government and the means of securing social improvement. Believing that man's natural destiny was perfect social harmony, he showed faith in the potential for prosperity and happiness that the Revolution offered. He also offered his services to the Convention, presenting himself as a "soldier in your cause," and hoping that a role could be found for him in the pursuit of agriculture, medicine or public instruction.

In the same year as his departure to Paris, Edwards published a pamphlet entitled, *Form and Foundation, Views and Laws Proposed for the Consideration of the Members of an Universal Society, or of a Society to be Established by some Similar Name, for the Purposes of Advancing and Completing Public Welfare, Private Happiness and Universal Peace*. The copy held at Harvard University contains a signature from Edwards and notes his address as Coleman Street, the same as that which featured on the Literary Fund list of subscribers.[65] Edwards must have been deeply involved in associational culture in the early years of

---

63 *Radical Means of Counteracting the Present Scarcity, and Preventing Famine in the Future :Including the Proposal of a Maximum Founded on a New Principle, to which is Prefixed, an Address to the Legislature, on a Plan for Meliorating the Condition of Society at Large* (London: Johnson, 1801); *A Plain Practical Plan, by which Great Britain may Extricate herself from her Present Difficulties, Procure the Blessings of Perfect Peace, Prosperity, and Happiness, and Dispense them to the Whole World* (London: [publisher unknown], 1808); *The true original scheme of human economy, applied to the completion of the different interests, and preservation, of the British empire; or, Heads, proposing the establishment of the third, the British dispensation* (Newcastle-Upon-Tyne: [publisher unknown], 1808).

64 *The Gentleman's Magazine*, vol. 134 (1823), p. 569. See also *Dictionary of National Biography*, vol. 17 (1885-1900), p. 118.

65 I have not yet seen this copy of the pamphlet, but the details are from the Bodleian Library holding note.

1792, nurturing a hope that such reforming initiatives would bring about social renewal and help to improve his own prospects. In his *Adresse aux citoyens législateurs*, Edwards makes reference to this hope of creating a far-reaching culture of universal benevolence. He extols the "universalists", those French citizens and foreign patriots dedicated to the pursuit of man's happiness and best-placed to realise the perfection of humanity that his integral system was designed to achieve.

The main tract itself does show some of the signs of the "unconscious humour of the egotist deeply persuaded of his mission" referred to in the *Dictionary of National Biography* entry. Edwards' contribution to the constitution debate is a plan for the renovation of the entire social system, which he believed would graft concern for "humanity" on to the core revolutionary values of liberty and equality. Although he does tackle the question of political reform, his major concern is about the need to overhaul society on a wider scale. He divides his tract into a series of thematic categories which included agriculture, education, medicine, national improvement, manufacturing and mechanics, the sciences and fine arts, the division of government, state administration, religion, laws, taxes, war and peace, the rights of man in society, the police and finally the cause of liberty and equality. There are some echoes in Edwards' tract of David Williams' ideal delegate, who must be well-versed in the arts, agriculture and manufacturing.

Edwards, unlike Williams however, takes little account of the precise context in which the constitution of France was to emerge, although he does laud republican government as being particularly effective at warding off public corruption. He sees his comprehensive social and economic vision as encompassing all countries, whether monarchical or not. Many of his ideas, as he acknowledges, were forged before the Revolution took place, but this did not make them any less applicable to the French context. His 'plan' had been previously presented to the British government, yet the funds required for its application (four to five hundred pounds) had been withheld, evidently a source of rancour for the author. He insists that governments must be prepared to invest in order to bring about the types of structural changes needed for social progress. For Edwards, this implied investment in the schemes of individual philosophers and improvers.

Edwards considers perfection in human development desirable and achievable as "men by nature are led towards greatness, and goodness."[66] Man had the capacity to eradicate misery and bring about far-reaching social change. He dwells on the idea of "regeneration" and how to inculcate "ordinary minds" with taste, sentiments, passions, virtue and knowledge.[67] Yet while fundamental changes in the social fabric were needed, any new system had to be based on both simplicity and a wide social reach. All

---

66 Edwards, *Idées pour former une nouvelle constitution*, p. 20.
67 Ibid, p. 12.

aspects of society – the political system, taxes, elections, agricultural improvement, laws – should be grasped by the "ordinary man". For this, he advocates the wide circulation of ideas, techniques and knowledge through the printing of books to be sold at low cost. New laws should be printed in language understandable to the ordinary person and circulated in one bound volume. All new advances, whether in science or the arts, should be shared. This repeated insistence on the coalescing of knowledge aimed at improvement was reminiscent of reforming societies more widely. The rules of many eighteenth-century societies included the fact that no new technique of improvement was to be concealed from another member in the interests of the general advancement of knowledge.[68]

Linked to the notion of simplicity, and with echoes of both the Jeffersonian vision of an ideal society and the theories of writers such as Mary Wollstonecraft, Edwards celebrates agriculture rather than commerce as the principal motor of human society. He added to this pillar of social life both medicine and education. It was in these three areas that he felt most competent and willing to offer his expertise to the revolutionary government. His views on medicine were primarily based on the work of Benjamin Franklin. On education, Edwards believed that crime would be eradicated if all people had received the necessary public instruction. He also argues that the state should bear the burden of paying for both the relief and education of the poor. While the rich were able to provide for their own families, they could not be expected to fund the improvement of the less well-off. As a result, he suggests the state should pay for the teaching of reading, writing, crafts and arithmetic to children from the lower echelons of society. Poor children with talent needed to be encouraged, while science and art textbooks had to be written in a language which was easily understood. Edwards was the only British contributor to the constitution debate to actively address the issue of economic redistribution and state funding of social reform. He had a utopian vision of the potential of medicine to remove the inequalities between the wealthy and the poor and eradicate destitution. Yet he laments the lack of doctors in England compared to the size of the population. His views pre-empt many of the actions begun in the early nineteenth century on poor relief and more equitable distribution of education and social care.[69]

Edwards sees republican government as preventing the exercise of illegal power by public servants as all would be directed to the good of the nation. While popular or primary assemblies should choose members of the

---

68 See Clark, *British Clubs and Societies*, p. 1.
69 In the early nineteenth century, radical activists were engaged in a debate over whether parliamentary reform was the best means by which to achieve a fairer society or whether politics was incidental in the quest towards fairer economic distribution of riches. In the mid-nineteenth century, the Chartist movement was characterised by this tension between the language of economic and political reform. See Gregory Claeys, 'Owenism and the emergence of social radicalism, 1820-35', *Politics and Anti-Politics in Early British Socialism* (Cambridge: Cambridge University Press, 1989), pp. 169-207.

legislative government, those executing power should be from the highest ranks of men, nominated by a supreme authority and with spotless public reputations. Even the simplest person could exercise the right to choose a representative: "It is time that we stopped looking at the people with disdain; as amongst all nations we are scathing of conditions we think beneath us; thus the people are everywhere demeaned."[70] In a passage reminiscent of the Jeffersonian celebration of the humble farmer, Edwards suggests that agriculture should replace etiquette, that people should supplant kings, and that the modest cottage should oust the palace.

On the finer details of the formation of government, Edwards, like David Williams, argues that the subdivision of authority is preferable as information could be spread more efficiently and communication between the people and their legislators facilitated. Overseeing the work of a legislative assembly would be a "revising assembly", which would present suggestions, defend the rights of the people, and process petitions from the districts. While Williams' constitutional council would simply inform the people of national decisions, Edwards's assembly would have a more active role in communicating objections and suggestions. The assembly would be renewed every year at the same time as annual elections to the legislature and elections to districts and departments. Its role would be to make sure no changes to the constitution were made unless they had been sanctioned by at least two successive administrations. This body was conceived of as a sort of constitutional guarantor or permanent convention of the people, with an overseeing capacity.

In his tract to the constitutional committee, Edwards put forward a wide-ranging vision of social and political reform applicable to any country. He had already attempted to secure support for his agricultural plan in Britain, to no avail, as he revealed in his introduction to the pamphlet. It was possibly this refusal of the British government to entertain his ideas which led him to involvement in both the SCI and the *SADH* and which may have had some influence in his decision to support the Literary Fund initiative. He was convinced of the benefits of universal benevolence and the need for collective action to alleviate poverty, ignorance and ill-health. Yet, over and above the particular ideas on social and political improvement put forward by Edwards, it is his place at the heart of the *SADH* which must also be fully acknowledged. Although he did not sign the address of 24th November 1792, the evidence points to his having had a relatively central role in the society. He was well-known to several core members of the group, had been involved in both the SCI and Literary Fund in 1792, and spent several months as a resident of White's hotel while in Paris. Cases such as those of Edwards corroborate the view that the club had a wide reach among emigrants in Paris and drew together both more established reformers and those who had hitherto had a marginal place in the reform movement. Its

---

70 Edwards, *Idées pour former une nouvelle constitution*, p. 60.

members negotiated their own terms of interaction with the club's public agenda and often drew little distinction between their reform initiatives in Britain and their interventions in France.

While it would be misleading to suggest that British activists were pivotal in French politics, Alger's categorisation of them as "imperceptible specks in the great eddy" probably more accurately reflects historiographical tradition than historical reality. They were not silent observers and their relative marginality could sometimes be a source of leverage. Michael Rapport contends that "through their writings and influence, such foreigners had intellectual or political influence beyond their small numbers."[71] The texts penned by emigrant commentators on the republican constitution represent a wide spectrum of opinions. In late 1792 and early 1793 there was still scope for disagreement over the ideal form of a new constitution and such discord was considered an essential facet of a healthy, enlightened culture in the late eighteenth century. While no consensus emerged, it does seem that the petitioners fell into two broad groups. There were those who were generally in favour of reformed representative government, modelled on the American example, and those who preferred a system of direct democracy and greater active participation by the people in political decision-making. The former group was more closely associated with the thinking of individuals who later became known as the Girondins, while the latter took inspiration from activists in the Cordeliers Club – such as Le Sueur, Robert and Desmoulins – who adhered to classical definitions of government of the people and popular citizenship. As Jack Censer has explained, "the guiding principle of these Cordeliers in their district, their section, and their club was that the populace itself was the rightful possessor of sovereignty. From the inception of the district, there were continuous efforts to safeguard popular sovereignty against the encroachments of any representative body."[72] For Cordeliers activists, while representative government signalled the confiscation of the people's rights through the pretence of popular verification of laws, democracy was the expression of the people's will through the direct law-making process.[73] Some Cordeliers members would later go on to take part in the Montagnard ascendancy from June 1793.

---

71 Rapport, *Nationality and Citizenship*, p. 113.
72 Jack Censer, *Prelude to Power*, p. 2.
73 For a discussion of the relationship between the Cordeliers and the Girondins see Patrice Gueniffey, 'Cordeliers and Girondins: The Prehistory of the Republic?', *The Invention of the Modern Republic*, ed Biancamaria Fontana, pp. 86-106. Gueniffey shows how the Brissotins in the National Convention of 1792 became associated with the movement for representative government, favouring limited public intervention and the delegation of sovereignty to national representatives. Brissot and Condorcet disagreed on the means by which a government should collect the views of the population but both concurred on the need for the delegation of sovereignty.

As Mark Philp has argued, "the historical evidence shows that most late eighteenth-century writers drew freely on a wide range of intellectual traditions and mobilised rhetoric from a variety of political languages."[74] This observation is relevant to the study of British contributions to the constitution debate. There was a high degree of liberty in what members of the *SADH* chose to express and how they conveyed both their thoughts on French regeneration and their hopes for subsequent change in Britain. Although new limits came to be imposed on foreign residents in the French capital after the outbreak of war with Britain and different counter-revolutionary upsurges in the Vendée, Marseille or Toulon, for a short time, British residents could express their ideas relatively openly. This freedom did not completely disappear during the years of 1793 and 1794, though it was severely proscribed. John Hurford Stone, writing to his brother during the period of emergency government, contended that "I am not affected by it myself: on the contrary, having the full enjoyment of liberty as an artist, and also the confidence of my not being hostile to the cause of liberty, I am more than free. I am respected, tho' I keep aloof from all political acquaintance."[75] Freedom was therefore dependent on emigrants' agreement not to enter into factional battles. Independence from political attachment allowed for a wealth of literature to be written on the constitutional debate. Such texts belie the deep contradictions in the attitudes of British radicals to political reform, the role of the people in government and the extent to which France could provide a blueprint for further European transformation. These contradictions were partly accepted within the tradition of enlightened enquiry that members of the Paris society subscribed to, however, they also created deep rifts under the pressure of emergency rule from 1793.

---

74 Philp, 'English Republicanism in the 1790s', p. 249.
75 *CCST*, p. 1226.

8

British experience in Paris under emergency rule, 1793-1794

The depositions and addresses to the constitutional committee were submitted at a crucial juncture in the Revolution, at a time when monarchy had been overthrown but uncertainty persisted over the fate of the king and the future shape of the new republic. The constitutional debates were overshadowed in late January 1793 by the outcome of the king's trial, his execution and the subsequent declaration of war between Britain and France, and the rallying of a counter-revolutionary alliance in Europe. Neither Condorcet's February 1793 proposal nor the Montagnard draft later in the same year culminated in an official and durable arrangement, overshadowed as they were by the fallout of and disputes following the death of the king and the eventual onset of emergency rule, under the auspices of the *Comité de Salut Public* and the *Comité de Sureté Générale* in mid-1793.

Captain Monro expected Louis XVI to be reprieved even as late as 7th January 1793, only two weeks before the king was sentenced to death. He wrote:

> There remains no doubt but the King has a great majority in his favour; when his trial will be finished is however uncertain, for there are a great number of deputies for and against him yet to speak. That with the different interruptions gives us every hope that things may take a favourable turn, and his life to a certainty be saved.[1]

---

1   Captain Monro to Lord Grenville, 7th January 1793. *Despatches of Earl Gower*, p. 273.

Even the most ardent British supporters of the Revolution and its republican departure balked at the prospect of regicide. Some had manifested their opposition to the death penalty in their writings, while others were acutely aware that the execution of Charles I during Britain's civil wars was seen as having undermined rather than furthered the cause of republicanism. The particular way in which the trial of Charles I had been conducted, the apparent ruthlessness of those who signed the king's death warrant and the timely and successful portrayal of the king as a martyr after his death on the scaffold were considered as elements crucial in the failure to establish enduring republican rule in the mid-seventeenth century.[2] Such issues were raised by both Thomas Paine and some French deputies in the debates in the Convention during the month of January. Paine, who favoured sending the king into exile, reminded the Convention of the role of Louis XVI in the American War of Independence and argued, in his opposition to regicide, that "what might appear today as an act of justice will later appear only as an act of vengeance."[3] Paine's friend Brissot voiced a similar point of view in the trial, stating that all hostile foreign powers wanted to see the death of the king as they believed it was the surest way of achieving the restoration of royalty.[4] Pierre Guyomar, speaking on 2nd January 1793, also showed concern that the people would suddenly be moved by the pathos of regicide to feel pity for the former ruler and insist on the restoration of monarchy in the person of an infant king.[5]

The execution of Louis XVI and the international diplomatic crisis it engendered proved a crucial turning point for British radical residents of Paris. Some were visibly shocked by the outcome of the trial. Many recognised that the decision would more than likely precipitate war with their

---

2   The full title of Charles I's confession was *Eikon Basilike, the Pourtracture of his Sacred Majestie, in his Solitudes and Sufferings. With a perfect Copy of Prayers used by his Majesty in the time of his sufferings. Delivered to Dr. Juxon Bishop of London, immediately before his Death* (London, 1649). The tract aimed at making a martyr of the deposed king who had been executed by the parliamentary tribunal.

3   *Le Moniteur Universel*, vol. 15, Wednesday 23rd January 1793.

4   "Opinion de Jacques-Pierre Brissot, sur le jugement de Louis XVI, prononcée dans la Séance du Premier janvier 1793", Supplément au no. 107 du *Journal des débats et des décrets*, vol. 41 (1795-1814): "Toutes les puissances veulent la mort de Louis...Elles veulent sa mort, parce qu'elle leur semble un garant de la restauration de la royauté, comme la mort de Charles Ier pour l'Angleterre ; elles la veulent enfin, la mort de Louis, et c'est un fait dont on ne peut douter, puisque non-seulement aucune n'a réclamé avec sincérité en sa faveur ; puisque toutes au contraire ont fait des armements et des menaces qui ne pouvaient qu'accélérer son supplice. Oui, citoyens, la même comédie qui s'est joué en Angleterre, lors de la mort de Charles Ier, elle s'est jouée de nos jours. Alors le cabinet de France avait l'air d'intercéder, et il payait les Cromwells qui le mirent à mort."

5   Pierre Guyomar, 'Suite de la discussion sur le jugement de Louis Capet', *Le Moniteur Universel*, vol. 15, 4th January 1793, p. 32: "Quant à moi, je craindrais bien plutôt que le peuple, égaré par les factieux qui l'agitent aujourd'hui, ne passât tout-à-coup de l'indignation à la pitié, et qu'il ne rendît à un enfant, ou à tout autre, les honneurs que les Anglais accordèrent à Charles II, et qu'il n'accusât ses représentants d'usurpation ou de tyrannie."

home country, a situation which would inevitably jeopardise their safety in Paris. David Williams embarked on an abortive mission to Britain on behalf of his Girondin associates, in an attempt to avert the course of war, yet on 1st February 1793, after the French ambassador the Marquis de Chauvelin was expelled and sent back to France, the Convention declared war and Britain headed up a counter-revolutionary assault on the new republic.

The deposition of the king and the founding of the new nation had a lasting and profound impact on the way in which foreign residents were perceived within the new regime. According to William Rogers Brubaker, the inscribing of cosmopolitanism in revolutionary ideology and the encouraging of foreigners to seek refuge in France paved the way for a rift once the nation replaced the monarchy as the source of sovereignty. Brubaker states, "The Revolutionary invention of the nation-state and national citizenship thus engendered the modern figure of the foreigner – not only as a legal category but as a political epithet, invested with a psychopolitical charge it formerly lacked, and condensing around itself pure outsiderhood."[6] Once war was underway and the republic threatened on all fronts, radical members of the Convention increasingly saw in the presence of foreigners, and in particular British nationals, the potent risk of counterinsurgency and the undermining of the Revolution. Robespierre complained, "All our miseries are the work of Pitt and his associates... Do you know Thomas Paine and David Williams? ... They are both traitors and hypocrites."[7]

By March 1793, in the prevailing atmosphere of war, all British residents had to obtain permission from their local section to leave Paris. As anxiety spread about counter-revolution inspired from both within and without, such individuals and their families were also monitored more closely by local *comités de surveillance*. Foreign residents now had to justify their adherence to the Revolution or risk expulsion. On 22nd March 1793, Nicholas Madgett, a translator for the revolutionary administration and Irish radical, put forward a list of twenty-two British, Irish and American residents who could be counted on for their loyalty to the republic and who could be entrusted with the mission of identifying known foreign spies working for the Pitt government. Among those named as trusted residents were four of the five petitioners who had shared their blueprints for reform with the constitutional committee. George Edwards, Robert Merry, Joel Barlow and John Oswald were on Madgett's list, as were those members of the *SADH* who appear to have continued to support the Revolution even after the trial and execution of the king. William Choppin, Robert Rayment, Robert Smith and Sampson Perry were all cited, as were William Jackson, Bernard MacSheehy and William Johnson. John Frost featured on the list, despite his

---

6 William Rogers Brubaker, 'The French Revolution and the Invention of Citizenship', *French Politics and Society*, 7.3 (1989), p. 44.
7 Quoted in Jones, *The Anvil and the Hammer*, p. 124.

waning enthusiasm after regicide, as did James Gamble, who had helped to raise funds for the victims of the Tuileries. Those individuals whose names were put forward appear to have been those whose adherence to the Revolution and its republican direction was most marked. The list also included Citizen Arthur however, an informant who later denounced John Hurford Stone to the National Convention.[8]

Those who went to France or remained in residence in late 1792 and early 1793 were individuals who welcomed the republican turn in France, yet they were ironically those for whom the repercussions of the measures against foreigners and emergency rule would be particularly acute. It was those who had arrived after, not before, 1789 who were considered most likely to be agents of counter-revolution sponsored by foreign tyrants since they were considered more likely to have been sent by the Revolution's detractors than those who had taken up residence before the overhaul of the *Ancien Régime*. This was one of the many ambiguities which characterised the treatment of foreigners, particularly those whose adherence to the Revolution remained strong, in the radicalised phase of the Revolution.[9] Philipp Ziesche summarises the paradox, noting "because they invested so much power in emotional honesty, which signified political integrity, French republicans and their foreign supporters harbored a profound, phobic suspicion that the most virtuous-looking exterior could mask a festering core of evil. The longing for transparency fed political paranoia.[10] Ziesche points out, "It was precisely the efforts of some foreigners to build a cosmopolitan community by making a spectacle of their sensibility and universal benevolence that raised suspicion among the Montagnards."[11] Authentic and vocal support for the Revolution, the membership of pro-republican societies and visits back and forth to Britain became, thus, sources of suspicion rather than proof of loyalty to the ongoing Revolution.

Yet despite the changing status of the foreigner within the new French republic, some foreign residents still managed to negotiate a tenable position within the nation. Michael Rapport suggests, "Foreigners could still find outlets for their political energies and could therefore exercise influence in revolutionary politics. The revolutionaries accepted these efforts provided they coincided with French interests and for as long as the foreigners concerned were ideologically committed to the Revolution."[12] Despite the

---

8   Archives Diplomatiques, Affaires Étrangères, Correspondance Anglaise, vol. 587, folio 28, quoted in Woodward, *Une Anglaise*, p. 102.
9   The importance of 1789 as a watershed, dictating responses to foreigner activities in France, is patent in the incarceration records of the *Comité de Salut Public*. Detainees such as *SADH* member Robert Rayment had to account for their revenues and profession "before and after the Revolution." The distinction would seemingly highlight any inconsistencies in behaviour which might betray counter-revolutionary intent hidden behind support for the Revolution.
10 Ziesche, *Cosmopolitan Patriots*, p. 85.
11 Ibid, p. 86.
12 Rapport, *Nationality and Citizenship in Revolutionary France*, p. 142.

apparent exclusivity of citizenship therefore, British residents were sometimes able to question these new boundaries and achieve a measure of leverage within the regime, benefiting from a degree of protection from the revolutionary authorities.[13]

Over the course of early 1793, the divides which had appeared in the Convention during the trial of the king widened, and by early June those labelled as 'Girondins' had been ousted from the National Convention and deputies from the 'Montagne', associated with *sans-culotte* activism in the Parisian localities, assumed effective control of government. After the Girondin expulsions, a significant core of British men and women sought to secure passports out of the country, fearing the repercussions of the conflict on foreigners resident in Paris. Some had themselves associated with Girondins, either in friendship circles or through political missions, and their connections marked them out as potential enemies of the nation, provoking suspicion among members of the ascendant revolutionary committees. Appeals to universal benevolence and common humanity, widespread at the height of revolutionary cosmopolitanism, were now perceived as sham attempts to secure passage out of the country and probably proof that those uttering such oaths of loyalty were actually enemies of the Revolution.

Alger suggests that John Hurford Stone had begun helping forty of his fellow countrymen to leave France and cross to Dover in February 1793, yet most passport requests were received by the French administrative authorities over the course of May to July 1793 when British residents began to struggle financially. Mary Wollstonecraft relied on Thomas Christie's visits for financial support, describing in a letter to Johnson in May 1793 how Christie had provided her with thirty pounds. In July of the same year she recorded a further personal financial transaction with Christie, presumably advancing her for contributions to the *Analytical Review*. Robert Merry, driven to distress by his inability to access funds or feed his family, noted the extreme financial insecurity of fellow British residents in Paris during the early months of 1793. In his petition for a passport out of France, written from Calais, Merry attempted to secure relief for other Britons stranded at the French port and for whom the passage back to Britain would prove costly: "If you could acquire a decree to ensure that the passage from Dover will be open for people to leave without any charge at all, you will do a great

---

13 Michael Rapport's work differentiates between the xenophobic rhetoric of the French government and the actual handling of foreigners by the revolutionary authorities. In looking at the pragmatic implications of the presence of alien nationals in revolutionary France, he identifies a significant discrepancy between principle, which was increasingly exclusive in the definition of citizenship, and practice, whereby foreigners retained some of their positions and privileges. He suggests that although the nation came to be a vital factor in the definition of civic belonging, foreigners were not simply excluded on the grounds of their origin. A cosmopolitan vein still ran through revolutionary politics, and if foreign nationals were persecuted it was more often because of their suspected political affiliations than their country of birth. The scope for political dissent narrowed and orthodoxy was increasingly the only legitimate mode of political expression.

service to a large number of unfortunate Englishmen who are here without any means and in absolute destitution."[14]

Writing to Jacques-Louis David on 9th May 1793, Merry requested a passport to leave the port of Calais and return to England, claiming material want as the primary reason for his and his family's departure. His request was granted by the *Comité de Sûreté Générale* on 13th May 1793. He grounded his plea in a portrait of his persistent loyalty to the Revolution. He expressed his ardent wish for the "good cause" to prevail over treachery and claimed to be a "true sans-culotte," hailing the Montagne in his conclusion.[15] He maintained that he would be more useful to the cause of liberty in England than in France. In Paris he could not serve the Revolution, but in England he could pursue activities and focus on the exporting of universal liberty. The letter conveys the acute desperation in which he and his family found themselves. It is abrupt and lacking the usual modes of politeness. Merry explained how his business affairs were calling him home and how he and his wife were in an unbearable financial predicament rendering their continued residence in France untenable. The recurrent spelling mistakes and one slip into English emphasise the desperate circumstances surrounding his appeal. A second letter a day later provided further arguments to support his request. He stated that his family would soon die of hunger if they were not permitted to leave the country.[16]

Robert O'Reilly petitioned the Convention on 12th June 1793 for a temporary passport to return to Britain in order to testify as a witness in a trial. In his plea, O'Reilly emphasised his status as a "fellow citizen." It was noted in the granting of his request that he had also served in the National Guard under the revolutionary authorities. O'Reilly did return to France after the trial as he would later edit the *Annales des Arts et Manufactures* with Barbier de Vémars. George Edwards also used his previous political activism to argue his case for a passport to return home in July 1793. He outlined his unequivocal support for the Revolution and reminded the committee that he had been the author of a number of political essays presented to the National Convention. He concluded by reiterating the unblemished nature of his principles and zealous support for the Revolution, portraying himself as a partisan of true republicanism. His request, sent on 7th July 1793, was granted.

It is difficult to determine whether service to and professed loyalty to the regime had any significant bearing on decisions to grant or refuse passports for British residents to return to Britain. Other foreign subjects who had no

---

14 AN F7/4412 contains Robert Merry's petition for a passport to Jacques-Louis David: "Si vous pourrez procurer un décret que la [*sic*] passage ici à Douvres soit ouverte pour les gens de sortir sans que personne pait [*sic*] entier, vous rendrai [*sic*] une très grande [*sic*] service à un grand nombre des malheureuses [*sic*] Anglois qui sont ici sans ressource et absolument dans la misère."
15 AN F7/4412 contains Robert Merry's passport petition to Jacques-Louis David.
16 AN F7/4412.

particular involvement with the *SADH* or with the political affairs of the Revolution more generally were also granted free passage, sometimes, but not systematically, with slightly more difficulty and without the intervention of influential individuals known to them personally. Two Irish medical students were granted passage out of France by the Convention after a first request had been turned down on account of their being "English". A doctor from the faculty of Edinburgh appealed for a passport to return home for urgent matters on 6th July 1793. His request was also accepted. William Kirby, a resident of Dunkirk for two years, who described himself as a negotiator, was granted a passport in response to his request of 28th June 1793 asking to return home to deal with family affairs in London. A collective petition was sent by a group of British inhabitants of Boulogne-sur-Mer on 19th June 1793. They claimed that they were no longer able to access their income and, without any financial means, were seeking passports to return to Britain.[17] While passports could therefore be granted to a varying set of individuals, those British residents who had been involved in revolutionary politics in France used this background as an argument to support their requests for passports to the respective committees. It is likely that, for some, these allusions to revolutionary partisanship had some impact on the success of their request.

RESIDENCE AFTER JULY 1793

Further decrees were promulgated in mid-1793 which targeted foreign residents who had arrived in France after 1789. Prompted by events such as the capture of Toulon by the British fleet and recurrent rumours of espionage activities, the Law of Suspects was enacted on 17th September 1793 and demanded strict ideological conformity with the Revolution's tenets. British residents also had their property seized and their assets frozen. According to Alger, "All British merchandise in stock was to be given up, an indemnity being promised, and ultimately even English placards and shop-signs were forbidden. A teacher of languages had even to announce lessons in *American*."[18] Maximillian Robespierre defended the arrest of all foreign nationals whose governments were at war with France, declaring:

> I distrust without exception all those foreigners whose face is covered with a mask of patriotism and who endeavour to appear more republican and energetic than us. It is these ardent patriots who are the most perfidious creators of our problems. They are the agents of foreign powers, for I am well aware that our enemies cannot have failed to say: Our emissaries must affect the warmest

---

17 AN F7/4412. Petitioners included Elizabeth O'Neill, Richard Bowater, Jane Price Wilson, Margaret Wilson and Charlotte Youd.
18 Alger, *Englishmen*, p. 144.

and most exaggerated patriotism to be able to insinuate themselves more easily into out Committees and into our assemblies.[19]

On 23rd September 1793, British and Irish nationals petitioned the authorities for special consideration in "an address presented to the National Convention, by the English, Irish, and Scottish residents of Paris and its environs, 23 September 1793, Year II of the Republic."[20] In the address, they reiterated their support for the Revolution and expressed understanding of the need to defeat its enemies. Yet they also argued the case for "justice" and "hospitality" in the light of the severe laws applicable to foreigners that had been introduced six days earlier. They reminded the Convention that, as foreign radicals, they had come to Paris to seek "asylum" as "friends of universal liberty" and requested that their plight be reconsidered. The fact that residents were now based in Paris and its "outskirts" hints at the decision taken by men and women such as Mary Wollstonecraft and Thomas Paine to seek a calmer environment away from the hub of events at this turbulent time. However, the presentation of such an address also suggests that the associational culture that had been fuelled by gatherings at White's hotel did not dissolve with the departure of some foreigners in the summer of 1793 and in spite of the increasing suspicion that foreign residents were held in. On the contrary, it was an essential source of support in the face of the punitive measures instituted against British nationals.

Sophie Wahnich and Marc Belissa suggest that from late 1793 a change of emphasis occurred in the discourse of the French revolutionary administration. While the liberticidal crimes of the British had hitherto been attributed to the corrupt Pitt ministry, and war declared on the apparatus of power rather than the people themselves, from late 1793 the British populace itself was seen as complicit in the crimes of its government and therefore a legitimate target in the ongoing war effort.[21] For the revolutionary leadership, the British people, in failing to resist their tyrannical rulers, had sullied the name of liberty. Failure to rise up in the face of oppression was considered an outright betrayal of universal natural law. It ultimately justified the decision, embodied in the decree of 7 Prairial (26th May 1794), of the French authorities to no longer take prisoners of war but to fight each man to the death.[22] Not to punish a guilty population would be to make the

---

19 'Séance du 16 octobre 1793' in Robespierre, *Oeuvres* quoted in Ziesche, *Cosmopolitan Patriots*, p. 83.
20 The address is held at the Archives des Affaires Étrangères at La Courneuve Paris. I am grateful to Mary-Ann Constantine for drawing my attention to this document and sharing its contents. Archives Diplomatiques, Affaires Étrangères, Correspondance Anglaise, vol. 588, folio 1.
21 See Sophie Wahnich and Marc Belissa, 'Les crimes des Anglais: trahir le droit', *Annales historiques de la Révolution française* 47 (1995), pp. 233-48. See also Sophie Wahnich, *L'Impossible citoyen: l'étranger dans le discours de la Révolution française* (Paris: A. Michel, 1997).
22 In her notes to the *Collected Letters of Mary Wollstonecraft*, Janet Todd provides an alternative explanation for the decision to no longer take prisoners of war. For Todd, this was due to French anxiety at the capacity of French jails to cope with the influx of foreign captives

French guilty themselves and tarnish their claim to be the custodians of universal liberty. This was a departure from the language used in the invitation to foreigners to become French citizens in August 1792 and in the Edict of Fraternity which drew a distinction between a tyrannical government and its suppressed, but ultimately righteous, people. The French revolutionary leadership used the accusation of liberticide to cast a collective shadow over a British population refusing to rise up against monarchical despotism.[23]

The irony was of course that British radicals themselves had chastised, and would continue to chastise, their fellow countrymen for their civic apathy and failure to shoulder the mantle of active citizenship. Many British residents of Paris believed a sea change in the moral sense and civic virtue of British people was needed as well as political reform to ensure the end of oligarchy, corruption and tyranny in their home country. As Margaret Jacob has argued, "in the last decades of the century, one theme seemed to dominate the international conversation in sociable circles: the meaning and nature of democratic republics, and after 1789, the kind of personal transformation needed to create the democratic subject."[24] British radicals, partisans of constitutional and political reform, nevertheless saw themselves cast as the embodiment of liberticidal foreign crimes as the war with Britain wore on.

SURVEILLANCE

Those who remained in the capital after July 1793 were subject to ever more stringent surveillance and, in such a climate, endeavoured to display their unblemished revolutionary record to guarantee their freedom. To this end, British residents sometimes signalled dubious correspondence they had received to the revolutionary authorities, fearing that if they did not, the onus would be on them to prove their innocence if their papers were ever

---

rather than an ideological decision to fight the British to the death. She argues, "anxieties about the increasing number of war prisoners contributed to the decision of 7 Prairial (26 May) that no British prisoners be taken." See Wollstonecraft, *Collected Letters*, p. 255.

23 Notions of liberticide were not new. Etienne de la Boétie had explored the idea of voluntary servitude in the sixteenth century in his *Discours de la servitude volontaire, ou le contre-un* (1549). In his view, the condition of slavery demanded not only an exploitative master but a willing slave. A century later, John Milton, Secretary for Foreign Languages in Cromwell's Commonwealth administration, was meditating on the conditions for a successful republic in his tracts on royal tyranny, *The Tenure of Kings and Magistrates* (1650) and *The Readie and Easy Way to Establish a Free Commonwealth* (1660). He believed that for a republic to flourish, a virtuous, liberty-loving citizenry was a prerequisite. Popular disaffection with the regime in the 1650s deeply troubled Milton and much of his thinking in the 1650s focused on how to transform a servile populace, repressed by monarchical culture, into a republican citizenry through the election of worthy leaders and popular education.

24 Margaret Jacob, 'Sociability and the International Republican Conversation' in Gillian Russell and Clara Tuite (eds.), *Romantic Sociability: Social Networks and Literary Culture in Britain, 1770-1840* (Cambridge: Cambridge University Press, 2002), p. 25.

scrutinised. The wife of Christopher White, the landlord of White's hotel, reacted quickly when, on encountering her former postman in the street shortly after the family had quitted their quarters for a new residence at rue des Filles-St-Thomas, he handed her an unexpected letter, without neither stamp, date, nor signature, in exchange for the payment of twelve *sols*. The short text, written in "bad English", expressed thanks for the information provided, asked for further news to be sent and hoped that British forces would soon be at Paris. White's wife wasted no time in showing the letter to her husband, who reported it immediately to the members of the Mail section in a formal deposition. He assured the section that it was a fraudulent letter from an enemy of the Revolution. At the head of the original letter is annotated, "This is a snare to entrap C. White rec'd by Mrs White July 31 and shall be sent to the Committee of Publick Safety by me. C White." The testimony to the section provides the details of Mrs White's whereabouts and movements before and after receiving the letter, showing just how meticulous British residents had to be in order to avoid suspicion. White's haste in rushing to rue Montmartre to deliver his statement to the justice of the peace of the section showed, in his words, "once again his civic spirit and total devotion to the French republic that he has adopted as his country."[25] The episode reveals the extent to which British residents, even those associated with radical activity, such as Christopher White, had to go to ensure their flawless reputation in the French capital.[26] Mary Wollstonecraft noted this atmosphere of suspicion in a letter written in March 1794. She wrote, "The French are, at present, so full of suspicion that had a letter of James's, improvidently sent to me, been opened, I would not have answered for the consequence."[27]

HARDSHIP

Many emigrants relied on their fellow countrymen for financial assistance once the harsher measures adopted against foreigners began to take their toll and during the prison terms of British residents. On 12th January 1794, Mary Wollstonecraft wrote to Gilbert Imlay, who was still away on business, revealing how money was increasingly in short supply.[28] Hurford Stone, from his own testimony, was one of the main sources of financial assistance for struggling British residents; he noted in April 1794, "We have advanced to

---

25 See the prison file of Christopher White, AN F7/4775/52.
26 David Williams also received a compromising letter in late 1792 while residing at Paris, requesting his assistance on behalf of an émigré family at St. Omer. The letter, which celebrated the English constitution and advocated the reprieve of Louis XVI, would have provoked further suspicion had it been made public. It is quoted in Whitney R. D. Jones, *David Williams: The Anvil and the Hammer* (Cardiff: University of Wales Press, 1986), p. 124.
27 Mary Wollstonecraft to Everina Wollstonecraft, Le Havre, 19th March 1794, Wollstonecraft, *Collected Letters*, p. 248.
28 Mary Wollstonecraft to Gilbert Imlay, 12th January 1794, Wollstonecraft, *Collected Letters*, p. 245.

some of them, but can do no more."[29] Writing to his brother, he claimed, "I have shared with my imprisoned countrymen my own money, till I have none left."[30] He went on to reiterate his role in the relief operations in later correspondence: "I am indeed the chief support of my unfortunate countrymen; and my time is employed in relieving and alleviating their wants."[31] Yet Stone's own financial situation was increasingly precarious, despite earlier reassurances to his brother William. He relied on sums deposited into his bank account from his brother and funds in Switzerland. Stone noted in April 1794, "The laws renewed against the foreigners, without distinction, will drive most if not all the English, who resided at Paris, to the extremest distress; there are no exceptions it seems."[32] Foreigners were barred from accessing their belongings, had their accounts frozen, were obstructed from withdrawing funds from bank accounts and were pursued for outstanding debts. Their political loyalty, despite untarnished records of supporting the Revolution, was cast into doubt. Robert Smith even provided financial receipts of donations offered to the cause of freedom as proof of his fidelity to the Revolution. Such difficulties, along with prolonged incarceration, had severe financial repercussions on British residents of Paris and many never recovered from the losses they incurred. Robert Rayment revealed his perilous financial situation in the information sheet filled out on his arrest on 17th November 1793. In the section reserved for details of his profession before and during the Revolution, the information given read, "his income, being dependent on his trade as a negotiator and cultivator, has suffered severely by the events of the moment and are as of today reduced to nothing."[33] Stone also finished his life in abject poverty after his printing enterprise collapsed in 1816, not long before his death. Some British nationals managed to leave the country, however, even as incarceration loomed. In November 1793, Thomas Paine helped to secure passports out of France for his fellow lodgers at rue du faubourg Saint-Denis, William Choppin and William Johnson, both of whom made their way to Basel in Switzerland.

INCARCERATION

Those British residents who did not seek or secure passage out of France in the spring and early summer of 1793 were for the majority detained in improvised French jails such as the Luxembourg, the Madelonnettes and the Benedictine convent. John Hurford Stone was arrested in October 1793, and

---

29 *CCST*, p. 1265.
30 Ibid, p. 1225.
31 Ibid, p. 1226.
32 Ibid, p. 1265.
33 AN F7/4774/88. In the file on Robert Rayment details are included of his situation during the Revolution: "Son revenu dépendant de son industrie comme Négociant et Cultivateur, a beaucoup souffert par les évenemens du tems, et se trouve aujourd'hui réduit à rien."

again in April 1794, after the decree of 27 Germinal An II which signalled the second, more intense phase of emergency rule.[34] Perry was imprisoned in the Madelonnettes jail until 22nd November 1794, having been arrested under the terms of the laws against foreigners in late 1793, while Henry Redhead Yorke also spent time in French jails before returning to Britain.[35] Thomas Christie was briefly detained from 2nd to 7th August 1793 under measures taken against foreigners arriving after 14th July 1789, though was quickly granted free passage to Switzerland with his daughter before continuing the pursuit of outstanding debts owed to him by the city of Paris.[36]

The archives of the *Comité de Salut Public* suggest that Robert Smith was detained a first time in August 1793 before being released by special order. He was taken into custody again however in October 1793, in view of his having been "born in England," this time to be held in the Maison des Ecossais until 16th October 1794. Two weeks before Smith's release was granted, he wrote to the members of his Le Pelletier section to request access to his private papers which had been locked away since his apprehension a year earlier.[37] Smith, who had come to France in 1791 partly to try to restore his own failing health (he was plagued by chronic asthma), suffered physically while in detention. He had a severe bout of gout and his asthma worsened, prompting the authorities to take the unusual step of granting permission for his own private doctor to visit him to treat his condition. Smith's wife also raised the issue of his deteriorating health in her plea to the authorities for his release in December 1793. Robert Rayment was arrested on 10th October 1793 in the same section as Robert Smith before also being transferred to the Maison des Ecossais on 18th November of the same year.[38] In his plea for liberation in August 1794, following the fall of Robespierre, he stated that he had been arrested "by virtue of the law against the English in France." The account goes on, "Or if there is another reason other than that of fortune and his birth in England, he is perfectly ignorant."[39]

Authorisation was given for the arrest of Thomas Paine and Anacharsis Cloots on 27th December 1793 after they were denounced in the National Convention. Their papers were also seized and examined and Paine was incarcerated in the Luxembourg the following day.[40] Paine's friend Sampson Perry wrote later that the author of *Rights of Man* had been imprisoned quite simply because he had been born in a country at war with France. Paine, who

---

34 AN F7/4775/23. This file includes documents relating to the arrest of John Hurford Stone. Stone's arrest had been provoked by the deposition of Citizen Arthur who denounced him as a British spy.
35 AN F7/4774/69 and F7/4775/13 provide details of the liberation of Sampson Perry.
36 AN F7/4648. Thomas Christie's prison file.
37 AN F7/4775/20/3. Sir Robert Smith's prison file.
38 AN F7/4774/88. Robert Rayment's prison file.
39 AN F7/4774/88.
40 AN F7/4774/61 Thomas Paine file.

also suffered from illness while in the Luxembourg prison, wrote to James Monroe: "Eight months I have been imprisoned, and I know not for what, except that the order says that I am a Foreigner."[41] British residents more readily linked their detention with laws passed against foreigners than with what might have been viewed as their problematic political affiliations.

While in prison British men and women crossed paths with fellow countryfolk before moving on to different locations or securing release. Some were involved in conspiracies or attempts at escape. Detention conditions were relatively lenient in most prisons, with detainees being able to move around, hold conversations and confer on their situations. Prisoners' material distress was often accentuated in prison however. Christopher White and his wife assumed responsibility for the care of Nicholas Joyce's daughters, after they had initially been separated from their parents. The White family's responsibility was made permanent once Joyce died in prison. Those British residents who managed to procure their freedom, or who avoided incarceration, visited compatriots or French acquaintances behind bars. Mary Wollstonecraft, exempted from the general arrest of British subjects by virtue of her association with Gilbert Imlay, visited a German prisoner in detention.

Helen Maria Williams drew a portrait of the prison conditions of British detainees in her *Letters Containing a Sketch of the Politics of France, from the thirty-first of May 1793, till the twenty-eighth of July 1794, and of the scenes which have passed in the prisons of Paris*.[42] She revealed that prison chambers were organised according to links of both rank and sociability, thanks to the attentions of the prison guard "Benoit", who attended to prisoners' comforts by "placing those persons together who were most likely to find satisfaction in each other's company."[43] Despite the fear inspired by the visits of police staff such as the notorious Henriot, the chief of the Parisian military, prisoners appear to have endured detention with relative serenity and good humour. The walls of the makeshift prisons were decorated with tapestries, and those incarcerated had access to newspapers where they read the latest stories of horror and conspiracy. For Williams, it was the female prisoners who demonstrated the greatest courage and constancy behind bars, making efforts to ease the suffering of fellow prisoners despite the risks such overtures might incur:

> Those prisons from which men shrunk back with terror, and where they often left their friends abandoned lest they should be involved in their fate – women, in whom the force of sensibility overcame the fears of female weakness, demanded and sometimes

---

41 Paine, "To James Monroe", Luxembourg, 17th August 1794, *CWTP* vol. 2, *p.* 1341.
42 The volume of letters was published in 1795 in Dublin and London.
43 H. M. Williams, *Letters Containing a Sketch of the Politics of France*, p. 14.

obtained permission to visit, in defiance of all the dangers that surrounded their gloomy walls.[44]

Iain McCalman has explored the circles of sociability which formed in Newgate prison in London during the period when notable radical reformers were incarcerated under the draconian measures instituted to counter suspected treason and sedition in the latter half of the 1790s.[45] A similar pattern may have emerged in the prisons of Paris, as British residents, often close acquaintances, radical associates or business partners, found themselves detained together during this radical phase of the Revolution. Paine and Perry may have been cellmates in the Madelonnettes prison while Thomas Paine, Helen Maria Williams, Nicholas Hickson, William Newton and Christopher White were all inmates of the Luxembourg. Newton and Nicholas Joyce underwent periods of incarceration in the English Benedictines convent on rue du faubourg Saint-Jacques, while Churchill, Hickson and Rayment were detained for a time in the Collège des Ecossais on rue des Fossés Victor. Charles Churchill's wife Elizabeth was an inmate of the English convent in rue des Courcines, while other British detainees found themselves in prisons on cul-de-sac de Vigne, rue des Costes, rue des Champs Fleury and the English Conceptionist college. Old acquaintances were reunited in prison and inmates passed their time drawing and reading. Many wrote prison journals or accounts of their incarceration, which would be published on their release or posthumously.

Previous involvement with radical activities had some bearing on the terms and conditions of imprisonment and on responses to requests for release during the later months of 1793 and into 1794. In August 1793 the Minister of the Interior tried to exempt William Newton, a member of the *SADH* and former serviceman in the French dragoons, from the general arrest of British residents, presumably in view of his engagement on behalf of the Revolution. However, the attempt was unsuccessful, Newton being confined to the Luxembourg and Benedictine prisons from October 1793 to June 1794 before being executed on 6th June 1794.[46] John Hurford Stone, on the other hand, despite being arrested in October 1793 and again in April 1794, secured relatively rapid release and boasted to his brother in January 1794 of being well-treated by the authorities. He confided, "A man who has established three different manufactories in a country, has a right to some consideration; thank god I enjoy more than my share."[47] It is revealing that Stone considered his privileged treatment to be linked to his business exploits rather than his service to the Revolution. Financial and entrepreneurial success in France may have had more weight in convincing

---

44 Ibid, p. 21.
45 Iain McCalman, 'Newgate in Revolution: Radical Enthusiasm and Romantic Counterculture', *Eighteenth Century Life* 22 (February 1998), pp. 95-110.
46 Alger, *Englishmen*, p. 179.
47 John Hurford Stone to William Stone, 24th January 1794, *CCST*, p. 1221.

leading members of the revolutionary committees to act leniently towards foreigners than political activism.

When British residents were imprisoned they were invariably subject to a range of probing questions aimed at revealing their loyalty to the republic or otherwise. The following were typical categories guiding the interrogation of British subjects incarcerated in French jails and the answers would be systematically recorded in a table for each individual prisoner:

> Name of the prisoner, residence before imprisonment, age, number of children, their age, where they are, if he is a widower or married; place of detention, since when, during which period, by which order, why?; profession before and since the Revolution; income before and since the Revolution; relationships and associations; nature of political opinions shown in the months of May, July and October 1789, the 10th August, the flight and death of the tyrant, the 31st May and the crises of the war; if he has signed petitions or decree against liberty.[48]

Questions for British prisoners distinguished between their pre- and post-revolutionary activities in an attempt to discover whether their allegiance to the Revolution was sincere or superficial. They focused on the individual circumstances of each detainee and their known associations and sympathies. What was particularly important was the way in which suspects had responded to the fall of the Bastille, the removal of the king and his family to Paris, the storming of the Tuileries, the flight and death of the king, the exclusion of the Girondin members from the Convention and foreign war. They were therefore asked about the key events which characterised the French Revolution and the subsequent turn to republicanism, and required to give their opinions, which would be kept on file and possibly influence future decisions made in regard to their case.

For British subjects who had not had any significant involvement with political or pro-revolutionary activities, many of these sections were left blank. Elizabeth Mayne Churchill, the American wife of Charles Churchill, was imprisoned in the English convent, faubourg Marceaux, rue de Courcine. Under the headings "relationships" and "political opinions" no details were given. Her plea for release was based primarily on her need to provide for her young children, the youngest of whom was still being breastfed. Also cited in her favour was the fact that her husband had given

---

[48] "Nom du détenu, son domicile avant sa détention, son âge, le nombre de ses enfans, leur âge, ou ils sont, s'il est veuf, garson ou marié : le lieu où il est détenu ; depuis quand, à quelle époque ; par quel ordre, pourquoi : la profession avant et depuis la Révolution ; son revenu avant et depuis la Révolution ; ses relations, ses liaisons ; le caractère et les opinions politiques qu'il a montrés dans les mois de mai, juillet et octobre 1789 ; au 10 août à la fuite et à la mort du tyran ; au 31 mai, et dans les crises de la guerre ; s'il a signé des pétitions ou des décrets liberticides." Taken from the table of personal information filled out for Robert Rayment. AN F7/4774/88.

shoes and weapons to the republic. Christopher White also spoke out in defence of the Churchills.[49]

This contrasts with the cases of Robert Rayment and Robert Smith, whose files give a number of indications of the importance of their political activities to the way in which their characters and loyalty to the Revolution were assessed by the committees considering appeals for release. In papers relating to Rayment, a witness from his section testified to his being an "excellent patriot with good principles." The citizen confirmed that there would be no risk in according him his liberty and explained he had been introduced to Rayment by another "excellent Republican, Stephen Sayre, an American." Sayre was one of the signatories of the British and Irish address and, due to his nationality, would have been a good character witness for a British national. It is quite likely that Sayre and Rayment had collaborated on banking initiatives in the French capital and Sayre, like Rayment, had tried to devise a solution whereby American national debt, owed to France, could be refinanced to the benefit of both nations by redirecting funds through London and Amsterdam to obtain lower interest rates.[50] In his own petition to the authorities, Rayment assured the Convention that he had always behaved as an "honest republican" and offered by way of proof his fund-raising project after the Tuileries confrontation on 10th August. He asked for freedom either to remain in France or to join friends in Philadelphia. He reassured the committee that there was no question of his returning to Britain. Unlike the case of the Churchills, Rayment's table is entirely filled with his pro-revolutionary activities.[51] Rayment cited his various actions as a radical resident of Paris, which he hoped would act in his favour. Nevertheless, Rayment was not released from prison until 18th January 1795, well after Thermidor, having been first incarcerated on 17th November 1793.

Two days after Rayment's petition for liberty, Christopher White drafted a plea for his own release. White had been the target of suspicion since May 1793 when the *Comité de Sûreté Générale* ordered the *comité de surveillance* of the Mail section to make a visit to his hotel and arrest both White and two captains named Fraser and Monro (the latter being the British spy), as well as

---

49 AN F7/4648/3, file on Charles and Elizabeth Churchill.
50 See Alden, *Stephen Sayre*, p. 166.
51 "La Révolution françoise lui parût l'évènement le plus glorieux, le plus nécessaire pour amener le bonheur de l'Europe, et le désir d'y contribuer autant qu'il étoit en lui, l'amena en France. Mais en offrant ses faibles lumières par les différens plans et mémoires mis sous les yeux de la Nation et de ses Magistrats, il n'a jamais prétendu s'immiscer sans vocation dans les affaires publiques, ou régler à sa fantaisie la marche révolutionnaire. Jamais il n'a signé, contribué ou adhéré à des pétitions ou arrêtés liberticides. Le quatrième jour après la mémorable victoire des Thuileries, il parut avec d'autres Anglois républicains de cœur, à la barre de l'assemblée nationale, pour y présenter leurs dons fraternels aux veuves et orphelins des hommes libre morts pour leur patrie le 10 août. Tous ses ouvrages, et la haine constante des aristocrates de toutes les nations, et de toutes les nuances, prouvent mieux en faveur de ses principes politiques, que ne pourroit faire une longue exposition." AN F7/4774/88.

to seize their papers and belongings.⁵² White described how, since the law of October 1793 authorising the arrest of all foreigners, his imprisonment and the confiscation of his possessions had led to his descent into poverty, exacerbating his poor health. He suffered from hydropsy and his physical fitness had been much depleted during his period of incarceration. He also complained of the extreme sorrow which his condition had plunged him into. In petitioning the authorities for his freedom, he requested that his belongings be restored and demanded either a return on the money invested in the Carmelite mill project or for his property to be returned to him. He highlighted that in his present condition he was deprived of all means of providing for his family.⁵³

In his appeal to the *Comité de Salut Public* for his release from prison, Christopher White mentioned the economic situation of the orphans of his business partner Nicholas Joyce, who were in a dire financial predicament, worsened by the fact that Joyce's debtors were pursuing outstanding sums, despite his having died in prison on 25th February 1794. While in prison, White also attempted to secure financial reparations for Joyce's orphaned children.⁵⁴ According to one of his daughters, Joyce had been detained "following one of the three laws of the National Convention of the 1st August, 6th and 7th September 1793 in relation to foreigners" and "was, as an Englishman, arrested and put behind bars in the English Benedictines prison or rue du faubourg Saint-Jacques."⁵⁵ Joyce's daughter was unable to discover the exact date of her father's arrest but had managed to learn that his belongings had been confiscated by the republican authorities following his incarceration. White provided more substantial details on the circumstances surrounding his partner's imprisonment and death in a testimony of 8th December 1794 which Joyce's daughter eventually managed to track down through tireless appeals to French archivists in the 1830s. It stated that he was detained sometime after the decree of October 1793, an event which had "reduced us to a deplorable state by depriving us of all industrial means of providing for our families."⁵⁶ Joyce's incarceration and death had exposed his orphaned children to severe want and White informed the members of the revolutionary committee that the three girls were "in absolute need and his creditors are waiting to be paid."⁵⁷

Sir Robert Smith also drew attention to his sustained commitment to the Revolution in his various petitions for release. Like Rayment, he too mobilised the support of a number of acquaintances from his local section,

---

52 AN F7/4775/52. The file contains an order of arrest and requisition at White's hotel.
53 AN F7/4775/52 folio 78. Account of Christopher White, an Englishman, to the *Comité de Sûreté Générale*.
54 It is not clear whether Nicholas Joyce was related to Jeremiah Joyce, a member of the SCI, although Alger suggests that there may have been some connection. See Alger, 'The British Colony in Paris', p. 683.
55 AN F7/4775/52 folio 73.
56 AN F7/4775/52 folio 71. Prison file for Christopher White and Nicholas Joyce.
57 Ibid.

including his grocer, a citizen named Billet, to testify to his dedication to the Revolution. Smith seems to be one of the few British radical activists imprisoned under the emergency measures whose previous political involvement materially influenced the decision of the French authorities to order his release. Smith was imprisoned twice under the different decrees instituted after August 1793. His first detention was brought to a swift end after five of the most hard-line members of the *Comité de Salut Public* accepted petitions in favour of his flawless character and concluded that his continued imprisonment was unnecessary. He was freed by a "special order" of the committee on 8th August 1793. Barère, Couthon, Thuriot, Saint-Just and Hérault, signed the order stating, "in view of the good accounts offered on behalf of Citizen Smith, Englishman, residing in rue du Choiseul, the committee declares that he will be freed."[58] This document was reproduced systematically both by Smith, in defence of his character, and by his wife, in her petition on his behalf, after his second arrest in September 1793. It constituted precious evidence that Smith had the formal backing of the members of the inner Montagnard circle.[59] After his second arrest, Smith remained behind bars for over a year, eventually being released in October 1794. During this further period of incarceration, Smith once again highlighted his various contributions to the advancement of liberty and his fidelity to the Revolution in petitions dated 22th September 1793 and 27th December 1793. In the first, addressed to the *Comité de Sûreté Générale*, he explained how he arrived in France in November 1791 "to free myself from a despotic government," recover his health and educate his children in the spirit of freedom. He celebrated the end of slavery, the triumph of liberty and the precedence given to justice and equality, attaching an account from his section testifying to his principles and loyalty. He also included other documents in support of his appeal, notably a list of his patriotic donations amounting to 1,910 *livres*. This sum was used for providing clothes for the National Guard, assisting troops quelling the royalist uprising in the Vendée and for the widows of those who died on 10th August 1792. A second petition from Smith, written in December, reiterated the injustice of his detention. He reminded the *comité* that he had lived in Le Pelletier district for two years and that no doubt had ever been cast on his principles. He stated that, after a thorough examination of his papers, nothing had shown that he had any other aim than the public good. He went on to urge the committee to allow him to return to his family, particularly as his health was rapidly deteriorating. On his release in October 1794, the authorities recorded that his petition had been considered and taken into account in their decision to free him.

---

58 AN F7 4775/20/3, the file is recorded under the name of Smyth.
59 Smith's petition for his release is dated 22nd September 1793 and was received by the committee two days later. Yet Smith also states that he was imprisoned under the law of 8th October 1793. This discrepancy in dates is perhaps explained by a prior arrest that pre-empted the decree of October.

Like other spouses, Smith's wife also lobbied the *Comité de Sûreté Générale* for the release of her husband. Her plea was sent in mid-December 1793 and, like her husband, she claimed that their arrival in France was prompted by a desire to educate their children and live under a government which matched their principles. She confirmed that her husband had followed the Revolution unfailingly and had celebrated France's triumphs over its enemies. His principles were unwavering and his arrest would not alter his view on the Revolution. Smith's wife also attached an extract from the local section register, which testified to Smith's being favourable to the constitution and national liberty and offered him special protection. She also enclosed the August judgement from the *Comité de Salut Public*. Smith's wife stated that, while her husband would have willingly remained in prison, hoping that his arrest would further the progress of the Revolution, his ill health necessitated his urgent release. Unable to see his regular doctor and deprived of the means of exercise and treatment, his health was rapidly worsening. Smith managed to mobilise an artillery of statements in support of his case. On 22nd August 1794, members of Le Pelletier section which Smith belonged to declared they had had no other reason for arresting Smith other than his nationality. There was nothing to make them question his loyalty, principles or civic responsibility. He had lived from his own income before and since the Revolution with a substantial revenue of 30,000 *livres* and was considered a friend of liberty. On 7th October 1794 the decision to free Smith was taken by his local revolutionary committee, after consent had been given by the *Comité de Sûreté Générale*.

Smith's case demonstrates a number of things. Firstly, it highlights the energy with which British radicals could defend themselves from any association with counter-revolution and argue their case for release, drawing on the precise details of their involvement in support of the Revolution. Secondly, it shows how some British residents were able to command a high level of backing from within both the central revolutionary committees and also among representatives of their section and even local tradesmen and acquaintances. These networks of solidarity would not necessarily secure the immediate release of British radicals, but they certainly proved crucial when the circumstances proved more propitious for liberation. They provided more weight to the case for release than mere familial, medical or financial reasons. As Smith's case shows, petitions were not always individual or family-led attempts to secure prisoners' freedom but could occasionally be drafted by friends, countrymen or French acquaintances. In the case of Smith and Rayment, local members of their respective sections testified on their behalf, probably at significant personal risk.

The case of Thomas Paine is slightly different. His former political role in the National Convention, his diplomatic position as well as his nationality, combined to ensure that he would remain the longest in prison compared to most of his compatriots. Paine's detention prompted a number of American citizens to plead the case for his freedom to the *Comité de Sûreté Générale* a few days after his seizure by the authorities.⁶⁰ Probably orchestrated by Joel Barlow, the petition requested that Paine be released so he could return to his adopted country of America where he would be welcomed with "open arms" into the republic. His service to the American Revolution was cited, as was the purity of his intentions in France, despite the fact that he was not exempt from "human error", a probable reference to his perceived miscalculation in supporting the exile and not the execution of the king. The signatories of the petition were drawn primarily from East coast states and cities such as Boston, Philadelphia, New York, Connecticut and Baltimore. Apart from Joel Barlow, the men did not have any visible links with the *SADH*. Yet Paine, by virtue of his role in the American Revolution and acquaintance with Jeffersonian Republicans and other luminaries of the New England political elite, was able to command support from the influential group which included Barlow's associate Mark Leavenworth. Despite the insistence in the petition on Paine's American citizenship however, the petition was not acted upon. Paine remained in jail until well after the fall of Robespierre, eventually being released in November 1794. Paine confided to Governor Morris's successor, James Monroe, that, "about three weeks after my imprisonment the Americans that were in Paris went to the bar of the Convention to reclaim me, but contrary to my advice, they made their address into a Petition, and it was miscarried."⁶¹ Paine preferred to keep a low profile while in prison, conscious that his case threatened to create tension between the American and French republics.

The American delegation was not the only group to draft a plea in support of Paine's release. In the wake of Robespierre's fall from power, Paine's interpreter and friend, Achille Audibert, sent a letter to Jacques Thuriot, member of the *Comité de Salut Public* and president during the events of 9 Thermidor, excusing Paine for his lack of political tact in denouncing Robespierre as a "monster who should be crossed off the list of human beings."⁶² Thuriot himself, along with Marat, had objected to the authenticity of Paine's plea for the respite of Louis XVI during the debates of January 1793. Like the American petitioners, Audibert cited Paine's involvement in the American Revolution as well as American disapproval of his incarceration and his estrangement from the British government as reasons for his release. Paine's translator, Lanthenas, also sent an appeal for Paine's detention to be reconsidered in the aftermath of Thermidor. Knowing Paine personally, he volunteered his time to explain in more detail his friend's record.

Paine did not address the National Convention nor its committees until August 1794, when he wrote a letter to the Convention detailing the ignominy he had suffered. He had addressed a brief appeal to Governor

---

60 AN F7/4774/61 Thomas Paine file.
61 Paine, "To James Monroe", Luxembourg, 18th August 1794, *CWTP* vol. 2, *p.* 1343.
62 AN F7/4774/61. See the letter from Achille Audibert, Paine's interpreter in Paris.

Morris, the American representative in Paris, in February 1794, yet apart from this, he had remained almost silent during his time in prison. In his first petition to the Convention he described himself as "the unceasing defender of Liberty for twenty years," and considered his incarceration in the Luxembourg as "the work of that hypocrite and the partisans he had in the place." Due to his particular quarrel with Robespierre, who had mobilised a denunciation of Paine amongst a section of his constituency, he had "submitted with patience to the hardness of my fate and waited the event of brighter days."[63] He wrote on numerous occasions to James Monroe between August and November 1794. Monroe had replaced Morris as US ambassador in 1794 and was more receptive to Paine's pleas and also allowing him to lodge in his quarters for eighteen months after his release from prison. Writing from the Luxembourg jail, Thomas Paine told Monroe, "I am now entirely without money. The Convention owes me 1800 *livres* salary which I know not how to get while I am here, nor do I know how to draw for money on the rent of my farm in America. It is under the care of my good friend General Lewis Morris. I have received no rent since I have been in Europe."[64] Paine's appeal to Monroe showed the extent of his financial ruin in Paris.

What seems clear from these examples is that those residents who were involved in pro-revolutionary authorship or activity, with the exception of Thomas Paine, who kept a studied silence throughout his incarceration, sought to promote and publicise these deeds, thinking that it would secure their passage out of jail or passport out of the country. They incurred the risk of suspicion to plead on behalf of acquaintances, associates or countrymen. Those who were members of the *SADH*, who had written tracts, given patriotic gifts or addressed the National Convention, did not fail to raise this background in their petitions, and particular emphasis was given to character references provided by others who were considered loyal to the regime. Robert Merry addressed his petition for a passport directly to Jacques-Louis David, a colleague and acquaintance, and Robert O'Reilly, in all likelihood because of his familiarity with revolutionary bureaucracy, was able to sift through depositions made to the *Comité de Salut Public* to receive confirmation that his petition had been lost without trace. This enabled him to return to his desk and present a new petition shortly after and salvage some of the time lost through administrative oversight.

Those who could not call upon previous political engagement, or had no direct links with revolutionary leaders, would rely more on personal argument to try to secure their liberty or departure. Private commitments, business engagements, ill health or economic distress were regularly reasons cited in support of passage out of the country or requests for release. Although pro-revolutionary residents believed their former actions would

---

63 Paine, 'Letter to the National Convention', 7th August 1794, *CWTP* vol. 2, pp. 1339-40.
64 Paine, 'To James Monroe', Luxembourg, 25th August 1794, *CWTP* vol. 2, *p.* 1344.

guarantee them special treatment, in reality it is far from sure that this had any significant bearing on the attitude of the authorities towards their cases. Such men and women may have had more backing from acquaintances in their sections, or may have been able to benefit from certain familiarity with key members of the regime, yet, apart from in the case of Robert Smith, few were able to reap substantial benefits from prior political activism.

Radical residents of Paris were not exempt from the measures taken against British citizens by the French authorities, despite their visible adherence to the changes occurring in France. Those members of the *SADH* who remained in Paris after August 1793 were invariably imprisoned, some, such as William Newton, even being executed under the measures adopted towards suspected agents of foreign enemies.

Incarceration gave rise to collective efforts to improve conditions of compatriots, access financial resources on behalf of detainees, or negotiate their release from prison. Conditions of detention also gave rise to imaginative attempts by British captives to convince the revolutionary authorities of their genuine loyalty to the Revolution. While many gave very practical reasons in petitioning for their own release, others continued to appeal to the fellow humanity of their jailers and demonstrated sustained belief in the principles evoked in the early stages of the Revolution. Those who succeeded in negotiating early release, or who continued to occupy positions within the revolutionary administration, were often those who had an excellent working knowledge of the French language combined with a sustained though not dogmatic or outspoken affiliation to revolutionary politics. Acquaintance with influential figures in the administration could often be of service to British residents struggling to justify their continued presence in the capital. After the fall of Robespierre, petitions also arrived to request renewed residence in the capital. Paine petitioned the post-Thermidor regime on behalf of Robert Smith and Robert Rayment to obtain permission for them to stay in Paris after their release from prison. Liberated foreigners were expected to leave the country, yet Paine pleaded Smith's case, citing his invaluable services rendered in aiding Paine with his writing activities.[65]

The emigrant community provided emotional, financial and professional assistance to each other during this period. Those who had more leverage within the revolutionary administration or influential acquaintances, such as John Hurford Stone, Robert Merry or Thomas Paine, actively petitioned

---

65 AN AFIII/1808/369 folios 114 and 28. Paine argued that Rayment was an excellent patriot, having established the best cotton stocking factory in France, which even rivalled English cotton manufacturing. He suggested the republic should consider him a friend. Paine's appeal on behalf of Smith was supported by his translator Lanthenas. Lanthenas claimed to know Smith personally and guaranteed that he was a friend to the republic. He went on to ask the Directoire to accord Paine's request to allow Smith's continued residence in Paris.

members of the government on behalf of fellow Britons who were either in distress, in prison, or awaiting repatriation. For those who were more intimately connected with members of the revolutionary leadership, such contacts with the French revolutionary elite could prove invaluable, both on arriving in Paris, in finding outlets for creative projects and in negotiating leniency during the period of emergency rule. The examples of such mutual assistance among countrymen who had gathered at White's hotel together in the late months of 1792 show the extent to which this associational culture survived during the difficult period of 1793 and 1794.

9

Sketchers of Revolution
Eyewitness histories

In 1889 John Alger noted that while "a multitude of French memoirs, authentic or spurious, are in existence, scarcely any English observers committed their recollections to writing."[1] Even those who did write down what they witnessed were more willing to give "reflections" rather than "facts", according to Alger, a trait which, in his view, diminished their utility as historical testimony. Considering the number of British visitors to Paris during the early years of the Revolution, it is true that few complete histories emerged, particularly from among members and associates of the *SADH*. Mary Wollstonecraft completed her *An Historical and Moral View of the Origins and Progress of the French Revolution* in 1794 and Sampson Perry wrote his *An Historical Sketch of the French Revolution*, covering the period 1789 to 1795, from Newgate jail in 1796 after his return from a two-year stay in France. Other more hostile eyewitness accounts emerged, such as William Playfair's *A History of Jacobinism*, published in the same year as Perry's *Historical Sketch* and Grace Dalrymple Elliott's *Journal of My Life during the French Revolution*. Playfair had been a spectator at the fall of the Bastille and was involved in one of Joel Barlow's speculative projects. By 1796, and probably a lot earlier, his initial enthusiasm for the Revolution had waned.

Although many participants in the Revolution did not convert their recollections into formal published accounts, some conveyed their perceptions of the events they had witnessed in alternative forms, including letters, historical fragments, precise descriptions of particular moments of

---

[1] Alger, *Englishmen*, p xi.

the Revolution, and later retrospective or biographical reflections. Helen Maria Williams wrote a series of epistolary observations and Joel Barlow sketched out a plan for a history of the Revolution intended to cover the years 1789 to 1796, which was never transcribed from scribbled notes. David Williams and Henry Redhead Yorke both published later autobiographical accounts, rewriting their experience in France during the early Revolution in the light of their later scepticism and writing out their fervent involvement in the process. Equally letters remain which give us an insight into the views that British radicals such as Mary Wollstonecraft and John Hurford Stone conveyed back to friends and relatives in Britain. Manuscripts were sometimes destroyed or lost before they were published and communication was also severely inhibited after the outbreak of war in February 1793. As Alger observed, "these emigrants mostly broke off intercourse with their kinsmen, especially as after a certain date war rendered communication very uncertain and difficult."[2] The necessity of silence or secrecy, the destruction of manuscripts, and the existence of unfinished projects all give important insights into the way in which channels of transmission could be obstructed.

This chapter will therefore look at the ways in which members of the radical British community in Paris wrote about the Revolution for a domestic readership. For many writers, living through a revolution resulted in the breakdown of all sense of conventional time and prevented them from providing a clear analysis of the events they had witnessed. They chose to describe the Revolution in sketch form, often openly acknowledging their inability to achieve the impartiality required of a more detached historian. Yet despite these inhibitions, eyewitness status could also confer authority on exiled writers who could claim authenticity in their accounts in contrast to what they saw as the erroneous reports published by editors in Britain. Writers often insisted upon their presence in Paris in their writings, focusing on observations which only the spectator could note and suggesting that authentic reporting was the preserve of the eyewitness. Some continued to support the Revolution, even in its most radical phase, seeing in it the prospect of the future regeneration of humanity. Others, concerned to convey an accurate reading of the Revolution to a misinformed public at home, tried to correct the errors they believed were circulating in the British public arena. Those radicals who had become more circumspect in their support for the Revolution also tried to revise prevailing misconceptions in Britain, while drawing back from condoning some of the excesses. Finally, some writers would later express their outspoken criticism of what the Revolution had become and how it had diverged from the principles which had animated the spirit of July 1789.

Jon Klancher makes a distinction which may be useful when considering the different ways in which British writers conveyed the Revolution back to Britain:

---

2 Ibid.

> To circulate is to follow a path, however circuitous or labyrinthine its windings, along an ordered itinerary; in this motion a cultural profit accrues... But to "disseminate" is to flood through interstices of the social network, into the social cracks of the ancien régime. Dissemination takes place where there is no circulation, where there are no pre-formed patterns to guide the flow of language or ideas. What is disseminated "propagates" or reproduces itself without the orderly expansion of circulation.[3]

The Revolution disrupted the channels of transfer that had existed under the *Ancien Régime*, channels which included official diplomacy, commercial exchange and the flow of aristocratic culture, Klancher's "ordered itinerary". Writing back to a British audience during the Revolution, British radicals had no official diplomatic role and they had, more often than not, been proscribed from engagement in public debate. Their contributions to the circulation of information were often inimical to the aims of the ruling authorities, existing in the "interstices of the social network" where there were no "pre-formed patterns", to use Klancher's paradigm. Equally, radicals were writing to an audience which had been subjected to a wave of official propaganda which conflicted with the news and accounts such pro-revolutionary writers were sending. Many accounts were written with the aim of contesting these loyalist portraits of the French Revolution. Yet most authors, many of whom had been in limited contact with friends and relatives in Britain since their departure to Paris, wrote with very little firm understanding of the exact temperature of opinion in their home country.

PERCEPTIONS OF TIME AND HISTORY IN THE WRITING OF THE FRENCH REVOLUTION

The French Revolution is often seen as having founded some of the institutions and notions associated with modern Western political life, such as equality, citizenship, democracy and nationhood. It is therefore granted a degree of stature and permanence which veils the uncertainty perceived by those living through the events as witnessed at the time. Yet the revolutionary period was above all a moment of profound flux. Roger Chartier has argued that, rather than forming the coherent intellectual origins of the French Revolution, the Enlightenment was itself perpetually defined and constructed by revolutionaries looking back in hindsight in search of an intellectual heritage.[4] Developments in the Revolution, though interpreted later as the building blocks of a new order, were profoundly troubling for those living through them. While onlookers and actors in the French Revolution would have been conscious of the momentousness of the

---

3 See Jon Klancher, *The Making of English Reading Audiences: 1790-1832* (Madison: University of Wisconsin Press, 1987) 34. Klancher's analysis of "circulation" and "dissemination" is based on an investigation of Arthur Young's *Travels in France*.
4 Roger Chartier, *Les origines culturelles de la Révolution française* (Paris: Seuil, 1991).

unfolding events, capturing them, understanding them and assessing their future portent was problematic.

The cultural historian Lynn Hunt has contended that "a new relationship to time would turn out to be the single greatest innovation of the revolution."[5] She suggests, "Revolution meant rejecting the past, introducing a sense of rupture in secular time, maximising and elongating the present in order to turn it into a moment of personal and collective transformation."[6] Signs of preoccupation with time and the regenerative potential of the Revolution were discernible in the establishment of the new revolutionary calendar which invoked images of spring and the revolving life cycles. There was also an insistence on the potency of *journées*, such as the "October days" and the "August days." Days in themselves could be transformative, effectuating rupture with the past and providing the Revolution with a new dynamic. Perceptions of the Revolution and the way in which observers wrote it down were heavily influenced by this sense of temporal readjustment. Those present at the scene, while undoubtedly aware of the enormity of the convulsions they lived through, were often aware of being unable to provide an immediate balanced assessment of the events. "From the very beginning," notes Hunt, "observers rushed to publish their accounts, as if writing down the events would give them a coherence they lacked intrinsically."[7]

British observers noted the distortions of time that the Revolution appeared to effectuate. They often perceived living through the Revolution as akin to witnessing whole ages of human existence condensed into shorter periods of time. Mary Wollstonecraft wrote to Gilbert Imlay on 1st January 1794:

> The 'peace' and clemency which seemed to be dawning a few days ago, disappear again. 'I am fallen,' as Milton said, 'on evil days;' for I really believe that Europe will be in a state of convulsion, during half a century at least. Life is but a labour of patience: it is always rolling a great stone up a hill; for, before a person can find a resting-place, imagining it is lodged, down it comes again, and all the world is to be done over anew![8]

Wollstonecraft saw no end to the instability that the Revolution epitomised and saw the perpetual remaking and refashioning of the world as characterising the revolutionary condition. The events had "almost rendered observation breathless," as she would put it in her account of the Revolution.[9]

---

5 Lynn Hunt, 'The World We Have Gained: The Future of the French Revolution', *American Historical Review* (2003), p. 6.
6 Ibid.
7 Ibid, p. 4.
8 Mary Wollstonecraft to Gilbert Imlay, 1st January 1794, Wollstonecraft, *Collected Letters*, p. 238.
9 *HMV*, p. 42.

Writing her final text, a retrospective autobiographical account of her time in France, published in 1828, Helen Maria Williams suggested that the time was still not ripe for reflection. She also revealed her own perception of how time was constricted during the Revolution and how the work of lifetimes had been fitted into the space of a few days: "Today, the time for reflection has not yet come. Events sweep us up through their quick succession; we have seen enough things to fill centuries: that which could have taken up entire ages hastily came to occupy a few days of our life."[10]

Joel Barlow noted a similar sense of temporal reordering in his fragmentary notes for a history of the Revolution: "Each day of the revolution becomes an age; & he that has seen it all has lived a thousand years."[11] Sampson Perry, writing a history of the Revolution in 1796, reiterated similar sensations, noting how "it would be difficult for an historian to follow and record the events of this surprising revolution, so rapidly did they roll on one after the other. One week presented the incidents of a century."[12] The disruption of ordinary time was consistently conveyed in texts which attempted to make sense of the Revolution through writing it down.

John Hurford Stone alluded to the unpredictability of the revolutionary context in a series of letters to his brother William. The Revolution, which he considered an irresistible and "almost miraculous impulse,"[13] prompted him to write with circumspection when trying to predict the future. He wrote, "I speak to you hesitatingly about everything, nor can I speak with more assurance, till I see the event of the 21st instant… the events of the last month will have given totally a new turn, and it presents to my mind the most pleasing prospects, not only for my own interest, but for that of mankind."[14] The times were so uncertain that Stone could not make any firm business plans or "speculate".[15] British observers were therefore conscious of the difficult task of capturing the Revolution. They were aware that what they were witnessing was an event which would have a significant impact on later generations and which deformed the perception of the passage of time for those living through it, yet they regularly showed their incapacity to determine its future shape and promise.

This specific relationship to time engendered by the Revolution meant that many observers chose unfinished, rough forms in which to convey their

---

10 "Aujourd'hui on n'est pas encore arrivé à l'époque de la réflexion. Les événemens nous entraînent par leur rapide succession ; nous avons été spectateurs de choses qui eussent suffi pour remplir des siècles: ce qui aurait pu occuper des époques entières est venu se presser dans quelques jours de notre vie." Helen Maria Williams, *Souvenirs de la Révolution française*, pp. 11-12.
11 'Notes for a hist. of the Fr. Rev.', Joel Barlow Papers, 1775-1935. HL MS Am 1448 (18) folio 7.
12 *HS* II, p. 506.
13 17th January 1794, *CCST*, p. 1218.
14 16th January 1794, *CCST*, p. 1175.
15 *CCST*, p. 1176.

impressions of it. Albert Boime has noted how sketch and caricature were the primary modes of representation used by contemporary witnesses of the Revolution. Unlike a painting by an accomplished master, distinguished by its precision and polish, the sketch was a quickly-drawn attempt to render the contours of an event with a minimum of detail and calling on the imagination of the onlooker to complete it. It was characterised by energy in both choice of subject matter and style of creation and represented a condensed image with coarse outlines, allowing room for error. In addition, the sketch was a form open to amateurs. It demanded openness, improvisation and impulse rather than the consciousness of an artistic heritage required by recognised craftsmen.

In this sense, as Boime points out, sketching the Revolution in words had ideological import. In opting for more spontaneous strategies of portrayal, those commenting were elevating innovation and experimentation above precedence and history. "In such a state," contends Boime, "the paradigm of the finished picture carries a conservative signification while only the crude approximations of the caricature and sketch maintain the integrity of the initiating impulse."[16] Thus choosing to sketch events could be a philosophical stance, encompassing the irreverent subversion of conservative views on political order, history and time, of social categories and literary endeavour. For sympathisers of the French Revolution, just as written texts could be improvised, unfinished, and impressionistic, the present states of countries and their political structures could be open to innovation and need not rely on the pillars of tradition and precedent for legitimacy. Helen Maria Williams claimed that "in France it is not what is antient [*sic*], but what is modern that most powerfully engages attention."[17] Eyewitnesses were not looking to the past for inspiration but were attentive to the changes taking place in the present.

Condorcet wrote *Esquisse d'un tableau historique des progress de l'esprit humain* (Sketch for a Historical Picture of the Progress of the Human Mind) a tract intended to be brought before the public in a moment of crisis and for immediate consideration. The title chosen by Sampson Perry for his 1200-page review of the Revolution was *An Historical Sketch*, and Perry referred to himself as a sketcher of history. Mary Wollstonecraft chose the term "sketch" to describe her outline of the French character in the first of her letters on the moral state of the French nation, written in February 1793. Yet by the time she had completed *An Historical and Moral View*, she felt equipped to provide a more comprehensive philosophical account of the development of the French national character since the early Revolution. Yet even in this text, which aims at providing an objective and coherent history,

---

16 Albert Boime, 'The Sketch and Caricature as Metaphors for the French Revolution', *Zeitschrift Fur Kunstgeschichte*. 55.2 (1992), p. 258.

17 Helen M. Williams, and Neil Fraistat, *Letters Written in France, in the Summer 1790, to a Friend in England: Containing Various Anecdotes Relative to the French Revolution* (Peterborough, Ontario: Broadview Press, 2002), p. 108.

Wollstonecraft recognised the impossibility of predicting the future outcome of the Revolution. Joel Barlow, although he wrote lengthy notes for a history of the French Revolution, never converted his hastily written ideas into finished prose. Barlow was perhaps too involved in business ventures to take time to write his planned history, or he may, like other writers, have sensed the difficulty of translating hasty impressions into a polished account for publication. British eyewitnesses of the French Revolution did not seek to provide conclusive accounts and often drew attention to the flaws in their testimonies and demanded the active participation of the reader. Perry acknowledged the inadequacies of his sketch and the futility of attempts at providing a master narrative in the preface to his *An Historical Sketch*:

> I have not presumed to call this a History of the French Revolution, but am contented in giving it the title of a Sketch... Many such sketches, under the denomination of Remarks, Observations, &c. will be required to the forming a perfect history; and, indeed, many partial histories of the different portions of the great whole, will doubtless be offered to the world ere the inquisitive, in search of the whole truth, will sit down contented.[18]

The "great whole" that Perry thought would one day emerge was inaccessible to those writing from their partial viewpoints. Commenting on the Revolution could only be done with subjective bias, in the form of personal "Remarks, Observations &c." As Joel Barlow wrote in his hastily composed notes:

> A complete picture of the Fr. Rev. would be an epitome of the history of man. All his predominant passions are there developed and acted out without disguise; all the shades of his moral character exhibited in their full force, each occupying without mixture the different canton of the piece. There every one of his virtues, & his whole legion of vices, all the Sciences as far as they are yet advanced, all the ignorance that is natural to men, & all that they have hitherto acquired, the head-strong hurry of experiment, the over-cautious step of experience, wisdom, folly and unexampled valour fill their distinguished places, we there note the downfall of so many states, the formation of so many others, alliances broken, changed, renewed, Constitutions formed, sworn to, idolised, violated & proscribed, so many new opinions, new laws, new men, brought into view, driven out of fashion and laid aside.[19]

---

18 *HS* I, pp. 1-2.
19 'Notes for a hist. of the Fr. Rev.', Joel Barlow Papers, 1775-1935. HL MS Am 1448 (18) folio 3R

For Barlow, whose introductory remarks were the most complete section of his notes, the entirety of human existence was summarised by the changes occurring under the Revolution. While the history of the Revolution would be a microcosm of human existence, he affirmed, "No one man can pretend to have seen it all. Some have been too near, others too far off, some blinded by their interest or prejudices, others rendered indifferent from their want of interest or sensibility; and no man can say he does not belong in some degree to one of these classes."[20] Like Perry therefore, Barlow concluded on the impossibility of writing a comprehensive history of the Revolution, whether that be because of an author's closeness of the event, his biased viewpoint, or the sheer scale of the events to be described. Yet the status of foreigner provided a different and valuable perspective:

> I have been generally near the centre of action, perhaps sometimes too near, tho' I never have been an actor. But, being a foreigner my acquaintance with the leaders, their connexions and motives has not been so particular as I could wish; but it would be difficult even for a native to have an acquaintance more particular and at the same time more general than mine has been.[21]

In a similar way to Barlow, Perry signalled the inadequacies of both the French and the foreign perspective in writing the history of the Revolution. No vantage point could give a perfect view:

> Who will be the qualified man which shall have accompanied it through its various stages? Of what country shall he be? If a native will he not be suspected of partiality, and a desire to conceal some of those sinister incidents, which tend to diminish the merit of the whole taken together? Against a foreigner there may be no fewer objections; such as his not having had access to persons and places from whence the choicest materials were to be gathered.[22]

Writers therefore constructed their histories having given thought to their own perspective, status and partiality. They wrote with an awareness of the potential objections that would be levelled at their work. They also showed clear-sightedness as to the flaws that any history of the Revolution would display and the inability of firsthand observers, whether foreign or native, to access the complete picture. Authors nevertheless saw the potential uniqueness of the outsider's viewpoint which could give their accounts particular value when read by a British audience.

---

20 'Notes for a hist. of the Fr. Rev.', Joel Barlow Papers, 1775-1935. HL MS Am 1448 (18) folio 3V.
21 'Notes for a hist. of the Fr. Rev.', Joel Barlow Papers, 1775-1935. HL MS Am 1448 (18) folio 4R-4V.
22 Perry, *An Historical Sketch* I, pp. 1-2.

"DO NOT TOUCH ON POLITICS": WRITING, SURVEILLANCE AND SILENCE

There were a number of restrictions on the circulation of correspondence and ideas. Letters written back to Britain could be opened and scrutinised for signs of treasonable intent and correspondence was also frequently intercepted by the French revolutionary authorities concerned about the threat of counter-revolutionary emissaries and their potential links with royalist émigrés. Radicals were aware of this prevailing culture of surveillance. They identified spies in their midst, noted the opening of letters and commented on the suspicion aroused by political references in their writings. They adapted their communication methods in response, sometimes choosing to write in language which through its very conscious elimination of all political references, only served to heighten the suspicions of the British and French authorities.

Home Office informant Charles Ross noted that British emigrants were aware of the monitoring of their correspondence: "Mr Frost mentions that all the letters he has received in France must have been broke open in England, Mr. Choppin says he wrote five letters to Mr. R _ two of which were only received which will make them cautious what they write."[23] John Frost and William Choppin changed their communication strategies in response to the discovery that their letters were being opened or going undelivered. Many emigrants would also have become more circumspect in what they said openly in meetings and with fellow radicals once it became clear that spies were working in their midst. A loyalist informant wrote, "My Lord ... the situation of this unfortunate city is critical. To the point that Mr Monro considers it wise to leave... He has already been noticed and observed by his villainous countrymen... If he leaves ... I will make sure to inform you of everything, maybe better than he."[24] British residents became increasingly reluctant to allude to politics and national and international affairs in their correspondence, aware that their letters would be scrupulously examined. John Hurford Stone thanked his brother for his caution in avoiding potentially dangerous topics in his letters: "I have received your various letters, which come to me safe and unopened. I thank you for the prudence you have observed in abstaining from everything that did not immediately refer to our own concerns, because this has inspired that confidence which leaves our correspondence unmolested."[25] Omission of political references afforded foreign residents greater immunity from the reprisals sweeping the country and encouraged a degree of leniency on the

---

23 TNA TS 11/965/3510/A2. 9th October 1792.
24 "My Lord... La situation de cette malheureuse ville est bien critique. Tellement que Mr Monro le juge prudent de se retirer... il est déjà remarqué et observé par des scélérats ses compatriots... s'il se retire... j'aurai soin de vous instruire de tout, peut-être mieux que lui ..." See TNA FO 27/40, folio 82.
25 CCST, p. 1219.

part of those in power. Joel Barlow wrote to his wife in May 1793 reassuring her that "I meddle with no politics."[26]

British radicals in Paris adjusted the terms of their debates and even the modes of communication they employed as a response to this awareness that their actions and words were being scrutinised. David Worrall has suggested that one of the outcomes of increased repression on the British reform scene was a growing preference for orality. Speech became less dangerous than the written word.[27] Captain Monro himself identified an inordinate level of secrecy in the activities of the *SADH*, pointing out that "they are ashamed of their proceedings they keep everything as secret as possible."[28] Monro's observations reveal the ways in which activists cautiously veiled their activities in response to the suspicion that their associational gatherings were held in, leaving very little written trace of their discussions.

In June 1793, writing to her sister Eliza, who still held out hopes of joining her sister in Paris, Mary Wollstonecraft expressed concern that letters were not arriving and those that did make it to their destination were being opened.[29] Wollstonecraft tried to communicate with her sisters through Gilbert Imlay's American business associates, but this channel of communication appeared precarious. She advised Eliza, "Do not touch on politics."[30] At the height of the executions decreed by the *Comité de Salut Public*, Wollstonecraft wrote to Joel Barlow's wife Ruth, carefully avoiding giving her opinion on the decision of the revolutionary government to arrest all British residents, whatever the views they expressed on the Revolution: "Of the state of things here, and the decree against the English I will not speak."[31] British observers censored their writings to avoid alerting the suspicion of the revolutionary authorities.

John Hurford Stone, who preserved his liberty during most of the period of emergency rule, followed Wollstonecraft's example, writing rarely and never mentioning politics. As he explained to his brother in England, "I am respected, tho' I keep aloof from all political acquaintance."[32] While personal correspondence seemed to reach its destination, Stone believed that any political discourse would be seized upon by the revolutionary authorities. If

---

26 Quoted in Buel, *Joel Barlow: American Citizen*, p. 171.
27 See David Worrall, *Theatric Revolution: Drama, Censorship, and Romantic Period Subcultures, 1773-1832* (Oxford: Oxford University Press, 2006).
28 Captain Monro to Lord Grenville, Paris, 31st December 1792, TNA FO 27/40 (Part 2).
29 Mary Wollstonecraft to Eliza Bishop, 13th June 1793, Wollstonecraft, *Collected Letters*, p. 226.
30 Mary Wollstonecraft to Eliza Bishop, 24th June 1793, Wollstonecraft, *Collected Letters*, p. 227. Wollstonecraft expressed her fear to Eliza that her letters were either being opened or "miscarried".
31 Mary Wollstonecraft to Ruth Barlow, Le Havre, 8th July 1794, Wollstonecraft, *Collected Letters*, p. 255. Wollstonecraft was probably referring to the laws of 27 Germinal (16th April 1794) and 7 Prairial (26th May 1794) which renewed measures against foreign residents and dictated that no British prisoners would be taken during the hostilities.
32 *CCST*, p. 1126.

letters were restricted to business, however, they would not be obstructed. On 21st April 1794 he wrote to his brother, telling him that "the post is sometimes negligent, though letters of business are rarely interrupted."[33] Two weeks earlier he advised his brother to avoid political commentary in his correspondence.[34]

British residents were subject to indiscriminate arrest from August to October 1793 and incarceration had considerable implications for the success and survival of writing projects. Thomas Clio Rickman noted the difficulty faced by Thomas Paine in drafting a history of the Revolution:

> It is unfortunate for mankind that Mr. Paine, by imprisonment and the loss of his invaluable papers, was prevented giving the best, most candid and philosophical account of these times. These papers contained the history of the French revolution, and were no doubt a most correct, discriminating, and enlightened detail of the events of that important era. For these papers the historian Gibbon sent to France, and made repeated application, upon a conviction that they would be impartial, profound, and philosophical documents.[35]

Rickman's recollections attest to the fact that Paine had made some headway in writing his version of the history of the French Revolution. The circumstances of his incarceration seem to have prevented these papers from being preserved or completed, despite later scholarly attempts to recover his manuscript.

Yet it was not just arrest and imprisonment which put pay to writing projects. In the prevailing atmosphere of suspicion and surveillance from mid-1793, radicals found it difficult to finish their histories as they had set out to do. Mary Wollstonecraft failed to realise her mission in going to Paris to provide regular reports of her observations of the Revolution for periodical publication in the *Analytical Review*. She went to France in December 1792, hoping to write a series of historical reflections on the Revolution, yet she only completed one such volume, which was published posthumously. Although in the preface to her account she revealed, "It is probable therefore, that this work will be extended to two or three more volumes, a considerable part of which is already written," the planned volumes were never published and Wollstonecraft's history only covered the period from May to October 1789.[36] In a letter to Ruth Barlow in February 1794 Wollstonecraft mentioned the sources that she hoped would form the basis of later volumes of her history of the Revolution:

---

33 Ibid, p. 1264.
34 John Hurford Stone to William Stone, 8th April 1794: "I shall write more frequent, but you need not answer but on business." *CCST*, p. 1267.
35 Rickman, *The Life of Thomas Paine*, p. 137.
36 *HMV*, p. 5.

I should be much obliged to Mr. Barlow, it he would get me the debates and decrees, from the commencement of that publication and order them to be sent to me here, in future, by post, – for I never see a paper. Tell him that I am now more seriously at *work* than I have ever been yet, and that I daily feel the want of my *poor Books*.[37]

In a letter to her sister Everina the following month, she announced that she had posted part of her manuscript for her history of the Revolution, probably to be read by her publisher: "I have just sent off great part of my M.S. which Miss Williams would fain have had [m]e burn, following her example. – And to tell you the truth, – my life would not have been worth much, had it been found."[38] The specific context of 1793-94 meant that writers could not plan further volumes, count on publication or even expect their manuscripts to survive.

EYEWITNESS AUTHORITY: "ONE MUST HAVE BEEN PRESENT"

As Bob Harris has noted, the French Revolution played a part in "stimulating the demand for news of the revolution, and ... through its proximity, it encouraged papers to experiment with new ways of gathering more immediate and up-to-date information, including direct reporting."[39] British observers who wrote accounts of the Revolution, either in published volumes or personal letters, invoked their physical intimacy with events as a marker of authority. They also emphasised the manner in which they gathered news to prove the worthiness of their accounts. Writers rejected calm distance from the event as a guarantee of trustworthy coverage, stipulating that a genuinely true judgement could only be formed through observation and inside knowledge. As Mary Wollstonecraft put it in March 1794, "I certainly am glad I came to France, because I never could have had else a just opinion of the most extraordinary event that has ever been recorded."[40] Immediacy and presence were held up by radicals as key factors in accessing the true nature of the Revolution. As John Hurford Stone noted, "Of the spirit of this people you can have little idea at a distance."[41] Presence in France during the revolutionary years was perceived as conferring a degree of authority on British radicals commenting on the events they witnessed, and prompted them to claim the power to provide a counter-narrative to that diffused in the British press. They did not consider

---

37 Mary Wollstonecraft to Ruth Barlow, [?Le Havre] February 3rd [1794], Wollstonecraft, *Collected Letters*, p. 247.
38 Mary Wollstonecraft to Everina Wollstonecraft, [Le] Havre, March 10th [17]94, Wollstonecraft, *Collected Letters*, p. 248.
39 Bob Harris, *Politics and the Rise of the Press: Britain and France, 1620-1800* (London: Routledge, 1996), p. 46.
40 Mary Wollstonecraft to Everina Wollstonecraft, [Le] Havre, March 10th [17]94, in Wollstonecraft, *Collected Letters*, p. 249.
41 *CCST*, p. 1300.

themselves as detached and indifferent witnesses and made no claim to impartiality, yet they did highlight the authenticity and legitimacy of their insights, suggesting that their presence at the revolutionary scene gave them a unique insight into the events they were living through.

Sampson Perry was conscious of the difficulty he faced in negotiating a route between objective history and personal testimony in his sketch of the Revolution. Piecing together his study from within Newgate prison, he claimed that the particular utility of his history was in the physical proximity he could claim to certain segments of the story he recounted rather than in its ability to provide a comprehensive view of events. Not only had he spent two years as an eyewitness and was acquainted with leading actors of the Revolution, but his friend John Hurford Stone, who remained in France, was supplying him with firsthand information to be included in his account, just as he had done in 1792 when Perry was editor of *The Argus*. The potential appeal of Perry's version of history for a British reading audience was its immediacy and the purported accuracy of the events it detailed:

> It is less in the first than in the succeeding volume, that the Sketcher of History pretends to build on materials exclusively his own. Driven by persecution from England, he was thrown into so peculiar a situation in France, that he may, without fear of contradiction, say, few had the same opportunity of investigating the causes of many of those incidents which the wondering world ascribed to chance or blind fatality.[42]

Perry acknowledged that his own particular insight was more clearly conveyed in the second of his two volumes, covering the years during which he was a resident of Paris. Aware of the rareness of his position as a British eyewitness in the months following the deposition of the king and the announcement of the republic, when many of non-republican bias had quickly negotiated a passage out of France, he presented his study as a considered investigation rather than blind conjecture. Unlike those in the "wondering world", reliant on speculation and imagination, Perry's account was based on verifiable facts and careful reporting.

For British activists, their proximity to events gave them a privileged insight therefore, which allowed them to contest reports of the Revolution which appeared inaccurate or inauthentic. Helen Maria Williams' first volume of letters are a vindication of the early progress of the Revolution and she reacts with astonishment on arriving back in Britain and hearing what she considers to be deceptive and erroneous portraits of the Revolution circulating widely and spread by émigrés:

> Every visitor brings me intelligence from France full of dismay and horror. I hear of nothing but crimes, assassinations, torture and death. I am told that every day witnesses a conspiracy; that

---

42 *HS* I, pp. vii-viii.

> every town is the scene of a massacre; that every street is blackened with a gallows, and every highway deluged with blood. I hear these things, and repeat to myself, Is this the picture of France? Are these the images of that universal joy, which called tears into my eyes, and made my heart throb with sympathy?[43]

In her first volume of letters written during the summer of 1790, Williams describes overhearing conversations on the boat back to Brighton, when returning to England, and explains, "I could not help being diverted with the comments on French customs, and French politics, which passed in the cabin."[44] Williams was not only surprised but *entertained* by the reports she heard. Such admissions of amusement undermined the validity of opposing views, which exaggerated and distorted the horrors of the Revolution. Gatherings of English-speaking residents in Paris, often drawing together men and women such as John Hurford Stone and Helen Williams, Mary Wollstonecraft, Joel and Ruth Barlow and Thomas Paine, would include discussions of the representations of the Revolution in the British papers. In a letter to his brother William, Hurford Stone wrote, "Nothing amuses us more than reading your news-papers, descriptive of the horrors of Paris."[45] Not only were reports of French violence in the British press erroneous, but they were risible, containing descriptions of gothic horrors which were not even worthy of riposte.

As the Revolution progressed, reactions in Britain to developments in France became more virulent. British radicals attempted to provide real-time commentaries on events in France with the aim of both correcting error in British press reports and elevating their own position as the arbiters of authentic history. They endeavoured to keep abreast of news on both sides of the Channel even when communication was increasingly difficult and as surveillance intensified. John Hurford Stone, writing to his brother in England, stated, "I have seen your papers to the 31st Dec. I receive them pretty constantly; am much amazed at your accounts of French politics. Heavens that you were wise and informed."[46] Stone had already provided Sampson Perry with information while the latter was still in London, as shown in this letter to his brother William from October 1792:

> You will have received from Verdun an immense packet of information, which you will have distributed according to the addresses; that to Perry contains an epitome of the campaign, and our present situation... I shall continue to send you Perry's letters, if I have time in future to write to him; but it is necessary that he

---

43 Helen M. Williams, *Letters Written in France, in the Summer 1790*, p. 147.
44 Ibid.
45 *CCST*, p. 1215.
46 Ibid, p. 1217.

should have them in the day, as a day of earlier intelligence is to him of some importance.[47]

Stone was providing Perry with information on the progress of the French armies to be included in his radical journal *The Argus*. He had spent a number of weeks in late 1792 travelling with a Prussian companion and following in the footsteps of Dumouriez's troops, stopping at Verdun, Rheims and other towns on the North-Eastern border. Stone's correspondence was included in Helen Maria Williams' third volume of published letters but may also have formed the basis of accounts published in *The Argus* in London. The emphasis on getting the news to Perry "in the day" highlights that one of the major preoccupations of British radicals was to provide immediate counter-readings of the events they witnessed.

Joel Barlow, sketching his notes of the French Revolution, began his eighth chapter, entitled "To the fall of Robespierre July 94" with his intended objective: "We are now to speak of the victory of the Republic. But that the deeds of this campaine [*sic*] many not appear to be the effect of inchantment [*sic*] & its history a romance, it is necessary to recapitulate the means that were employed by the Com ee of Sal. Pub. to collect the vigour that it was to display."[48] He aimed to correct the exaggerated reports of emergency rule by giving the necessary background to the measures taken by the *Comité de Salut Public*, collated during his time in Paris and essential to understanding the reasons for the violence. Much of the eyewitness reporting by foreign residents aimed at rationalising episodes in the Revolution which had been portrayed as spontaneous eruptions of senseless brutality by their detractors. Hurford Stone signalled his proximity to news sources in letters to his brother:

> The letter I sent you of the retreat of the Prussians was, I am certain, the only information of the event to be met with in England, for the news arrived at the assembly at ½ past 12: I heard it from a deputy; a minute after I ran into the box and spoke with one of the secretaries; and at one the post went off to Calais; and my letter was put on board a boat that was then going to England. In any future affairs of this sort, you may depend on the authenticity of the intelligence, for I have access to the secretary's table.[49]

It was not only the content of the news that was significant, but the manner in which it was acquired and transferred. Stone insisted he heard the information with his own ears and conveyed it within the hour, from his privileged place at the heart of French affairs, literally at the "secretary's

---

47 Ibid, p. 1302.
48 Barlow, "Notes for a hist. of the Fr. Rev.," folio 10.
49 Paris, 24th October 1792, *CCST*, p. 1298.

table". Such efficient channelling of news allowed Stone to claim that his reports had particular value that could not be found in other testimonies.

In a similar way, Sampson Perry suggested that it was important for readers of *An Historical Sketch* to be aware of the manner in which he had gained access to the information contained in his account. It was for this reason that he had reluctantly highlighted his own experience in Paris in the preface:

> The repugnance I feel in becoming the topic of my own discourse (short as I mean to make it), is greatly qualified by what I conceive an indispensable necessity of thereby enabling my readers of The Sketch of the French Revolution, to understand how I obtained a knowledge of many of those incidents and anecdotes, which, though abstractedly appearing to be unimportant to the grand work, had, nevertheless, very considerable, but remote influence upon some of its most striking parts.[50]

British presence in Paris represented a potential threat to the stability of reports generated by the British government on the French descent into anarchy. In correcting the errors they perceived in official portraits of developments in France, in expressing shock at the deceptive vision of the Revolution portrayed by commentators across the Channel, or in describing their amusement at the scenes played out in the British press, radicals undercut official versions of the Revolution and acquired a degree of leverage in determining which knowledge was to be deemed authentic and reliable.

To highlight their own presence at the scene, British commentators often emphasised the aural, sensory and visual aspects of the events they witnessed. In Helen Maria Williams' depiction of a visit to the French National Assembly, it is not the content of speeches themselves, which were easily transcribed, reprinted and accessible in Britain, which take precedence, but the behavioural aspects of oratory and debate. Williams makes references to manners and gestural style, the "haranguing" of the audience, or the posture of the president, who "stretches out his arms and endeavours to impose silence."[51] As Matthew Bray has pointed out, Williams implied that it was "only those people, such as Edmund Burke, who have not witnessed the Revolution firsthand who do not understand its transformative effects."[52] She systematically included precise detail, bolstering the text's claim to realism from the scenes she saw. In her description of the *Fête de la Fédération*, the one-year anniversary celebration of the fall of the Bastille, Williams points out the quantity of seats for the spectators, the number of days' preparation required, the exact route of the procession and the inscription written on the royal altar. Further into the text she provides a precise

---
50 *HS* I, p. 3.
51 Helen M. Williams, *Letters Written in France, in the Summer 1790*, pp. 72, 82.
52 Bray, 'Helen Maria Williams and Edmund Burke: Radical Critique and Complicity', p. 9.

description of Madame de Sillery's medallion, which could only be penned by someone who had been present. The accumulation of extraneous detail provides at once incontestable proof of the veracity of her representation while at the same time making her own presence in person the focal point of the reader's attention.

Bray has suggested that Williams created a "sensocracy", which he defines as "a society predicated upon an equality of feeling among all people," and therefore open to female commentators.[53] Williams portrayed the sounds, sights and spirit of events in her accounts. At the *Fête de la Fédération*, the music "had the power of electrifying the hearers," and the "discords" of the composer produced "a melancholic emotion" on those present and the performance of the sacred drama "affected the audience in a very powerful manner." The spirit of liberty is "displayed" in dancing, singing, performance, demonstration and decoration.[54] She focuses on sound and sight, detailing pauses in the procession, the suspension of cries of joy, the "solemn silence", and the cries of the people which "still ring in my ear!"[55] Presence gave Williams the authority to read emotional meaning into signs, gestures and the tenor of shouts and cries, meaning that could never be discovered from distant observation. In suggesting that the crowd "called out with exultation rather than regret," or explaining the instinctive reactions of onlookers as "the sudden impulse of feeling," she was interpreting reactions which could not be objectively verified.[56] Helen Maria Williams allowed the multiple voices of the Revolution to resonate in her texts, inserting anecdotes recounted to her personally by individuals present at the scene and relaying the ephemeral shouts that only a listener could seize upon.

In a letter to her publisher and friend Joseph Johnson from Paris in December 1792, Mary Wollstonecraft described the scene from her window during the trial of Louis XVI. She was struck by the silence of the streets, where "not a voice could be heard" after the tumult of the preceding days. As an onlooker, Wollstonecraft had a privileged place as an eyewitness of the events. She identified the expressions on faces, the movement of the national guards, the sounds of drums, and the body postures of the crowd.[57] In a similar way to Williams, she invoked her presence at the scene and took advantage of her eyewitness position to convey a sensory view of the atmosphere during the trial. She would also call upon her role as an "observer of mankind" in the first of a series of commentaries on the "present character of the French nation", written in February 1793. In her portrait she claimed to have identified key elements of French culture:

---

53 Ibid, p. 18.
54 Helen M. Williams, *Letters Written in France, in the Summer 1790*, p. 63.
55 Ibid, p. 73.
56 Ibid, pp. 69, 66.
57 Mary Wollstonecraft to Joseph Johnson, Paris, 26th December 1792, Wollstonecraft, *Collected Letters*, pp. 216-17.

> The whole mode of life here tends to render the people frivolous, and, to borrow their favourite epithet, amiable. Ever on the wind, they are always sipping the sparkling joy on the brim of the cup, leaving satiety in the bottom for those who venture to drink deep. On all sides they trip along, buoyed up by animal spirits, and seemingly so void of care, that often, when I am walking on the Boulevards, it occurs to me, that they alone understand the full import of the term leisure; and they trifle their time away with such an air of contentment, I know not how to wish them wiser at the expense of their gaiety.[58]

The gaiety and levity of people's behaviour and "mode of life" resulted in a loss of wisdom and gravity. Although Wollstonecraft held back from reproaching the French people for this preference for superficial pleasure over deeper concerns, she would later consider this national trait as incompatible with the rapid establishment of rational and enlightened society. While in letters and sketches she called upon her status as an eyewitness observer to describe the revolutionary scene, in her philosophical account of the "origins and progress" of the Revolution she judged the early Revolution based on the studied enquiry of official texts rather than the observations of the onlooker.

Presence at the scene conferred authority on spectator-writers, in that they considered their descriptions to be firsthand and authentic, yet writers also highlighted the impossibility of accurately conveying their experiences in words. For Helen Maria Williams, the scenes depicted in her letters were accurately drawn because they were the result of her own firsthand observation. However, they also proved insufficient, as words were unable to describe events which were first and foremost an emotional experience: "I am well aware how very imperfectly I shall be able to describe the images which press upon my mind. It is much easier to feel what is sublime than to paint it; and all I shall be able to give you will be a faint sketch, to which your own imagination must add colouring and spirit."[59] Her written text was a thus flawed rendering of what she had witnessed. Williams also called on the reader to embellish the text, using his or her own power of invention and imagination to complete the portrait. Writing about the celebrations at the *Fête de la Fédération* Williams exclaimed, "It is not to be described! One must have been present, to form any judgment of a scene, the sublimity of which depended much less on its external magnificence than on the effect it produced on the minds of the spectators." She wondered, "How am I to give you an adequate idea of the behaviour of the spectators. How am I to paint the impetuous feelings of that immense, that exulting multitude?"[60]

---

58 'Introductory to a series of letters on the present character of the French nation', Paris, 15th February 1793, Janet Todd and Marilyn Butler (eds.), *The Works of Mary Wollstonecraft* (London: Pickering, 1989), p. 443.
59 Helen M. Williams, *Letters Written in France, in the Summer 1790*, p. 63.
60 Ibid, p. 64.

Writers therefore found themselves confronted with the ambiguity of being in a place which allowed them privileged access to the events captivating Europe but unable to put those events into words. Sampson Perry wrote of the near impossibility of successfully portraying the French Revolution in written form since "no language can come up to the grandeur of the object – no artificial eloquence can equal the natural sublimity of the scene."[61] The Revolution was "one of those occurrences which cannot be magnified by the power of language."[62] For Perry, the extent of the events was such that even "the pen of Tacitus" would not have been able to faithfully render the proceedings.[63] Such admissions were in part genuine expressions of bewilderment in the face of events which they felt ill-equipped to describe. Yet they also constituted attempts to shield their writings from criticism and deny the primacy of the perfect picture over the partial sketch. Hostile readers of Perry, Williams and Wollstonecraft frequently made reference to their flawed style and poor writing technique, suggesting they were not equal to the task of describing an event as historic as the French Revolution. However, if the Revolution was primarily an emotional experience, then the brilliance and accomplished style of one's writing was secondary. Mary Wollstonecraft, writing to her sister Everina, emphasised the difficulty in conveying one's impression of the Revolution to those following it at a distance. She stated, "It is impossible for you to have any idea of the impression the sad scenes I have been a witness to, have left on my mind."[64]

British emigrants, writing of their experience of the Revolution in sketches, fragments, letters and published form, held up their presence in Paris as a marker of the veracity of their accounts. Their eyewitness status gave them a privileged position, allowing them to see the events from the inside and acknowledge its psychological, emotional and sensory impact. Yet for such observers, the events could ultimately defy description and language alone failed to capture the magnitude of an event which had a profound effect on those who witnessed it, disrupting ordinary conceptions and experience of time. For some British witnesses, their attempts at capturing the Revolution in writing were frustrated by the prevalence of surveillance and the climate of suspicion which led many to refrain from expressing their views in both private correspondence and published testimony. Other manuscripts did not survive the period during which many British men and women underwent some form of incarceration. Despite these common points, British radical onlookers nevertheless varied in their degree of support for the Revolution and in their views on events they chose to write about. This was partly due to the fact that they were writing at different times in the Revolution's course,

---

61 *HS* I, p. 489.
62 Ibid, p. v.
63 Ibid, p. vii.
64 Mary Wollstonecraft to Everina Wollstonecraft, 10th March 1794, Wollstonecraft, *Collected Letters*, p. 248

sometimes during the heat of emergency rule and on other occasions in retrospect, but it also reflects the heterogeneity of opinions within the British radical community at this time and the different ways in which they attempted to comprehend the contradictions and uncertainties generated by the developments in the early republic.

10

'It would be rash to hazard any prediction of the future'
The historical accounts of Helen Maria Williams and Mary Wollstonecraft

As women, neither Mary Wollstonecraft nor Helen Maria Williams signed the official declaration of the *SADH* in November 1792, yet both were central figures in the gatherings that took place in tandem with official meetings and were key members of the international radical community in Paris. Williams and Charlotte Smith were both toasted at the signing of the November address, while Wollstonecraft regularly read the English newspapers with Paine, Hurford Stone and the Barlows. Helen Williams facilitated communication between emigrants through her salon assemblies and both Williams and Wollstonecraft contributed to the conveying of impressions of the Revolution to Britain in written accounts. Helen Williams' epistolary eyewitness reports of the Revolution extend to eight volumes published between 1790 and 1796 while Wollstonecraft's account was written during her stay in Paris at the height of emergency rule in 1793-94. While Williams went to Paris to witness what she considered to be the advent of liberty, Wollstonecraft arrived at the end of 1792 with the aim of discovering the inner workings of the Revolution which would enable her to give a philosophical interpretation of its progress. She also intended to publish a series of moral portraits of France for the *Analytical Review*, although only one reached publication, posthumously, in 1798. In her *Historical and Moral View of the French Revolution* (1794), Wollstonecraft wrote that the object of the historian was to "trace the hidden springs and secret mechanism, which have put in motion a revolution, the most important that has ever been recorded in the annals of man."[1] She was already aiming at uncovering some of the long historical causes of the Revolution, despite the fact she was writing in the midst of emergency government when predicting the future was a perilous endeavour. Williams, on the other hand, while setting out to draw a portrait of what she saw, acknowledged her lack of "coolness" and "impartiality" and the "indistinct" nature of her account due to her closeness to the events she witnessed.[2] As she conceded in volume four of the first series:

> Placed amid circumstances where the great events that are passing succeed each other so rapidly, that it is almost as difficult to consider them separately, with attention, as it is impossible to calculate their effects, you impose a task on me which I am incapable of fulfilling: for so new and unexpected are they, and so little relation do they bear to the past, that it would be rash to hazard any prediction of the future, from what we now behold.[3]

Williams' letters abound with personal anecdotes and stories related by individuals she knew and met or whose views had been relayed to her by acquaintances. Her perception of the ills of *Ancien Régime* France and the levelling spirit inspired by the Revolution, but also its abuses, are conveyed either through what she saw or what she was told. The reader follows her different visits – to Orléans, to Rouen, to former royal palaces, the National Assembly, the Jacobin Club and the Lycée. Wollstonecraft, unlike Williams, who preferred human testimony, drew on purely written sources for the core material informing her reflections on the progress of the Revolution. She used accounts from Thomas Christie's *Letters on the Revolution in France* (1791) and Helen Williams' own writings, but mainly official French sources, which included *Le Moniteur Universel, Le journal des débats et des décrets* and *Les Archives parlementaires*.[4] She also read the *New Annual Register* and Mirabeau's published letters. Wollstonecraft's account, by her own admission, is based on studied reflection and the perusal of accounts of the Revolution. Unlike Williams, she gives no indication of any failings or inadequacies in her reading of events, nor does she cite her aim as correcting the errors circulating in Britain. Wollstonecraft's history is framed as a self-standing piece of philosophical enquiry into the progress of the early Revolution, tinged with the author's knowledge of its later excesses.

Yet despite the very different aims of these two authors, we know that they were acquaintances in Paris and mixed in similar circles and were writing some of their work at the same time. Wollstonecraft was one of the first

---

1 *HMV*, p. 42.
2 H. M. Williams, *Letters from France* IV, p. 82.
3 Ibid, p. 74.
4 These texts gathered together all the debates carried out in the National Assembly and National Convention and also transcribed the texts from different laws voted on by the national representatives.

visitors to Williams' salon when she arrived in Paris in December 1792 and Williams included a text by Wollstonecraft's editor at the *Analytical Review*, Thomas Christie, in the third volume of her first series of letters. Wollstonecraft was a frequent guest at gatherings attended by John Hurford Stone, with whom Williams entered into a longstanding relationship while in Paris, and Stone wrote to his brother in late 1793, informing him that Wollstonecraft was writing a historical account of the Revolution. Stone would also contribute the vast majority of the material to Helen Williams' third volume of letters. The influence of this lettered, radical community was significant for both writers.

HELEN MARIA WILLIAMS' *LETTERS FROM FRANCE* (1792-1793)

Although Helen Maria Williams began her writing on the Revolution full of enthusiasm, her writings, from volume III of the first series onwards, reveal her progressive disillusionment. She has, with reason, been portrayed as an admirer of the Girondins, whose principal leaders she played host to at her salon and celebrated unreservedly in her writings. She saw figures such as Roland, Brissot, Pétion and Condorcet as the philosophical lights of the Revolution, capable of great eloquence in the cause of liberty. Her abhorrence of Robespierre, the Paris Commune, and the band of "conspirators" that she blamed for the degeneration of the Revolution is also patent in her writings. She dates the descent of the Revolution into "anarchy" from the period of August to September 1792, although it is the expulsion of the Girondin members from the Assembly after the armed assault on the National Convention on 31st May 1793 which she sees as the crucial turning point. It was this event which signalled the substitution of wise, enlightened leadership by the rule of the mob, sanctioned by imprudent and vain despots. Yet as Stephen Blakemore has argued, while writers such as Williams, Wollstonecraft and Thomas Paine highlighted the flaws in the progress of the Revolution, they did not entirely renege on their admiration. Such writers put pen to paper, in Blakemore's view, "not as a renunciation of their revolutionary faith, but as a way of reclaiming both their faith and the Revolution."[5] In this study of Williams, I will focus on three of her volumes of letters, written between 1792 and 1793.[6] Rather than emphasising Williams' progressive disillusionment with the Revolution or the conscious rewriting of the Revolution that Blakemore notes, I intend to highlight the complexities faced by writers like Williams who were trying to reconcile the changing nature of the Revolution with their fundamental and

---

5   Blakemore, *Crisis in Representation*, pp. 20-1.
6   These works are *Letters from France: Containing Many New Anecdotes relative to the French Revolution, and the present state of French Manners* (1792) and *Letters from France: Containing A Great Variety of Interesting and Original Information concerning the most important events that have lately occurred in that country, and particularly respecting the campaign of 1792*, vol. III and vol. IV (1793).

underlying approval of its reforming potential, often with very little analytical distance.

In her little-studied second volume of letters, Williams continues her relatively light-hearted celebration of the spirit of the Revolution, in a similar vein to her much-read first volume. Yet volumes three and four are more problematic, revealing the deep contradictions that British eyewitnesses felt during the course of 1793. In volume three Williams offers an often misshapen and chronologically disordered patchwork of texts, making no claim to organisational unity or ideological stability. A denunciation of the Revolution's excesses and the tyranny of the Paris Commune, epitomised by the trial of the king, is followed by a jubilant account of the success of the French armies, written by John Hurford Stone, and a more reticent account of the republic's military successes by Thomas Christie. Volume three is a polyvocal work without logical or argumentative cohesion; in many ways a showcase of the diversity of opinions espoused by members of the British community in Paris at this period. In volume four, while portraying the September massacres in the introduction as an event which had blackened the historical record of the Revolution, Williams goes on to give a rational explanation of its origins. The volume contains criticism of the way in which British newspapers purposefully manipulated reports of the Revolution and Williams even manages to lay the blame for Louis XVI's death on Edmund Burke. These two volumes show that, as well as being a resolute critic of Montagnard rule and the municipality of Paris, Williams was also attentive to alternative readings put forward by her compatriots and associates. She may have struggled to reconcile these contradictions given her deep personal and intellectual commitment to the idea of liberty the Revolution epitomised. Her membership of the Dissenting community, dislike of hierarchy and abhorrence of institutional repression led her, despite her many reservations, to continue her undertaking to correct errors circulating in Britain, even though she was "prepared for censure" in adopting such a view.[7]

Volume II of *Letters from France* was dismissed by M. Ray Adams as "quite superficial."[8] He judged that Williams "seems not yet to have sensed the extreme towards which some of the members of this famous revolutionary society were tending," suggesting, as many subsequent critics have done, that British observers should have foreseen the events that were to follow in their immediate commentaries.[9] Volume II widely follows the general spirit of volume I, using anecdotal evidence overheard by Williams on her travels through France to illustrate the culture of benevolence the Revolution had engendered amongst all ranks of people. The letters also serve to confirm the acquiescence of the majority of the French population in the changes wrought by the Revolution. Williams recounts the story of a couple who overcame the arbitrary restrictions on inter-rank marriage under the *Ancien*

---
7 H. M. Williams, *Letters from France* IV, p. 265.
8 M. Ray Adams, 'Helen Maria Williams and the French Revolution', p. 103.
9 Ibid, p. 102.

Régime to find union with the advent of the Revolution, and celebrates public instruction programs and the attempts to give a veritable education to children with hearing and speaking difficulties. The author highlights the moderation and humanity of the soldiers of the Château-Vieux regiment, who refused to fire on ordinary citizens who had resisted foreign onslaught from invading armies. Their defiance was seen as a blow to arbitrary power. She also notes the saintly vocation of nuns, working to ease suffering in the Hôtel-Dieu. Their devotion contrasts with "that unfeeling indifference which prevails in the world."[10] She details sacrifices and transformations in the common revolutionary cause and holds up the virtues of benevolence and simplicity as being the markers of the new revolutionary mindset. Liberty is seen as infiltrating all ages, generations and ranks, bringing the French together in a community of universal harmony where "every selfish interest is sacrificed with fond alacrity at the altar of the country."[11] Williams notes that even the games of young children generally had a reference to liberty.

Frequent comparisons are made with the cultural practices and social fabric of England. In these parallels, the advances of the French nation are generally seen as superior. Williams praises the system whereby French wives take an active part in the running of their merchant husbands' business, allowing them to take over their affairs in the case of death, pass on their knowledge to their children, or anticipate eventual bankruptcy.[12] French theatres and audiences, with their "love of gaiety and pleasure", surpass the London stage and "the English idea of finding ease, comfort, or festivity, in societies where women are excluded, never enters the imagination of a Frenchman."[13] Yet Williams is nostalgic for the English custom of spending Sundays "in the bosom of your family, or consecrated to friends and connections you love most," suggesting that Sunday in France was indistinguishable from any other day.[14] On social custom, the French fare better in Williams' portrait. While English guests are so afraid of censure and ridicule that they keep "their minds in complete armour," the French are more good-natured and allow the expression of feeling. Similarly, in political debate, Williams suggests that in French legislative chambers "eloquence may have an impression on the vote" while in the House of Commons everything is decided in advance of the debate.[15] The "minute deformities" which might be noticed in the broad view of the Revolution pale in comparison with the "overwhelming majesty of the whole".[16] France is considered an example for mankind as a whole, a view that would be attenuated in later volumes. Williams calls on her native country to follow the

---

10 H. M. Williams, *Letters from France* II, p. 194.
11 Ibid, p. 5.
12 Ibid, p. 63.
13 Ibid, pp. 79-80.
14 Ibid, pp. 94-95. Williams would go on to qualify this criticism in her later volumes, where she defended the French population from accusation of free-thinking atheism.
15 Ibid, pp. 99, 110.
16 Ibid, pp. 22-3

French example, but makes it clear that this should be by "wise and temperate means" and "with no other arms than reason."[17] The "detestable crimes" committed by "fanatics" should not detract from the fact that liberty is preferable to "the gloomy tranquillity of despotism."[18] The crimes, which she does not specifically name, are to be attributed to the fact the French liberty is in its infancy and the people are not yet accustomed to the advantages of benevolence, having been maintained in ignorance and slavery for so long. This tendency to blame the vices of the Revolution on former oppression is repeated in Williams' later volumes, and also in the writings of her compatriots. Volume II therefore, despite sparse references to aristocratic attempts at defaming the Revolution and a few lines mentioning some unnamed wrongdoings, portrays the Revolution as sending a message to mankind. The author notes how "the liberal opinions of philosophy, liberty, and truth, are everywhere bursting forth like the fresh leaves of spring."[19]

In the third and fourth volumes of the first series of *Letters from France*, Williams was confronted with a much more complex diplomatic and political context in which to publish her writings. The result, in the third volume, is a collage of different views and authors, expressing a variety of opinions on the king's trial and the subsequent Montagnard ascendancy but primarily on the military campaigns of the revolutionary armies in late 1792. As Williams herself specifies in her advertisement, the letters were "not all the production of the same pen," and provided a triple perspective on the events of late 1792 and early 1793. Williams tackles the subject of Parisian politics and the trial of the king, while Hurford Stone and Christie focus on military material, with some limited philosophical commentary. The letters are not published in chronological order. Williams' letter is dated 25th January 1793, while Stone's reports on the military campaigns are written between October and December 1792 and sent from locations such as Clermont, Verdun and Rheims, where he was pursuing the army's progress in the company of a Prussian friend and "patriot". Williams' first letter, detailing the ignominy of the king's trial is therefore a perplexing introduction to the letters that follow, which celebrate Dumouriez's army and the moral and physical defeat of the Duke of Brunswick. Writing in late January 1793, Williams would have been aware, if not of the certainty of war with Britain, at least of its likelihood and imminence; yet she does not interfere with or comment on the accounts provided by Stone of the French military victories, leaving them intact and unedited.

In the introductory letter, Williams cites her presence at the scene as proof of authority: "I am placed near enough the scene to discern every look and every gesture of the actors, and every passion excited in the minds

---

17 Ibid, p. 116.
18 Ibid, p. 204.
19 Ibid, p. 155.

of the audience."[20] She outlines the tyranny of the Commune of Paris, made up of three principal protagonists – Robespierre, Marat and Danton – and deplores the decline of the "golden age" of the 14th July 1789 compared with the vision of people "dragging forth those victims to modes of death at which nature shudders."[21] Scenes of celebration had become "the desolation of the wilderness" and the triumvirate from the municipality of Paris were guilty of "baseness", their crimes provoked by "some deep and extraordinary malignity."[22] Williams attributes the crimes of 2nd September 1792 to the machinations of the Commune. Only the mayor of Paris, Jérôme Pétion, emerges unscathed in her report for having attempted to prevent the atrocities. Liberty was threatened by the designs of profligate men who "endeavour to lead the people to the last degree of moral degradation" and instil a spirit of permanent insurrection.[23] Education and intellectual capacity had become synonymous with aristocracy and Williams sees the Commune as waging war on everything that "embellishes human life" or "softens and refines our nature."[24] The portrait of the vulgar, Spartan and philistine Montagnard leaders in contrast to the enlightened Girondins was familiar at the time among supporters of the deposed members from the Gironde. Williams even accuses the "faction" of being in league with foreign courts and, in the case of Jean-Paul Marat, of being an aristocrat and ally of Austria, another common strand of Girondin propaganda. She reminds her readers that it was the Montagnards, dominated by the Commune and under the influence of the sections of Paris, who demanded the death of the king.

This account is then followed without any form of transition or clarification by a series of five letters by John Hurford Stone from his station with the French army in the north-east of France in late 1792. Stone begins his correspondence with the treasonable conduct of the court, which attempted to league with the Duke of Brunswick to bring about the invasion of Paris by the foreign alliance.[25] He suggests that the 10th August 1792 "disconcerted this well-arranged system" as did the superior strategic skills of Dumouriez, who made Brunswick, reputed as a "general and a negotiator", appear as the simple "dupe" of the émigrés.[26] Providence and the "genius of Liberty" aided the French armies.[27] Stone outlines the Duke's

---

20 Ibid, p. 2.
21 Ibid, p. 5.
22 Ibid, pp. 6-8.
23 Ibid, p. 23.
24 Ibid, p. 24.
25 The Duke of Brunswick was at the head of the Austrian army and delivered a proclamation which reached Paris in July 1792. The proclamation expressed determination to quell the anarchy reigning in France and restore the monarchy to its rightful place. The Duke also intimated that the people of France were, in the main, opposed to the upheavals that had occurred under the Revolution and would welcome the arrival of the royalist armies at the re-establishment of order.
26 H. M. Williams, *Letters from France* III, pp. 45, 105, 106.
27 Ibid, p. 59.

misconception that the people of France would welcome an invading force and "he felt the full force of their courage in the opposite direction," while the republican army was so totally divested of monarchical elements that there was no threat of defection.[28] He celebrates the assertion of popular sovereignty and the decision to bring the king to justice: "See assembled those patriots, re-clothed with power by the people, declaring the kingdom a republic, about to establish a still more popular constitution, and ordering the immediate trial of him whom they were to have felt as a tyrant, but who is now sunk into contempt with them as a traitor."[29] The enthusiasm felt by a number of British observers at this republican outcome and the optimism prompted by the drafting of a new constitution is given clear voice in Stone's letter.

Where the author does contest the conduct of the revolutionaries is in the decision to secularise the Church. Stone, a Dissenter and member of Richard Price's Unitarian congregation at Newington Green in Hackney, disapproved of the contempt for religion shown in the decision to make the Church dependent on the state. On founding morality purely on "public utility" rather than religious faith, the leaders of the Revolution had acted improvidently, as "they have taken away that which furnishes the strongest motives for its observance, the motives furnished by the prospects and assurances of revelation."[30] Yet apart from this denunciation of the civil oath, Stone's letters are a broad celebration of the advance of liberty that the republic represented. He dismisses the charge that "the lightness of the French character but ill accord with that sentiment which belongs peculiarly to free men" and suggests that, far from being frivolous, the French character had been transformed from "the effeminacy of the Sybarite" to "Roman firmness and Tartarean ferocity." He confirms the readiness of the French population for liberty, suggesting that "there is sufficient energy, and firm foundation to build up a people zealous of good works, worthy of the principles they have now adopted, and of the destiny to which they aspire."[31] Even if there were some chapters of the Revolution that friends of liberty would want to erase from history, he believed that liberty would emerge triumphant. Stone's final letter from Rheims of 2nd November 1792, only two weeks before he would chair the meeting of the *SADH* which celebrated the advances of the revolutionary armies, suggested that liberty could be obtained without sacrifice:

> The triumphs even of liberty appear glorious but at a distance. Those who have the highest relish for the blessing, and prize it most, must have the love of it deeply rooted in their hearts not to shudder at the measures by which it is obtained. Rousseau, in his

---

28 Ibid, p. 65.
29 Ibid, p. 76.
30 Ibid, p. 141.
31 Ibid, pp. 149-50.

declaration, that a revolution was too dear, if it cost but the life of one citizen, had never wandered over a field of battle, or his sensibility, too exquisite to advise its acquisition by means so ferocious, would have destroyed, in its embryo, that fine offspring of his genius, what has nerved the arm of the republic in its greenest infancy.[32]

Stone dismisses Rousseau's maxim that denied the need for bloodshed in a revolution and suggests that for liberty to prosper some loss of life had to be anticipated. In this viewpoint, he also pre-empts the view of Sampson Perry who concluded that violence was an inevitable stage in the passage towards freedom.

The final letter of the volume was written by Stone's one-time business associate and fellow member of the Literary Fund, Thomas Christie, a Scottish radical who had written his own account of the Revolution in 1791 and who had translated the French constitution of that year into English. Stone and Christie later became estranged after financial disagreements soured their business relationship. Christie contributed the final letter to Williams' third volume, a letter from Lille on the progress of the Revolution in the north of France. Christie's opinions are more conservative than Stone's. He warns against the forcible imposition of French liberty on other countries and forecasts that the trial of the king, gripping Paris as he wrote and inspired by a "spirit of rancour and undue severity," would make the Convention "lose sight of the more important fate of the country, and spend those precious moments, in which they should prepare for the future, in unnecessary invectives against the abuses of the past."[33] Christie suggests that there were countless dangers to liberty in France, particularly due to the "ferocious anarchy" and factional strife that beleaguered the country.[34] Yet he concludes that France is too enlightened to suffer a similar fate to the Roman republic and that, with so many foes from without, the viciousness and suspicion of the revolutionaries is understandable.

Volume III therefore contains texts which differ in style and argument, reflecting the triple authorship of the letters. Although the following volume, which bears the same title, appears to have been written mostly by Williams without any other authorial input, the letter from 17th April 1793 includes an account by Stone of Dumouriez's defection. Volume IV is a testimony to the way in which British radicals struggled to reconcile the contradictions in the Revolution in their writing. The first letter was written on 10th February 1793, only days after the entry into war with Britain and not long after the execution of the king. In this account, Williams is moved to pathos by the image of the fallen sovereign, recollecting his dignity in the face of the "faction of the anarchists" who showed to what extent they were "aloof

---

32 Ibid, p. 182.
33 Ibid, pp. 233-4.
34 Ibid, p. 237.

from all the ordinary feelings of our nature."³⁵ She reminds her reader of Louis's religious temperament, his "devotion" and courage in the face of death. Williams rouses compassion for the dethroned monarch, recounting how the king's children tried to prevent the deputies from decreeing the death of their father. In a reversal of many of the views expressed on the culpability of Louis XVI, Williams suggests that the king should inspire greater compassion than ordinary men, not only because he had already endured enough humiliation, but because, being educated in the art of delusion, his faults should be treated with greater leniency. In focusing on the sentimental impact of the king's death and the personal goodness of Louis XVI, Williams contributed to what Linda Colley sees as a trend towards privatising the relationship between the people and monarchy in the late eighteenth century, a trend which led to the strengthening of the authority of the Crown.³⁶

Despite her compassionate apology for the king, Williams is more equivocal on the general progress of the Revolution, seeing continued justification for the revolutionary momentum. Like Stone in volume III and Perry in his *Historical Sketch*, she refers to the fact that "temporary evil" is necessary in the passage from tyranny to liberty, and while upbraiding Santerre for refusing to allow the king to utter his last words from the scaffold, she then paradoxically acknowledges that the decision may have been justified in the interests of public order.³⁷ Had the pity of the crowd been incited, the repercussions could have led to massacre and civil war. Santerre's action, though considered as a gesture of inhumanity, is nevertheless explained as being a legitimate desire to ensure the maintenance of peace. These internal dissonances in Williams' argument seem to belie the deep contradictions that British observers felt in witnessing some of the events of 1793. Rather than being a sign of incoherence, such paradoxes and transformations show the difficulties faced in determining a plain and unambiguous stance on some of the Revolution's defining events. This was particularly the case for those, like Williams, writing from immediate observation.

Three more letters followed, revealing similar reversals and ambivalence. In a letter from 17th April 1793, Williams suggests that members of the Montagne were in league with aristocrats to perpetuate disorder and

---

35 H. M. Williams, *Letters from France* IV, p. 1
36 See in particular Linda Colley, 'The Apotheosis of George III: Loyalty, Royalty and the British Nation 1760-1820', *Past and Present* (1984), p. 94-129. John Barrell discusses the pathos inspired by the last interview between Louis XVI and his family and its impact on representations of George III in *Imagining the King's Death*, pp. 49-86.
37 H. M. Williams, *Letters from France* IV, p. 12. Antoine Joseph Santerre had been appointed by the National Convention to preside over the king's imprisonment and inform Louis XVI of any decisions emanating from the Convention. It was Santerre who told the king of the verdict of death and who, as the legend goes, brought a rapid end to the proceedings on the scaffold by preventing Louis from delivering a final speech with the call for a drum roll. This story was reiterated by Williams in her account.

conspired to murder the Girondin members. She also includes an account of Dumouriez's defection to the counter-revolutionary cause by Hurford Stone and laments the fact that Marat's reputation had increased with the knowledge of the renowned General's treason. At the end of the letter she admits to being unsure as to whether liberty would prosper under the republic or whether ancient privileges would be renewed. A further letter from 10th April 1793, included after the one written on the 17th April, again not following a clear chronological order, reiterates her inability to foretell the future. Williams suggests that she is "too near the events" to judge them with accuracy and finds it difficult to determine the causes of "such an inundation of distress" from her eyewitness vantage point.[38] A letter from 7th May 1793 provides an account of the rallying capacity of the French military and the legal sanction given to allow the arming of citizens, a topic unconnected with the other themes in the collection. The correspondence of 7th May 1793 calls on foreign princes to retreat and seek peace with the republic and concludes with the ambivalent remark that "if freedom be a blessing, it must be known by its fruits."[39] By mid-1793 Williams was no longer sure whether French freedom in its latest iteration was something to celebrate.

The final epistolary account in this collection is dated March 1793. Once again Williams shuns strict time order in the reproduction of her correspondence and saves her earliest letter of the volume and most resounding indictment of the British press and lettered classes for her conclusion. She begins by noting the "erroneous opinions in England" respecting the French Revolution, pointing out how ironic it was that a people who had struggled for their liberty had "looked with an evil eye on the efforts of another nation to obtain the same valuable blessing." It was not only since the later events of 1792-93 that the Revolution had been "viewed in a dubious light," but from the outset. Such criticism came not only from hostile politicians, uneducated men or a population in wartime, but from the bourgeoisie, "the most disinterested and the most judicious class of society."[40] Towards the end of the letter, Williams accuses the British population of collective amnesia in overlooking the fact that they had been "the first bold experimenters in the science of government in modern Europe – the first who carried into practical execution the calumniated principle of EQUALITY – the first people who formally brought a monarch to the scaffold – the first asserters of the neglected *rights of man*."[41] As well as reminding her readers of the execution of Charles I, she suggests that the Glorious Revolution had not been a bloodless insurrection, and counsels against overlooking the fact that liberty in Britain had been achieved at a price. In France all the stages in the progress of liberty, which in Britain had

---

38 Ibid, p. 82.
39 Ibid, p. 153.
40 Ibid, pp. 155-7.
41 Ibid, p. 225.

been progressive, had been crowded into a shorter space of time. Williams asserts that "no people ever travelled to the temple of Liberty by a path strewn with roses," and many of the "imprudences" of the Revolution were to be blamed on the antipathy of other nations who had impeded and denounced the pursuit of liberty in France.[42] The court is held responsible for many of the misfortunes that had blighted the country since 10th August 1792, particularly the monetary excesses of the civil list, the machinations of aristocrats, and the provocative behaviour of the king. The advent of the republic also signalled the advent of a more complex set of circumstances than those of 1789.

The greatest misrepresentation in the British press, however, concerned the events of 2nd September 1792. While introducing the massacres in her opening letter of March 1793 as the "sullen rapacity of the vulture", in her final letter Williams denies the portrait circulating in London of "a mere wanton and unprovoked effusion of the cruelty and ferociousness of the French populace," and sets out the rational basis of the actions as well as their place in the annals of human history.[43] She recalls how the impending arrival of the Duke of Brunswick had disseminated fear among the populace. Ordinary citizens believed that if the Duke was successful in taking Paris, he would release all prisoners, prompting a wave of vengeance against those whose actions had put them there. Williams prefers the term "savage justice" to "indiscriminate massacre" to describe the events and gives examples of the fairness of some of the makeshift trials. One citizen-judge spared a royalist because his opinions were not considered to have harmed the people. He then escorted the royalist to his home and refused to take money in return for his benevolence. Silence was respected when death sentences were pronounced and even the most enthusiastic of the perpetrators had legitimate reasons for their ferocity. Williams drew the conclusion that the prison massacres could not be blamed on the perpetrators themselves but on the chain of betrayals that preceded and prompted the actions. A volume of letters which begins therefore with the expression of horror and repugnance at the unspeakable events of 2nd September 1792 ends which a rational and even sympathetic portrait of the perpetrators who had been wronged by the court on 10th August and brutalised by the cruel apathy of the justice system.

For Williams, the misrepresentations of the French Revolution in British newspapers were the result of speculation based on flawed information. It was only the discerning foreign observer who could accurately convey the events:

> It is easy to obtain a superficial knowledge of a foreign nation: but to delineate justly its history; to trace events to their sources in its character and habits, so as to appreciate their real nature, and fix

---

42 Ibid, pp. 227-8.
43 Ibid, p. 182.

the degree of approbation or censure which belong to them, requires such an intimate acquaintance with a people as cannot be obtained without living amongst them, and possessing opportunities of information and a capacity of profiting from them that do not fall to the share of many of the class of writers now alluded to.[44]

Williams warns against cultural prejudice and counsels the importance of taking into account the particular circumstances of France and the specificities of the national character, reminding her reader of the unreliability of first impressions. In her view, no newspaper in England had succeeded in providing an accurate depiction of the Revolution, even though *The Morning Chronicle*, reliant on French sources and helped by the impartiality of its editors, had almost succeeded. Even French journals were not entirely accurate, as they focused their reports on Paris, the centre of turbulence and disorder, rather than the much more peaceful provinces.

Williams also denounces Edmund Burke, whose prescience in anticipating the vices of the Revolution she contests. Burke's warnings in his *Reflections on the Revolution in France* of 1790 appeared to have been realised when the Revolution became bloodier during the course of 1792. Yet Williams undoes this interpretation, suggesting that when people make bold guesses, they will always be partially right. She accuses him of error in identifying the causes of the Revolution's evils and condemns him for nonchalantly writing off the Revolution before it had even begun rather than taking the risk of faith: "It is easy to argue in this way, but generous minds hope the best, and see with pleasure the commencement of enterprises, that promise to improve the condition of humanity; rejoice in their progress, and mourn at their fall."[45] She also argues that Burke's predictions of evil may have produced the very deeds they describe. It was likely, she contends, that Burke's description of the probable death of the king and queen caused the French royalty concern, while until the publication of his text they had been satisfied with the progress of the Revolution. Burke was guilty of "painting to [the king] delusive pictures" of how monarchs should live and had sowed the seed of the idea that royalty was being ill-treated and that the king should not comply with the demands of the revolutionaries. She advances the opinion that "but for Mr. Burke and his associates in France, it is highly probable Louis the sixteenth might now have been reigning peaceably on his throne."[46]

In endeavouring to refute reports in British newspapers, Williams, though a defender of the need for order and severely critical of excessive violence, nevertheless provided a rational explanation of events in France that had been fervently denounced in Britain. Despite her repugnance at the rule of

---

44 Ibid, p. 209.
45 Ibid, p. 216.
46 Ibid, p. 218.

the Montagnard "conspirators", the loss of her enlightened friends and the disgrace of the king's execution, Williams could not regret having supported the Revolution and still ventured to give a balanced portrait of its most radical phase. The ordinary weaknesses of men struggling for their freedom are taken into account and she brings out the benevolence, generosity and virtue of the French people as well as their vices. Williams was under no illusion that her views would shock the British public and was prepared for much of the intense criticism she received. In 1795, *The Gentleman's Magazine* reported that, in Williams' eyes, "we are given to understand that liberty has been innocent of the horrible outrages committed in France under the sanction of her name."[47] Even on the eve of her death in 1821, *The Anti-Jacobin Review* was exhorting its readers to "remember the day when Helen Maria Williams was held up as the model of female patriots, for striding over the mutilated carcasses of the murdered Swiss, and examining what ravages had been committed upon them!"[48] Later commentators also reprimanded her for having apparently condoned revolutionary violence: "There is a troubling sense in *Letters Written in France* that the act of revolution itself – the actual process of opposing the ancient regime through necessary, yet also sublime violence – is much more satisfying than the calm, beautiful order that emerges from this violence."[49]

Undoubtedly Williams did become disillusioned with the Revolution, although, as Steven Blakemore has contended, she rewrote and reclaimed it rather than renounced it entirely. Yet, through an emphasis on the patchwork and dissonant nature of her 1793 letters, what emerges is her willingness to combine her views with those of other members of the British contingent and her interweaving of the most severe denunciation of the Revolution with the starkest justifications. This shows just how problematic it was for writer-spectators, intent on giving immediate firsthand portrayals of the Revolution, to judge events with clarity at a time when the contradictions thrown up were increasingly difficult to assess. Williams was not just reclaiming the Revolution in 1793 from its uninformed detractors, but she was working out her own personal reaction as she wrote, drawn as it was from the many inconsistencies the Revolution generated.

MARY WOLLSTONECRAFT'S RETROSPECTIVE VIEW OF THE EARLY REVOLUTION

Helen Williams' compatriot in Paris, Mary Wollstonecraft, did not claim to be providing a firsthand report of the Revolution when she began writing her *An Historical and Moral View of the Origins and Progress of the French Revolution; and the Effect it has Produced in Europe* in mid-1793, but addressed the philosophical and moral grounding of the Revolution from a universal

---

47 *The Gentleman's Magazine and Historical Chronicle*, vol. 65 (1795), p. 1030.
48 *The Anti-Jacobin Review and Protestant Advocate* (1821), p. 358.
49 Bray, 'Helen Maria Williams and Edmund Burke: Radical Critique and Complicity', p. 12.

historical perspective.[50] The first of a planned three-volume account was published in 1794 and covered the early Revolution from May to October 1789, a period which she had observed from afar while living in England. After an abortive attempt in the summer of 1792, Wollstonecraft eventually travelled to Paris in December 1792 and quickly found herself among the members of the British circle that she would have met with or heard of prior to her departure. She became involved in working on the constitutional committee's plan for education, guided by Condorcet, and began a relationship with the American speculator Gilbert Imlay, with whom she would have a daughter, Fanny, in May 1794. She wrote *An Historical and Moral View* at the height of emergency rule and, as Steven Blakemore has pointed out, her account is as much a reflection of the period in which she was writing as of 1789. The account brims with a sense of foreboding and frequent allusions are made to the Revolution's later descent into violence. Yet, Wollstonecraft, like Williams, despite her reservations, does not completely renounce her support for the Revolution. She explains the reasons for its vices and laments the lack of moral readiness of the French people for liberty, a fact which had ultimately prevented a smooth transition from despotism to enlightenment.

Isabelle Bour has suggested that Wollstonecraft's reliance on two opposing literary models produces incompatible contradictions in her account of the Revolution. While following the arguments of the Scottish school of Enlightenment philosophers, who saw historical development as the progress of humanity from barbarity towards perfection, she was also influenced by notions of sensibility common to gothic literature. Bour sees the use of these competing paradigms as resulting in "irreconcilable readings of the French Revolution." Historical figures become dark intriguers and "such passages are more an efflorescence of gothic-romantic fantasies of the kind one found in the cheap novels of the Minerva Press than the balanced assessment of the historian."[51] For Bour, such "psychological" readings are fundamentally irreconcilable with the Scottish model of moral economy she purported to rely on. Bour is not the only scholar to have pointed out inconsistencies and shortcomings in Wollstonecraft's history. Bour herself mentions Ralph Wardle's description of the *An Historical and Moral View* as "her least original work."[52] Even John Hurford Stone, part of Wollstonecraft's inner circle in Paris and a contributor to Williams' collections of letters, wrote disparagingly of the author's attempt at historical

---

50 Although there has been some interest in this text by Wollstonecraft, as Audrey Tauchert has pointed out in her abstract to the following article, it is "one of the most neglected of her mature writings." See Ashley Tauchert, 'Maternity, Castration and Mary Wollstonecraft's *Historical and Moral View of the French Revolution*', *Women's Writing* 4.2 (1997), pp. 173-203.
51 Isabelle Bour, 'Mary Wollstonecraft as Historian in *An Historical and Moral View of the Origins and Progress of the French Revolution; and the Effect it has Produced in Europe* (1794)', *Études Épistémè* 17 (2010), pp. 121, 125.
52 Quoted in Bour, 'Mary Wollstonecraft as Historian', p. 120.

coverage. In a letter to his brother in December 1793 he noted that "Right of Women is writing a huge work; but it will be as dull as Dr. Moore's Chronicle, and probably as inaccurate."[53]

What will be the focus here is not the quality or coherence of Wollstonecraft's account in terms of the philosophical or moral traditions on which she draws, but the ways in which her account reflects and contrasts with broader trends within the British community in 1793-94. Her attempt at providing an objective, rational historical account jarred with the inherent confusion the Revolution inspired among British observers during this period. In a similar way to Helen Maria Williams, Mary Wollstonecraft was writing in circumstances where contradictions were not only common, but an essential facet of all reporting on the Revolution. Commentators had not worked out the implications of the latest phase in the Revolution's course, even if they often agreed on its causes. Therefore, while Wollstonecraft claimed to be writing with the "cool eye of observation", at a distance from the events she was relating, and without pretensions of eyewitness recording, her account nevertheless reflects the impact of the period of the Revolution she was writing in. This was evident as much in Wollstonecraft's arguments as her style of writing. While she celebrated the principles of the Revolution, she denounced their flawed implementation, while she showed faith in the general improvement of society and the French nation, she lamented the descent into terror and the inadequacies of national leaders. Equally, as Bour has shown, while she used the language of Enlightenment rationality to describe the progress of morals and general understanding among the French population, she portrayed the intrigue of the court, the degeneracy of the king and queen and eventually the dissoluteness of popular despotism with all the excess of gothic story-telling. She confirmed the overall superiority of the virtues of liberty and justice that the Revolution embodied, yet she elevated, in Burkean language, the superiority of experience over ungrounded theory. These discordances, as much as revealing inherent stylistic or ideological contradictions in her writing, reflect the ambiguities and conflicting perceptions that the Revolution prompted in 1793-94, bewildering writer-observers and precluding the writing of conclusive history.

While Wollstonecraft does give some insight into her own emerging views on the current state of the French Revolution, she also makes considerable use of material from other authors, a technique which was common to most writers of the time including her fellow British compatriots in Paris. Sampson Perry inserted whole passages of texts from speeches, letters and reports into his *Historical Sketch* and the author of *A Circumstantial History* relied entirely on the report from the *Révolutions de Paris* for his account of the August Days. Such techniques were not frowned upon by contemporaries and were widely employed by newspaper editors of the time.

---

53 *CCST*, p. 1216.

Accounts of the Revolution as it occurred were not revered for their originality, but rather for their authenticity, and as Williams suggested in her letters, authenticity was synonymous with proximity. Quoting French debates, newspapers, statesmen or eyewitnesses all revealed that the author has access to reliable sources rather than demonstrated the intellectual inadequacies of the writer.

Writing at the height of emergency rule, Mary Wollstonecraft's account of the 1789 Revolution conjugates both optimism at the early advances of liberty and an awareness of its later descent into violence. Joy at the heroism of those who brought about the fall of the Bastille is constantly eclipsed by an awareness of how the failings of those who assumed power led to future calamities. On many occasions, she hints at the later Revolution for instance when alluding to "the tumults that have since produced so many disastrous events."[54] Yet despite the influence of her experience in France in 1793 which permeates her account, Wollstonecraft remains wedded to a belief in the Revolution's contribution to the advance of human society, judging that "it is perhaps, difficult to bring ourselves to believe, that out of this chaotic mass a fairer government is rising than has ever shed the sweets of social life on the world. – But things must have time to find their level."[55] Despite the nation's lack of readiness for the moral rigours of liberty, a better order would ultimately prevail.

Unlike Helen Williams, whose sympathy for the fate of the king and queen are conveyed in sentimental pathos, Wollstonecraft shows no compassion for the royal couple. Their passivity and "ruinous vices" were the catalyst for their downfall and their moral depravity, the principal flaw in *Ancien Régime* France, had infiltrated the population to such an extent that the just principles which led to the Revolution had subsequently faltered in their application.[56] Writing after the execution of the king and at the time of Marie-Antoinette's death on the scaffold, Wollstonecraft portrays the court as a dissolute hive of superficial pleasure, connivance, and indolence. Detailing the vices of the court, the author recalls the scheming and plundering conduct of royalist ministers such as Charles Alexandre de Calonne and the vanity of those who constituted the king's inner circle. Étienne-Charles de Loménie de Brienne, the king's cardinal and minister, is portrayed as an "obsequious slave" of power and the king's advisors weak and vengeful, plotting in the "dens of their nefarious machinations."[57] Jacques Necker is also criticised for his "rhetorical flourishes", "trivial observations", and propensity to appease the king and conciliate with the priesthood while purporting to speak on behalf of the people.[58] *Ancien Régime* France had thus lacked true statesmen who were capable of wise and

---

54 *HMV*, p. 32.
55 Ibid, p. 47.
56 Ibid, p. 30.
57 Ibid, pp. 36, 39.
58 Ibid, p. 57.

independent judgement, uninfluenced by the "general impulsion" and guided by their "own centre."[59] It is this lack of virtuous leadership, the legacy of pre-revolutionary France, which blighted the Revolution after 1789. While the country needed noble men, capable of sincerity, selflessness and enlightened guidance, the members of the National Assembly had fallen prey to the vices that had characterised the rule of their predecessors. In protecting their self-interest, capitulating to fear and elevating showy eloquence over true magnanimity, the Assembly had sacrificed the gains brought about by the underlying noble principles of the Revolution. Most leaders were guided by "a vain desire for applause" rather than true patriotism and constancy.[60] In an echo of both David Williams and Helen Maria Williams, Wollstonecraft laments the fact that "good lungs" prevailed over "sound arguments" in national debate. Even as admirable a statesman as Mirabeau secured the attention of his audience more through the "thundering emphasis" of his rhetoric than the "striking and forcible association of ideas" he was reputed for.[61] Such men had been "educated and ossified" under the *Ancien Régime* and proved unequal to the demands of high public office.[62]

Part of the reason for the failings of the early Revolution was the haste with which it had been propelled forward at a time when social relations were still characterised by slavishness. Rather than concentrating on the gradual moral improvement of the nation, the revolutionaries had tried to bring about change immediately, when the country as a whole was not equipped and the people were straining under the weight of servitude. Leaders had attempted to implement a system suited to a nation in the highest stages of civilisation which was "improper for the degenerate society of France."[63] The monarchy was transformed into a branch of government without any actual power and Wollstonecraft criticises the duplicity of retaining the Court while depriving it of all means of exerting its influence. Although she does not express a preference for monarchy, Wollstonecraft argues that "while crowns are a necessary bauble to please the multitude, it is also necessary, that their dignity should be supported, in order to prevent an overwhelming aristocracy from concentrating all authority in themselves."[64] If a monarchy was to be retained, it should be more than a mere empty figurehead. Constitutions should be altered peaceably and gradually, in line with the slow improvement in the science of government and the moral education of the people.

In her demand for progressive adjustment in the political system, in her distinguishing between men "acting from a practical knowledge, and men

---

59 Ibid, p. 43.
60 Ibid, p. 141.
61 Ibid, p. 156.
62 Ibid, p. 143.
63 Ibid, p. 162.
64 Ibid, p. 164.

who are governed entirely by theory, or no principle whatever," and in her warning against the dangerous innovations of unwise theorists, Wollstonecraft began to sound strikingly like her adversary Edmund Burke, whose views she had criticised in *Vindication of the Rights of Men* (1790).[65] Yet Wollstonecraft does not deny the need for "absolute change" in a nation, or the establishment of a constitution according to principles, as Burke had done, but she counsels against its hasty application.[66] Many British observers of the Revolution, including David Williams, came to defend the notion of gradual progress, having witnessed the sudden and violent changes brought about under the French Revolution. Williams himself began to withdraw his support for the Revolution on returning to Britain, condemning the members of the National Convention who had been "collected principally from the dregs of society" for attempting to overhaul the fundamental laws of the nation.[67] Wollstonecraft, on the other hand, employed the language of gradual and progressive reform while not renouncing the fundamental benefits of the changes in France for humanity at large.

Despite noting how the Revolution had diverged in practice from the principles which had underpinned it, Wollstonecraft's assessment of the future state of France belies optimism about the eventual establishment of just and free government. She concludes positively on the general advancement of the people towards a state of higher moral awareness. As Bour has pointed out, this stadial vision of gradual human progress towards perfection drew on the tradition of thinkers of the Scottish Enlightenment. Wollstonecraft considered herself "confident of being able to prove that the people are essentially good, and that knowledge is rapidly advancing to that degree of perfectibility, when the proud distinctions of sophisticating fools will be eclipsed by the mild rays of philosophy, and man be considered as man, acting with the dignity of an intelligent being."[68] This expression of optimism in regard to the potential for future perfection is often couched in terms that reflect the savagery of the natural world. Freedom is personified as "a lion roused from his lair" that "rose with dignity, and calmly shook herself." The émigré armies are characterised as a "tiger, who thirsts for blood," while government ministers are "the reptile who crawls under the shelter of the principles he violates."[69] In the latter allusion, Wollstonecraft seems to make a reference to the Montagnard rule of the era in which she was writing and the way in which leaders such as Robespierre held themselves up as the embodiment of the people while exacting cruel punishments on them in the name of defending the republic. She also uses

---

65 Ibid, p. 185.
66 Ibid, p. 62.
67 See D. Williams, *Incidents in My Own Life Which Have Been Thought of Some Importance*, Peter France (ed.) (Brighton: University of Sussex Library, 1980), p. 27.
68 *HMV*, p. 46.
69 Ibid, pp. 106, 216.

sentimental language to exult in the glory of the fall of the Bastille and the heroes of the 14th July, calling for the triumph of human knowledge:

> Down fell the temple of despotism; but – despotism has not been buried in it's [sic] ruins! – Unhappy country! – when will thy children cease to tear thy bosom? – When will a change of opinion, producing a change of morals, render thee truly free? When will truth give life to real magnanimity, and justice place equality on a stable seat? – When will thy sons trust, because they deserve to be trusted; and private virtue become the guarantee of patriotism? Ah! – when will thy government become the most perfect, because thy citizens are the most virtuous![70]

Wollstonecraft's account, far from being a clear and unambiguous assessment of the early Revolution, is layered with complex narratives. While she bewailed how the "cavalcade of death moves along, shedding mildew over all the beauties of the scene, and blasting every joy," she also contended that the alteration in the system of France "must ultimately lead to universal freedom and happiness."[71] The national character of the nation was depraved and "the french [sic] were in some respects the most unqualified of any people in Europe to undertake the important work in which they are embarked," yet liberty would eventually be secured and the Declaration of Rights, because of its simplicity, was a resounding example to the whole world. While the mob was "barbarous beyond the tiger's cruelty," the people were fundamentally good, emboldened by liberty and had begun to think for themselves.[72] Wollstonecraft also refused to hold up Britain as a model of constitutional stability. In her view, 1688, rather than being a founding act of justice, had stifled discussion and given the false impression that perfection had already been achieved in constitutional matters. British freedom, once a model for other nations, had descended into corruption, arrogance and complacency. The British, repressed by the pretence of power-seeking elites who had hijacked liberty, could not envisage further change and were thus unable to secure their true rights. Wollstonecraft did not explicitly set out to undermine the constructed image of Britain as a model of liberty, yet in her history of the Revolution, she, like other British radical writers, contributed to the subversion of a view of British perfection which hailed 1688 and a constitutional heritage of moderate reform as the beacon of civilised society.

The writings of British residents such as Williams and Wollstonecraft can appear contradictory and dissonant, combining different styles, registers, contributors, sources, and objectives. Yet they provide a reading of the French Revolution which was ultimately entirely in keeping with the broader experience of the British community at this crucial period of the Revolution,

---

70 Ibid, p. 85.
71 Ibid, pp. 212, 222.
72 Ibid, p. 234.

whatever the literary or political traditions they subscribed to. As enthusiastic observers of the Revolution at both the time of the fall of the Bastille, but also during the more troubled months after the declaration of the republic, by 1792-93, British radical residents were confronted with all the ambiguities and contradictions of a more complex political landscape where violence existed alongside heightened popular political participation, and where eloquence was considered both a mask of intrigue and a way of "impressing the results of thinking on minds alive only to emotion," giving "wings to the slow foot of reason, and fire to the cold labours of investigation."[73] This was also what Helen Williams was referring to when she noted the passage from the simplicity of 1789 to the complexity of the later period. Emigrants were also writing for a British audience whose general approbation of the Revolution in 1789 had been replaced by more widespread antipathy, fuelled by loyalist propaganda and a broadly hostile press. It is not surprising, therefore, that British eyewitness reports contained stylistic and ideological incongruity. Writings to Britain meshed original reflection with the insertion of second-hand material, they veiled their criticism of the British constitution in historical accounts of a foreign revolution, they allowed contingent writers to insert reflections which did not fit neatly with their own, and, as in the case of Mary Wollstonecraft, they merged optimistic readings of the progress of humanity with doubt at the course the revolutionaries had pursued. The polyphony of the accounts produced by British eyewitnesses was testimony to the complex standpoint they adopted after the foundation of the republic, when dejected withdrawal, zealous tenacity or muted optimism about the Revolution's future could be grafted on to general enthusiasm at its founding principles. It is also a reflection of the different ways such writers chose to portray the Revolution to a British audience whose opinions they could only judge from afar and where the temper of public opinion often jarred with their open approval for the republican turn.

---

73 Ibid, p. 61.

11

'A spectacle worthy of heaven and earth'
Sampson Perry's *An Historical Sketch of the French Revolution* (1796)

Sampson Perry was one of the members of the British emigrant community who had been forced into exile after repeated prosecutions for seditious libel over the course of 1791 and 1792. He had failed to rein in his outspoken criticism of the government in his radical newspaper and had consequently become a target of ministerial repression. A militia surgeon turned captain before taking on the editorship of *The Argus* in March 1789, Perry is one of the most defiant yet least known radicals of his time. Although his attempts to secure the republication of his newspaper in Paris seem to have failed, Perry's brief stay in France was transformative. He regularly met with Thomas Paine, whom he knew from London, and was one of the regular visitors to the latter's residence in rue du faubourg Saint-Denis, where he also became acquainted with William Choppin and William Johnson. He was involved in the hub of radicalism at White's hotel and, though he joined the *SADH* after the presentation of the November 1792 address to the National Convention, he revitalised the group and contributed to its initiatives at the end of the year.

Perry was also respected by members of the revolutionary administration. After being identified as one of a number of British residents considered loyal partisans of the republic, he accepted a diplomatic mission on behalf of Hérault de Séchelles, a member of the *Comité de Salut Public*. In May 1793 he appeared as a witness at the trial of Jean-Paul Marat, a man he greatly esteemed and would go on to celebrate in his *Historical Sketch*. At the hearing,

Perry stated his continued admiration for the Revolution and deplored the publication of a supposed suicide note from William Johnson in Brissot's newspaper, *Le Patriote français*, which blamed Marat for the degeneration of the Revolution. In his testimony on 24th April 1793, Perry conceded, "I was distressed to see [the note] in the *Patriote français*, because it gave the impression in England that, Marat, whom I consider a useful man, was setting France ablaze."[1] Jeanbon Saint-André, a permanent member of the *Comité de Salut Public* and apologist of the September massacres, tried to secure Perry's exemption from the measures taken against foreigners in late 1793. Despite special pleas on his behalf by members of the ruling Montagnard administration, Perry spent fourteen months in different French jails, including the Luxembourg and the Madelonnettes, only narrowly escaping execution. He returned to Britain in the spring of 1795 to be indicted for previous sedition charges and sent to Newgate prison for seven years.

Perry was not the only radical to suffer from incarceration in both Britain and France, yet he was one of the few to emerge from the Luxembourg even more convinced of the merits of the ideals he considered the Revolution to stand for and was the only British radical to have publicly acclaimed Jean-Paul Marat, a man whom Helen Maria Williams, writing two years before Perry, accused of "villainy" and of being a "determined aristocrate [sic]" in league with the tyrannical heads of European monarchies.[2] In Newgate, Perry began a major writing venture inspired by persecution in Britain and his firsthand experience of the Revolution in France. His previously banned newspaper, *The Argus*, reappeared in two bound volumes which drew on new material, he printed his own self-defence entitled *Oppression!!!: The Appeal of Captain Perry, Late Editor of the Argus, to the People of England: Containing a Justification of his Principles and Conduct* (1795) and wrote *An Historical Sketch of the French Revolution* (1796), published by one of his fellow inmates, H. D. Symonds, in 1796. In 1797 *The Origin of Government Compatible with and Founded on the Rights of Man* was published by J. S. Jordan. Perry also wrote for the *Monthly Magazine* while he was in prison in 1796, penning a series of portraits of the leading figures of the Revolution.[3]

---

1   See Sampson Perry's testimony in the trial of Jean-Paul Marat: "J'ai été très affligé de la voir dans le Patriote français, parce qu'elle tendait à faire croire en Angleterre que Marat, que je regarde comme un homme utile, mettait toute la France en combustion." *Le Moniteur Universel*, vol. 16, Friday 3rd May 1793.
2   H. M. Williams, *Letters from France*, III, p. 70.
3   See *The Monthly Magazine*, vol. 2 (1796) and vol. 3 (1797). The portraits are anonymous, yet what suggests that the author of the portraits was Perry, however, are a series of remarks on the importance of rewarding merit rather than social standing, the scourge of birth advantage and the regrettable way in which writers were persecuted, all perennial themes of the radical editor. The notice also ends with the statement that "the anecdotes will be regularly continued and the conductors request the assistance of all persons who, by a recent residence in France, are qualified to communicate original and interesting facts." Perry had regularly claimed that his residence in Paris meant that he was knowledgeable enough to comment on the Revolution. This along with the reference to themes familiar

Perry had left Britain in late November or early December 1792, when radical writers and editors were beginning to become the target of government repression.[4] Yet by the time of his return in 1795 the political context had changed significantly. In late 1793 the so-called 'Scottish Martyrs' had been sentenced to transportation for their role in the convening of the British Convention in Edinburgh, while in May 1794 key members of the radical London Corresponding Society had been arrested and detained in Newgate prison or the Tower of London on charges of treason. Their acquittal in November and December 1794 had not substantially eased the pressure on radical activists, and the 1795 Two Acts, or "Gagging" Acts as they were dubbed, revised the terms of treason offences and banned large-scale public gatherings in an attempt to dissipate popular association.[5] From the mid-1790s therefore, despite the fact that very few prosecutions were actually brought against radicals under the terms of the Two Acts, perceptions of how dissent could be expressed and what form public protest could take had changed. Reformers refrained from articulating opposition in the same vociferous and public ways they had done in the early years of the decade. Expressions of protest thus found outlets in either underground militant movements or through more codified defiance.

Not only had the terms of reference changed for radical activists, with dissent, now narrowly contained by the letter of the law, being manifested in more covert and ambiguous ways, but many now found themselves detainees in political wings of prisons. Although, on the one hand, the conditions of incarceration restricted the expression of dissent, in that behaviour and writing would have been heavily policed, publications vetted and associations closely monitored, on the other hand the prison experience could intensify grievances, foster alliances between fellow inmates and, in the case of Newgate jail, prompt the forging of a hub of radical exchange which fuelled rather than dissipated a culture of resistance. Iain McCalman has delved into the subculture located within the walls of Newgate jail during the last years of the 1790s. Civilian detainees, behind bars for political misdemeanours, were incarcerated together, often sharing living quarters and social spaces

---

in his work, hints that he had probably been commissioned to write the portraits.

4   Perry, although in France throughout the month of October 1792, returned to SCI meetings for three weeks in a row in November 1792. His last recorded attendance was on 23rd November 1792, and it is likely that he set off for Paris shortly after this date. The SCI ordered an advertisement to be published in *The Argus* for a week after the 23rd November 1792 (see TS 11/965/3510/A1), so the date of Perry's departure was more likely to have been early December. Captain Monro reported Perry's arrival in Paris on 7th January 1793 and his arrival is also recorded in *La Chronique du Mois* of January 1793. *The Times* indicated on 5th January 1793 that Perry was already in Paris.

5   The "Two Acts" banned political lecturing (Treasonable and Seditious Practices Act) and public meetings attended by more than fifty people, unless they had been authorised by a local magistrate (Seditious Meetings Act). Such legislation was effectively an attempt to repress the public and open nature of the radical reform movement in the 1790s yet in reality very few actual prosecutions were brought against radical leaders. For more on the impact of the Two Acts see Barrell, *Imagining the King's Death*.

while they purged their sentences. Radical editors, publishers, writers and artists provided momentum for a number of collective publication projects which would emerge from Newgate, providing inspiration not only for contemporary radical activists but also for later writers, poets and authors of the post-1815 era. The radical engraver Richard Newton sketched the atmosphere within Newgate prison in two works entitled *Soulagement en Prison, or Comfort in Prison* (1793) and *Promenade on the State Side of Newgate* (1793). Newton and those publishing from within Newgate set out to counter the authorities' detrimental portrait of civil prisoners behind bars for political dissent, portraying the rectitude, civility and egalitarian spirit of those in Newgate.[6]

McCalman, who has called for more interest to be devoted to Perry's account of the French Revolution, argued that "[Perry] is one of the 1790s ultraradicals whose political extremism crystallised as a direct consequence of counterrevolutionary repression."[7] For Perry, repression and firsthand witnessing of the French Revolution were not only politicising but were paradoxically a form of public salvation, bringing him back from the brink of anonymity and providing his writing with purpose. Having been disappointed in both his military and journalistic careers, the latter by "deceiving friends", he believed himself to be the victim of wilful persecution. His public existence after 1792 was forged around the reiteration of this perceived persecution, and through this he achieved a certain prestige that he may never have had access to otherwise. His status as "late editor of the Argus," appeared on the title pages of almost all his Newgate works and he prefaced his *Historical Sketch* with "The Particulars of s. PERRY's Case – of the Occasion of his leaving England." No longer known for his satirical jibes at ministers, he gained recognition as the "persecuted editor", and his reputation was forged through reference to his outlawry and alienation rather than the particular causes for which he had previously fought.

Perry, with a keen sense of his own persecution, believed himself to have been "attacked at all points at once," during the early 1790s libel battles, and considered his lengthy stay in Newgate to have been the result of a "prison-keeper's whisper" and "personal resentment" rather than "the most powerful logic and rhetoric."[8] Perry also used the collapse of his paper as a recurring epithet in Paris. References to him in French archives without mention of the "persecuted" *Argus* are scarce. In the Marat trial papers, one citizen

---

6 John Barrell discusses the visual message conveyed by the representation of British radicals in prison in Newton's engravings in 'Radicalism, Visual Culture, and Spectacle in the 1790s'. There is also a discussion of Newton in McCalman, 'Newgate in Revolution: Radical Enthusiasm and Romantic Counterculture', *Eighteenth Century Life* 22 (1998), pp. 95-110. See also David Alexander, *Richard Newton and English Caricature in the 1790s* (Manchester: Manchester University Press, 1998).

7 See McCalman, 'Sampson Perry, Jacobin Doctor and Journalist', *Dictionary of Literary Biography*, p. 158.

8 *HS* I, p. 22.

described him as "a gallant man, a victim of his love for the French Revolution, he fled his country where he had a price on his head for having defended republican principles in a paper he wrote under the name of the argus of the people."[9] Similarly, *La Chronique du Mois*, announcing the imminent publication of his newspaper in Paris, recounted that Perry had "come to find true friends amongst the directors of the Cercle Social press, who are going to publish in France the persecuted newspaper, *The Argus of the People*."[10] From 1792 onwards, it was his reputation as a target of ministerial persecution which cemented Perry's reputation in the radical movement.

Perry saw this general misrepresentation of his own case as mirroring the way the French Revolution had been maligned in Britain. Equally, the virtues that Perry judged to be the bedrock of the changes occurring in France were those he coveted in his own character. He prided himself on his constancy, gravity, attachment to principle, sincerity and dignity, the antithesis of those "worn-out patriots" that he chastised in the preface to his *Historical Sketch* and blamed for the dissolution of *The Argus*. In the prospectus to the republished *Argus*, Perry wrote:

> The part which I had in establishing a literary work under this name, though of a different nature, justifies my pretensions, more especially as the same reverence for principle and truth which pervaded, which so peculiarly distinguished that work, is the great motive for my commencing this. In the conduct and prosecution of it, it will be seen whether my Political Principles, by which alone I desire to be known to, or estimated by, my Fellow-Citizens, have been shaken, or whether they are not rather confirmed.[11]

He went on "I declare myself beginning the world again" and introduced himself to his readers in "new dress". It was against this backdrop of renewal and with the aim of vindicating the steadfastness of his principles that Perry wrote his *Historical Sketch*, an optimistic historical account of the French Revolution from 1789 to 1795 but also a veiled attack on the British government, constitution and apathetic populace.

---

9   Letter from Citoyenne Moreau, Affaire Marat, AN W 269/16 folio 30: "un galant homme victime de son amour pour la révolution française il a fui son pays où sa tête est mise à prix pour avoir défendu les principes républicains dans une feuille qu'il rédigeait sous le nom de l'argus du people."
10 *La Chronique du Mois*, January 1793, p. 80. "To the Friends of Truth. *Sampson Perry*, auteur d'un journal républicain, en Angleterre, *The argus of the People* (*La Sentinelle du Peuple*) pour avoir défendu avec énergie les droits de l'homme, la révolution françoise, Horne-Tooke et Thomas Payne, son ami, n'a échappé que par sa fuite à des bourreaux. Perry et un autre écrivain anglois, Merry…sont venus trouver de francs amis, chez les Directeurs de l'Imprimerie du Cercle Social, qui vont publier en France, le journal persécuté, *The Argus of the People*."
11 Perry, *Prospectus of a new and interesting work, The Argus*, p. 3.

PERRY'S ACCOUNT OF THE REVOLUTION

Although Perry did not deny the excesses that took place during the later stages of the Revolution, he still considered the events of France as setting an example to other nations and having the potential to create a new source of happiness through the establishment of freedom. Despite its length, it is worth quoting the preface to volume two in full, which charts the events that he had witnessed in part:

> Writing first volume was a more "pleasing task" than second. In that part of the Revolution reason only presided; passion and vengeance by turns have since been seen to triumph. It is impossible however, without injustice, to condemn the design, on account of the errors of those who were appointed to carry it into execution.
>
> The Author is aware of the unpopularity he may lie under at present, for not condemning the Revolution altogether, as other writers who have gone before him have done: he is, nevertheless, not afraid to appeal to impartial posterity, as to whose opinion of it is best founded. It is true, that in following up the progress of this Revolution, (as new in its nature, as wonderful in its effect) the eye will necessarily sometimes be arrested by scenes of horror and of pity, the painful instances of human ferocity arising out of the former debasement of the People; but if this event from first to last be seen only with a philosophic eye, and those humiliating evidences of the joint imperfection of man and of government be overlooked, what a delightful prospect will present itself to the view! For though the sun of freedom at its rising in France should have been obscured by passing clouds, and sometimes veiled with almost impenetrable darkness, yet is it expected henceforward to shine with meridian lustre, and to extend its beaming influence to the happy guidance of every politically bewildered country in the world.[12]

Although the "horrors" and "impenetrable darkness" of the gloomier phases of the Revolution are not omitted, he recommends that they be "overlooked" and that the events be seen with a broad, "philosophic eye." Such a perspective would, he believed, help to convince those in doubt of the ultimate benefits of the Revolution. In the main body of the account, the flaws and machinations of the privileged class are set in sharp contrast to the justice and boldness of the people. While the violence of the September massacres and later emergency rule are not justified, they are explained on rational grounds, and if the king, his ministers, the Girondin members and Robespierre are heavily criticised, leading members of the Montagne, the

---

12 *HS* II, pp. iii-iv.

members of the first Constituent Assembly and Jean-Paul Marat are given more sympathetic treatment.

Perry's criticism of Louis XVI is unreserved throughout the two volumes. From the outset he condemns the former king's want of character and resolution and his underhand strategies and calculating manipulation of the Assembly.[13] Although he explains how some of the king's speeches in 1789 and 1790 and his professions of loyalty to the Revolution had been well-received by the population, "the subsequent conduct of this monarch taught the people, at length, to set less and less value upon such declarations and professions."[14] As Perry pursues the history of the Revolution during the course of 1791, the verdict on Louis XVI is even more damning. Perry again denounces the character of the king after his interrupted journey to St Cloud, asserting that any glimpses of courage were "solitary efforts" and he had no "innate quality", all his best speeches having been written by others.[15] He concludes his first volume with an attack on the French monarch, whose "inglorious" conduct and "duplicity" could not be overlooked:

> The gross ignorance the king of France shewed in men, in things, in nature, by all his actions, is the best excuse to the French nation for depriving him of his power. It is a miserable reflection on the head of a king, that he knows nothing of the hearts of men. It is a phrenzy in a chief magistrate, whether king or emperor, to desire to reign longer than he is willing to consult the good of the people. Under any other tenure, the sceptre is always liable to be wrested from the hand that would wield it, and the life of him who disputes its relinquishment put into imminent hazard.[16]

Perry's denunciation of the hypocrisy and weakness of the king continues in volume two where the author lists Louis's crimes and presents him as "the restorer of French liberty, yet giving way to perfidy and perjury." Again the king's character comes under assault as Perry describes the "conduct of this unhappy man" as "at one time inflated with pride; at another peevish with ill humour; and lastly, condescending and even humble from fear." Louis is accused of having refused to listen to the concerns of the people at the *Fête de la Fédération*. Perry reminds his reader, "Did not the people speak out and speak plainly to him?"[17] As a result of such blatant disregard for the views of the populace, the king could not be reprieved by shifting the blame on to the corruption of his court.

The king's ministers, guards, queen and faithful followers also come under attack as the representatives of privilege, "speculating on the miseries of the poor." He exposes the profligacy of state pensions, that "despotic

---

13 *HS* I, pp. 19, 192-3.
14 Ibid, p. 374.
15 Ibid, p. 570
16 Ibid, p. 623.
17 *HS* II, pp. 40, 109, 194.

waste of national wealth," and suggests that considerable sums of public money were given to prostitutes and opera performers. He highlights the "underhand and treasonable proceedings" of the aristocracy and the "self-interest" of the émigrés, "those ungrateful children of their country" who would only return to France once they knew their property was under threat.[18] The king's ministers, "obnoxious to the nation," are contrasted with the upstanding representatives of the National Assembly and strong criticism is reserved for the non-juring priests, as well as the king's guards, who carried out an unrelenting attack on the people at the Tuileries on 10th August 1792. Those who were still attached to royalty in October 1792 were "a coalition of bigoted priests and fanatic nobles."[19]

Yet it is Perry's verdict on the execution of the king which is one of the most notable examples of his radical stance and which illustrates how far he had diverged from the views of those representing the events in Britain and even many of his compatriots in Paris, including Helen Maria Williams. Far from condemning the judgement reached by the Convention, he holds it up as a lesson to other "despots and tyrants."[20] He reveals how the king showed no bravery, but only "repugnance" in the face of his imminent execution and justifies the decision not to allow three days' respite to Louis before he went to the guillotine. Regicide is blamed on the king's allies rather than his enemies:

> It was, however, not out of the limits of possibility that an issue, much less disastrous to Louis XVI. than the one we have witnessed, might have been obtained. But royalty, like a dazzling meteor, as long as it is not utterly extinguished in darkness, is followed by infatuation... If this unhappy monarch had gained the knowledge which he affirmed he had acquired by his journey to Varennes; then is there no doubt but that *his friends*, as they were willing to be thought, were the authors of his death, and of a major part of those evils, which were brought upon their country.[21]

The responsibility for the king's death lay therefore with the associates that had corrupted his judgment after his ignominious return from Varennes. After a summary account of the king's execution, which is void of all pathos, Perry immediately goes on to contrast the king's behaviour with that of "this martyr of liberty", Le Pelletier, who was assassinated only days after the king's death.[22] The celebration of a figure of the Revolution in the immediate wake of the passage dealing with regicide demonstrates Perry's refusal to

---

18 *HS* II, p. 283, p. 292, *HS* I, p. 360, *HS* II, p. 42.
19 *HS* I, p. 518, *HS* II, p. 267.
20 *HS* II, pp. 306, 307.
21 Ibid, p. 156.
22 Ibid, p. 308.

show the least compassion for the former monarch and his determination to celebrate those he saw as the true heroes of the Revolution.

Not only does Perry direct severe criticism towards the king, his ministers and guards, and the non-juring clergy, but, in contrast to Helen Maria Williams, he also denounces the Girondin members of the Convention, who refused to countenance the execution of the king. He accuses the representatives of having wanted to spare the king's life "to remove as much as possible the responsibility from themselves." He charges Madame Roland, who had been eulogised by Williams, with having been "a very ambitious woman; she possessed considerable talents for either business or intrigue."[23] He considers the Girondins as detached from the people and, having "studied books and man in the abstract" were "unacquainted with man in the mass." For Perry they were out of touch with the people: "These men were silly enough to think nothing of the people; they were too much of *statesmen* to contemplate the actions and opinions of *common men*."[24] No friends to the poor, "they might wish to level downwards, but it does not appear that they wished to raise upwards."[25]

In contrast to many British commentators therefore, Perry was unreservedly critical of the Girondins, even with the knowledge of the period of emergency rule which followed. He provides justification for the decision to oust the members from the Convention at the end of May 1793, referring to the ambition of the excluded men, their lack of understanding of the people, and their refusal to accept their rightful responsibility. He concludes, "That these men were republicans there can be no doubt… But they were republicans too much spoiled by diplomacy to love equality. A republic with inequalities which they might fill up, would have been more congenial to their dispositions. Their lives were useful to liberty; their deaths will not be less so."[26] This final statement is rare in its bold and barely veiled defence of the execution of the Girondins and its admission of the utility of their deaths to the cause of the Revolution. This was a position that was almost unique among British accounts and came close to echoing the discourse offered by the leading members of the Montagne who saw the purging of the seats of power as essential to maintaining the purity of the Revolution. While very few British observers would have gone as far as to justify the violence committed during the period of emergency rule, Perry was one of the only members of the *SADH* who did so in a frank and unrepentant way.

While Perry criticises the Girondins' lack of empathy for the poor, he celebrates the legacy of Jean-Paul Marat, whose trial he had testified at and whose journal, *L'Ami du Peuple*, had claimed to represent the plight of the ordinary man. According to Perry, Marat was not a counter-revolutionary but

---

23 Ibid, pp. 303, 342
24 Ibid, p. 347.
25 Ibid, p. 385.
26 Ibid, p.426.

an ultra-revolutionary. He was denounced in newspapers and pursued with "unavailing, endless persecution" which explained (if not justified) his vengeful behaviour.[27] Perry may have personally identified with Marat, whose persecution he saw as mirroring his own at the hands of the authorities in Britain. He alludes to Marat's speech of 26th May 1793 against luxury, in which the French revolutionary spoke of the necessity of "*republican manners*":

> Thus it is obvious that this man, so generally execrated for his sanguinary disposition, did by his discourses most essentially serve the cause of the revolution. He was a bitter enemy to the idle and ostentatious aristocracy; and every one knows how much their bad example impedes the virtuous efforts of the sincere and good republican.[28]

Out of all the revolutionaries mentioned in Perry's account, it is Jean-Paul Marat who receives the most glowing praise and who is portrayed as the closest to understanding the plight of the people.

While the Girondins are criticised and Marat celebrated, Perry is more reticent on the overall merits of Montagnard rule. He admits that of those who were executed as "Dantonists" in April 1794, there had been "two honest patriots" among them, although he does not specify which.[29] He evokes the wickedness of Robespierre, calling him a "tyrant" and portraying him as inimical to the freedom of the people. Yet he also suggests that Robespierre's downfall unfortunately allowed royalists to gain ground again: "With the fall of Robespierre, who was *bad*, much of that which the best friends of France thought *good* was destroyed, and the re-action of opinion had well nigh allowed *royalism* again to set up its standard in the month of December, of the same year":

> It is hoped the reader will do the author the justice to believe, he does not mean to sully the lustre of the revolution of France, by perhaps too minutely detailing the enormities of one of its professors. The merits of that revolution stand distinct from those of any of its abettors or opposers. He is not of the opinion of some, who believe it to be the work of a few men's hands: on the contrary, he thinks these characters and personages the natural production of revolutions; and he is almost at a loss to guess how that in France could have been carried forward without them.[30]

Perry refuses to detail the crimes of Robespierre for fear of damaging the reputation, or "lustre", of the Revolution as a whole, indicating once again

---

27 Ibid, pp. 386, 384.
28 Ibid, p. 402.
29 Ibid, p. 518.
30 Ibid, pp. 537, 539.

his determination to portray the Revolution as broadly beneficial despite its violent excesses.

If Perry directs criticism at most of the principal actors of the Revolution, apart from a handful of patriotic leaders of the Montagne, including Jean-Paul Marat, he celebrates the enlightened statesmen of the first National Assembly unreservedly. He praises their conduct, despite their having had to face difficulties due to the popular ferment unleashed after the people recovered their liberty.[31] He celebrates the genius of the leaders of the first Assembly and recounts their contributions to human progress. The replacement of the king's loyal servants by national statesmen meant that the ministry had been filled with "men, promoted not by intrigue, but by supposed merit – whose honorary distinctions were not derived from their ancestors, but from the esteem of their fellow citizens."[32] He contends:

> If ever a body of men, admired for their wisdom, had occasion to counsel with their understandings, it was now the case with the senators of France. To be *firm*, – to be *just* – to evince their *constituent* power – and yet display their *individual* tenderness, called up the best faculties of the human mind.[33]

The National Constituent Assembly was dissolved on 30th September 1791 and gave way to the Legislative Assembly. In retrospect the Constituent Assembly "appears uncommonly brilliant" and "has given a new character or reputation to the country itself; and that eloquence, which before was only accounted bright and sparkling, has since acquired the qualities of *force* and *dignity*."[34]

Perry also rectifies errors concerning the guillotine and the Revolutionary Tribunal, set up to try suspected enemies of the Revolution. While the guillotine had been portrayed as an instrument of terror and bloodshed, an example of the incivility of the French Revolution, Perry reminds his readers that it had initially been devised to equalise punishment for all offenders. Rather than allowing the privileged classes to be executed by decapitation and the poor by the much more barbaric method of hanging, the guillotine was a means to lessen the torture of the death penalty. Its objective was to minimise rather than increase pain and provide balance between the punishment of rich and poor. Similarly, the Revolutionary Tribunal, in Perry's view, was set up to provide fairer treatment for citizens under the law.

Perry reserves his greatest eulogy however for the "people" – who he defines as the poor and those without power. He criticises Louis XVI for having refused to listen to their voices and chastises the Girondin ministers for seeking to direct power away from them. Throughout the sketch, the justice of the ordinary men and women of France is celebrated and the

---

31 *HS* I, p. 278.
32 Ibid, p. 530.
33 *HS* II, p. 25.
34 Ibid, p. 106.

efforts made at different stages of the Revolution to equalise the fortunes of the wealthy and impoverished are praised. The celebration of the people is often achieved through direct and poignant contrasts with the unscrupulous behaviour of those who belonged to the privileged classes. Discussing the decision to reward those who took part in the capture and demolition of the Bastille, Perry states:

> That part of society which is denominated the people, has been always regarded by the privileged few with contumely; when, however, we consider the eagerness with which the latter run after titles and distinctions, it must be insisted on that the following instance of forbearance in the crowd, is as deserving to be recorded as that of any sacrifice we have heard of.[35]

He praises the convergence of civil liberty with practical equality, contending, "Whatever ridicule may at different times have been thrown on the *levelling* principle, the true spirit of *liberty* is inseparable from a spirit of *equality*. But if distinctions of rank are supposed to be incompatible with a genuine freedom, the enjoyment of hereditary honours must have a still more dangerous tendency."[36] Perry would later consider "civil *equalization*" and the tendency of the people to propel the Revolution to "a perfect *democratic* station" as two of the driving forces of the Revolution. The principle of equality, "like the tendency of water to find its level, will rush forward, unless some unnatural obstacle intervene."[37] Perry's praise of the desire to seek equality would have come into contrast with the views of members of the ruling administration, such as Lord Auckland, who had denounced the levelling tendencies of radical reformers.

The civility of the people is also emphasised in the *Historical Sketch*. Perry extols the boldness of ordinary men and women in demonstrating against the conduct of the king's ministers and demanding their dismissal, and celebrates the "pacific, confidential, and legal dispositions of the people, who shewed themselves highly worthy of defending their liberty."[38] In his second volume, Perry dwells on the events of the 10th August 1792 and the September massacres, revising reports of the brutal and bloodthirsty mob conveyed to Britain by hostile observers. Writing of the invasion of the Tuileries, he, like Robert Merry, reminds his readers that it was the king's Swiss guards who began firing first. In an allusion to the story of David and Goliath, Perry describes how the people riposted with "small arms and cannon." Their spirit of vengeance was rooted in real cause, namely the "fury" they felt as "their comrades fell dead by their side."[39] Again, he follows Merry in mentioning the restraint of the popular militias. One

---

35 *HS* I, p. 331.
36 *HS* II, p. 482.
37 Ibid, pp. 344-45.
38 *HS* I, pp. 530, 610.
39 *HS* II, p. 207.

volunteer is described as having rescued a Swiss guard who was on the point of death. Rather than exacting his revenge, the volunteer brought him before the Assembly and demanded that he be given leave to take the guard home and provide him with the necessary care and treatment for his wounds. For Perry, this was "proof that generosity and courage usually inhabit the same breast."[40]

The September massacres however were even more difficult to defend than the events of 10th August 1792, and many leading revolutionaries sought to distance themselves from the wave of summary justice that swept through the Paris prisons in early September 1792. Perry introduces his discussion of the events by referring to accounts of "the licentious and extravagant behaviour of the prisoners under accusations for high treason," from the outset therefore refusing to consider the prisoners as innocent victims of popular barbarity.[41] He goes on to suggest that "in every crisis of the revolution the people have been pushed to some lamentable or fatal excess." While he accepts the massacres as regrettable therefore, he insists that the perpetrators had been driven to their actions by external forces: "The French are a people naturally mild, though lively, and forgiving, though sensitive; but when goaded by danger, or stung by treachery, they are soon driven mad, and, in that furious paroxysm, are to be governed by no rule, nor are their actions to be scanned by any measure."[42] By giving the reasons for the unleashing of madness – the danger of the approaching enemy, the betrayal of counter-revolutionary insurgency, the possible undoing of the Revolution by its detractors – Perry explains the actions in the prisons, if not going as far as justifying them.

Perry also revises the portrait of the specific proceedings that occurred within the prisons during the massacres. Those who had been wounded on 10th August 1792 took brutal measures against the Swiss guards who had been detained in prison, yet showed clemency towards schoolteachers or those parents whose children pleaded mercy for them. There was no blind slaughter but a careful and essentially humane calculation of those who deserved death. In each prison a kind of jury was set up. Perry insists on the legal pretensions of the people, setting up makeshift courts to judge the accused, particularly those charged with firing on the people on 10th August. When a prisoner was "acquitted" by jury he was spared death. The trials were organised with modes of retribution or reprieve which had been well-defined in advance. Those exercising popular justice were revolted by acts of uncivilised behaviour and killed a member of their group who had been searching the pockets of a headless prisoner. Any money found was taken to the municipal authorities and bodies were buried.[43]

---

40 Ibid, p. 208.
41 Ibid, p. 224.
42 Ibid, p. 228.
43 Ibid, pp. 228-34.

The account of the massacres is once again audacious in its defence, or at least comprehension, of acts which most British observers, even in revolutionary France, had roundly condemned. In Britain, the purge of the prisons gave rise to graphic accounts of bloodshed, particularly of notable aristocrats such as the Princesse de Lamballe, whose death is not even mentioned by Perry. Perry describes the swift restitution of order after the events, giving the impression that the massacres may even have had a cathartic effect. He also suggests that France was plagued by fewer foreign enemies afterwards. What emerges therefore from Perry's report is a view that the massacres had occurred not out of spontaneous popular madness but because of comprehensible grievances. Even when executions were carried out, victims were subject to a makeshift trial, some were reprieved and the killings were followed by civilised burials. He concludes by stating that those outside France must suspend judgement, considering that revolutions in general give rise to actions which would not be conceivable in times of peace. Those from the local *comités de surveillance* knew the guilty from the innocent better than anyone and should not be condemned based on outside judgement: "They would offer a number of those revolutionary excuses which a country not in a revolution, and a people not under the agony of multiplied dangers and sufferings, would consider no excuses at all."[44] As eyewitnesses, radicals such as Perry could begin to understand the exceptional circumstances which had led people to acts considered as barbarous to foreign onlookers.

Perry's view of the Revolution is remarkable for its defence of events that had contributed to the renunciation of the Revolution in Britain. While for Perry the violence of the period of emergency rule was lamentable, it was the result of unrelenting pressure from external and internal enemies rather than the conscious design of a group of tyrannical revolutionary leaders directing a violent and unrestrained mob. Such excesses were only to be expected in "the tumultuary movements of a sensitive suffering people, driven almost mad by powerful foes without, and insidious enemies within."[45] As this extract clearly states, Perry concurred with the prevailing Montagnard narrative of 1793-94 which insisted that the Revolution was embattled and threatened by its detractors, the "conspiracy of kings" and their émigré followers. In such circumstances, Perry understood why men were prepared to violate laws in order to defend the brand of liberty they were striving to establish:

> The French now began to be more sensible than ever of their newly acquired liberty. Its value was not depreciated by the danger of obtaining it, and the difficulty of preserving it. They saw it exposed to hazard as much be the insidious designs of professed but deceiving friends and apostates, as from the powerful attacks

---

44 Ibid, p. 238.
45 *HS* I, p. 15.

of inveterate enemies. It is no wonder their fears, their alarms, their jealousies should be carried to the greatest excess, or that their vigilance and caution should lead them to infringe those very rights, and that sacred freedom, which they wished to preserve and perpetuate.[46]

Perry's account dismissed the darker phases of the Revolution as "passing clouds". In similar phlegmatic fashion, he acknowledged that a period of tumult was necessary before order could be restored: "The revolution, like a ship that has to sail through a narrow strait, had to pass over a critical period."[47] Even the several months that Perry spent incarcerated in Paris did not make him doubt that the Revolution would ultimately triumph. The author confirmed that great human sacrifices had to be made to ensure its success: "For my own part, were I one of ten millions of men, and the transition from slavery to freedom should cost the lives of all but ten, I would take my chance to survive – I would run at the prize!"[48]

In his major Newgate work therefore, Sampson Perry delivered a resounding defence of the French Revolution. This in itself was an extremely radical position in 1795-96. As Amanda Goodrich has noted, by 1795 "events in France had diluted enthusiasm for Paineite republicanism among many radicals."[49] Loyalist writings on the events in France multiplied. William Frend concluded that "the assassinations, murders, massacres, burning of houses, plundering of property, open violations of justice, which have marked the progress of the French Revolution, must stagger the boldest republican in his wishes to overthrow any constitution".[50] Critic of the Revolution, William Playfair, wrote:

> I am a greater advocate for liberty than those who call themselves reformers and patriots... I appeal therefore to the history of the sect against which I have written, to shew that the most disorderly and cruel despotism was exercised under the appearance of liberty and justice; that far from being an enemy to liberty, I am its friend, though I do not chuse to join in the general deception that has been practised with regard to what has been called French liberty.[51]

---

46 Ibid, p. 466.
47 *HS* II, pp. 267-8.
48 Ibid, p. 447.
49 Amanda Goodrich, *Debating England's Aristocracy in the 1790s* (Woodbridge: Boydell, 2005), p. 125.
50 William Frend, *Peace and Union Recommended to the Associated Bodies of Republicans and Anti-Republicans* (1793), quoted in Goodrich, *Debating England's Aristocracy*, p. 125. The very title of Frend's work shows how writers were beginning to direct their appeals to both reformers and loyalists alike, considering that the language of British constitutionalism could resonate with both.
51 William Playfair, *The History of Jacobinism, Its Crimes, Cruelties and Perfidies: Comprising an Inquiry Into the Manner of Disseminating, under the Appearance of Philosophy and Virtue, Principles Which are Equally Subversive of Order, Virtue, Religion, Liberty and Happiness* (Philadelphia: Cobbett, 1796), pp. 19-20. Playfair, identified by Alger as a spectator at the fall of the

Perry's prose ran counter not only to loyalist literature, but also to the more moderate stance taken by British reformers who were repelled by the violence that had occurred in France. The radical author nevertheless maintained his faith in the French version of liberty, noting in his preface:

> A people long distinguished for the refinement of their manners, and for the brilliancy of their wit and genius, setting to surrounding nations a glorious example, by vindicating the injured rights of man, against opposition the most formidable that can be conceived, is one of those occurrences which cannot be magnified by the power of language. To spurn under foot the idols of tyranny and superstition by the influence of reason, – to erect, on the ruins of arbitrary power, the glorious edifice of civil liberty, – is a spectacle worthy of earth and heaven.[52]

It took courage – or perhaps a deep sense of disaffection – to utter such praise for the Revolution in 1796, with the memory of the violence of the Revolution still vivid, although of course Perry was already behind bars and therefore posed little tangible threat. He wanted to educate British citizens on the true nature of the Revolution now that the era of Thermidor had begun. Yet a key aim of his writing project was also to call into question the portrait of British liberty which had gained ascendancy, even among former supporters of the Revolution, under the early republic. In his writing, Perry exposed implicitly through a historical account of a foreign revolution what, as editor of *The Argus*, he had denounced explicitly, namely the decadence of British political culture, the lack of transparency in decision-making, the moral vacuity of kings, the need for external reform of government and the unaccountability of ministers. His political agenda had not been shaken, neither had his faith in a French brand of liberty, but his methods had radically altered. Perry now adopted much more covert means of perpetuating a culture of opposition to the British status quo than before his departure to Paris.

While lauding the accountability of deputies in the National Convention, Perry asserts, "The members had not sat long enough to forget the limits of the authority given to them by their *diplomas*."[53] The allusion to the unreformed British parliament is unmistakable, as British Members of Parliament had been consistently criticised for attending to their own

---

Bastille, had also been a far-from-trusted associate of Joel Barlow in Paris. See Buel, *Joel Barlow: American Citizen*, pp. 114-17. I am grateful to Jean-François Dunyach for sharing some of his views on Playfair and for arranging for me to have access to early drafts of Richard Buel's biography of Joel Barlow. See also 'Les réseaux d'un excentrique: vies et parcours de William Playfair (1759-1823)' in Ann Thomson, Simon Burrows, Edmond Dziembowski (eds.), *Cultural Transfers: France and Britain in the Long Eighteenth Century* (Oxford: Oxford University Press, Studies on Voltaire and the Eighteenth Century 4, 2010), pp. 115-27.

52 *HS* I, pp. v-vi.
53 Ibid, p. 261.

interests instead of those of the public at large. Equally, Perry puts forward the protests of different deputations against the Plenary Court after the establishment of the States General, seen as a body which would usurp the rights of Commoners:

> The parliaments all cried out against this new institution; and that of Britanny sent up a deputation to protest against it as *illegal*, upon the principle that the nation was dissatisfied with the government; that it insisted upon a *reform*, but that the government had no right to reform itself; that it was unnatural to expect it would be done effectually, as it was presumptuous to attempt it at all.[54]

Here Perry reiterates what Paine had railed against in his *Letter Addressed to the Addressers* of September 1792, namely the self-reforming capacities of governments:

> I consider the reform of Parliament, by an application to Parliament, as proposed by the Society, to be a worn-out, hackneyed subject, about which the nation is tired, and the parties are deceiving each other. It is not a subject which is cognizable before Parliament, because no government has the right to alter itself, either in whole or in part. The right, and the exercise of that right, appertains to the nation only, and the proper means is by a national convention, elected for the purpose, by all the people.[55]

David Williams had also picked up this issue in his *Letters on Political Liberty* of 1782. Thomas Morris noted in his short biographical review of the Welsh reformer how Williams believed that, "where the absurdity of petitioning an offending body to reform itself is strikingly represented; the necessity and practice of national conventions to regulate the legislative and executive powers is historically as well as logically proved."[56] Perry therefore draws upon many of the themes that had animated radical reforming debate in the 1780s and 1790s in his account of the French Revolution.

In discussing how the nobility had taken up their place in the National Assembly, not because of their commitment to reform but primarily because they had been deprived of court favour, Perry appears to make a barely veiled attack on those Whigs who presented themselves as friends of the people: "Since now that a real opportunity offered of proving their disinterestedness, they not only kept aloof, but concerted in private how to wound their professed cause, and plunge the oppressed in greater, because more *confirmed* slavery."[57] As discussed earlier, many radicals began to denounce the reforming Whigs, gathered as the Society of the Friends of

---

54 Ibid, p. 20.
55 Paine, "Letter Addressed to the Addressers" in *CWTP*, p. 477.
56 Morris, *A General View of the Life and Writings of the Rev. David Williams*, p. 16.
57 *HS* I, p. 50.

the People, for abandoning the cause of reform and preferring to court the favour of the Pitt ministry, fearing their own indefinite exclusion from power. Perry also revises prevailing assumptions about the French populace as a bloodthirsty and violent mob, alluding to their republican responsibility and political vitality: "Nothing less than calling a national council seemed likely to satisfy the people."[58] In his portrait of French civic duty, the author implicitly chastises both the British people for their want of robustness in campaigning for greater representation and the authorities for punishing attempts at establishing a National Convention.

Perry's *Historical Sketch* was undoubtedly subversive on an explicit level through its alternative reading of the Revolution, rare for its time and radical in the extent of its defence of what had become a stigmatised event in Britain. Yet it seems undeniable that the text was also defiant in less overt ways. The echoes of core British reforming platforms permeate the text and, in allowing the voices of key figures of the Revolution to be included in unmediated fashion, Perry refrained from engaging in direct criticism of the British political structure, while at the same time actively selecting the arguments put forward to undermine the legitimacy of the *status quo*. Finally, the very medium he chose, the sketch, an immediate rendering based on feeling rather than studied enquiry, subverted claims that true history could only be written with distance and reflection.

REVIEWS OF PERRY'S *HISTORICAL SKETCH*

The Critical Review gave a scathing verdict on Perry's *Historical Sketch* in February 1797. Calling it "a work, which neither for matter nor style possesses any considerable degree of merit," the reviewer suggested that "the candid, even of those who agree in the republican sentiments of the author, will scarcely fail to notice its gross deficiencies on the score of historical impartiality."[59] The work was seen as flawed on account of the author's style but also in its flagrant subjectivity, something Perry himself had anticipated. The same periodical had reviewed Perry's republished *Argus* the previous year, concluding that it "has very slender claims to merit, and many exceptionable articles included in it."[60] The unfavourable reviews continued with *The Monthly Review* of 1797, which considered both the *Historical Sketch* and the republished *Argus* as poorly written and lacking in interest. The reviewer suggested that these "bulky volumes will afford copious food for those politicians, who, having been warmly interested in the passing scenery of the eventful period commencing with the French Revolution, wish to recall to memory the principal transactions, and to view them in a connected form." Yet after issuing such reserved views on the usefulness of Perry's work, the critic went on to censure his style of writing:

---

58 Ibid, p. 21.
59 *The Critical Review, or, Annals of Literature*, vol. 19 (1797), p. 180.
60 *The Critical Review, or, Annals of Literature*, vol. 18 (1796), p. 339.

> We must observe, however, that the narration is calculated for politicians on one side only; that it is for the most part mere compilation and transcription; and that it can boast of little merit of style or composition. The French Revolution is not a theme for a common mind or a dashing pen; still less for a professed party writer, except for the use of party readers.[61]

Perry was, put plainly, a bad writer whose explicit political bias and determination to show the favourable side of the Revolution deprived his account of any true value. His preference for including the texts of speeches, letters and declarations provoked the scorn of the reviewer who saw such strategies as revealing his lack of skill as a writer. It is doubtful that Perry's account of the French Revolution was widely read, even among so-called "party readers". Very few political leaders, even from among the Opposition, would have concurred with Perry's radical reading of the French Revolution. His *Historical Sketch* may have been read by his fellow inmates within Newgate as they worked concurrently on publishing projects and joint ventures which attempted to perpetuate a culture of resistance to the prevailing national discourse of loyalism.

Perry was an expert in self-fashioning. From surgeon to lieutenant to editor, he carved out an unexpected yet ultimately fruitless publication project for himself in revolutionary Paris only weeks after his newspaper had been closed down in London. He also generated a reputation for himself as an unswerving partisan of the French Revolution among the Parisian authorities and orchestrated a substantial publication enterprise from Newgate jail while imprisoned for libel on his return to England. Perry combined criticism of an unreformed political system with an attack on an apathetic British populace and faith in the underpinnings of the French Revolution, even during and following the period of emergency rule. It was the "seed of liberty" and the "philosophic light" of the French Revolution which galvanised his radicalism. Moral ignorance and political servitude, catalysts of the Revolution in his eyes, remained the scourge of British political life. He clung to a rationalist view of government and liberty and, with few acquaintances and resources, did not disguise his admiration for French justice, even seeing terror and violence, dramatised by artists like Gillray and Rowlandson in harrowing satire, as "passing clouds". Just like that of the Revolution, Perry's reputation in Britain was beleaguered. He spent a large part of his later life in prison, either for libel or debt. Yet Perry is a breed of radical who defied categorisation. His independent commitment to protest, his place at the crossroads of British and French culture, his capacity for reinvention and the mobilisation of *The Argus* as a symbol of opposition were attempts both to resist and harness infringement on radical expression in late 1790s Britain. The Recorder of Birmingham, Matthew Davenport Hill, summed up Perry's life in an 1817 letter:

---

61 *The Monthly Review, or Literary Journal*, vol. 22 (1797), p. 103.

> While I was writing to you this morning I was interrupted by the entrance of an old patriot, Captain Sampson Perry, a friend of Tom Paine and author of an excellent history of the French revolution. He was imprisoned by our Government, during the suspension of the Habeas Corpus Act [probably in 1794], for seven years on account of what they were pleased to call a libel in the Argus, a paper of which he was proprietor and conductor. He is a fine old man, possessing all the fire of youth. His face, which is furrowed with age and care, is every now and then lighted up with the enthusiasm of boyhood, and though his hopes are lowered by disappointment his heart is not shut against confidence.[62]

Writing two years before the Peterloo massacre, in an era when the French Revolution had less traction within a more national-focused radical movement, the Recorder of Birmingham nevertheless described the "old patriot" Perry with nostalgia, as a figure who embodied the idealism and resilience of the 1790s.[63]

---

62 To Margaret Bucknall, Temple, 29th January 1817, Rosamond D. Hill and Florence D. Hill, *The Recorder of Birmingham: A Memoir of Matthew Davenport Hill; with Selections from his Correspondence* (London: Macmillan, 1878), pp. 22-3.

63 The massacre at St. Peter's Field in Manchester on 16th August 1819 occurred during a peaceful demonstration by people requesting the right to elect their own parliamentary representatives. The violent reaction of the local yeomanry calvary, leading to the death of eighteen people and the injury of over 700, had a lasting legacy on the British reform movement and was recalled in the later Chartist campaign.

12

British Girondins?

The political sympathies of British nationals resident in Paris during the early republic have been, in the main, judged in retrospect, whether by later commentators considering their involvement in French politics over a long span of the revolutionary period, or by British participants themselves, looking back on their experience in France in the wake of the overthrow of emergency government in 1794. Those radicals who wrote retrospective autobiographical accounts of their role in the French Revolution, such as Helen Maria Williams, David Williams or Henry Redhead Yorke, often allowed opinions constituted after the events to filter through into their versions of the early republican period. Helen Williams' *Souvenirs de la Révolution française* (1828), not translated into English, is filled with sorrow at the loss of her Girondin friends, while David Williams and Henry Yorke both regretted the Revolution itself by the turn of the century and wrote their enthusiasm of 1792 out of their later autobiographical accounts. For Whitney Jones, David Williams' case "is surely the embodiment of that pattern of transition from euphoric approval to disillusioned discomfiture which typified so much of British reaction to events in France."[1] Commentators from the time noted a trend towards dejected withdrawal from the Revolution among British eyewitnesses as it wore on. Thomas Rickman wrote of Thomas Paine:

---

[1] Jones, *The Anvil and the Hammer*, p. 113.

It is well known that Mr. Paine always lamented the turn affairs took in France, and grieved at the period we are now adverting to, when corrupt influence was rapidly infecting every department of the state. He saw the jealousies and animosities that were breeding, and that a turbulent faction was forming among the people that would first enslave and ultimately overwhelm even the convention itself.[2]

Yet, Michael Sonenscher's counselling of "proceeding prospectively rather than retrospectively" in relation to the supposed causal relationship between the Enlightenment and the French Revolution might be useful when considering the position of British participants in revolutionary Paris.[3] Onlookers frequently revised their earlier views in line with their opinions at the time of writing as part of a drive to re-establish or revise their reputations.

Retrospective revisionism is equally identifiable in the accounts of French contemporaries who sought to transcribe the events they witnessed firsthand in later accounts. Paul Barras, who would eventually go on to be a key figure in the Directoire, described the political coup of 31st May 1793 as "having seen one of the two factions in the assembly, the right side, the Girondins, succumb in the struggle against the left side, the Montagnards."[4] Writing his memoirs, Barras, whose reputation would eventually be built on his involvement in the post-Thermidorian regime, had an interest in portraying the Convention of 1793 as wrought by binary and factional infighting which would ultimately only be quelled by the more stable and moderate republican regime.

While analytical distance can sometimes prove useful in judging historical events, in the case of the British emigrant community in Paris, distance has tended to confer a dubious coherence not only on the social and political networks they belonged to but also on the ideas they were considered to have espoused. A prevailing portrait of British pro-revolutionary residents of Paris is that they were, by and large, associated with the Girondins, a political category whose usefulness has been brought into question.[5]

---

2 Rickman, *The Life of Thomas Paine*, pp. 137-8.
3 Michael Sonenscher, 'Review Article: Enlightenment and Revolution', *The Journal of Modern History* 70 (1998), p. 380.
4 "La journée du 31 mai [1793] où la représentation nationale avait été violée, avait vu l'une des deux factions de l'assemblée, le côté droit, les Girondins, succomber dans la lutte contre le côté gauche, les Montagnards." Paul Barras, *Mémoires* 1769-1793, vol. 2 (Clermont-Ferrand: Paléo, 2004), p. 96.
5 Scholars such as William Doyle have brought into question the accuracy of the traditional distinction between the "moderate" Girondins, committed to the advance of capitalism and commercial society, and the "radical" Montagnards, drawing on classical political models for inspiration, pursuing a pure ideal of revolution, opposed to commercialism and committed to popular governance.

Alison Patrick has carried out a painstaking exploration of affinities in the first French republican Convention.[6] Patrick's quantitative study of voting patterns in the *appels nominaux* during the course of 1793 demonstrates the behaviour of representatives and re-examines traditional perceptions of party allegiance. Her study contributes to undermining the thesis that there was a consistent and clearly identifiable "Girondin" block in the Convention during the course of 1793.[7] Patrick shows that Girondins were a rough grouping broadly opposed to the influence of the Parisian sections and with certain values in common, but they were also men who were classed together because of their ties of friendship. This was the case for Roland, Brissot and Pierre Vergniaud. Patrick points out that while Vergniaud was seen as a member of the Girondin grouping, he also voted in favour of the death of the king. Voting for execution in the trial was generally interpreted as a sign of sympathy with the Montagne.[8] Michael Sydenham has also argued that the divisions between Girondins and Montagnards were more pragmatic than ideological. Historians have expressed doubt therefore concerning the usefulness of political categorisation. Some have suggested that such terms were more propaganda tools serving immediate political purposes – such as in the case of Barras – than true determinants of principle or affiliation. There is, therefore, no historical consensus on the categories themselves which have been used to describe the political affiliations of British nationals resident in the French capital. Given these considerations, we may wonder how relevant it is therefore to talk about British "Girondins."

Allusions to British residents' Girondin affinities abound, however, in the historical record. John Hurford Stone has been described as having "totally identified himself with France and the Girondins," despite his decision to publish John Oswald's very un-Girondin text.[9] Steven Blakemore has suggested that on the whole British and American admirers of Revolution had "a quasi-Girondist perspective of the Revolution," while Helen Maria Williams was described as being "a warm adherent of the Girondist party."[10]

---

6 Alison Patrick, *The Men of the First French Republic: Political Alignments in the National Convention of 1792* (Baltimore & London: Johns Hopkins University Press, 1972). Patrick's study, as she readily admits, cannot pretend to account for behaviour before January 1793 as there were no *appels nominaux* before this date. The period immediately after the declaration of the republic is therefore immensely difficult to qualify in terms of party allegiance and behaviour.
7 See in particular the chapter entitled 'The Problem of Political Divisions in the Convention', *The Men of the First French Republic*, pp. 3-36.
8 See Vergniaud's speech during the trial of Louis XVI: "Quant à moi, mon choix est fait. Que Louis périsse, que le peuple soit sauvé, et que tous les maux dont on nous menace retombent ensuite sur ma tête, s'il le faut. Je les brave ; on n'est jamais malheureux quand on s'est sacrifié pour son pays." *Le Moniteur Universel*, vol. 14, Wednesday 2nd January 1793.
9 Christina Bewley and David K. Bewley, *Gentleman Radical: A Life of John Horne Tooke, 1736-1812* (London: Tauris Academic Studies, 1998), pp. 143-4.
10 Steven Blakemore, *Crisis in Representation*, p. 17; Clayden, *The Early Life of Samuel Rogers*, p. 77.

Such a portrait of British residents of Paris is not restricted to the work of Anglo-American historians. Writing in the immediate wake of the Russian Revolution, Albert Mathiez wrote of the key figures in the British circle as "true Girondins" and suggested that most of the Anglo-American colony in Paris had affiliated to the Girondin party. Lionel Woodward, largely relying on Mathiez's Marxist view that the Girondins were part of a bourgeois betrayal of the popular masses, wrote in his biography of Helen Maria Williams that she saw events from a "Girondist" point of view, while Paul Gerbod reiterated Woodward's conclusions in his work on British visitors to France. Jacques Godechot suggested that the British nourished links with the Girondins, sharing their cultivated spirit, taste for philosophical abstraction and respect for the law.[11]

Historians who have categorised British radicals as Girondins have done so with sometimes conflicting intentions. Some have sought to situate these individuals politically, attempting to ally their ideas with those being expressed in the Convention, in political pamphleteering or in the wider international debate. This is often linked to an attempt to demonstrate the relative moderation of British spectators of the Revolution, their penchant for enlightened leadership, and their abhorrence of the violence associated with the period of emergency rule in 1793-1794. Yet for others, the term "Girondin" has been employed with the aim of describing the patterns of sociability of members of the British community in Paris and their French associates. Gary Kates has argued that Thomas Paine was drawn to members of the *Cercle Social* such as Bonneville, Condorcet and Lanthenas because they were among the few revolutionaries who could converse in English. Kates has also suggested that the *Cercle Social* leaders themselves were connected more by friendship than intellectual affinity.[12] If British radicals socialised with certain figures in the revolutionary authorities, political alignment with these same individuals was not a necessary corollary.

The shoe-horning of British residents into a political camp begins to unravel when we examine their activities more closely. The constitutional texts published at the turn of 1792 and 1793 show that some, though not all, had a significant interest in the merits of a greater degree of popular participation in government, semi-direct or direct democracy, and held the representative system in mistrust, if not contempt; ideas that went counter to what has become the commonly-held interpretation of Girondism. Robert Merry put forward the merits of classical republican virtue over commercial republicanism and John Oswald believed that the people should have a boisterous role in national government. Oswald's view contrasts therefore with what William Doyle sees as a core element of the Girondin stance: the belief that the opportunity to create an enlightened republic would be squandered "if the ignorant were allowed to override with their prejudices

---

11 Godechot, *La Grande Nation*, pp. 95-6.
12 See Kates, *The Cercle Social*, pp. 120-75.

the benevolent convictions of educated men."[13] Oswald was scathing of elite legislators or enlightened chaperons of the people. He agreed with the Cordeliers position that "representatives had confiscated the right of the people to express the general will." As Patrice Gueniffey has put it, "[The Cordeliers] did not mean giving *citizens* the right to *verify* the conformity of laws with their rights, but returning to the *people* the power to *make* the law, in order to establish, thanks to the immediate exercise of sovereignty, the absolute reign of the general will."[14] Robert Merry's pamphlet on the new republican constitution is much more reticent on the vocal presence of the people, but he was deeply sceptical about the merits of representation.

Some studies have nevertheless highlighted how a number of members of the British community did hold views which gave them some leeway in a regime which was increasingly dominated by revolutionary figures who wanted to protect the Revolution from foreign and internal subversion.[15] Such scholars have begun to deconstruct the portrait of British radicals as Girondins, testifying to the range of opinions and positions found within the British emigrant community. This diversity of views and affiliations is apparent in the behaviour of those British nationals that remained in Paris after January 1793, though any evidence must be tempered by the fact that outspoken adherence to the regime in place at this time could be interpreted as a way of guaranteeing personal liberty or the preservation of life or property.

Robert Merry professed his loyalty to the Montagne in a letter to Jacques-Louis David, while Sampson Perry was held in high esteem by leading members of the revolutionary government as late as April 1793. His 1796 *Historical Sketch* is one of the most partisan, pro-revolutionary histories that appeared in Britain in the latter half of the decade. Merry's friend David signed Perry's certificate of civic duty and Perry, with the aid of Robert Smith, agreed to take on a diplomatic mission on behalf of Hérault de

---

13 William Doyle, 'Thomas Paine and the Girondins', p. 216.
14 Gueniffey, 'Cordeliers and Girondins: The Prehistory of the Republic?', p. 106.
15 Michael Rapport, though accepting that the majority of British radicals in Paris had "publicly supported the Girondins," argues that a radical minority, in which he includes John Oswald, were "true Jacobins." Rapport, *Nationality and Citizenship*, pp. 180-1. Albert Mathiez also identified Scottish radicals John Oswald and Thomas Christie as being dedicated to the Montagne, despite the vast majority of foreigners being allied to the Girondins or under the influence of counter-revolutionary elites. See Mathiez, *La Révolution et les étrangers*, pp. 46-7. F. M. Todd acknowledged that Helen Maria Williams had "connexions with the Girondin party," but suggested that her partner, John Hurford Stone, was closer to the Montagnard faction. See F. M. Todd, 'Wordsworth, Helen Maria Williams and France', *Modern Language Review* 43.4 (1948), p. 458. Furthermore, Deborah Kennedy has argued that while the majority of British residents of Paris were disillusioned by the Revolution's course by the end of 1793, some, such as Sampson Perry, did not withdraw their support from the Jacobin leadership. See Deborah Kennedy, 'Responding to the French Revolution: Williams' Julia and Burney's The Wanderer' in Laura Dabundo (ed.), *Jane Austen and Mary Shelley and Their Sisters* (Lanham: University Press of America, 2000), pp. 3-17.

Séchelles.[16] A member of the *Comité de Salut Public*, Hérault would go on to be executed with Danton in April 1793. Perry recalled the incident in his *Historical Sketch*:

> He called upon me a few days afterwards, paid many compliments to my nation, and, after a preface, in which he was pleased to say he considered me as the friend to my fellow creatures, on which ever side the channel they might be situated, and that I must abhor war, and deplore its consequences, he made no hesitation to say, that it was the desire of the committee to open a communication with England again, if it could be done consistently with the honour of France, and the views of the people."[17]

Perry was to send a female relative, resident in France, with letters for Sheridan. The intention of the correspondence was to open negotiations with the British opposition in order to negotiate a possible peace treaty. Perry, imprisoned with Robert Smith, believed that his close acquaintance with Hérault would bring about a summons before the Revolutionary Tribunal. He learnt that he was to be reprieved due to the decision to forego the trial of the 'Dantonists' and proceed directly to execution. Perry's close association with, and agreement to undertaken a mission on behalf of, one of the members of the *Comité de Salut Public* only confirms that British residents had very wide-ranging associations in Paris. Although they often admired the intellectual brilliance of the Girondins, they were not uniform in affiliating politically with a group that promoted the merits of enlightened leadership.

John Oswald's views on direct democracy would have chimed with those of leading members of the revolutionary committees, of Cordeliers heritage, and despite his earlier involvement with the *Cercle Social*, he was not averse to espousing more radical ideas on the issue of popular involvement in law-making. His early death in the Vendée in September 1793 means that we cannot judge his view on the Montagnard ascendancy with sufficient accuracy. We might surmise however that he would have adopted a similar position to Perry. Both Robert Smith and Robert Rayment had generated enough confidence in the Parisian sections of their place of residence to prompt impassioned pleas by citizens and section leaders on their behalf once in prison. While Joel Barlow would later go on to state his repugnance for the violence of emergency rule, he wrote to Thomas Jefferson in March 1793 bemoaning critical accounts of the Revolution by those who had not seen the events firsthand. He voiced his concern "lest some of the late transactions in France should be so far misrepresented to the Patriots in America as to lead them to draw conclusions unfavourable to the cause of liberty in this hemisphere."[18] Some emigrants therefore cannot be easily

---

16 For Perry's account of how he secured an extension on his liberty, see his *HS* I, p. 15.
17 *HS* I, pp. 12-13.
18 Joel Barlow to Thomas Jefferson, 8th March 1793, in Thomas Jefferson Papers 25, p. 336,

classed as Girondins, and even those who were more clearly linked to a particular group, such as Paine or Williams, sometimes showed ambivalence. Paine for example, perhaps sensing the risk he faced after the purge of the National Convention on 31st May 1793, offered his services to the *Comité de Salut Public*. He was heavily dependent on the Girondin members for translation services, and indebted to them for publicising his earlier writings, but, despite the opinion given during the trial of the king, did not consider himself as part of a defined political faction.

In a similar vein, members of the *SADH* have also been seen as Paineites. Moncure Conway christened the Paris society a "Paine Club", seeing Paine as the principal convenor whom the other members "gathered around."[19] Wil Verhoeven, describing the context in which Gilbert Imlay arrived in Paris in February 1793, has recently suggested that "a constant stream of Revolution tourists, as well as British spies, would come to get a hearing with the notorious guru of British radicalism."[20] There is some credence in the argument that members of the group that met at White's hotel were strongly influenced by Paine. Sampson Perry and Robert Merry, among others, seem to have maintained strong affinities with the veteran radical. Members had also supported the widespread circulation of Part Two of *Rights of Man* as members of the SCI.

Yet the very notion of "Paineite" loses much of its resonance when transplanted to the French context. In Britain, the term can be read as implying a certain degree of democratic thought, sympathy for natural rights theory, the denial of the existence of a British constitution, a celebration of the present over precedent and the elevation of France as a model of liberty, deriving from Paine's influential work, *Rights of Man*. Yet in France, Paine's influence and reception were very different. By 1793, his views were considered less subversive than part of the mainstream of revolutionary and republican thinking. He was perceived as on the radical republican wing after June 1791, when he became involved in the drafting of a republican manifesto, but was discredited after his contribution to the trial of the king in January 1793, when he voted for the banishment of Louis XVI rather than his death. Paine's official duties in the Convention meant that he became associated with decisions which could be held against him in the vengeful climate of 1793-94. He also showed a firm preference for representative government at a time when some of his compatriots were discussing the possibility of direct democratic models of government. While Paine developed his thinking on representative government, in line with his Girondin allies, other British activists bluntly rejected the very term "representation". While Paine did arrange meetings between his countrymen and the revolutionary administration, he was careful not to get too closely

---

quoted in Ziesche, *Cosmopolitan Patriots*, p. 80.
19 Moncure D. Conway (ed.), *The Writings of Thomas Paine*, vols. 3 and 4 (1893; New York, AMS Press, 1967), p. xii.
20 Verhoeven, *Gilbert Imlay*, p. 150.

involved in emigrant politics, appearing to consider his responsibilities as a representative of the French nation and member of the constitutional committee as precluding his active involvement in a grassroots associational culture.

While there is little doubt that many British emigrants began their residence in Paris in the company of the men and women from the Girondin grouping therefore, it is a step too far to consider them as having been Girondins themselves. Very few British radicals had clearly identifiable circles of sociability organised along lines of political opinion and many associated with a wide range of revolutionary leaders and thinkers from Brissot and Condorcet to Danton and Hérault de Séchelles. While Helen Maria Williams celebrated the brilliance of the Girondins, Sampson Perry hailed Jean-Paul Marat as the embodiment of revolutionary audacity and the voice of the people. While any study of British political engagement in the years 1792 to 1794 must come up against the dilemma of the reliability of written testimony in an era where divergence from established conventions and prevailing political tendencies could be punished by death, based on the disparate array of sources available to the historian, it appears that there was no uniform affiliation among British residents to a particular political group in early republican France. This view is only reinforced by an awareness of the flaws in the categorisations of such groupings.

SOME CONCLUSIONS

British radicals lived in Paris where they gathered with each other and with members of the local, municipal and national revolutionary administration, to discuss politics, pursue editorial projects, and monitor the progress of the French Revolution. Ostracised to a certain extent from British political and social life, they also found themselves confronted with the French administration's increasingly exclusive view of citizenship over the course of 1793. In some ways therefore, their experience was akin to that of Conway's "man without a country". Yet the community that British emigrants forged at White's hotel with their Irish, French and American acquaintances, was also a displaced hub of counter-culture and site of open and fierce exchange in line with many of the debating societies and circles of improvement that had emerged over the course of the eighteenth century in Britain. The founding of the *SADH* consolidated and reshaped pre-existing channels of communication between Britain and France and helped to forge a cross-Channel network of ideas, commerce and sociability which was at once linked to and distinct from the respective reform scenes in Britain and France.

The society was established in Paris at a time of rapid and mesmerising transformation in French political culture, when the king had been removed from the throne, the people had manifested their vital energy in a series of *journées*, and the country was threatened on all fronts by foreign armies.

Though the events from August 1792 through to the late months of 1793 and early 1794 can now be slotted into a neat chronology, those observing the developments at the time felt deep contradictions and uncertainty. The difficulties British radicals encountered in trying to work out their individual positions and reactions are evident in the accounts of the Revolution sent back to Britain. The forms that these writings took – hastily-written sketches, spontaneous reflections, eyewitness letters or commissioned observations – also hint at the particular relationship that British residents in France had with the notion of time and history. While they could conceive of their privileged place as outsiders and observers and while they understood that the changes they were witnessing were historic, they recognised the near-impossibility of providing coherent and impartial readings of events which appeared so momentous.

Residing in France during the years 1792-94 was formative for British radicals, both in terms of how they fitted the French Revolution into their own worldviews and conceptions of politics, but also in the way they were seen by others, particularly the British press. Temporary emigration gave radicals a different perspective on both the Revolution and their own political culture, sometimes precipitating support for more democratic and wholesale constitutional change, at other times leading them to ultimately concur with the ideas of their former political adversaries. British nationals' emigration to Paris prompted a number of broadly hostile writers and observers in Britain to portray them as having sacrificed their claim to national belonging and protection. By their very presence in the French capital, members of the *SADH* were perceived as infectious agents, capable of spreading revolutionary contagion back to their home country.

As well as their political interest in the Revolution, British residents were also involved in collective initiatives to establish publishing houses, set up commercially-successful business ventures and make headway in journalism and writing. Yet very few of their private pursuits in Paris could be divorced from their support for the Revolution. Even cotton manufacturing, the supplying of grain or property development had a political angle in 1792 and 1793. The associational culture and network of mutual reliance that emerged within the Paris society provided a source of constant support and information for members of the community, both on arrival in the French capital as well as at times of hardship during the period of emergency rule. Although the *SADH*, as an organised society, seems to have dissolved after the outbreak of war between Britain and France, the friendships and connections its existence helped to forge endured well after February 1793.

The tracts examined in the context of the republican constitution debate and written by foreign observers of the Revolution have rarely been studied in terms of how they reflect the collective engagement of British emigrants with the Revolution. The writings of Robert Merry and George Edwards to the constitutional committee have attracted no scholarly attention while those of Barlow, Oswald and Williams have been considered in isolation within specialist biographies, often with a focus on the development of an individual's political thought rather than the interaction of those ideas with those of other writers in the context in which they were written. While these tracts contributed to a debate which was quickly overshadowed by the trial of Louis XVI and emergency rule, they nevertheless provide some insight into the political preoccupations of British residents in Paris at this critical junction in the French Revolution. The variety of opinions expressed, the different forms that these depositions took and the way in which they constructed a subtle interplay between French and British political culture are all aspects which add to the portrait of British radicalism in this period. British emigrants disagreed on the extent to which the people should be involved in constitutional questions and law-making. While most concurred that the ordinary citizen should be informed, educated and inspired by a spirit of civic energy and enquiry, there was much contention as to how far the people should be able to give their assent or disapproval on legislative issues. Such tensions were also evident in the struggles and disputes which characterised the *SADH* in the early months of 1793. The society brought together an eclectic range of individuals whose commitment to free speculation and enquiry had to be tempered when the repercussions of holding political opinions at odds with those accepted by the ruling majority in the National Convention were recognised.

The desire to write down the Revolution for a British audience was in a way a result of a perceived need to rewrite the Revolution, correcting the many errors and misjudgements, many of them voluntary, which emigrant writers believed had been published in the British press. Yet this process of revision was not as considered nor as conscious as has sometimes been suggested. Writers certainly set out to attempt to adjust the portrait of the Revolution being conveyed to their home country, but they did not necessarily feel equipped to provide an impartial or comprehensive history. Many used the term "sketch", others wrote of their inability to predict the future and all recognised how the Revolution had interfered with how they perceived time and the progress of history. Accounts of the Revolution blended different influences, styles, contributors and messages, giving a strong impression that such writers, with perhaps the exception of Mary Wollstonecraft, felt more able to provide immediate eyewitness impressions than measured historical analysis. How they wrote the Revolution was just as important as what they said about it, and it was their proximity to the events, their ability to call upon firsthand witnesses to corroborate their views, their physical presence and their knowledge of the most reliable sources which bolstered their claims to having provided authentic accounts. British writers drafted their texts with an awareness of the limitations of their viewpoints, their partiality and their status as outsiders. The process of writing itself was a way of trying to understand the Revolution and its impact on posterity, a way of working out uncertainties during a period of incessant change.

The period from August 1792 when the first French republic was in the making, to the middle of 1794, was not only crucial in the history of the French Revolution, but also saw the forging of a displaced British radical movement in France. While the fall of the Bastille induced many British visitors to travel to Paris to witness the progress of the Revolution, it was the fall of the monarchy and the establishment of a republic which was perhaps the true catalyst for the making of a British associational culture in France. If revolutionary sight-seeing was the principal mode of visiting France in the early years after July 1789, by the middle of 1792 taking up residence in revolutionary Paris was a political and ideological decision. It implied support for a Revolution which was much maligned by the political class and the press in Britain. It was no coincidence that British radicals chose to establish a pro-revolutionary society at this crossroads in both the French Revolution and British political culture. The destitution of the king, the decision to open a debate on the constitutional settlement of the new republic and allow foreigners to have a stake in this discussion were aspects of French political culture which appealed to British radicals, many of whom were not wondering whether to leave Britain, but when, and to which destination. The willingness of French revolutionaries to entertain new theories of government and law-making was welcomed by British men and women who objected to the hierarchical and strictly delineated political culture of Britain. Many had felt the force of the government's decision to persecute the dissemination of radical ideas, whether through the increased policing of the private sphere, the assault on newspaper editors or the clampdown on artistic forms which criticised the *status quo*. The associational culture which emerged on French soil was closely connected with the movement for reform in Britain therefore. In addition to the fact that its core members had been involved in radical gatherings in Britain prior to their stay in Paris, the political discussions, writings and accounts of the Revolution which emerged during this period highlight how interest in revolutionary France could never be entirely divorced from hope for reform at home.

Appendices

Map of Paris Showing the Location of White's hotel

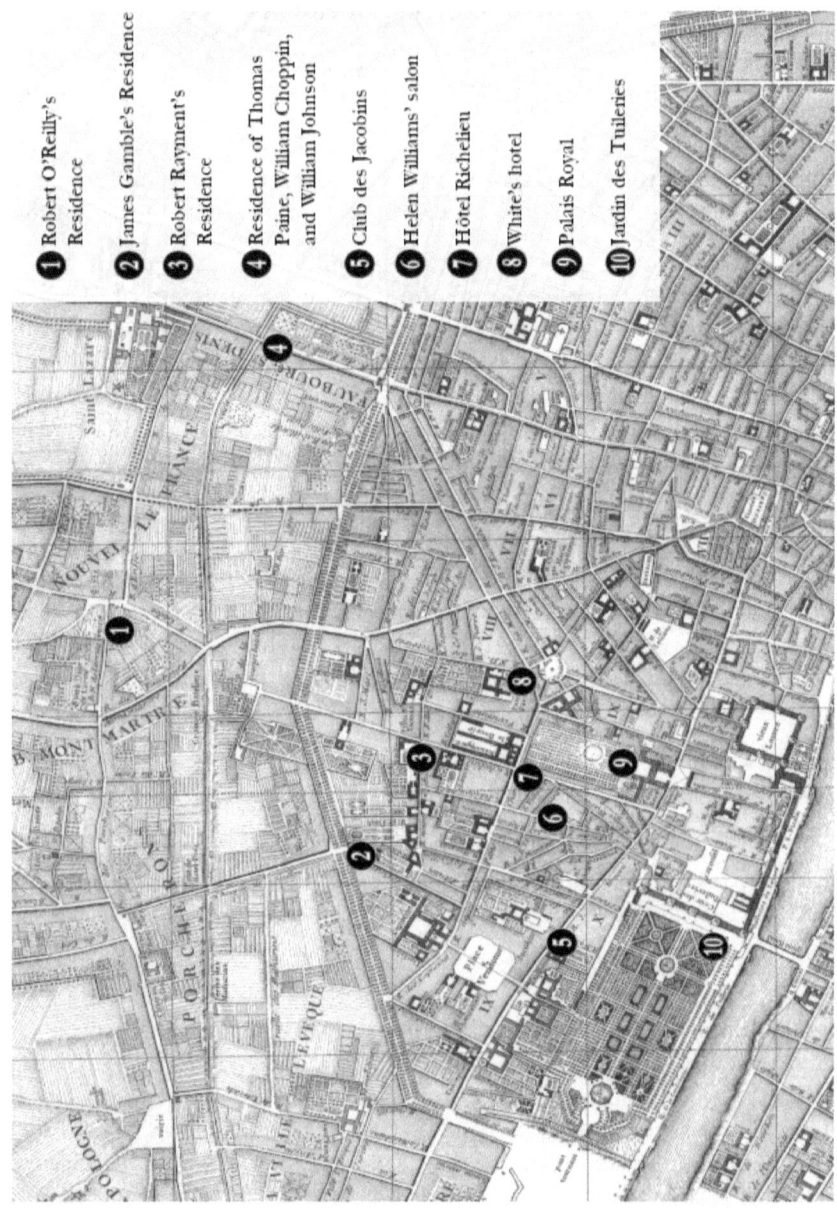

Map of Paris showing the location of White's hotel in relation to some of the key arenas of revolutionary activity and a selection of landmarks relating to British residents. Plan de Paris, dédié à Messieurs les échevins de la Ville par M. L'Abbé Delagrive, Géographe de la Ville de Paris de la société roiale de Londres 1741 (*Bibliothèque Nationale de France*).

Short Biographies of British Politicians mentioned

William Eden, Lord Auckland (1744-1814), served under William Pitt in the diplomatic service from 1785, taking up a post as ambassador in The Hague from 1790-1794.

James Bland Burges (1752-1824) was under-secretary of state for Foreign Affairs from 1789-1795 and a close ally of William Pitt from the early 1780s.

Henry Dundas (1742-1811), a Scottish politician and close ally of William Pitt, acted as Home Secretary from 1791, becoming Secretary of War from 1794-1801. Dundas was known for his intransigence towards the radical reform movement during his time at the Home Office. Thomas Paine's correspondence with Dundas from 1792 gives a flavour of this animosity. (See Paine, 'To Mr. Secretary Dundas', Foner (ed.), *The Complete Writings of Thomas Paine*, pp. 446-56).

Charles James Fox (1749-1806) was a Whig politician who was disliked by King George III and who, as a result, spent most of his career in opposition. George III dismissed the Fox-North coalition from government in 1783, precipitating the start of the Pitt ministry. Fox was an initial admirer of the French Revolution, though began to withdraw his support with the outbreak of war in 1793. He concentrated instead on arguing the case for the negotiation of peace with France.

George Granville Leveson Gower, Earl Gower (1758-1833) was the British ambassador in Paris from 1790-1792. He was recalled by the Pitt government from France with the destitution of the king in August 1792.

Charles Grey (1764-1845), a later leader of the Whig Party and British Prime Minister in the 1830s, he was at the head of a group called the "New Whigs" in the early 1790s who supported the cause of parliamentary reform in Britain.

Lord William Wyndham Grenville (1759-1834) entered parliament in 1782 and was considered a close ally of William Pitt. He served as Home Secretary, Leader of the House of Lords, and Secretary of State for Foreign Affairs. He was at the head of the Foreign Office during the French revolutionary and Napoleonic wars, resigning in 1801 with Pitt. Grenville received regular updates from Captain George Monro at the end of 1792 and in early 1793 on the foreign radical community based in Paris.

Evan Nepean (1752-1822) was a British civil servant who served as under-secretary of state at the Home Office from 1782 to July 1794 and as under-secretary of state for War from 1794 to 1795. From 1791 onwards, he worked under the leadership of Henry Dundas and was considered an able ally of the Home Secretary. Nepean was the recipient of letters from British spy Charles Ross who had infiltrated the SCI and who sent regular reports to the Home Office during the course of 1792.

William Pitt the Younger (1759-1806) was Prime Minister from 1783 to 1801 and from 1804 to his death in 1806. He was at the head of the government when the French Revolution began and also led Britain during the revolutionary and first Napoleonic wars. Although known for his sympathy with the cause of parliamentary reform at the time of his appointment as Prime Minister in 1783 (consolidated by an election victory in 1784), he became the notorious adversary of both the reforming Whigs, under Charles Fox, and radical reformers during the course of his premiership.

Short Biographies of Revolutionary Leaders mentioned

Jacques-Pierre Brissot de Warville (1754-1793) was considered one of the leaders of the Girondins (sometimes known as Brissotins) and cultivated links with American revolutionaries and abolitionists in the 1770s and 1780s. He was also well-known to British radicals such as Thomas Paine and David Williams. He edited a revolutionary newspaper, *Le Patriote français*, and adopted a republican stance after the king's flight to Varennes in June 1791. He was involved in launching the military campaigns of the early republic, in an attempt to rid France of its royal enemies and consolidate the Revolution. He was arrested along with other Girondins on 2nd June 1793 and died on the scaffold in October 1793.

Marie-Jean Antoine Nicolas de Caritat, marquis de Condorcet (1743-1794), was a French philosopher and an exponent of Enlightenment ideas of progress, educational reform and human improvement. He was heavily involved in the republican movement after the king's attempt to leave France in 1791, editing *Le Républicain* with Thomas Paine. Condorcet also had a crucial role in drafting the Girondin constitution of February 1793 which was eclipsed by the Jacobin proposal of June 1793. He also worked on a proposal for education. When the Girondins were ousted from the National Convention, Condorcet was outlawed for his opposition. After a period in hiding, he was discovered and imprisoned, where he died in March 1794.

Georges Danton (1759-1794) was an early advocate of popular sovereignty as president of the Cordeliers district in 1789-90 and later as member of the Cordeliers Club. He gained national prestige after 1791 when, on returning from refuge in London following the massacre at the Champs de Mars in July, he was elected to the National Assembly and the Paris Commune. He credited himself with starting the insurrection which led to the overthrow of the king in August 1792 and was held responsible by many for provoking the popular rage vented during the September massacres. Initially prominent in the *Comité de Salut Public*, his increasing reticence about the merits of emergency government led to his indictment and death in April 1794.

Jacques-Louis David (1745-1825) was a French painter who became known for his sympathy with the Montagnards and his political art. He voted for the death of Louis XVI as a member of the National Convention in 1793 and was involved in bringing the arts in line with Montagnard standards of republican virtue.

Marie-Jean Hérault de Séchelles (1759-1794), a member of the *Comité de Salut Public* who had delivered the Jacobin draft of the republican constitution of June 1793 to the Convention. He fell out of favour because of his unconventional lifestyle, which did not match up to the standards of republican virtue demanded by the Montagnards. He was imprisoned in March 1794 before being executed.

François Xavier Lanthenas (1754-1799) was considered part of the Girondin grouping in the Convention due to his close affinity with Jean-Marie Roland. However, he voted for the death of Louis XVI in January 1793 with certain conditions, eschewing association with a particular political faction. Lanthenas was also Thomas Paine's regular translator in Paris.

Jean-Paul Marat (1743-1793) was a politician and journalist whose newspaper *L'Ami du Peuple* gained fame as a mouthpiece of popular reform. Marat spoke out in favour of a more democratic political system and other measures to help the poor, fleeing to England in 1790 after his attacks on aristocracy. As a member of the National Convention from September 1792 he continued to argue for democratic reform and condemned counter-revolutionaries and émigrés. Helen Maria Williams held him responsible for inciting the people to commit the prison massacres. He survived an appearance before a tribunal in April 1793 and was instrumental in ousting the Girondins. Yet in July 1793 he was killed by Charlotte Corday in his bath.

Jérôme Pétion de Villeneuve (1756-1794) was an ally of Robespierre in 1789 but, after having served as Mayor of Paris in 1791-92 and associated with the Girondins as President of the Convention in September 1792, he was ousted from the National Convention in June 1793. His role in both the *journées* of 20th June 1792 and 10th August 1792 remain obscure. He did not attempt to quell the insurrection of June but neither did he wholly vindicate the popular seizure of power in August 1792. He committed suicide after escaping arrest in the purge of the National Convention of June 1793.

Maximilien Robespierre (1758-1794) is known principally for his orchestration of the Terror as a member of the *Comité de Salut Public* from 1793 to his death in July 1794. Given the name the Incorruptible, he was also famed for stating, "I am the People," an illustration of his view that the "general will" could be understood by a devoted legislator without the need for consultation, voting or deliberation. In the first years of the Revolution he did not express anti-monarchical views, although he quickly became renowned as someone who spoke his mind, who lived an austere lifestyle and who demanded high standards of virtue from French representatives. He died on the scaffold after his adversaries in the *Comité de Salut Public* allied against him and his supporters.

Jean-Marie Roland (1734-1793), a member of the Girondin grouping in the National Convention. He had been appointed as an advisor to Louis XVI as part of the king's concessions to republican leaders in March 1792. He was dismissed from the king's counsel in June 1792. In the National Convention, he opposed Louis XVI's conviction for treason and resigned. He fled Paris during the purge of the National Convention in early June 1793, and committed suicide on learning of the death of his wife.

Jeanne-Marie 'Manon' Roland (1754-1793) was the wife of the French politician Jean-Marie Roland and was largely known for her role as a salon leader and as a strong influence on the political affairs of her husband. She was imprisoned and executed with the Girondin leaders in October 1793.

Jeanbon Saint-André (1749-1813) played a minor role in the Revolution until September 1792 when he was elected as one of the ten representatives from the department of the Lot to sit in the National Convention. During the trial of the king he voted for a guilty verdict and the death of the king without recourse to a popular referendum. He was a member of the *Comité de Salut Public* and was responsible for nominating Robespierre as a replacement for Gasparin. During the Terror he was sent on regional and military missions, only returning after 9 Thermidor. Although imprisoned temporarily for crimes committed at Brest, he was released under the general amnesty of October 1795. He died from typhus in 1813.

Louis de Saint-Just (1767-1794) was, along with Robespierre, considered one of the most fervent exponents of emergency rule. He spoke out eloquently in the National Convention and was considered an ideologue of the "Republic of Virtue," serving on the *Comité de Salut Public* during the course of 1793-94 in close consultation with Robespierre. He was arrested and executed after the events of 9 Thermidor.

Glossary of Revolutionary Terms

Comité de Salut Public   (Committee of Public Safety) The governing body set up by the National Convention in April 1793 to help France deal with the problems of foreign and civil conflict. Initially dominated by Georges Danton, it became quickly associated with the Reign of Terror (September 1793-July 1794) instituted when France resorted to emergency rule and suspended the constitution in mid 1793. During the years of emergency government, the make-up of the committee did not change and its members included Marie-Jean Hérault de Séchelles, Maximilien Robespierre, Louis de Saint- Just and Georges Couthon. Rivalries within the committee led to the downfall of Robespierre on 9 Thermidor An II and, although the committee survived after the Terror, its powers were drastically limited.

Comité de Sûreté Générale   (Committee of General Security) Set up in 1792, the committee ran the police force under the early republic and during the period of emergency rule. It also liaised with the Revolutionary Tribunal to exact revolutionary justice.

Comité de surveillance   Set up in March 1793 to monitor foreign residents in France and keep track of their movements and attitude towards the Revolution; the committees were responsible for dispensing "certificates of loyalty" or *certificats de civisme* to those who could prove their continued adherence to the Revolution. The committees were particularly active after the law of 17th September 1793 known as the Law of Suspects.

Gironde / Girondins   Term used to describe the politicians in the Convention who opposed the Montagne. Seen as mostly from the outer-lying regions of France (although some were from Paris), they have been considered as the moderate wing of the Convention, preferring enlightened, commercial republicanism to classical ideals of a virtuous citizenry and wary of an increase in popular involvement in government.

Le Marais, La Plaine The main bulk of the members of the National Convention who did not conspicuously ally with one particular grouping in key votes (*les appels nominaux*) during the course of 1793. The term "marais," meaning "swamp" or "marsh", was a derogatory term used by those who scorned the representatives' place in the middle ground.

Montagne, Montagnards Term given to the representatives in the National Convention by virtue of their preference for the highest seats in the chamber. The group gained ascendancy in the Convention during the trial of Louis XVI, when most Montagnards voted not only for the destitution of the king but also his execution.

National Assembly The representative body which replaced the States-General and worked to establish a constitutional monarchy from July 1789 to September 1791. After the king signed the constitution of 1791, the National Constituent Assembly was superseded by the Legislative Assembly.

National Convention After the destitution of the king following the uprising of the 10th August 1792 a National Convention was instituted on 20th September 1792 with the aim of devising a new constitution. Monarchy had officially been brought to an end and a republic declared on 21st September 1792. Once the republican constitution had been drafted, the Convention would theoretically dissolve itself to be replaced by a legislative body. The first phase of the Convention was dominated by struggles between the Girondins and the Montagnards, the former being excluded from the Convention on 31st May 1793 and their key members sent to the guillotine in October of the same year.
From June 1793 to July 1794, the Convention

	was dominated by the Montagne, who set up emergency rule under the *Comité de Salut Public*. The Convention was eventually superseded in October 1795.
Revolutionary Tribunal	Also set up in March 1793 to try political crimes against the Revolution at a time when foreign armies threatened the security of France and when the threat of civil war inspired by royalist émigrés and counter-revolutionaries was rife. The uprising in the Vendée in March 1793 was only one example of this general unrest. Antoine Fouquier-Tinville (1746-1795) was the most famous of the public prosecutors to direct the Revolutionary Tribunal.
Thermidor	Name given to the regime change which took place on 9th July 1794 (9 Thermidor An II) when Robespierre was removed from power and executed. The deposition of the leader of the *Comité de Salut Public* made way for a more moderate constitutional settlement in 1795 which tempered the radical reforms of the Montagne and protected more restricted property qualifications in voting rights.

Timeline of Key Events in Britain and France, 1792-94

BRITAIN	DATE	FRANCE
	1792	
Foundation of the London Corresponding Society.	**January**	
Publication of Part Two of Thomas Paine's *Rights of Man*.	**February**	
The establishment of the Society of the Friends of the People.	**April**	Declaration of war against Austria.
SCI organises the cheap distribution of Paine's *Rights of Man*.	**May**	
Royal Proclamation Against Seditious Writing targeted radical authors and booksellers, including Thomas Paine (21st).		
	June	Louis XVI dismisses his Girondin ministers. *Journée* of 20th June when the people of Paris converged on the royal residence at the Tuileries.
	August	10th August revolution, or "August Days", which brought an end to monarchy.
Thomas Paine escapes to France. LCS declaration to the National Convention.	**September**	Massacres in the prisons of Paris from 2-6th September, seen as a wave of vengeance in a climate of war and paranoia. Declaration of the Republic on 21st September.

Addresses of support from British reforming societies to the National Convention (including the SCI and the *SADH*).	**November**	Declaration of fraternity to foreign peoples struggling under the yoke of tyranny (19th November).
Foundation of the Association for the Protection of Liberty and Property against Republicans and Levellers at the Crown and Anchor Tavern.		
First general Convention of Scottish Reformers in Edinburgh.	**December**	Convention decides to try Louis XVI for treason.
Widespread fear of popular insurrection in Britain.		
King's Proclamation calls out the British militia		
	1793	
	January	Conclusion of Louis XVI's trial, judgement and execution (21st January).
Outbreak of war with France.	**February**	War declared on Britain (1st).
	March	Revolutionary Tribunal and committees created. Royalist uprising in the Vendée.
The second general Convention of reformers in Edinburgh.	**April**	Creation of the *Comité de Salut Public*. Defection of General Dumouriez.
	May	(31st) Demonstrations against the Girondin members of the Convention.

	June	Ousting of the Girondin members from the Convention (2nd). Hérault de Séchelles achieved the ratification of the Jacobin Constitution.
	July	Marat killed by Charlotte Corday. Danton resigns from *Comité de Salut Public*, Robespierre joins the committee.
	August	Capture of Toulon by British fleets.
	September	Law of Suspects (17th) and beginning of the Reign of Terror.
	October	Trial and execution of the Girondins. Execution of Marie-Antoinette. Revolutionary calendar adopted.
Third meeting of reformers in Edinburgh is designated as the British Convention.	**November**	
Arrest of members of the British Convention, known as the "Scottish Martyrs", who would subsequently be sentenced to 14 years' transportation.	**December**	Revolt in the Vendée quelled. Thomas Paine imprisoned.
	1794	
	March	Arrest and execution of Hébertists.
	April	Arrest and execution of Dantonists.

Arrests of members of the SCI and LCS on charges of high treason, including Thomas Hardy, John Thelwall and John Horne Tooke.	**May**	
Suspension of Habeas Corpus		
Defection of Burke and the Portland Whigs to the Tories under William Pitt.	**June**	Law of 22 Prairial, accelerates the executions under emergency rule..
	July	Fall of Robespierre, 9 Thermidor.
	August	Law of 22 Prairial repealed, meaning that most British prisoners would shortly be released.
Treason trials begin, Thomas Erskine acts as defence for the reformers.	**October**	
Trials of members of the LCS and SCI result in their acquittal.	**November**	

Engravings from contemporary editions of the newspaper *Révolutions de Paris*

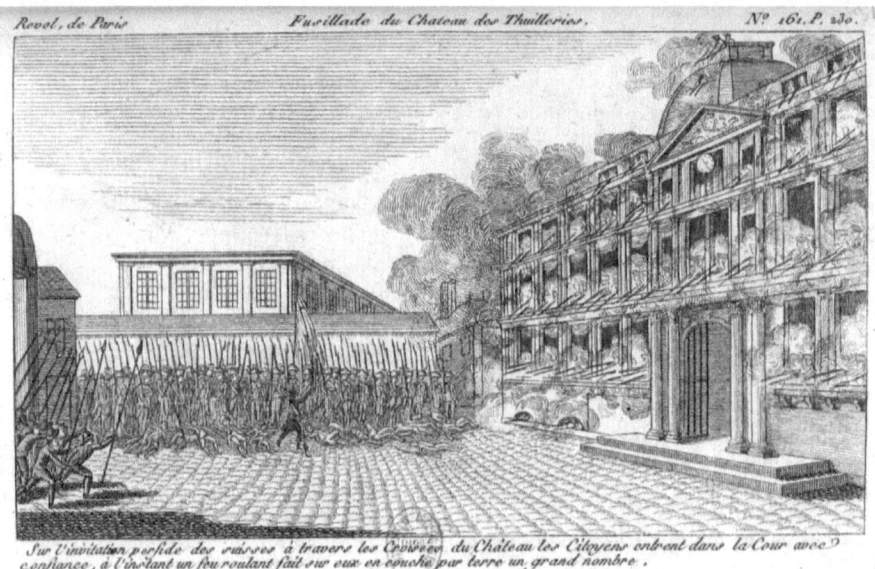

Engraving from the edition of the *Révolutions de Paris*, No. 161, 4th to 10th August 1792, The account from the newspaper was used by Robert Merry as his template for *A Circumstantial History* and Sampson Perry reiterates the same viewpoint in his *An Historical Sketch*. The plate is entitled "Gun Fire at the Château des Tuileries" and contrasts the "perfidious" Swiss Guards, with the confident citizens of Paris, many of whom fell when the king's guards opened fire in the courtyard of the palace.

Pompe funèbre en l'honneur des Citoyens tués au massacre du 10 Aoust, et à laquelle tout Paris assista.

This engraving is taken from the *Révolutions de Paris* No. 164, 25th August to 1st September 1792 and portrays the funeral held "in honour of the citizens killed in the massacre of the 10th August" and attended by all of Paris.

Another plate from the *Révolutions de Paris* edition of 4th to 10th August 1792. This engraving shows the Parisians pulling down the statue of the reputed king Henry IV at the entrance to the Pont Neuf and that of Louis XIII at the Place Royale. The editors suggested they were "wrong not to have taken" such measures on the 20th June, when the citizens first marched to the Tuileries.

Statues of previous French kings were removed during the August Days. These depictions, published in *Révolutions de Paris*, no. 161, show, in the words of the editors, "the people of Paris taking actions that they should have taken on 20th June 1791 [the date of Louis XVI's flight from Paris via Varennes]. They toppled the statues of Louis XIV at the place des Victoires at at place Vendôme".

Two depictions, published in *Révolutions de Paris* (No. 161), of the toppling of *Ancien Régime* statues from the place de l'Hôtel de Ville and place Louis XIV. In the caption, it is mentioned that the same actions were taken in the 83 other *départements* of France in the aftermath of these removals.

This plate shows the Swiss Guards' barracks on fire on 10th August 1792 (*Révolutions de Paris*, no. 161). The caption reads: "The Carrousel was like a huge raging furnace; to get into the castle you had to go through two residences which had been entirely burnt down; it was impossible to get in without going past a burning beam or stepping on a fresh corpse."

Title Pages of Tracts and Pamphlets by British Observers

AN

HISTORICAL SKETCH

OF THE

FRENCH REVOLUTION.

COMMENCING WITH ITS

PREDISPOSING CAUSES,

AND CARRIED ON TO THE

ACCEPTATION OF THE CONSTITUTION,

IN 1795.

BY
SAMPSON PERRY.

VOL. THE FIRST.

LONDON:
PRINTED FOR H. D. SYMONDS, N° 20, PATERNOSTER-ROW.

1796.

Title page to the first volume of Sampson Perry's pro-revolutionary *An Historical Sketch of the French Revolution*, published in 1796 in two volumes by Perry's fellow Newgate inmate H. D. Symonds.

Oppreffion!!!

THE
APPEAL
OF
CAPTAIN PERRY,
(LATE EDITOR OF THE ARGUS,)

TO THE PEOPLE OF ENGLAND;

CONTAINING

A JUSTIFICATION OF HIS PRINCIPLES AND CONDUCT WHICH HAVE RENDERED HIM OBNOXIOUS TO MINISTERIAL TYRANNY; WITH A FEW REMARKS ON THE PEOPLE OF FRANCE, TO REFUTE THE BASE CALUMNIES OF THOSE INTERESTED IN THIS RUINOUS CRUSADE AGAINST THE LIBERTY AND HAPPINESS OF MAN.

TO WHICH IS ADDED

A DEVELOPEMENT

OF SOME OF THE

MYSTERIES OF THE SPY TRADE,

PROVING THE DETESTABLE INIQUITY OF THE PRACTICE, AND THE NECESSITY OF ITS IMMEDIATE ABOLITION.

LONDON:

PRINTED FOR CITIZEN LEE, AT THE BRITISH TREE OF LIBERTY, NO. 47, HAYMARKET: SOLD LIKEWISE BY J. SMITH, PORTSMOUTH-STREET, LINCOLN'S-INN FIELDS; J. S. JORDAN, FLEET-STREET, AND H. D. SYMONDS, PATER-NOSTER-ROW.

1795.

Title page of Sampson Perry's published self-defence Oppression! in which he details his persecution at the hands of the British government. The pamphlet was printed by radical publisher Richard "Citizen" Lee in 1795 while Perry was serving in Newgate prison. In the title is included the epithet of Perry's later career, "late editor of the Argus."

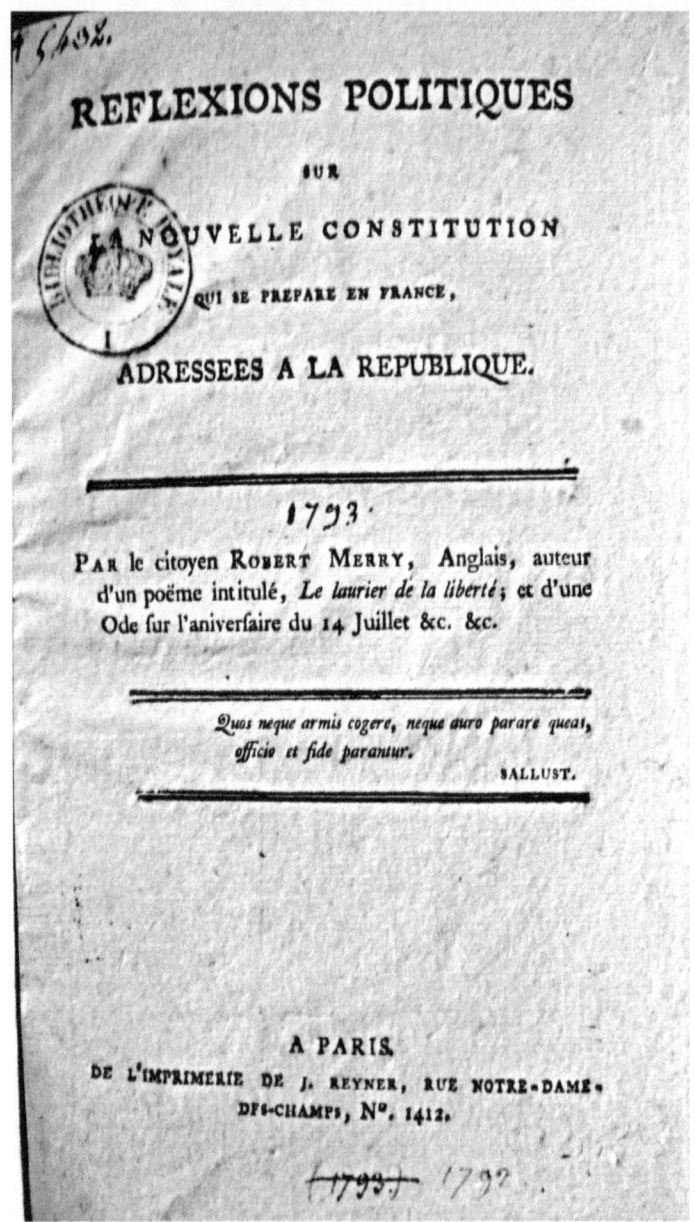

Title page of Robert Merry's tract, sent to the French constitutional committee in October 1792, in which he outlines his thoughts on the republican constitution being drawn up after the deposition of the king.

Some Extracts from Manuscript Sources

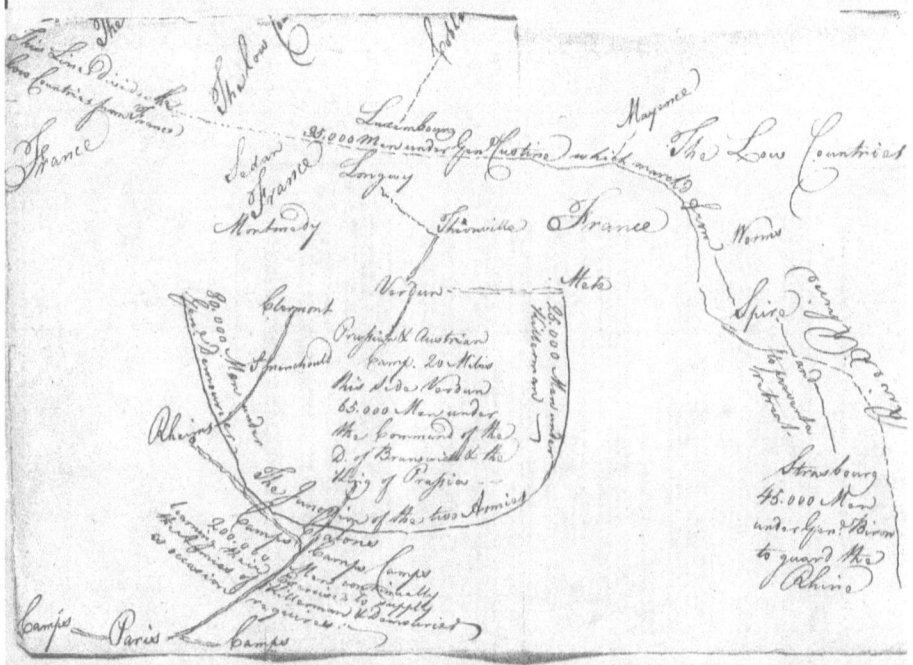

Map of the advance of the French revolutionary armies sent by *SADH* member William Choppin to Thomas Rickman, but intercepted by spy Charles Ross and shown to Evan Nepean at the Home Office. Ross wrote, "This was copied from a rough sketch sent from Mr Choppin in France to Mr. R _ and which he mentions was copied from a Plan sent to Mr Paine with whom he is very intimate. Received in London Monday Oct 8 th 1792." See TS 11/965/3510/A2, 9th October 1792.

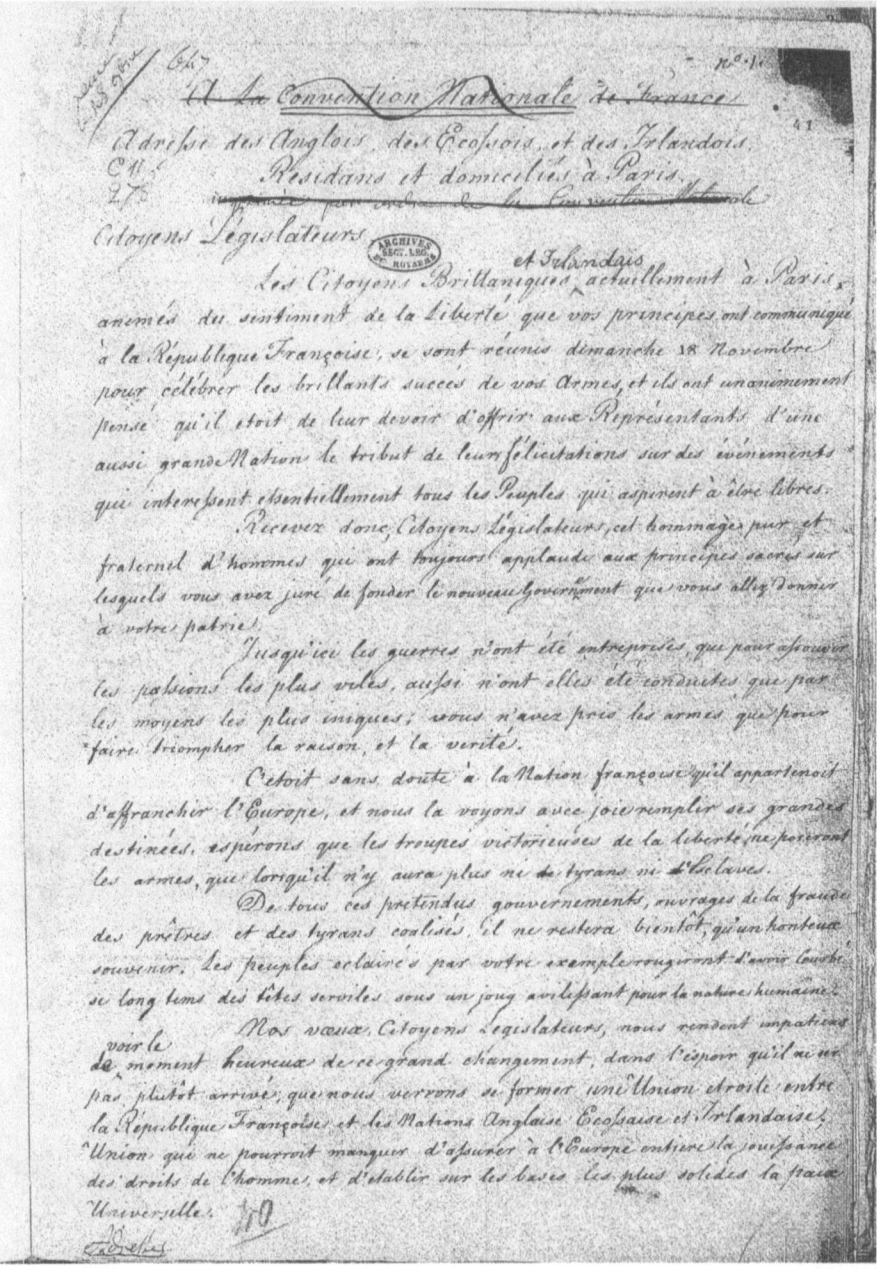

Address to the National Convention by members of the *SADH*, signed on 24th November 1792 and presented to the Convention on 28th November 1792. AN C 11/278/40. Page 1/3.

Nous ne sommes pas les seuls animés de ces sentimens, nous ne doutons pas qu'ils ne se manifestent également, chez la grande majorité de nos compatriotes, si l'opinion publique y étoit consultée comme elle devroit l'être dans une Convention Nationale.

Quant à nous qui faisons dans ce moment notre résidence à Paris, nous saisirons avec joie cette occasion pour déclarer que dans tout le cours de la Revolution, et nonobstant le brusque départ de notre Ambassadeur, ou plutôt de l'ambassadeur de la Cour de Londres, nous avons constamment éprouvé de la part de la Nation Françoise les sentimens de la cordialité la plus franche, et de l'amitié la plus sincere.

Paris, 24 Novembre 1792.

l'an premier de la République Françoise.

Signée par nous membres & Comité nommée à cet effet

J. H. Stone Président
Francis Tweddell
Mat'o Bellew   Joseph Webb
W. Frost   W'm Newton
W'm Joyce   J. Tickell
Joseph Green   Harold Mowatt
J. Hall   Pierre Lower
                                Ber'd Mac Shehey
David Gibson   Jeremie ...
Tho' Armfield   Wm. Chrison
Edw'd Fitzgerald   W'm Mardell
W'm Duckett   N. Madgett
                                Jas Gamble
Edw'd Ferris   Tho' Ma'Dermott
P. Murray   W'm Richets
                                Rob't Rayment

Wm Francis Jackson
Robert Merry
W. [?] O'Reilly
J. E. Macdonnel
Wm Watts
Ths Marshall
John Oswald
Jno Walker Sen.
And Potier
L. Marquerier
Rie m[?]
N. Hickson
F. J. Gastineau
Stephen Sayre
Henry Sheares
John Sheares
Rose
[?]
[?]
B. Palmer
[?]

J. H. Stone P.dt
Rob.t M O'Reilly Sec.re

suivent les Sig.res au nombre de 50, Commission nommée par la Société à cet Effet

en N.o 50

attendre la réponse du président.

Page 3/3.

Signatories of the *SADH* Address to the National Convention, 24th November 1792

[Arranged in order of signature]

Francis Tweddell
Matthew Bellews
John Frost
Nicholas Joyce [Erdman reads "Richard Joyce"]
Joseph Green
J. Skill
J. Usher Quartermain
David Gibson
Thomas Armfield
Edward Fitzgerald
William Duckett
J. O'Neill
Edward Ferris
B. Murray
J. H. Stone (President)
Joseph Webb
William Newton
J. Tickell
Harrold Mowatt
Pearce Lower
Bernard MacSheehy
Jeremie Curtayn
William Choppin
William Wardell
N. Madgett
James Gamble
Thomas MacDermott
William Ricketts
Robert Rayment
William Francis Jackson
Robert Merry
Robert May O'Reilly (Secretary)
D. E. MacDonnell [Erdman reads J. E. MacDonnell]
William Watts
Thomas Marshall
John Oswald
John Walker Snr
Thomas Potier
L. Masquerier
R. Smyth
N. Hickson
T. J. Gastineau
Stephen Sayre
Henry Sheares
John Sheares
Rose
John Bradley
William Maxwell
B. Bulmer
Caesar Colclough

Prison records for British residents of Paris

Prison record of Robert Rayment, showing the table filled out when he entered the Maison des Ecossais on 18th November 1793, imprisoned as a foreigner. AN F7/4774/88. Page 1/2.

Prison record of Robert Rayment, showing the table filled out when he entered the Maison des Ecossais on 18th November 1793, imprisoned as a foreigner. AN F7/4774/88. Page 2/2.

> Dons Patriotiques.
>
> | | | Livres |
> |---|---|---|
> | 1° | — | 500 : 0 |
> | 2° pour habiller six gardes Nationales | — | 900 : 0 |
> | 3° deux hommes par Compagnie allant à la Vendée | — | 60 : 0 |
> | 4° pour les Veuves des Citoyens tués les 10 d'Aout | — | 400 : 0 |
> | 5° Buste de Marat & Le Pelletier | — | 50 : 0 |
> | | Total | 1910 : 0 |
>
> Extrait du Registre de la Section de 1792
>
> Le C. Smith nous ayant requis de le mettre autant qu'il est en notre pouvoir, Lui, sa femme, & ses Enfans, sous la Sauvegarde de la Loy & de la Nation, & sous la protection Speciale de la Section de 1792, Ce que nous lui avons accordé plus volontiers que nous sommes instruis & convaincus de principes Politiques de C. Smith favourables à notre Constitution & à notre Liberté Nationale, en foy duquel nous avons signé le present pour lui servir & valoir en cas de besoin & suivant les Circonstances : fait au Comité &c &
>
> Signé : Raffy Commissaire
> & plusieurs autres

A note from a representative of Robert Smith's section, attesting to his revolutionary loyalty and detailing his patriotic gifts during the Revolution. AN F7/4775/20/3.

APPENDICES

Extract from *La Chronique du Mois; ou Cahiers Patriotiques*

To the Friends to Truth.

Sampson Perry, auteur d'un journal républicain, en Angleterre, *The Argus of the People* (*La Sentinelle du Peuple*) pour avoir défendu avec énergie les droits de l'homme, la révolution françoise, Horne-Tooke et Thomas Payne, son ami, n'a échappé que par la fuite *à des bourreaux*. Perry et un autre écrivain anglois, Merry, célèbre par une pièce de théâtre, des vers républicains, et autres écrits philosophiques que nous ferons connoître, sont venus trouver de francs amis, chez les Directeurs de l'imprimerie du Cercle Social, qui vont publier en France, le journal persécuté, *The Argus of the People*, La société angloise *des Droits de l'Homme*, et Thomas Payne *et autres* y contribueront avec zèle. Amis de la liberté, vous leur devez secours, alliance et fraternité. — Voilà la lettre de Sampson Perry, à ses amis persécutés à Londres.

„ It must however give some satisfaction to the advocates for European Freedom, and to the friends of the human race in general, should they find that *their* Argus is not banished from the world, but that it has been only transplanted from the region of tyranny, injustice and oppression to his happy soil of Liberty and Equality.

Argus of the People. „

Les Directeurs de l'imprimerie du Cercle Social viennent de mettre en vente :

La grammaire de Miège et Boyer, nouvelle édition. Ils attendent incessamment une collection de classiques anglois.

Sous presse.

Les Poésies de N. Bonneville.

A PARIS, de l'Imprimerie du CERCLE SOCIAL, rue du Théâtre-François, n°. 4.

Extract from *La Chronique du Mois; ou Cahiers Patriotiques* of January 1793, advertising the imminent publication of Sampson Perry's *The Argus* in Paris and followed by an address from Perry to his readers.

Bibliography

I. MANUSCRIPT SOURCES

The National Archive, Kew

Treasury Solicitor's Papers

TS 11/959	Report from Captain George Monro dated 6th December 1792.
TS 11/962/3508	Record of meetings of the London Society for Constitutional Information, Friday 9th December 1791 to Friday 9th May 1794.
TS 11/962/3508 A2	Declaration by the Constitutional Whigs.
TS 11/965/3510 A1	Report from a meeting of the SCI 23rd November 1792.
TS 11/965/3510 A2	Memoranda from spy Charles Ross to Evan Nepean, under-secretary to Henry Dundas at the Home Office, 8th August 1792; 9th October 1792; 22nd October 1792; 1st November 1792; 13th November 1792.
TS 11/965/3510 A3	Undated spy report of a planned foreign landing on British soil and papers seized in the position of Rev. William Jackson.

Foreign Office Papers

FO 27/40 (Part 1)	Letters and papers from Mr. Lindsay at Paris, to the Secretary of State for Foreign Affairs, with drafts to him from August 23rd to September 8th 1792.
FO 27/40 (Part 2)	Letters from Captain George Monro to Lord Grenville, 17th December 1792; 20th December 1792; 21st December 1792; 24th December 1792; 27th December 1792; 31st December 1792.
FO 27/41	Letters from Captain George Monro from January 1793; Letter from Monro's successor in Paris, Mr. Somers.

British Library, British Museum

BM Add. MS 25388. 399-404	Two letters from Morgan John Rhys to the Reverend John Rippon, from France November 23rd 1791 and February 20th 1792

Royal Literary Fund Archive

RLF 1.514:	Sum granted to Sampson Perry's widow after his death.
MS 10 333 E	John Oswald relief grant from the Literary Fund.
RLF 2	Literary Fund Committee Minute Book.

National Library of Wales

Cardiff MS 2.192   Manuscript in English of David Williams' *Observations sur la dernière constitution de la France, avec des vues pour la formation de la nouvelle constitution* (1793). David Williams: On the French constitution.

Cardiff MS 5.36   Letter from David Williams to Jean-Marie Roland. David Williams Papers (1776-1816).

Houghton Library, Harvard University, Cambridge, Mass

MS Am 1448 (18)   Joel Barlow Papers, 1775-1935, "Notes for a Hist. of the Fr Rev.".

Archives Nationales, Paris

Fonds du Comité de Salut Public

AFII/380/49/5   Original letters from Thomas Paine to the French National Convention.

Archives du Directoire

AFIII/57/221   Foreign relations with England, letter from Hérault de Séchelles to people of England.
AFIII/57/223
AFIII/1805   Letter from François Xavier Lanthenas requesting continued resident in Paris of Sir Robert Smith.
AFIII/1808/369   Letters from François Xavier Lanthenas and Thomas Paine requesting that Sir Robert Smith be permitted to reside in Paris, 12th May 1796. Resident request for Robert Rayment.

Ministère de la Justice

BB/3/72   Denunciation of Thomas Paine.

Archives des Assemblées Nationales (1787-2007)

C/11/278/40   Address from the Society of Constitutional Information and the *SADH* to the National Convention, dated 24th November 1792.

Police Générale

F7/4223   Laws relating to foreign passports.
F7/4368   Documents relating to William Stone.

F7/4412	Passport demands sent to the *Comité de Sûreté Générale*, Robert Merry, 8th & 9th May 1793; Charlotte Smith, 2nd September 1793; George Edwards, 7th July 1793; James Eyles, 3rd June 1793; [?] O'Brien & Magher[y?], 21st June 1793; G. O'Connell, 6th July 1793; Robert O'Reilly, 12th June 1793; Mr. Somers, 5th June 1793; William Kirkby, 28th June 1793.
F7/4648/3	Files on Charles Churchill and Thomas Christie.
F7/4750	Prison file of Jacobite exile, [?] Johnstone, 18th October 1793.
F7/4774/61	Prison file of Thomas Paine.
F7/4774/69	Short file on Sampson Perry, with details of his release from prison.
F7/4774/70/458	Letter from [?] Wetherill to Jérôme Pétion, 11th January 1793.
F7/4774/70/459	Letter from John Hurford Stone to Jérôme Pétion, 12th February 1792.
F7/4774/70/460	Letter from Philip Thicknepe to Jérôme Pétion, 21st August 1792.
F7/4774/70/461	Letter from W. S. Smith to Jérôme Pétion [n.d.].
F7/4774/70/462	Letter from [T?] Jones to Jérôme Pétion, 2nd November 1792.
F7/4774/70/463	Letter from David Williams to Jérôme Pétion, 10th March 1792.
F7/4774/70/464	Letter from Thomas Walker to Jérôme Pétion, [n.d.].
F7/4774/70/465	Letter from Thomas Christie to Jérôme Pétion, 14th February 1792.
F7/4774/70/466	Letter from [?] Montfort to Jérôme Pétion, 20th April 1792.
F7/4774/70/467	Letter from John Tuffin to Jérôme Pétion, 13th April 1792.
F7/4774/70/468	Letter to Jérôme Pétion, [n.a.] [n.d.].
F7/4774/70/471	Letter to Jérôme Pétion, [n.a.], 13th February 1792.
F7/4774/88	Prison file of Robert Rayment, including numerous petitions and letters of appeal against incarceration.
F7/4775/13	Prison file of Sampson Perry, details of his release, 22nd November 1794.
F7/4775/20/3	Prison file of Sir Robert Smith, including numerous petitions and letters of appeal against incarceration.
F7/4775/23	Police statement of Citizen Arthur, denouncing John Hurford Stone, and the latter's prison file.
F7/4775/52/70-81	Prison files of Christopher White and Nicholas Joyce.
F7/4775/52	Prison file of Helen Maria Williams.
F7/4779	List of foreign residents and sums owed to foreigners by the authorities.

Jurisdictions Extraordinaires

W/269/16/29   Papers from the trial of Jean-Paul Marat.
W/269/16/30   Papers from the trial of Jean-Paul Marat.

II. MAPS

Plan de Paris dédié à Messieurs les Prévôt (1761). Bibliothèque Nationale de France, Paris.

III. CONTEMPORARY NEWSPAPERS AND PERIODICALS

The Analytical Review. London: Johnson, 1788-1799.
Annales des arts et manufactures: ou, mémoires technologiques sur les découvertes modernes concernant tous les arts et métiers, les manufactures, l'agriculture, le commerce, la navigation, etc. Paris: Imprimerie de Chaignieau Aîné, 1800-.
The Annual Register, or a View of the History, Politics and Literature for the Year 1792. London: Rivington, 1798.
The Anti-Jacobin Review; and Protestant Advocate. London: Sherwood, Neely and Jones, 1821.
The Argus. London: Powell, 1789-1792.
La Chronique du Mois, ou, les cahiers patriotiques. Paris: Imprimerie du Cercle social, 1791-1793.
Le Courier de l'Europe ou mémoires pour servir à l'histoire universelle puis gazette anglo-française. London: Cox, 1776-.
The Critical Review, Or, Annals of Literature. London: Hamilton, 1796.
The European Magazine, and London Review. London: Philological Society of London, 1782-1826.
The Evening Mail. London: Walter and Holl, 1789-1800.
The Gazetteer and New Daily Advertiser. London: Say, 1764-1796.
The Gentleman's Magazine: and Historical Chronicle. London: Nichols, 1736-1856.
The Mirror of Literature, Amusement, and Instruction. London: Limbird, 1823-1847.
The Monthly Magazine, Or, British Register. London: Phillips, 1796-1836.
The Monthly Review, Or, Literary Journal. London: Griffiths, 1752-1825.
The Morning Chronicle. London: Westley, 1770-1800.
The Morning Post. London: Norris, 1773-1800.
The New Monthly Magazine. London: Chapman and Hall, 1857.
Notes and Queries: A Medium of Intercommunication for Literary Men, General Readers etc. London: [publisher unknown] 1849-1921.
The Oracle. Or Bell's World. London: Millan, 1790.
Réimpression de l'Ancien Moniteur: seule histoire authentique et inaltérée de la Révolution française depuis la réunion des États-Généraux jusqu'au Consulat (mai 1789-novembre 1799). Paris: Plon, 1858.
Révolutions de Paris, dédiées à la nation et au district des Petits-Augustins. Paris: Prudhomme, 1789-1794.

IV. PRINTED PRIMARY SOURCES

Literary Fund: An Account of the Institution of the Society for the Establishment of the Literary Fund: the Transactions of the Committee for the Application of the Subscriptions: Poems on Anniversaries, &c.: the Constitutions of the Society, Alterable Only at the Desire of a General Meeting: and a List of the Subscribers. London: Nichols, 1795.

────── *Biographical Sketch of the Revd John Stevens Henslow* (London, 1861).

M. De Viette's Translation from the French of the Life, Portrait, Character, and Trial at Large, of the Late Queen of France: Containing Particular Detail of the Execution and Whole Sufferings in Prison, of That Unhappy Princess; Also the Treatment of the Princess Lamballe, Whose Naked Body, Without Head, Was Dragged Through the Streets of Paris in Horrid Procession.-Likewise an Authentic Account of the First Cause of the French Revolution, and of the Manner in Which It Burst Forth on the Memorable Tenth of August, 1792, on Which Day the Blood of Fifteen Thousand Persons Deluged the Streets of Paris, to Which Is Added, the Trial of the Unfortunate Louis Xvi. Late King of France: Giving an Account of His Parting with the Queen, His Sister, and Two Children, the 21st of January, 1793.-Also, of His Noble Behaviour When He Ascended the Scaffold. with a Description of La Guillotine; or Beheading Machine: by Which the King and Queen Suffered. to Which Is Prefixed, an Exact Copy of His Will. London: Eves, 1794.

Proceedings in the Society of Friends of the People; associated for the purpose of Obtaining a Parliamentary Reform, in the Year 1792. London: Westley, 1793.

ADAMS, J., *A Defence of the Constitutions of Government of the United States of America, Against the Attack of M. Turgot in his Letter to Dr. Price, dated the Twenty-Second Day of March, 1778.* London: Freeman, 1788.

AUCKLAND, W. E., AND AUCKLAND. R. J. E., *The Journal and Correspondence of William, Lord Auckland.* London: Bentley, 1861.

BARÈRE, B., CARNOT, H., AND D'ANGERS, P.-J. D., *Mémoires de B. Barère: membre de la Constituante, de la Convention, du Comité de Salut Public, et de la Chambre des Représentants.* Paris: Labitte, 1842.

BARLOW, J., *A Letter to the National Convention of France: On the Defects in the Constitution of 1791 and the Extent of the Amendments Which Ought to Be Applied.* London: Johnson, 1792.

BARRAS, P., *Mémoires.* Clermont-Ferrand: Paleo, 2004.

BURKE, E. AND MITCHELL, L. G., *Reflections on the Revolution in France.* Oxford: Oxford University Press, 2003.

CHRISTIE, T., *Letters on the Revolution of France, and on the New Constitution Established by the National Assembly: Occasioned by the Publications of the Right Hon. Edmund Burke, M.P. and Alexander de Calonne ... Illustrated with a Chart of the New Constitution: to which is Added, an Appendix, Containing Original Papers and Authentic Documents Relative to the Affairs of France: Addressed to Sir John Sinclair, Bart. M.P.* London: Johnson, 1791.

COLERIDGE, S. T., *The Watchman.* Bristol, 1796.

CONDORCET, J-A-N DE C., *Aux citoyens français, sur la nouvelle constitution*. France: [s.n.], 1793.
——— *Esquisse d'un tableau historique des progrès de l'esprit humain*. Paris: [s.n], 1793.
COOPER, T., *A Reply to Mr. Burke's Invective against Mr. Cooper, and Mr. Watt, in the House of Commons on the 30th of April, 1792*. London: Johnson, 1792.
EDWARDS, G., *Idées pour former une nouvelle constitution et pour assurer la prospérité et le bonheur de la France et d'autres nations*. Paris: Jansen, 1793.
——— *Adresse au corps législatif contenant l'exposé d'un nouveau système politique*. [s.n.], [n.d.].
——— *The Royal and Constitutional Regeneration of Great Britain: Or, Properly Speaking, the Effectual Advancement of All the Different National Interests of the Kingdom ... Being the Discovery of the Practical Means of Advancing and Completing the Political Economy, the National Improvements and Civilization; the Church, Medicine, and Law; the Government, Politics, and Finances of the Kingdom*. London: Debrett, 1790.
——— *The Great and Important Discovery of the Eighteenth Century, and the Means of Setting Right the National Affairs: By a Great Addition of Numerous and Inestimable Useful Designs and Public Improvements, by Which the Nation Is Still Capable of Being Infinitely Benefited; to Which Are Added Addresses to the Several Different Classes of Society, Pointing Out the Measures, Which They Ought to Pursue As Their Respective Duties, in Redressing Public Affairs. by George Edwards, Esq. MD: Author of the Aggrandisement of Great Britain; of the National Perfection of Finance; and of the Royal Regeneration of Great Britain*. London: Ridgway and Debrett, 1791.
ELLIOTT, G. D., *Journal of My Life during the French Revolution*. London: Rodale, 1955.
FORSTER, G., AND GILLI, M., *Un révolutionnaire allemand, Georg Forster (1754-1794)*. Paris: CTHS, 2005.
FREND, W., *Peace and Union Recommended to the Associated Bodies of Republicans and Anti-Republicans*. St. Ives: Croft, 1793.
FROST, J., AND MR. RAMSEY, *The Trial of John Frost for Seditious Words, in Hilary Term, 1793*. London: Ridgway and Symonds, 1794.
GENLIS, S. F., *Mémoires inédits de Madame la Comtesse de Genlis sur le dix-huitième siècle et la Révolution française, depuis 1756 jusqu'à nos jours*. Paris: Ladvocat, 1825.
GIRARDIN, R. L., *Discours sur la nécessité de la ratification de la loi: par la volonté générale*. Paris: Creuset, 1791.
GODWIN, W., *An Enquiry Concerning Political Justice and Its Influence on General Virtue and Happiness*. London: G. G. and J. Robinson, 1793.
GOWER, G. G. L., AND BROWNING, O., *The Despatches of Earl Gower, English Ambassador at Paris from June 1790 to August 1792, to Which Are Added the Despatches of Mr. Lindsay and Mr. Monro, and the Diary of Viscount Palmerston in France During July and August 1791*. Cambridge: Cambridge University Press, 1885.

HAWKINS, L. M., *Letters on the Female Mind, Its Powers and Pursuits: Addressed to Miss H.M. Williams, with Particular Reference to her Letters from France.* London: Hookham and Carpenter, 1793.

HOWELL, T. B, HOWELL, T. J., COBBETT, W., AND JARDINE, D., *A Complete Collection of State Trials and Proceedings for High Treason and Other Crimes and Misdemeanors from the Earliest Period to the Year 1783.* London: Longman, Rees, Orme, Brown & Green, 1816-1828.

JOHNSON [?], *A Genuine Narrative of the Proceedings at Paris: From the 16th of December, 1791, to the 1st of February, 1793: Containing, Among Other Interesting Anecdotes, a Particular Statement of the Memorable Tenth of August and Third of September, to which is Annexed the Life, Trial, and Execution, of Louis XVI. by Mr. Johnson, Who Was Eye-Witness of the Whole of the Transactions.* London: Turner, 1793.

LAURENS, H., HAMER, P. M., ROGERS, G. C., CHESNUTT, D. R., AND LYLES, M. E., *The Papers of Henry Laurens.* Columbia: University of South Carolina Press, 1968.

LE SUEUR T, AND VAUGHAN, B., *Idées sur l'espèce de gouvernement populaire qui pourroit convenir à un pays de l'étendue et de la population présumée de la France: essai présenté à la Convention Nationale.* Paris: Mayer et Compagnie, 1792.

MAXWELL, W., *Déclaration De W. Maxwell relativement à l'assemblée qui devait se tenir chez lui à Londres, le 12 septembre 1792, pour ouvrir une souscription en faveur des patriotes français, imprimée dans le "Morning Chronicle"... et traduite sous les yeux de l'auteur.* Paris: Imprimerie du Cercle Social, 1792.

MERRY, R., *Réflexions politiques sur la nouvelle constitution qui se prépare en France, adressées à la république.* Paris: Reyner, 1792.

——— [?] *A Circumstantial History of the Transactions at Paris on the Tenth of August: Plainly Shewing the Perfidy of Louis XVI and the General Unanimity of the People, in Defence of Their Rights.* London: R. Thomson, R. Lyttlejohn, H.D. Symonds, 1792.

MOORE, J., *A Journal During a Residence in France: From the Beginning of August, to the Middle of December, 1792: to Which Is Added, an Account of the Most Remarkable Events That Happened at Paris from That Time to the Death of the Late King of France.* London: G. G. and J. Robinson, 1793.

MORGAN, G. C. AND MORGAN, R. P., *Travels in Revolutionary France and A Journey Across America.* Ed. Mary-Ann Constantine and Paul Frame. Cardiff: University of Wales Press, 2013.

MORRIS, T. AND WILLIAMS, D., *A General View of the Life and Writings of the Rev. David Williams, Drawn Up for the Chronique du Mois, a French Periodical Publication, at the Request of Messrs. Condorcet, Claviere, Mercier, Auger, Brissot, &c.* London: Ridgway, 1792.

NARES, R., *A Short Account of the Character and Reign of Louis XVI. Shewing how little he deserved, from his Ungrateful people, the name of Tyrant. To which is subjoined, a corrected translation of his last will.* London: Downes, 1793.

OSWALD, J., *The Triumph of Freedom!: An Ode to Commemorate the Anniversary of the French Revolution.* Paris: Printed for the Author, 1790.

―――― *The Government of the People, or a Sketch of a Constitution for the Universal Commonwealth*. Paris: The English Press, 1792.

―――― *Le gouvernement du peuple; ou plan de constitution pour la république universelle, traduit de l'anglais de J. Oswald, etc*. Paris, [s.n.], 1793.

―――― *Review of the Constitution of Great-Britain*. London, [s.n.] 1792.

O'REILLY, R., *Essai sur le blanchiment avec la description de la nouvelle méthode de blanchir par la vapeur, d'après le procédé du citoyen Chaptal: et son application aux arts*. Paris: Imprimerie des Annales des Arts et Manufactures, 1801.

PAINE, T. AND KRAMNICK, I., *Common Sense*. 1776; Harmondsworth: Penguin, 1976.

PAINE, T. AND FONER, E., *Rights of Man*. 1791; 1792: Harmondsworth: Penguin, 1984.

PAINE, T. AND CONWAY, M. D., *The Writings of Thomas Paine*. New York: G.P. Putnam's Sons, 1899.

PAINE, T. AND FONER, P. S., *The Complete Writings of Thomas Paine*. New York: Citadel, 1945.

PAINE, T., MACDONALD, A., ERSKINE, T. E., MACDONALD, A., ANDREWS, E. T., THOMAS, I., LARKIN, E., AND WEST, D., *The Trial of Thomas Paine, for a Libel, Contained in the Second Part of Rights of Man: Before Lord Kenyon, and a Special Jury, at Guild Hall, December 18, 1792. with the Speeches of the Attorney General and Mr. Erskine at Large*. Boston: Thomas and Andrews, 1793.

PERRY, S., *A Disquisition of the Stone and Gravel; with Strictures on the Gout, When combined with those Disorders*. London: Reynell, 1785.

―――― *The Argus; Or, General Observer: a Political Miscellany. Containing the Most Important Events of Europe, and the Principal Occurrences in England, from the Meeting of the Parliament, October 29, 1795, to its Dissolution, May 18, 1796. with a Variety of Original Letters and Reflections on the Interesting and Critical Situation of the British Empire*. London, Symonds, 1795.

―――― *Oppression!!!: The Appeal of Captain Perry, Late Editor of the Argus, to the People of England : Containing a Justification of His Principles and Conduct, to which is Added, a Development of Some of the Mysteries of the Spy Trade*. London: Citizen Lee, 1795.

―――― *Prospectus. on Saturday, the 24th of October, 1795, Will Be Published, by H.D. Symonds: A New and Interesting Work, to be Called the Argus, Or, General Observer of the Moral Political, and Commercial World*. London: Symonds, 1795.

―――― *An Historical Sketch of the French Revolution: Commencing with Its Predisposing Causes, and Carried on to the Acceptation of the Constitution, in 1795*. London: Symonds, 1796.

―――― *The Origin of Government Compatible with and Founded on the Rights of Man: With a Few Words on the Constitutional Object of the Corresponding Society: the Whole Addressed to the Common Sense of Every Englishman*. London: Jordan, 1797.

PIGOTT, C., *The Jockey Club, Or, a Sketch of the Manners of the Age*. London: Symonds, 1792.

———— *Persecution. the Case of Charles Pigott: Contained in the Defence He Had Prepared, and Which Would Have Been Delivered by Him on His Trial, If the Grand Jury Had Not Thrown Out the Bill Preferred against Him*. London: Eaton, 1793.

PIOZZI, H. L., BLOOM, E. A., AND BLOOM, L. D., *The Piozzi Letters: Correspondence of Hester Lynch Piozzi, 1784-1821 (formerly Mrs. Thrale)*. Newark: University of Delaware Press, 1989.

PLAYFAIR, W., *The History of Jacobinism: Its Crimes, Cruelties and Perfidies: Comprising an Inquiry into the Manner of Disseminating, Under the Appearance of Philosophy and Virtue, Principles Which Are Equally Subversive of Order, Virtue, Religion, Liberty and Happiness*. Philadelphia: Cobbett, 1796.

PRICE, R., *A Discourse on the Love of Our Country: Delivered on Nov. 4, 1789, at the Meeting-House in the Old Jewry, to the Society for Commemorating the Revolution in Great Britain : with an Appendix, Containing the Report of the Committee of the Society, an Account of the Population of France, and the Declaration of Rights by the National Assembly of France*. London: Cadell, 1789.

RICKMAN, T. C. AND PAINE, T., *The Life of Thomas Paine: Author of Common Sense, Rights of Man, Age of Reason, Letter to the Addresses, &c. &c*. London: Rickman, 1819.

RIGBY, E., *Dr. Rigby's Letters from France &c in 1789 edited by his daughter Lady Eastlake*. London: Longmans, Green, 1880.

ROBERT, F., *Le républicanisme adapté à la France: par F. Robert, membre de la Société des Amis de la Constitution de Paris*. Paris: L'Auteur, 1790.

ROLAND, M., *An Appeal to Impartial Posterity: By Citizenness Roland, Wife of the Minister of the Home Department: Or, a Collection of Pieces Written by Her During Her Confinement in the Prisons of the Abbey, and St. Pélagie. Translated from the French*. London: Johnson, 1795.

ROLAND, M. AND DE ROUX, P., *Mémoires de Madame Roland*. Paris: Mercure de France, 1986.

SAINT-JUST, L. A., *Theorie politique: textes établis et commentes par Alain Lienard*. Paris: Seuil, 1976.

SEWARD, A. AND CONSTABLE, A., *Letters of Anna Seward: Written between the Years 1784 and 1807*. Edinburgh: Constable and Co., 1811.

STONE, J. H. AND PRIESTLEY, J., *Copies of Original Letters Recently Written by Persons in Paris to Dr. Priestley in America: Taken on Board of a Neutral Vessel*. London: Wright, 1798.

THALE, M., *Selections from the Papers of the London Corresponding Society, 1792-1799*. Cambridge: Cambridge University Press, 1983.

THELWALL, J., *Poems Written in Close Confinement in the Tower and Newgate, Under a Charge of High Treason. by John Thelwall*. London: Ridgway, 1795.

WATLINS, J., SHOBERL, F. AND UPCOTT, W., *A Biographical Dictionary of the Living Authors of Great Britain and Ireland: Comprising Literary Memoirs and Anecdotes of Their Lives ; and a Chronological Register of Their Publications, with the Number of Editions Printed*. London: Colburn, 1816.

WILLIAMS, D., *The Philosopher: in Three Conversations*. London: Becket, 1771.

―――― *Letters on Political Liberty: Addressed to a Member of the English House of Commons, on His Being Chosen into the Committee of an Associating County*. London: Evans, 1782.

―――― *Observations sur la dernière constitution de la France, avec des vues pour la formation de la nouvelle constitution*. Trans. Jean-Baptiste Maudru. Paris: Imprimerie du Cercle Social, 1793.

WILLIAMS, D. AND FRANCE, P., *Incidents in My Own Life Which Have Been Thought of Some Importance*. Brighton: University of Sussex Library, 1980.

WILLIAMS, H. M. AND FRAISTAT, N., *Letters Written in France, in the Summer 1790, to a Friend in England: Containing Various Anecdotes Relative to the French Revolution*. Peterborough, Ontario: Broadview, 2002. Print.

WILLIAMS, H. M., *A Farewell, for Two Years, to England. a Poem*. London: Cadell, 1791.

―――― *Letters from France: Containing A Great Variety of Interesting and Original Information concerning the most important events that have lately occurred in that country, and particularly respecting the campaign of 1792*. London: G. G. and J. Robinson, 1793.

―――― *Letters from France: Containing Many New Anecdotes relative to the French Revolution, and the present state of French Manners*. London: G. G. and J. Robinson, 1796.

―――― *Letters Containing a Sketch of the Politics of France, from the 31st of May 1793, Till the 28th of July 1794, and of the Scenes Which Have Passed in the Prisons of Paris*. London: G. G. and J. Robinson, 1796.

―――― *A Tour in Switzerland: Or, a View of the Present State of the Governments and Manners of Those Cantons: with Comparative Sketches of the Present State of Paris*. London: G. G. and J. Robinson, 1798.

―――― *Sketches of the State of Manners and Opinions in the French Republic, Towards the Close of the Eighteenth Century: In a Series of Letters*. London: G. G. and J. Robinson, 1801.

―――― *A Narrative of the Events Which Have Taken Place in France: With an Account of the Present State of Society and Public Opinion*. London: Murray, 1815.

―――― *Letters on the Events Which Have Passed in France Since the Restoration in 1815*. London: Baldwin, Cradock and Joy, 1819.

―――― *Souvenirs de la Révolution française*. Paris: Dondey-Dupré, 1827.

WOLLSTONECRAFT, M. AND TODD, J. M., *The Collected Letters of Mary Wollstonecraft*. New York: Columbia University Press, 2003.

WOLLSTONECRAFT, M., TODD, J. M. AND BUTLER, M., *The Works of Mary Wollstonecraft: An Historical and Moral View of the French Revolution. Letters to Joseph Johnson. Letters Written in Sweden, Norway and Denmark*. London: Pickering, 1989.

YORKE, H. R., *Reason urged against precedent: in a letter to the people of Derby*. London: G. G. and J. Robinson, 1793.

―――― *These Are the Times That Try Mens Souls!: A Letter Addressed to John Frost, a Prisoner in Newgate*. London: Eaton, 1793.

――― *Thoughts on Civil Government: Addressed to the Disfranchised Citizens of Sheffield*. London: Eaton, 1794.

――― *The Trial of Henry Yorke, for a Conspiracy, &c. Before the Hon. Mr. Justice Rooke, at the Assizes, Held for the County of York, on Saturday, July 10, 1795. Published by the Defendant, from Mr. Ramsay's Short-Hand Notes*. York: Peck, 1795.

――― *On the Means of Saving Our Country*. Dorchester: Lockett, 1797.

――― *A Letter to the Reformers*. Dorchester: Lockett and Symonds, 1798.

――― *Elements of Civil Knowledge*. Dorchester: Lockett, 1800.

――― *A View of a Course of Lectures to Be Commenced on Monday, May 11, 1801, on the State of Society, at the Opening of the Nineteenth Century: Containing Inquiries into the Constitutions, Laws, and Manners, of the Principal States of Europe*. London: Clement, 1801.

YORKE, H. R. AND SYKES, J. A. C., *France in 1802: Described in a Series of Contemporary Letters*. London: Heinemann, 1906.

YOUNG, A. AND BETHAM-EDWARDS, M., *Arthur Young's Travels in France During the Years 1787, 1788, 1789*. London: Bell, 1892.

V. SECONDARY SOURCES

Journal Articles and Chapters from Edited Collections

ADAMS, R. M., 'Helen Maria Williams and the French Revolution', in Griggs, E. L. (ed.), *Wordsworth and Coleridge: Studies in honour of George Mclean Harper*. New York, Russell, 1967, pp. 87-117.

――― 'Della Cruscanism in America', *Publications of the Modern Language Association of America*, 79:3 (1964), pp. 259-65.

――― 'Robert Merry: Political Romanticist', *Studies in Romanticism*, 2 (1965), pp. 23-37.

AGNEW, J., 'Representing Space: Space scale and culture in social science', in Duncan J. and Leys, D. (eds.), *Place, Culture, Representation*. London: Routledge, 1993, pp. 251-71.

ALGER, J. G., 'The British Colony in Paris, 1792-1793', *The English Historical Review*, 13.52 (1898), pp. 672-94.

ANDERSON, W., 'John Oswald', *The Scottish Nation*, 3 (1863), pp. 268-9.

ANDREW, D. T., 'Popular Culture and Public Debate: London 1780', *Historical Journal*, 39.2 (1996), pp. 405-23.

APPLEBY, J., 'America As a Model for the Radical French Reformers of 1789', *The William and Mary Quarterly: a Magazine of Early American History*, 28.2 (1971), pp. 267-86.

AZIMI, V., 'L'étranger sous la Révolution', in Vovelle. M. (ed.), *La Révolution et l'ordre juridique privé, rationalité ou scandale?: Actes du colloque d'Orléans, 11-13 Septembre 1986*, Paris: Presse Universitaire de France, 1988, pp. 699-705.

BARRELL, J., 'Radicalism, Visual Culture, and Spectacle in the 1790s', *Erudit: Romanticism on the Net* 46 (2007).

BLAKEMORE, S., 'Revolution and the French Disease: Laetitia Matilda Hawkins's Letters to Helen Maria Williams', *Studies in English Literature, 1500-1900*, 36.3 (1996), pp. 673-91.

BOIME, A., 'The Sketch and Caricature as Metaphors for the French Revolution', *Zeitschrift Fur Kunstgeschichte*, 55.2 (1992), pp. 256-67.

BOUR, I., 'Mary Wollstonecraft as Historian in An Historical and Moral View of the Origins and Progress of the French Revolution; and the Effect it has Produced in Europe (1794)', *Études Épistémè*, 17 (2010), pp. 119-29.

BRAY, M., 'Helen Maria Williams and Edmund Burke: Radical Critique and Complicity', *Eighteenth Century Life*, 16.2 (1992), pp. 1-24.

BRUBAKER, W. R., 'The French Revolution and the Invention of Citizenship', *French Politics and Society*, 7.3 (1989), pp. 30-49.

BRUBAKER, W. R. AND COOPER, F., 'Beyond "Identity."', *Theory and Society*, 29.1 (2000), pp. 1-47.

BURKE, P., 'Performing History: The Importance of Occasions', *Rethinking History*, 9.1 (2005), pp. 35-52.

CENSER, J. R., 'Review Essay – Social Twists and Linguistic Turns: Revolutionary Historiography a Decade After the Bicentennial', *French Historical Studies*, 22.1 (1999), pp. 139-67.

CLIFFORD, J., 'Robert Merry, A Pre-Byronic Hero', *Bulletin of the John Rylands Library*, 27.1 (1942), pp. 74-96.

COLLEY, L., 'The Apotheosis of George III: Loyalty, Royalty and the British Nation 1760-1820', *Past and Present*, (1984), pp. 94-129.

—— 'Britishness and Otherness: an Argument', *Journal of British Studies*, 31.4 (1992), pp. 309-29.

CONSTANTINE, M.-A., 'The Welsh in Revolutionary Paris." "Footsteps of Liberty and Revolt' in Constantine, M.-A. and Johnston, D. (eds.), *Essays on Wales and the French Revolution*. Cardiff: University of Wales Press, 2013, pp. 69-92

CRAWFORD, J., '"At This Period Peculiarly Necessary': the Republication of Milton's Political Tracts in the 1790s', *Journal for Eighteenth-Century Studies*, 32.1 (2009), pp. 69-86.

CUNNINGHAM, H., 'The Language of Patriotism, 1750-1914', *History Workshop*, 12 (1981), pp. 8-33.

DUNYACH, J.-F., 'Les réseaux d'un excentrique: vies et parcours de William Playfair (1759-1823)' in Thomson, A, Burrows, S., Dziembowski, E. (eds), *Cultural Transfers: France and Britain in the Long Eighteenth Century, Studies on Voltaire and the Eighteenth Century* 4, Oxford: Oxford University Press, 2010, pp. 115-27.

DYCK, I., 'Local Attachments, National Identities and World Citizenship in the Thought of Thomas Paine', *History Workshop*, 35 (1993), pp. 117-135.

EASTWOOD, D., 'Patriotism and the English State in the 1790s' in Philp, M. (ed.), *The French Revolution and British Popular Politics*. Cambridge: Cambridge University Press, 1991, pp. 146-98.

EDELSTEIN, M., "Une élection purement populaire': l'impact de la démocratie sur les élections municipales dans les plus grandes villes à l'automne 1792', *Annales historiques de la Révolution française*, 349 (2007), pp. 29-49.

ELLIOTT, M., 'The "Despard Conspiracy" Reconsidered', *Past and Present*, 75.1 (1977), pp. 46-61.

EMSLEY, C., 'An Aspect of Pitt's 'Terror': Prosecutions for Sedition During the 1790s', *Social History*, 6.2 (1981), pp. 155-84.

―――― 'The London 'Insurrection' of December 1792: Fact, Fiction, or Fantasy?', *Journal of British Studies*, 17.2 (1978), pp. 66-86.

EPSTEIN, J., "Our Real Constitution:' Trial Defence and Radical Memory in the Age of Revolution' in Vernon, J. (ed.), *Re-reading the Constitution: New Narratives in the Political History of England's Long Nineteenth Century*. Cambridge: Cambridge University Press, 1996, pp. 22-51.

―――― 'Spatial Practices, Democratic Vistas', *Social History*, 24.3 (1999), pp. 294-310.

―――― "Equality and No King': Sociability and Sedition: The case of John Frost' in Russell, G. and Clara Tuite, C. (eds.), *Romantic Sociability: Social Networks and Literary Culture in Britain 1770-1840*. Cambridge: Cambridge University Press, 2002, pp. 43-61.

EPSTEIN, J. AND KARR, D., 'Playing at Revolution: British "Jacobin" Performance', *The Journal of Modern History*, 79.3 (2007), pp. 495-530.

ERDMAN, D, V., 'The Dawn of Universal Patriotism: William Wordsworth among the British in Revolutionary France' in Johnston, K. R. and Ruoff, G. W. (eds.), *William Wordsworth and the Age of Romanticism*. New Brunswick, New Jersey: Rutgers University Press, 1987, pp. 3-20.

FERRADOU, M., 'Histoire d'un 'festin patriotique' à l'hôtel white (18 novembre 1792): les Irlandais patriotes à Paris, 1789-1795', *Annales historiques de la Révolution française*, 382 (2015), pp. 123-43.

FRUCHTMAN, J., 'Public Loathing, Private Thoughts: Historical Representation in Helen Maria Williams' Letters from France', *Prose Studies*, 18.3 (1995), pp. 223-43.

GERBOD, P., 'Visiteurs et résidents britanniques dans le Paris révolutionnaire de 1789 à 1799' in Vovelle, M. (ed.), *Paris et la révolution*. Paris: Publications de la Sorbonne, 1989, pp. 335-51.

GILMARTIN, K., 'Popular Radicalism and the Public Sphere', *Studies in Romanticism*, 33 (1994): pp. 549-57.

GREENE, J. P., 'Paine, America, and the "Modernization" of Political Consciousness', *Political Science Quarterly*, 93 (1978), pp. 73-92.

GUENIFFEY, P., 'Cordeliers and Girondins: The Pre-History of the Republic?' in Fontana, B. (ed.), *The Invention of the Modern Republic*. Cambridge: Cambridge University Press, 1994, pp. 86-106.

HUNT, L., 'The World We Have Gained: the Future of the French Revolution', *The American Historical Review*, 108.1 (2003), pp. 1-19.

JACOB, M., 'Sociability and the International Republican Conversation' in Russell, G. and Tuite, G. (eds.), *Romantic Sociability: Social Networks and Literary Culture in Britain, 1770-1840*. Cambridge: Cambridge University Press, 2002, pp. 24-42.

JONES, C. B., 'Helen Maria Williams and Radical Sensibility', *Prose Studies*, 12 (1989), pp. 3-24.

KATES, G., 'From Liberalism to Radicalism: Tom Paine's Rights of Man', *Journal of the History of Ideas*, 50.4 (1989), pp. 569-87.

KENNEDY, D., 'Responding to the French Revolution: Williams' Julia and Burney's The Wanderer' in Dabundo, L. (ed.), *Jane Austen and Mary Shelley and Their Sisters*. Lanham: University Press of America, 2000, pp. 3-17.

KITSON, P. J., '"Not a Reforming Patriot but an Ambitious Tyrant": Representations of Cromwell and the English Republic in the Late Eighteenth and Early Nineteenth Centuries' in Morton, T. and Smith, N. (eds.), *Radicalism in British Literary Culture, 1650-1830: From Revolution to Revolution*. Cambridge: Cambridge University Press, 2002, pp. 183-200.

KRAMNICK, I., 'The "Great National Debate": The Discourse of Politics in 1787', *The William and Mary Quarterly*, 45.1 (1988), pp. 3-32.

LOTTES, G., 'Revolution and Political Culture: An Anglo-French Comparison' in Philp, M. (ed.), *The French Revolution and British Popular Politics*. Cambridge, Cambridge University Press, 1989, pp. 78-98.

MARQUIS, H., 'L'espionnage britannique et la fin de l'Ancien Régime', *Histoire, économie et société*, 17.2 (1998), pp. 261-76.

MCCALMAN, I., 'Newgate in Revolution: Radical Enthusiasm and Romantic Counter-culture', *Eighteenth Century Life*, 22 (1998), pp. 95-110.

MACDONALD, S., 'English-language Newspapers in Revolutionary France', *Journal for Eighteenth-Century Studies*, 36.1 (2013), pp. 17-33.

MEE, J., "'Reciprocal expressions of kindness': Robert Merry, Della Cruscanism and the Limits of Sociability' in Russell, G. and Tuite, C. (eds.), *Romantic Sociability: Social Networks and Literary Culture in Britain, 1770-1840*. Cambridge, U.K: Cambridge University Press, 2002, pp. 104-22.

———— 'The Strange Career of Richard 'Citizen' Lee: Poetry, Popular Radicalism and Enthusiasm in the 1790s' in Morton, T. and Smith, N. (eds.), *Radicalism in British Literary Culture, 1650-1830: From Revolution to Revolution*. Cambridge: Cambridge University Press, 2002, pp. 151-66.

———— 'A bold and free-spoken man": the strange case of Charles Pigott' in Womersley, D., Bullard, P. and Williams, A. (eds.), *"Cultures of Whiggism": New Essays on English Literature and Culture in the Long Eighteenth Century*. Newark: University of Delaware Press, 2005, pp. 330-50.

———— 'The Magician No Conjuror: Robert Merry and the Political Alchemy of the 1790s' in Pickering, P. A. and Davis, M. T. (eds.), *Unrespectable Radicals?: Popular Politics in the Age of Reform*. Aldershot, England: Ashgate, 2008, pp. 41-56.

―――― 'Popular Radical Culture' in Clemit, P. (ed.), *The Cambridge Companion to British Literature of the French Revolution in the 1790s*. Cambridge: Cambridge University Press, 2011, pp. 117-28.

―――― '"The Use of Conversation": William Godwin's Conversable World and Romantic Sociability', *Studies in Romanticism*, 50.4 (2011), pp. 567-90.

PAGE, A., 'The Dean of St Asaph's Trial: Libel and Politics in the 1780s', *Journal for Eighteenth-Century Studies*, 32.1 (2009), pp. 21-35.

PHILP, M., 'Vulgar Conservatism, 1792-3', *English Historical Review*, 110.435 (1995), pp. 42-69.

―――― 'English Republicanism in the 1790s', *The Journal of Political Philosophy*, 6.3 (1998), pp. 235-62.

PIERRE, J., 'Notes autour de Parmentier', *Revue de l'histoire de la pharmacie*, 275 (1987), pp. 307-18.

RAPPORT, M. G., 'A Community Apart? the Closure of the Scots College in Paris During the French Revolution, 1789-1794', *Innes Review*, 53.1 (2002), pp. 79-107.

―――― 'Deux nations malheureusement rivales : les Français en Grande-Bretagne, les Britanniques en France, et la construction des identités nationales pendant la Révolution française', *Annales Historiques de la Révolution Française*, 342 (2005), pp. 21-46.

RIGBY, B., 'Radical Spectators of the Revolution: The case of the Analytical Review' in Crossley, C. and Small, I. (eds.), *The French Revolution and British Culture*. Oxford: Oxford University Press, 1989, pp. 63-83.

ROGERS, N., 'Pigott's Private Eye: Radicalism and Sexual Scandal in Eighteenth-Century England', *Journal of the Canadian Historical Association / Révue de la Société Historique Canadienne*, 4.1 (1993), pp. 247-63.

ROGERS, R., 'The Society of the Friends of the Rights of Man, 1792-94: British and Irish Radical Conjunctions in Republican Paris', *La Révolution française*, 11 (2016).

SAGRADINI, L., 'La plèbe entre dans la surface de jeu', *Multitudes*, 39.4 (2009), pp. 205-10.

SCHOFIELD, T. P,. 'Conservative Political Thought in Britain in Response to the French Revolution', *The Historical Journal*, 29.3 (1986), pp. 601-22.

SCRIVENER, M., 'John Thelwall and the Revolution of 1649' in Morton, T. and Smith, N. (eds.), *Radicalism in British Literary Culture, 1650-1830: From Revolution to Revolution*. Cambridge: Cambridge University Press, 2002, pp. 119-50.

SHEPS, A., 'Ideological Immigrants in Revolutionary America' in Fritz, P. and Williams, D. (eds.), *City and Society in the Eighteenth Century*. Toronto: Hakkert, 1973, pp. 231-46.

SONENSCHER, M., 'Review Article: Enlightenment and Revolution', *The Journal of Modern History*, 70 (1998), pp. 371-83.

STERN, M. B., 'The English Press in Paris and Its Successors, 1793-1852', *Papers of the Bibliographical Society of America*, 74 (1980), pp. 307-59.

―――― 'The Franco-American Book Trade in the Late Eighteenth and Early Nineteenth Centuries', *Publishing Research Quarterly*, 10.1 (1994), pp. 47-54.
TAUCHERT, A., 'Maternity, Castration and Mary Wollstonecraft's *Historical and Moral View of the French Revolution*', *Women's Writing*, 4.2 (1997), pp. 173-203.
THALE, M., 'London Debating Societies in the 1790s', *The Historical Journal*, 32.1 (1980), pp. 57-86.
THOMPSON, E. P., 'Hunting the Jacobin Fox', *Past and Present*, (1994), pp. 94-140.
TODD, F. M., 'Wordsworth, Helen Maria Williams and France', *Modern Language Review*, 43.4 (1948), pp. 456-64.
VERNON, J., 'Notes Towards an Introduction' in Vernon, J. (ed.), *Re-reading the Constitution: New Narratives in the Political History of England's Long Nineteenth Century*. Cambridge: Cambridge University Press, 1996, pp. 1-22.
VINCENT, E., '"The Real Grounds of the Present War": John Bowles and the French Revolutionary Wars, 1792–1802', *History*, 78.254 (1993), pp. 393-420.
WAHNICH, S. AND BÉLISSA, M., 'Les crimes des Anglais: trahir le droit', *Annales historiques de la Révolution française*, 300.1 (1995), pp. 233-48.
WILLIAMS, D., 'The Missions of David Williams and James Tilly Matthews to England (1793)', *The English Historical Review*, 53.212 (1938), pp. 651-68.
WOODWARD, L. D., 'Les projets de descente en Irlande sous la Convention, et les réfugiés irlandais et anglais en France: d'après des documents inédits', *Annales historiques de la Révolution française*, 8 (1931), pp. 1-30.
ZIZEK, J., '"Plume De Fer": Louis-Marie Prudhomme Writes the French Revolution', *French Historical Studies*, 26.4 (2003), pp. 619-60.

Books

ALDEN, J. R., *Stephen Sayre: American Revolutionary Adventurer*. Baton Rouge and London: Louisiana State University Press, 1983.
ALDRIDGE, A. O., *Man of Reason: The Life of Thomas Paine*. London: Cresset Press, 1959.
ALENGRY, F., *Condorcet: guide de la Révolution française*. Paris: Giard et Brière, 1904.
ALEXANDER, D., *Richard Newton and English Caricature in the 1790s*. Manchester: Manchester University Press, 1998.
ALGER, J. G., *Englishmen in the French Revolution*. London: S. Low, Marston, Searle and Rivington, 1889.
―――― *Glimpses of the French Revolution: Myths, Ideals, and Realities*. London: Low, Marston and Co., 1894.
―――― *Napoleon's British Visitors and Captives, 1801-1815*. New York: AMS Press, 1970.
―――― *Paris in 1789-94: Farewell Letters of Victims of the Guillotine*. London: Allen, 1902.

ANDERSON, B. R. O. G., *Imagined Communities: Reflections on the Origin and Spread of Nationalism*. London: Verso, 2006.

ANDREWS, A., *The History of British Journalism from the Foundation of the Newspaper Press in England to the Repeal of the Stamp Act in 1855*. London: Bentley, 1859.

ARENDT, H., *The Origins of Totalitarianism*. New York: Harcourt, Brace and World, 1966.

AVENEL, G., *Anarcharsis Cloots: l'orateur du genre humain*. Paris: Lacrois, Verboeckhoven and Co., 1865.

BARKER, H., *Newspapers, Politics and English Society, 1695-1855*. Harlow: Longman, 2000.

BARNARD, T., *Anna Seward: A Constructed Life: A Critical Biography*. Farnham: Ashgate, 2009.

BARRELL, J., *Imagining the King's Death: Figurative Treason, Fantasies of Regicide, 1793-1796*. Oxford: Oxford University Press, 2000.

—— *The Spirit of Despotism: Invasions of Privacy in the 1790s*. Oxford: Oxford University Press, 2006.

BART, J., NAUDIN-PATRIAT, F., AND ABERDAM, S., *La constitution du 24 Juin 1793: L'utopie dans le droit public français?: Actes du colloque de Dijon, 16-17 Septembre 1993 organisé par le Centre Georges Chevrier pour l'histoire du droit*. Dijon: Editions Universitaires de Dijon, 1997.

BELCHEM, J., *Popular Radicalism in Nineteenth-Century Britain*. New York: St. Martin's Press, 1996.

BEWLEY, C., AND BEWLEY, D. K., *Gentleman Radical: A Life of John Horne Tooke, 1736-1812*. London: Tauris Academic Studies, 1998.

BEWLEY, C., *Muir of Huntershill*. Oxford: Oxford University Press, 1981.

BILLINGTON, J. H., *Fire in the Minds of Men: Origins of the Revolutionary Faith*. New York: Basic Books, 1980.

BIZARDEL, Y., *Les Américans à Paris sous Louis XVI et pendant la Révolution: notices biographiques*. Paris: Clavreuil, 1978.

BLACK, J., *The English Press in the Eighteenth Century*. Philadelphia: University of Pennsylvania Press, 1987.

BLAKEMORE, S., *Crisis in Representation: Thomas Paine, Mary Wollstonecraft, Helen Maria Williams, and the Rewriting of the French Revolution*. Madison: Fairleigh Dickinson University Press, 1997.

BLANC, O., *Les hommes de Londres: histoire secrète de la Terreur*. Paris: A. Michel, 1989.

BLUM, C., *Rousseau and the Republic of Virtue: The Language of Politics in the French Revolution*. Ithaca: Cornell University Press, 1986.

BUEL, R., *Joel Barlow: American Citizen in a Revolutionary World*. Baltimore: Johns Hopkins University Press, 2011.

BURSTIN, H., *Une révolution à l'œuvre. Le faubourg Saint Marcel 1789-1794*. Seyssel: Champ Vallon, 2005.

BUTLER, M., *Burke, Paine, Godwin, and the Revolution Controversy*. Cambridge: Cambridge University Press, 1984.

CENSER, J. R., *Prelude to Power: The Parisian Radical Press, 1789-1791*. Baltimore: Johns Hopkins University Press, 1976.

CHARTIER, R., *Les origines culturelles de la Révolution française*. Paris: Seuil, 1990.

CLAEYS, G., *The Political Writings of the 1790s*. London: Pickering and Chatto, 1995.

────── *Thomas Paine: Social and Political Thought*. Boston: Unwin Hyman, 1989.

────── *The French Revolution Debate in Britain: The Origins of Modern Politics*. Basingstoke: Palgrave Macmillan, 2007.

────── *Politics and Anti-Politics in Early British Socialism*. Cambridge: Cambridge University Press, 1989.

CLARK, P., *British Clubs and Societies 1580-1800: The Origins of an Associational World*. Oxford: Oxford University Press, 2000.

CLAYDEN, P. W., *The Early Life of Samuel Rogers*. London: Smith, Elder and Co., 1887.

COLLEY, L., *Britons: Forging the Nation, 1707-1837*. New Haven: Yale University Press, 2009.

COMPAGNON, A., *Les Antimodernes: de Joseph de Maistre à Roland Barthes*. Paris: Gallimard, 2005.

COQUELLE, P., *Les projets de descente en Angleterre: d'après les archives des Affaires Étrangères*. Paris: Typ. Plon-Nourrit, 1902.

CORBIÈRE, A., *Jacobins ! Les inventeurs de la République*. Paris: Perrin, 2019.

CRANSTON, M., *Philosophers and Pamphleteers: Political Theorists of the Enlightenment*. Oxford: Oxford University Press, 1986.

CURRAN, S., *The Cambridge Companion to British Romanticism*. Cambridge: Cambridge University Press, 2000.

DANN, O. AND DINWIDDY, J. R., *Nationalism in the Age of the French Revolution*. London: Hambledon Press, 1988.

DICKINSON, H. T., *The Politics of the People in Eighteenth-Century Britain*. New York: St. Martin's Press, 1995.

────── *Liberty and Property: Political Ideology in Eighteenth-Century Britain*. New York: Holmes and Meier Publishers, 1977.

DOYLE, W., *Officers, Nobles and Revolutionaries: Essays on Eighteenth-Century France*. London: Hambledon, 1995.

────── *The Oxford History of the French Revolution*. Oxford: Oxford University Press, 1989.

DUFFY, M., *The Englishman and the Foreigner*. Cambridge: Chadwyck-Healey, 1986.

DUPUY, P., *Face à la Révolution et l'Empire: caricatures anglaises 1789-1815*. Paris: Paris Musées, 2008.

DUREY, M., *Transatlantic Radicals and the Early American Republic*. Lawrence: University Press of Kansas, 1997.

DUTHILLE, R., *Le discours radical en Grande-Bretagne, 1768-1789*. Oxford University Studies in the Enlightenment 2017:11, Oxford: Oxford University Press, 2017.

DYBIKOWSKI, J., *On Burning Ground: An Examination of the Ideas, Projects, and Life of David Williams*. Oxford: Voltaire Foundation, 1993.

ELLIOTT, M., *Partners in Revolution: The United Irishmen and France*. New Haven: Yale University Press, 1982.

EPSTEIN, J., *Radical Expression: Political Language, Ritual, and Symbol in England, 1790-1850*. London: Breviary Stuff Publications, 2014.

ERDMAN, D. V., *Commerce Des Lumieres: John Oswald and the British in Paris in 1790-93*. Columbia: University of Missouri Press, 1986.

FAUVILLE, H., *La France de Bonaparte vue par les visiteurs anglais*. Aix-en-Provence: Edisud, 1989.

FONTANA, B., *The Invention of the Modern Republic*. Cambridge: Cambridge University Press, 1994.

FURET, F., *Interpreting the French Revolution*. trans. E. Forster. Cambridge: Cambridge University Press, 1981.

FURET, F. AND OZOUF, M., *Dictionnaire critique de la Révolution française: 5*. Paris: Flammarion, 2007.

GERBOD, P., *Voyages au pays des mangeurs de grenouilles: la France vue par les Britanniques du XVIIIe siècle à nos jours*. Paris: A. Michel, 1991.

GILMARTIN, K., *Writing against Revolution: Literary Conservatism in Britain, 1790-1832*. Cambridge: Cambridge University Press, 2007.

GODECHOT, J. L., *La Grande Nation: l'expansion révolutionnaire de la France dans le monde de 1789 à 1799*. Paris: Aubier Montaigne, 1983.

GOODRICH, A., *Debating England's Aristocracy in the 1790s: Pamphlets, Polemics, and Political Ideas*. Woodbridge: Boydell, 2005.

GOODWIN, A., *The Friends of Liberty: The English Democratic Movement in the Age of the French Revolution*. London: Hutchinson, 1979.

GUÉRIN, D., *La lutte de classes, sous la première république, 1793-1797*. Paris: Gallimard, 1968.

HAIG, R. L., *The Gazetteer: 1735-1797: A Study in the Eighteenth-Century English Newspaper*. Carbondale: Southern Illinois University Press, 1960.

HAMMERSLEY, R., *French Revolutionaries and English Republicans: The Cordeliers Club, 1790-1794*. Rochester: Boydell, 2005.

HARGREAVES-MAWDSLEY, W. N., *The English Della Cruscans and their Time, 1783-1828*. The Hague: Martinus Nijhogg, 1967.

HARRIS, B., *The Scottish People and the French Revolution*. London: Pickering & Chatto, 2008.

——— *Politics and the Rise of the Press: Britain and France, 1620-1800*. London: Routledge, 1996.

HEFFERNAN, J. A. W., *Representing the French Revolution: Literature, Historiography, and Art*. Hanover, NH: Dartmouth College, 1992.

HELLMUTH, E., *The Transformation of Political Culture: England and Germany in the Late Eighteenth Century*. London: German Historical Institute, 1990.

HETHERINGTON, K., *The Badlands of Modernity: Heterotopia and Social Ordering*. London: Routledge, 1997.

HIGONNET, P., *Sister Republics: The Origins of French and American Republicanism.* Cambridge, Mass: Harvard University Press, 1988.
HILL, R. D. AND HILL, F. D., *The Recorder of Birmingham: A Memoir of Matthew Davenport Hill, with Selections from his Correspondence.* London: Macmillan, 1878.
HILTON, B., *A Mad, Bad, and Dangerous People?: England, 1783-1846.* Oxford: Oxford University Press, 2006.
HUNT, L., *Politics, Culture, and Class in the French Revolution.* Berkeley: University of California Press, 1984.
JARRETT, D., *Three Faces of Revolution: Paris, London, and New York in 1789.* London: Philip, 1989.
JONES, C., *Britain and Revolutionary France: Conflict, Subversion, and Propaganda.* Exeter: University of Exeter, 1983.
JONES, C. B., *Radical Sensibility: Literature and Ideas in the 1790s.* London: Routledge, 1993.
JONES, SIR E. D. AND VAUGHAN, H. M. (eds.), *The Welsh Book-plates in the Collection of Sir Evan Davies Jones M.P. of Pentower, Fishguard. A catalogue, with biographical and descriptive notes.* London: Humphreys, 1920.
JONES, W. R. D., *David Williams: The Anvil and the Hammer.* Cardiff: University of Wales Press, 1986.
KATES, G., *The Cercle Social, the Girondins, and the French Revolution.* Princeton: Princeton University Press, 1985.
KEANE, J., *Tom Paine: A Political Life.* London: Bloomsbury, 1995.
KENNEDY, D., *Helen Maria Williams and the Age of Revolution.* London: Buckness University Press, 2002.
KLANCHER, J. P., *The Making of English Reading Audiences, 1790-1832.* Madison: University of Wisconsin Press, 1987.
LANDES, J. B., *Women and the Public Sphere in the Age of the French Revolution.* Ithaca: Cornell University Press, 1988.
LOUNISSI, C., *Thomas Paine and the French Revolution.* Palgrave Macmillan, 2018.
MACKENZIE, P., *The Life of Thomas Muir, Esq. Advocate, Younger of Huntershill, Near Glasgow; Member of the Convention of Delegates for Reform in Scotland etc. etc. Who was Tried for Sedition Before The High Court of Justiciary in Scotland, and sentence to Transportation for Fourteen Years with a Full Report of his Trial.* Glasgow: McPhun, 1831.
MALONE, D., *The Public Life of Thomas Cooper, 1783-1839.* Columbia: University of South Carolina Press, 1961.
MATHIEZ, A., *La Révolution et les étrangers: cosmopolitisme et défense nationale.* Paris: La renaissance du livre, 1918.
MCCALMAN, I., *Radical Underworld: Prophets, Revolutionaries and Pornographers in London, 1795-1840.* Cambridge: Cambridge University Press, 1988.
MCLEAN, I. AND HEWITT, F., *Condorcet: Foundations of Social Choice and Political Theory.* Hants: Edward Elgar, 1994.
MEE, J., *Romanticism, Enthusiasm and Regulation: Poetics and the Policing of Culture in the Romantic Period.* Oxford: Oxford University Press, 2003.

MICHELET, J., *Les femmes de la Révolution*. Paris: Chamerot, 1863.
DE MONTLUZIN E. L., *The Anti-Jacobins, 1798-1800: The Early Contributors to the Anti-Jacobin Review*. New York: St. Martin's Press, 1988.
MOORE, T., *The Life and Death of Lord Edward Fitzgerald*. Paris: Baudry's European Library, 1935.
MORIEUX, R., *Une mer pour deux royaumes: la Manche, frontière franco-anglaise, XVIIe-XVIIIe siècles*. Rennes: Presses universitaires de Rennes, 2008.
NEWMAN, G., *The Rise of English Nationalism: A Cultural History, 1740-1830*. London: Macmillan, 1997.
NEWMAN, I., *The Romantic Tavern: Literature and Conviviality in the Age of Revolution* (Cambridge University Press, 2019).
PARRA, P. C., *Miranda et la Révolution française*. Paris: Dumoulin, 1925.
PATRICK, A., *The Men of the First French Republic: Political Alignments in the National Convention of 1792*. Baltimore: Johns Hopkins University Press, 1972.
PHILP, M., *Paine*. Oxford: Oxford University Press, 1989.
——— *The French Revolution and British Popular Politics*. Cambridge: Cambridge University Press, 1991.
POCOCK, J. G. A., *Virtue, Commerce, and History: Essays on Political Thought and History, Chiefly in the Eighteenth Century*. Cambridge: Cambridge University Press, 1985.
RAPPORT, M. G., *Nationality and Citizenship in Revolutionary France: The Treatment of Foreigners 1789-1799*. Oxford: Clarendon, 2000.
RAYNARD, P., *Trois révolutions de la liberté: Angleterre, Amérique, France*. Paris: Presses Universitaires de France, 2010.
READ, D., *Press and People: 1790-1850*. London: Arnold, 1961.
REINHARD, M. R., *La chute de la royauté, 10 août, 1792*. Paris: Gallimard, 1969.
ROSE, R. B., *The Making of the Sans-Culottes: Democratic Ideas and Institutions in Paris, 1789-92*. Manchester: Manchester University Press, 1983.
RUIZ, A., GRAB, W. AND KUHN, A., *Les jacobins allemands en France*. Marseille: CRDP, 1986.
RUSSELL, G., *The Theatres of War: Performance, Politics, and Society, 1793-1815*. Oxford: Clarendon Press, 1995.
SAHLINS, P., *Unnaturally French: Foreign Citizens in the Old Regime and After*. Ithaca: Cornell University Press, 2004.
SCRIVENER, M., *Seditious Allegories: John Thelwall & Jacobin Writing*. University Park, Pa: Pennsylvania State University Press, 2001.
SERNA, P., *La république des girouettes. 1789-1815 et au-delà. Une anomalie politique : la France de l'extrême centre*. Paris: Champ Vallon, 2005.
SMITH, O., *The Politics of Language, 1791-1819*. Oxford: Clarendon Press, 1984.
SOBOUL, A., *Les sans-culottes parisiens en l'an II: mouvement populaire et gouvernement révolutionnaire, 2 juin 1793 - 9 Thermidor an II*. Paris: Librairie Clavreuil, 1958.
ST. CLAIR, W., *The Godwins and the Shelleys: The Biography of a Family*. LONDON: FABER AND FABER, 1989.

SWORDS, L., *The Green Cockade: The Irish in the French Revolution 1789-1815*. Sandycove, Co. Dublin, Ireland: Glendale, 1989.
SYDENHAM, M. J., *The Girondins*. London: Athlone Press, 1961.
TAYLOR, I. A., *The Life of Lord Edward Fitzgerald, 1763-1798*. New York: Brentano's, 1904.
TAYLOR, J., *Records of My Life*. New York: J and J Harper, 1833.
THOMIS, M. I. AND DAVIS, M. T., *Radicalism and Revolution in Britain, 1775-1848: Essays in Honour of Malcolm I. Thomis*. New York: St. Martin's Press, 2000.
THOMIS, M. I, AND HOLT, P., *Threats of Revolution in Britain, 1789-1848*. Hamden, Conn: Archon Books, 1977.
THOMPSON, E. P., *The Making of the English Working Class*. London: Victor Gollancz, 1963.
THOMPSON, J. M., *English Witnesses of the French Revolution*. Oxford: Blackwell, 1938.
TILLYARD, S., *Citizen Lord Edward Fitzgerald 1763-1798*. London: Chatto and Windus, 1997.
TOCQUEVILLE, A., *L'Ancien Régime et la Révolution*. Paris: Calmann Lévy, 1887.
TODD, C. B., *Life and Letters of Joel Barlow: Poet, Statesman, Philosopher: With Extracts from His Works and Hitherto Unpublished Poems*. New York: G. P. Putnam's Sons, 1886.
TODD, J., *Mary Wollstonecraft: A Revolutionary Life*. New York: Columbia University Press, 2000.
TULARD, J., *Les Thermidoriens*. Paris: Fayard, 2005.
VERHOEVEN, W. M., *Gilbert Imlay: Citizen of the World*. London: Pickering & Chatto, 2008.
VOVELLE, M., *La Révolution française: 1789-1799*. Paris: A. Colin, 1992.
WAHNICH, S., *L'impossible citoyen: L'étranger dans le discours de la Révolution française*. Paris: A. Michel, 1997.
WALTER, G. AND MARTIN, A., *Catalogue de l'histoire de la Révolution française*. Paris: Bibliothèque Nationale de France, 1936-43.
WALTON, G. C., *Policing Public Opinion in the French Revolution: The Culture of Calumny and the Problem of Free Speech*. Oxford: Oxford University Press, 2009.
WELLS, R., *Insurrection: The British Experience, 1795-1803*. London: Breviary Stuff Publications, 2013.
WERKMEISTER, L. T., *A Newspaper History of England, 1792-1793*. Lincoln: University of Nebraska Press, 1967.
—— *The London Daily Press, 1772-1792*. Lincoln: University of Nebraska Press, 1963.
WILLIAMS, G. A., *Artisans and Sans-Culottes: Popular Movements in France and Britain During the French Revolution*. London: Libris, 1988.
WOODWARD L. D., *Une Anglaise amie de la Révolution française: Hélène-Maria Williams et ses amis*. Paris: Champion, 1930.
WORRALL, D., *Radical Culture: Discourse, Resistance and Surveillance, 1790-1820*. London: Breviary Stuff Publications, 2019.

―――― *Theatric Revolution: Drama, Censorship, and Romantic Period Subcultures, 1773-1832*. Oxford: Oxford University Press 2006.

ZIESCHE, P., *Cosmopolitan Patriots: Americans in Paris in the Age of Revolution*. Charlottesville: University of Virginia Press, 2010.

Index

Alger, John Goldworth, 4-8 12, 22, 60, 88, 90, 92, 110-11, 120, 129, 134, 141, 143, 161, 162
An Historical and Moral View, see Wollstonecraft, Mary
An Historical Sketch of the French Revolution, see Perry, Sampson
Analytical Review, 47, 55, 103, 141, 171, 181, 183,
Annales des Arts et Manufactures, 30, 48, 142
Annual Register, 17, 69, 182
Anti-Jacobin Review, 194
Argus, The, 19, 30, 49-54, 81, 173-75, 203-7, 218, 220, 221, 222, 254, 264
Arthur, Citizen, 58, 60, 71, 74, 140, 148
Auckland, Lord, 18, 65, 214, 238
Audibert, Achille, 156

Bancal des Issarts, Henri, 44
Barbier de Vémars, J. N., 142
Barère, Bertrand, 39, 85, 109, 154
Barlow, Joel, 10, 34, 36, 37, 41, 44, 45, 55, 57, 58, 59, 60, 61, 64, 71, 78, 79, 81, 82, 88-9, 91, 93-96, 109, 125, 139, 156, 161, 162, 165, 167-168, 170, 174, 175, 218, 228
Barlow, Ruth, 37, 38, 41, 90, 170, 171, 172, 174
Barras, Paul, 224, 225
Bland Burges, James, 18, 80, 238
Bonneville, Nicholas de, 8, 39, 55, 226
Brienne, Étienne-Charles de Loménie de, 197
Brissot de Warville, Jacques-Pierre, 8, 44, 81, 85, 88, 93, 97, 98, 99, 100, 101, 106, 115, 134, 138, 183, 204, 225, 230, 240
Brissotins, 113, 134, 240
British Convention, 205, 248
Brunswick, Duke of, 16, 21, 186, 187, 192
Brunton, Anne, 35
Burke, Edmund, 15, 17, 18, 19, 54, 105, 124, 176, 184, 193, 194, 196, 199, 249

Calonne, Charles Alexandre de, 197
Cartwright, John, 77

Cercle Social, 53, 54, 55, 87, 89, 99, 106, 111, 122, 127, 207, 226, 228
Charles I,
    execution of, 138, 191,
    personal rule, 116
Chaumette, Pierre Gaspard, 25
Choppin, William, 44, 48, 54, 70, 78, 82, 83, 92, 139, 147, 169, 203, 256, 260
Christie, Thomas, 26, 30, 35, 44, 47, 55, 61, 80, 91, 141, 148, 182, 183, 184, 186, 189, 227
Chronique du Mois, 36, 52, 53, 55, 81, 101, 122, 127, 205, 207, 264
Churchill, Charles and Elizabeth, 41, 150, 151-152
Cloots, Anacharsis, 3, 10, 148
Collot d'Herbois, Jean-Marie, 36
Comité de Salut Public, 12, 25, 32, 41, 112, 129, 137, 140, 148, 153, 154, 155, 156, 157, 170, 175, 203, 204, 228, 229, 240, 241, 242, 243, 245, 247, 248
Comité de Sûreté Générale, 12, 41, 48, 63, 137, 142, 152, 153, 154, 155, 243
comités de surveillance, 139, 216
Commune (Revolutionary Commune of Paris), 16, 17, 20, 75, 183, 184, 187, 240
Condorcet, Marquis de, 39, 85, 86, 88, 97, 99, 112, 113, 114, 115, 134, 137, 166, 183, 195, 226, 230, 240
Constituent Assembly, 2, 16, 94, 96, 100, 125, 127, 208
Conway, Moncure, 6, 229, 230
Coope, Rachel, 35, 36, 41, 44, 45
Cooper, Thomas, 9, 31, 47, 78, 91, 92
Cordeliers (club and activists), 16, 17, 55, 86, 87, 112, 116, 134, 227, 228, 240
Courier de l'Europe, 49
Couthon, Georges, 154, 243
Critical Review, 220
Cromwell, Oliver, 109, 138, 145
Crown and Anchor Tavern, 52, 53, 78, 83, 129, 247
Curtayn, Jeremie, 70, 260

Danton, Georges, 40, 112, 187, 228, 230, 240, 243, 248

295

Dantonists, 25, 212, 228
David, Jacques-Louis, 31, 113, 142, 157, 227, 240
Declaration of the Rights of Man and of the Citizen, 100
Desmoulins, Camille, 42, 112, 134
Duc d'Orléans, 40
Duckett, William, 70, 260
Dumouriez, General, 175, 186, 187, (defection of) 189, 191, 246

Edict of Fraternity, 2, 70, 121, 145, 247
Edwards, George, 12, 31, 40, 48, 78, 80, 88, 91, 110, 126, 127, 128-34, 139, 142, 231
English Benedictines, prison of, 150, 153
English Conceptionist college, prison of, 150
Erdman, David V., 7-8, 12, 21, 36, 48, 55, 63, 68, 75, 80, 122, 128, 129, 260
Esquisse d'un tableau historique des progress de l'esprit humain, Condorcet, Marquis de, 166
European Magazine, The, 73
Evening Mail, The, 51

Fabre d'Églantine, Philippe, 25
Fête de la Fédération, 92, 176, 177, 178, 209
Fitzgerald, Lord Edward, 9, 20, 21, 34, 40, 46, 47, 50, 63, 68, 69, 76, 78, 129, 260
Fox, Charles James, 45, 238, 239
Foxite Whigs, 15
Franklin, Benjamin, 48, 128, 132
Frost, John, 5, 30, 34, 37, 54, 71, 72, 78, 79, 81, 82, 83, 129, 139, 169, 260

"Gagging Acts", *see* Two Acts
Gamble, James, 19, 38, 41, 45, 60, 63, 68, 140, 260
Gazetteer, The, 30, 49, 68
General Advertiser, The, 49
Gentleman's Magazine, The, 5, 36, 49, 130, 194
George III, King, 7, 76, 190, 238
Gillray, James, 221
Girondins (Gironde/Girondism), 3, 4, 11, 16, 25, 31, 40, 43, 55, 58, 77, 85, 87, 91, 97, 99, 106, 107, 112, 118, 134, 139, 141, 151, 183, 187, 191, 208, 211, 212, 213, 223-30, 240, 241, 242, 243, 244, 246, 247, 238
Glorious Revolution (1688), 13, 15, 103, 104, 191, 200
Godwin, William, 62, 77, 101, 106
Grenville, William Wyndham (Lord), 48, 54, 68, 72, 74, 75, 76, 137, 170, 238
Grey, Charles, 15, 238
Gulliver's Travels, Jonathan Swift 65
Guyomar, Pierre, 138

Hamilton Rowan, Archibald, 32
Hardy, Thomas, 249
Hérault de Séchelles, Marie-Jean 85, 154, 203, 227, 228, 230, 240, 243, 248
Hickson, Nicholas, 150, 260
Horne Tooke, John, 53, 77, 78, 91, 93, 207, 225, 249

Idées pour former une nouvelle constitution, see Edwards, George
Imlay, Gilbert, 10, 32, 33, 35, 38, 43, 44, 45, 60, 64, 146, 149, 164, 170, 195, 229
Irish Colleges, 70
Irish Rebellion (1798), 9, 32, 81

Jacobin Club, 36, 37, 54, 61, 75, 89, 182, 240, 248
Jefferson, Thomas, 58, 95, 96, 132, 133, 156, 228
Johnson, Joseph, 55, 79, 141, 177
Johnson, William, 21, 44, 48, 81, 139, 147, 203, 204
Joyce, Jeremiah, 78, 153
Joyce, Nicholas, 44, 63, 68, 74, 78, 149, 150, 153, 260

L'Ami du Peuple, Marat's journal, 211, 241
La Bouche de Fer, 55
Lanthenas, François, 39, 156, 158, 226, 241
Lauderdale, Lord, 92
Law of Suspects, 143, 243, 248
Le Républicain, 55, 240
Le Sueur, Théodore, 86, 87, 134
Lessons to a Young Prince, Williams, David, 98

Letter Addressed to the Addressers, see Paine, Thomas
Letters from France, see Williams, Helen Maria
Letters on Political Liberty, Williams, David, 98, 219
Letters Written in Sweden, Norway and Denmark, Wollstonecraft, Mary, 33
Literary Fund, 18, 79-81, 89, 101, 106, 107, 113, 129, 130, 133, 189
Lyttlejohn, R., 21
Loffe, Capel, 77, 89
London Corresponding Society (LCS), 19, 30, 32, 49, 71, 78, 82, 205, 246, 249
Louis XVI, trial and execution of, 2, 16, 17, 22, 25, 38, 42, 72, 86, 90, 92, 107, 109, 112, 137, 138, 146, 156, 177, 184, 190, 193, 209, 210, 213, 225, 229, 232, 241, 244, 246, 247
Loustalot, Elisée, 25
Luxembourg, prison of, 3, 6, 9, 44, 63, 147, 148, 149, 150, 157, 204

MacDonnell, D. E., 20, 68, 72, 260
MacSheehy, Bernard, 70, 139, 260
Madelonnettes, prison of, 3, 147, 148, 150, 204
Madgett, Nicholas, 21, 36, 111, 129, 139, 260
Manchester Constitutional Society, 36
Marat, Jean-Paul, 38, 45, 52, 156, 187, 191, 203, 204, 206, 207, 209, 211-12, 213, 230, 241, 248
Maréchal, Sylvain, 25
Matthews, James Tilly, 41, 97
Maxwell, Dr. William, 48, 68, 78, 260
Merry, Robert, 2, 12, 19, 20, 21-27, 29, 30, 31, 33, 34, 35, 36, 47, 52, 53, 68, 69, 70, 71, 72, 73, 76, 78, 80, 81, 88, 91, 93, 100, 110-122, 127, 129, 139, 141, 142, 157, 158, 207, 214, 226, 227, 229, 231, 250, 255, 260
Miranda, General Francisco de, 44, 58
Moniteur Universel, 63, 70, 75, 182
Monro, Captain George, 5, 8, 12, 22, 37, 48, 54, 63, 67-76, 81, 90, 137, 152, 169, 170, 238
Monroe, James, American ambassador in Paris, 149

Montagne (Montagnards), 11, 20, 38, 40, 77, 85, 86, 87, 88, 105, 112, 113, 118, 134, 137, 140, 141, 142, 154, 184, 186, 187, 190, 194, 199, 204, 208, 211, 212, 213, 216, 224, 225, 227, 228, 240, 243, 244, 245
Montesquieu, 15, 86, 98, 112, 115, 116
Monthly Magazine, The, 111, 204
Monthly Review, The, 220
Morgan, George Cadogan, 89
Morning Chronicle, The, 22, 49, 50, 193
Morning Post, The, 49, 68
Morris, Gouverneur, 156, 157
Morris, Thomas, 80, 81, 101, 219
Muir, Thomas, 9

National Assembly of France, 17, 19, 26, 30, 70, 100, 102, 124, 125, 126, 176, 182, 183, 198, 210, 213, 215, 219, 240, 244
National Convention of France, 1, 2, 3, 6, 10, 11, 17, 19, 25, 30, 31, 34, 36, 37, 38, 39, 40, 47, 48, 51, 54, 55, 59, 60, 62, 63, 67, 68, 70, 71, 72, 75, 76, 79, 82, 83, 84, 85, 86, 87, 89, 90, 91, 92, 93, 94, 96, 97, 102, 103, 104, 107, 110, 111, 112, 118, 121, 125, 127, 128, 129, 130, 134, 138, 139, 140, 141, 142, 143, 144, 148, 151, 152, 153, 155, 156, 157, 182, 183, 189, 190, 199, 203, 210, 211, 218, 220, 224, 225, 226, 229, 232, 240, 241, 242, 243, 244, 245, 246, 247, 248, 257, 260
Necker, Jacques, 42, 197
Nepean, Evan, under-secretary of state for the Home Office, 53, 82, 238-239, 256
New Whigs (Society of the Friends of the People), 15, 19, 20, 21, 56, 78, 238, 246
Newgate, prison of, 2, 36, 150, 161, 173, 204, 205, 206, 217, 221, 253, 254
Newton, Richard, 206
Newton, William, 48, 68, 150, 158, 260

O'Reilly, Robert, 30, 31, 41, 47, 48, 68, 70, 76, 142, 157, 260
Observations sur la dernière constitution de la France, see Williams, David

Onslow, Lord, 50
Oswald, John, 2, 7, 8, 12, 18, 30, 34, 36, 39, 47, 48, 55, 57, 58, 68, 70, 76, 80, 89, 91, 100, 110, 115, 122-7, 128, 139, 225, 226, 227, 228, 231, 260
Otto, Louis-Guillaume, 39

Paine, Thomas, 1, 2, 3, 5, 6, 8, 9, 10, 19, 20, 21, 24, 29, 30, 31, 36, 37, 38, 39, 40, 43, 44, 45, 47, 48, 49, 50, 51, 52, 53, 54, 55, 57, 63, 72, 74, 75, 77, 78, 81, 82, 83, 85, 86, 91, 92, 93, 94, 95, 96, 97, 101, 103, 123, 124, 127, 138, 139, 144, 147, 148, 150, 155-7, 158, 171, 174, 181, 183, 203, 217, 219, 222, 223, 224, 226, 229, 238, 240, 241, 246, 248, 256
Palais Royal, 40, 41, 42, 43
Perry, Sampson, 1, 6, 12, 19, 20, 21, 23, 27, 30, 31, 34, 36, 40, 45, 47, 48, 49-54, 55, 68, 69, 76, 78, 80, 81, 89, 110, 112, 120, 125, 139, 148, 150, 161, 165, 166, 167, 168, 173, 174, 175, 176, 179, 189, 190, 196, 203-22, 227, 228, 229, 230, 250, 253, 254, 264
Pétion, Jérôme, 25, 26, 37, 56, 61, 87, 106, 183, 187, 241
Philadelphia Hotel, 40
Pitt the Younger, William, 4, 51, 65, 139, 238, 239, 249
Playfair, William, 161, 217, 218
Price, Richard, 56, 89, 188
Priestley, Joseph, 32, 56, 57, 58, 91, 92
Prud'homme, Louis-Marie, 22

Rayment, Robert, 12, 19, 31, 35, 41, 62, 68, 70, 72, 74, 76, 139, 140, 147, 148, 150, 151, 152, 153, 155, 158, 228, 260, 261-262
Association for preserving Liberty and Property against Republicans and Levellers, 247
Reeves, John, 80, 107
Reflections on the Revolution in France, see Burke, Edmund
Réflexions politiques, see Merry, Robert
Revolution Society, 56, 71, 89, 90
Revolutionary Tribunal, 25, 38, 48, 213, 228, 243, 245, 247

Révolutions de Paris, 22, 25, 27, 196, 250-252
Rhys, Morgan John, 38, 41
Ricketts, William, 48, 260
Rickman, Thomas Clio, 6, 8, 44, 82, 83, 171, 223, 256
Rights of Man, see Paine, Thomas
Robert, Pierre-François, 16, 115
Robespierre, Maximilien, 31, 36, 88, 92, 112, 118, 139, 143, 148, 156, 157, 158, 175, 183, 187, 199, 208, 212, 241, 242, 243, 245, 248, 249
Roland, Jean-Marie, 97, 98, 100, 101, 106, 183, 225, 241, 242
Roland, Manon (Madame Roland), 43, 97, 102, 106, 107, 211, 242
Ross, Charles, 12, 53, 82-3, 89, 92, 169, 239, 256
Rousseau, Jean-Jacques, 87, 95, 101, 112, 114, 115, 117, 124, 188, 189
Rowlandson, Thomas, 18
Royal Proclamation Against Seditious Writings, 246

Saint-Just, Louis-Antoine de, 85, 86, 118, 154, 242
Santerre, Antoine Joseph, 190
Sayre, Stephen, 40, 59-60, 68, 70, 152, 260
Sciotto Company, the, 93
Scotch College, prison of or, Maison des Ecossais, 148, 261, 262
sedition (accusations of, trials for), 2, 24, 25, 50, 150, 204
September massacres, 7, 17, 18, 20, 184, 187, 192, 204, 208, 214, 215, 240, 246
Seward, Anna, 5, 17, 19
Sheares, John and Henry, 68, 76, 81, 260
Sieyès, Abbé, 85
Smith, Charlotte, 31, 35, 181
Smith, Robert (Sir), or Smyth, 12, 19, 35, 36, 41, 47, 68, 69, 72, 74, 75, 139, 147, 148, 152, 153-5, 158, 227, 228, 260 263
Society for Constitutional Information (SCI), 1, 19, 20, 21, 30, 37, 50, 52, 53, 54, 71, 77-9, 81-84, 93, 129, 133, 153, 205, 229, 239, 246, 247, 249

Society of the Friends of the People, *see* New Whigs
Somers, Mr. British spy, 75, 76
Stone, John Hurford, 7, 18, 20, 26, 29, 32, 34, 35, 36, 40, 41, 44, 45, 46, 47, 55, 56-9, 61, 63, 65, 68, 71, 78, 80, 88, 106, 122, 135, 140, 141, 146, 147, 148, 150, 158, 162, 165, 169, 170-6, 181, 183, 184, 186, 187-189, 190, 191, 195, 225, 227, 260
Swift, Johnathan, 24, 65
Symonds, H. D., 21, 22, 204, 253

Times, The, 21, 27, 28, 51, 54
Thelwall, John, 32, 106, 249
Thermidor, 9, An II, (Thermidorian constitution, 1795), 3, 8, 31, 33, 87, 88, 152, 156, 158, 218, 224, 242, 243, 245, 249
Thomson, Robert, 21, 22
Thuriot, Jacques-Alexis, 38, 129, 154, 156
Treaty of Amiens (1802), 31
True Briton, 51
Tuileries, siege of (10th August 1792) (August Days), 1, 2, 3, 15-28, 41, 60, 62, 68, 109, 111, 140, 151, 152, 154, 164, 187, 192, 196, 210, 214, 215, 241, 244, 246, 250, 251, 252
Tweddell, Francis, 34, 78, 81, 260
Two Acts, 1795 ("Gagging" Acts), 205

Universal Patriot, The, 30, 55, 122

Varennes, king's flight via, 16, 33, 55, 94, 210, 240

Vicomterie, Louis de la, 16
Vindication of the Rights of Men, Wollstonecraft, Mary, 199
Voltaire, 112

Walker, Thomas, 61, 92
War of American Independence (American Revolution), 34, 96, 123, 138
Watt Junior, James, 36, 61, 91
Watts, William, 18, 78, 260
White, Christopher, owner of White's hotel, 2, 12, 41, 44, 60, 62-3, 146, 149, 150, 152, 153
Williams, David, 2, 10, 16, 18, 26, 37, 43, 47, 79, 80, 88, 89, 97-107, 109, 111, 112, 115, 127, 129, 131, 133, 139, 146, 162, 223, 229, 231, 240
Williams, Helen Maria, 5, 7, 9, 20, 21, 29, 30, 32, 35, 41, 45, 46, 55, 57, 58, 59, 71, 149, 150, 162, 165, 166, 172-9, 181, 182, 183-94, 195, 196, 197, 198, 199, 200, 201, 204, 210, 211, 219, 223, 225, 226, 227, 230, 241
Wollstonecraft, Mary, 24, 32, 33, 35, 37-8, 42, 43, 44, 45, 47, 55, 62, 64, 66, 90, 104, 106, 132, 141, 144, 146, 149, 161, 162, 164, 166, 167, 170, 171, 172, 174, 177, 178, 179, 181-183, 194-201, 232
Woodward, Lionel D., 7, 12, 36, 226

Yorke, Henry Redhead, 6, 31, 34, 47, 48, 61, 68, 71, 72, 76, 78, 81, 82, 83, 148, 162, 223
Young, Arthur, 42, 163

Also from
BREVIARY STUFF PUBLICATIONS

Victor Bailey, CHARLES BOOTH'S POLICEMEN, *Crime, Police and Community in Jack-the-Ripper's London*
£17.00 • 162pp *paperback* • *2 colour and 8 b/w images* • 140x216mm • ISBN 978-0-9564827-6-1

Victor Bailey, ORDER AND DISORDER IN MODERN BRITAIN, *Essays on Riot, Crime, Policing and Punishment*
£15.00 • 214pp *paperback* • 5 *b/w images* • 191x235mm • ISBN 978-0-9570005-5-1

Roger Ball, Dave Beckwith, Steve Hunt, Mike Richardson, STRIKERS, HOBBLERS, CONCHIES & REDS, *A Radical History of Bristol, 1880-1939*
£18.50 • 366pp *paperback* • *101 b/w images* • 156x234mm • ISBN 978-0-9929466-0-9

John Belchem, 'ORATOR' HUNT, *Henry Hunt and English Working Class Radicalism*
£17.50 • 248pp *paperback* • 191x235mm • ISBN 978-0-9564827-8-5

Alastair Bonnett & Keith Armstrong (eds.), THOMAS SPENCE: THE POOR MAN'S REVOLUTIONARY
£15.00 • 214pp *paperback* • 156x234mm • ISBN 978-0-9570005-9-9

Norah Carlin, REGICIDE OR REVOLUTION?, *What Petitioners Wanted, September 1648 - February 1649*
£18.50 • 358pp *paperback* • 156x234mm • ISBN 978-1-9161586-0-3

Nigel Costley, WEST COUNTRY REBELS
£20.00 • 220pp *full colour illustrated paperback* • 216x216mm • ISBN 978-0-9570005-4-4

Simon Hannah, RADICAL LAMBETH 1979-1991
£16.00 • 224pp • 156x234mm • ISBN 978-1-9161586-3-4

Ariel Hessayon (ed.), THE REFINER'S FIRE, *The Collected Works of TheauraJohn Tany*
£25.00 • 552pp *paperback* • 156x234mm • ISBN 978-0-9570005-7-5

Catherine Howe, HALIFAX 1842, *A Year of Crisis*
£14.50 • 202pp *paperback* • 156x234mm • ISBN 978-0-9570005-8-2

Philip Ruff, A TOWERING FLAME, *The Life & Times of the Elusive Latvian Anarchist Peter the Painter*
£17.00 • 284pp *paperback* • 156x234mm • ISBN 978-0-9929466-5-4
£25.00 • 284pp *hardback* • 156x234mm • ISBN 978-0-9929466-8-5

David Walsh, MAKING ANGELS IN MARBLE, *The Conservatives, the Early Industrial Working Class and Attempts at Political Incorporation*
£15.00 • 268pp *paperback* • 191x235mm • ISBN 978-0-9570005-0-6

David Walsh, THE SONS OF BELIAL, *Protest and Community Change in the North-West, 1740-1770*
£16.00 • 272pp *paperback* • 156x234mm • ISBN 978-0-9929466-9-2

For further information visit
www.breviarystuff.org.uk

Also from
BREVIARY STUFF PUBLICATIONS

Ralph Anstis, WARREN JAMES AND THE DEAN FOREST RIOTS, *The Disturbances of 1831*
£17.00 • 242pp *paperback* • 191x235mm • ISBN 978-0-9564827-7-8

John E. Archer, BY A FLASH AND A SCARE, *Arson, Animal Maiming, and Poaching in East Anglia 1815-1870*
£17.00 • 282pp *paperback* • 156x234mm • ISBN 978-1-9161586-2-7

Bob Bushaway, BY RITE, *Custom, Ceremony and Community in England 1700-1880*
£16.00 • 206pp *paperback* • 191x235mm • ISBN 978-0-9564827-6-1

Malcolm Chase, THE PEOPLE'S FARM, *English Radical Agrarianism 1775-1840*
£12.00 • 212pp *paperback* • 152x229mm • ISBN 978-0-9564827-5-4

Malcolm Chase, EARLY TRADE UNIONISM, F*raternity, Skill and the Politics of Labour*
£17.00 • 248pp *paperback* • 191x235mm • ISBN 978-0-9570005-2-0

James Epstein, THE LION OF FREEDOM, *Feargus O'Connor and the Chartist Movement, 1832-1842*
£17.00 • 296pp *paperback* • 156x234mm • ISBN 978-0-9929466-1-6

James Epstein, RADICAL EXPRESSION, *Political Language, Ritual, and Symbol in England, 1790-1850*
£15.00 • 220pp *paperback* • 156x234mm • ISBN 978-0-9929466-2-3

Chris Fisher, CUSTOM, WORK & MARKET CAPITALISM, *The Forest of Dean Colliers, 1788-1888*
£14.00 • 198pp *paperback* • 156x234mm • ISBN 978-0-9929466-7-8

Barry Reay, THE LAST RISING OF THE AGRICULTURAL LABOURERS, *Rural Life and Protest in Nineteenth-Century England*
£15.00 • 192pp *paperback* • 191x235mm • ISBN 978-0-9564827-2-3

Buchanan Sharp, IN CONTEMPT OF ALL AUTHORITY, *Rural Artisans and Riot in the West of England, 1586-1660*
£15.00 • 204pp *paperback* • 191x235mm • ISBN 978-0-9564827-0-9

Dorothy Thompson, THE CHARTISTS, *Popular Politics in the Industrial Revolution*
£17.00 • 280pp *paperback* • 191x235mm • ISBN 978-0-9570005-3-7

E. P. Thompson, WHIGS AND HUNTERS, *The Origin of the Black Act*
£16.00 • 278pp *paperback* • 156x234mm • ISBN 978-0-9570005-2-0
£30.00 • 278pp *hardback* • 156x234mm • ISBN 978-0-9929466-6-1

Roger Wells, INSURRECTION, *The British Experience 1795-1803*
£22.00 • 372pp *paperback* • 191x235mm • ISBN 978-0-9564827-3-0

Roger Wells, WRETCHED FACES, *Famine in Wartime England 1793-1801*
£23.00 • 412pp *paperback* • 191x235mm • ISBN 978-0-9564827-4-7

David Worrall, RADICAL CULTURE, *Discourse, Resistance and Surveillance, 1790-1820*
£15.00 • 186pp *paperback* • 156x234mm • ISBN 978-0-9929466-4-7